SO IT WAS TRUE

So It Was True

*The
American Protestant Press
and the Nazi
Persecution of the Jews*

ROBERT W. ROSS
*Religious Studies
University of Minnesota*

UNIVERSITY OF MINNESOTA PRESS
Minneapolis

Published by the University of Minnesota Press,
2037 University Avenue Southeast,
Minneapolis, Minnesota 55414
Printed in the United States of America

Library of Congress Cataloging in Publication Data

Ross, Robert W
  So it was true.

  Bibliography: p.
  Includes index.
  1. Holocaust, Jewish (1939–1945)—Public
opinion. 2. Journalism, Religious—United
States. I. Title.
D810.J4R664   943.086   80–196
ISBN O–8166–0948–9
ISBN 0–8166–0951–9 pbk.

In remembrance of those who died
and of those who survived
and
For Sally Jo, Becky, and
David, my family

Acknowledgments

M y thoughts, concerns, and questions were nourished and the
project was encouraged by those who have attended the Bernhard E. Olson Annual Scholars' Conference on the Church Struggle
and the Holocaust, which was named in honor of a friend and col-
league of many years. The memory of Bernhard Olson lives on with
his many friends as well as in the annual conference named in his
honor by the National Conference of Christians and Jews.

A. Thomas Kraabel and Robert B. Tapp, each at times chairperson
of the Program in Religious Studies at the University of Minnesota,
have consistently encouraged both the research and the "doing" of
this study. And Jasper S. Hopkins has been that valued faculty col-
league and friend who has patiently listened in spite of his own
heavy schedule in teaching philosophy courses. My special thanks to
Jasper.

Libraries, academic and private, house the resources that make a
study such as this one possible. It is, therefore, with a special sense
of obligation that I wish to thank the head librarians and staffs of the
library of Bethany-Northern Theological Seminaries, Oak Brook, Illinois; the Jesuit-Kraus-McCormick Library, Chicago, Illinois; the University of Chicago library; the Presbyterian Historical Society, Philadelphia, Pennsylvania; the Library of the American Jewish Committee,
New York City; the YIVO Institute for Jewish Research, New York
City; the Library of Princeton Theological Seminary, the Luther-
Northwestern Seminaries, the United Theological Seminary, Bethel
College and Seminary, and Hamline University, Minneapolis–St.
Paul, Minnesota; St. Paul Bible College; and especially the staff of the
O. Meredith Wilson Library of the University of Minnesota, who pro-
vided me a writing room and innumerable services, some beyond
that considered reasonable.

I wish to thank the Board of Regents and the Office of Student

Affairs of the University of Minnesota, the former for granting and the latter for supporting a sabbatical leave for one full year to complete this study. At a timely point, the Center for Studies on the Holocaust of the Anti-Defamation League of B'nai B'rith provided a grant, which hastened the completion of the manuscript. My thanks to Theodore Freedman, director of the National Program Division of the Anti-Defamation League and coordinator of the center, for making such a grant possible, and my thanks also to Rabbi Solomon S. Bernards, director of the Department of Interreligious Cooperation, whose personal interest in this study brought me into contact with the Anti-Defamation League.

Sue Brown and Toni Ziegler transformed the handwriting in my manuscript into typescript. I can only thank them by saying that we became and remain good friends and that they are both very good typists and advisers on form and style. Also, my thanks to Richard M. Abel and Marcia Bottoms, who so ably shepherded the manuscript through all phases to publication.

Errors of omission, commission, and judgment are my own. One can wish, now and always, to have done better while awaiting the advice of friendly critics.

Finally, three persons are particularly important in my life. Their encouragement, enthusiasm, and joyful optimism that the book would be completed was a constant incentive to keep at it. My children, Becky and David, though grown and gone, were boosters par excellence through their letters and telephone calls. A long- distance cheering squad. Sally Jo, my wife, postponed her own major writing task for a year. Two in the same home consumed by a writing task would have been too much. She became my researcher, taking a leave of absence from the university in order to help gather data. Then, back in the routine of home, writing, and work, she gave me strength and initiative, encouragement and a ready ear. The debt of gratitude I owe to her is boundless.

Contents

Introduction

The questions are serious. What information did members of American Protestant churches regularly receive through their religious periodicals (magazines published weekly, semimonthly, or monthly) about what was happening to the Jews in Germany during the Nazi era? In what form within these periodicals was this information conveyed? Was the information continuous from January 1933 to the end of World War II and after to December 1945 and to some extent into 1946? If information about the plight of the Jews under the Nazis was being systematically and regularly reported in these periodicals, what was the nature of this reporting? Did it change over the span of twelve years? What cautions, caveats, evaluations, judgments, and opinions accompanied the reporting of this information? Did these opinions, judgments, warnings, and cautions change over time? How did the reporting of the information concerning the plight of the Jews under the Nazi regime relate to other significant issues of the times, that is, the Church Struggle taking place at the same time in Germany and the problems of anti-Semitism and racism in the United States? Finally, if the persecution of the Jews was known by the average reader of denominational and interdenominational American Protestant periodicals, what was done through the churches to respond to what was being reported?

Add to these questions those raised by Lucy S. Dawidowicz in her aptly titled book, *The War against the Jews: 1933–1945*[1]

1. How was it possible for a modern state to carry out the systematic murder of a whole people for no reason other than that they were Jews?
2. How was it possible for a whole people to allow itself to be destroyed?
3. How was it possible for the world to stand by without halting this destruction?

In Dawidowicz's appendix A, "The Fate of the Jews in Hitler's Europe: By Country," the third of these questions is given a partial answer or answers. Within these "partial answers," the role of the Christian religions of Europe—Roman Catholic, Protestant, and Orthodox—is discussed. It is in this context that another and equally important question needs to be raised, a question not asked by Professor Dawidowicz but one related to her discussion of the three Christian religions of Europe. The question is: What is the relationship of the Christian religions in the United States of America, particularly Protestant Christianity, to the persecution and destruction of the Jews in Europe?

It is within the context of these questions that the charge that the American Protestant churches were silent (or, if not silent, then unresponsive and uncaring) must be faced. This is a very serious charge. When Jews speak of the Silence, they are referring to the failure of Christians generally (including American Protestants) to respond adequately or to intervene on behalf of beleaguered Jews in Germany from 1933 to as late as 1943–1944, when something could have been done to save the lives of Jews in Germany and Europe. More particularly, the Silence refers to the death camps and the consequent charge of guilt by association, if not complicity by association. By and large, from the time of the discovery and liberation of the "death factories" to the war crimes trials at Nuremberg to the present-day considerations of what is now labeled the Holocaust, the Jews have asked—where were the Christians, German, European, and American?

Perhaps no better witness to the problem of American Protestant Christians and the whole Jewish question, including the Holocaust, exists than in the difficulty that became central at the meeting of the World Council of Churches at Evanston, Illinois, in 1954. Alan T. Davies, in his *Anti-Semitism and the Christian Mind*, told of the conflict that arose quite unexpectedly among the delegates at the second assembly of the World Council of Churches in Evanston.[2] He used a quotation from the editor of *The Ecumenical Review*, whose statement was about the issue "which would provoke the greatest misunderstanding and . . . heated discussion, . . . the attitude and relation of the Church to Israel"[3] Davies briefly described the confrontation between European neo-Orthodox theologians and American Protestant theologians. To the former, Israel transcended time, place, and ethnic connotation; for the latter, Israel connoted a political and ethnic entity embodied in the state of Israel. The discussion that ensued resolved nothing and only served to widen the misunderstanding, but Davies's comment made the point that should be emphasized here.

> Auschwitz is a village in Poland, and liberal Protestant Christianity, with its "Anglo-Saxon" coloration, is mainly—though not exclusively—British and American in its genius. For this reason perhaps, and because Great Britain and the United States opposed Germany by force of arms in the Second World War, the significance of Auschwitz as an exposure of Western, rather than German, sinfulness has been slow in penetrating the American churches. *Not many Americans have seen themselves disclosed as guilty participants in its fires* [emphasis mine].[4]

If this assessment by Davies is correct or even partially correct and if the silence of the American Protestant churches about what happened to Jews in Germany under the Nazis (implied in an article by Roy and Alice L. Eckardt, "Again, Silence in the Churches," which discussed the 1967 war and the threatened destruction of the state of Israel)[5] is also correct or even partially correct, then it is imperative that all of the information and knowledge available be gathered and assessed in order to understand more fully American Protestant churches, the Nazi era, and what Davies (by implication) defined as the ultimate anti-Semitism, the Holocaust. A sentence in the article by Eckardts about the 1967 war is equally applicable to the Holocaust and to this study, "The few voices that were raised merely help to make the general stillness louder"[6] Thirty-three years (at this writing) after the Holocaust, the "general stillness" of American Protestantism still hangs like a pall over all Holocaust studies. It is, therefore, time to speak to the issue of what the American Protestant churches knew about what was happening to Jews in Germany from 1933 through 1945 and beyond. In truth, it is past time.

But where should such an effort be undertaken? The choices were several: (1) denominational "official" pronouncements; that is, the sort of statements that might conceivably be issued by denominational officials as speaking "for the denomination"; (2) interdenominational agencies and committees, such as the Federal Council of Churches of Christ in America or the several committees that were formed on behalf of intervention, refugees, and boycotts or for fund raising for the relief of the persecuted in Germany—Jews, non-Aryans, Hebrew Christians, and others; (3) sermons preached from the pulpits of Protestant churches; and (4) regularly published religious periodicals. For a number of reasons, I decided to examine in detail a selected number of American Protestant periodicals, commonly referred to as the religious press in America. Two reasons were paramount. Such periodicals are available from various denominational seminaries, church colleges, and archives; also, denominational "official" statements, significant sermons, and pronouncements of interdenominational agencies and committees tend to be printed in these religious periodicals. In addition, American Protestant periodicals, in the main, depend heavily on subscriptions purchased and renewed annually by the members of the churches of the various denominations, and even interdenominational and nondenominational religious periodicals depend on subscriptions purchased at the parish level by church members. In other words, it can be assumed that the American Protestant press regularly reported information about the plight of the Jews in Germany between 1933 and 1946 and that these religious periodicals were subscribed to by church members and those affiliated with churches at the parish level.

An aggregate of fifty-two Protestant periodicals from the years 1933 through 1945, with some from 1946 and a smaller number from 1947, were examined. These periodicals were selected according to a typology of four categories representative of American Protestantism during the period between 1933 and 1946: (1) liberal, (2) mainstream Protestant, (3) evangelical-conservative, and (4) fundamentalist. A "finer" theological differentiation was not made, and some periodicals used would not neatly fit into these categories. My object was to be as representative as possible without being excessively repetitive. Another researcher might well have made other selections, but the information would probably not be significantly different. (See appendix A for a list of religious periodicals used in this study.)

All the periodicals for every year were not used for a variety of reasons. Some were not published for all the years from 1933 through 1945 or 1946 or 1947; some were difficult or impossible to locate for some of the years; some, such as the Lutheran and Southern Baptist periodicals, tended to print the same items, often quoting each other, and so for some Lutheran and Southern Baptist periodicals only certain years were used. Some religious periodicals were victims of the Great Depression and had either ceased publication or had merged into other publications of their denominations. *The Presbyterian Banner* had merged into *The Presbyterian* in 1937, for example.

Some interdenominational and nondenominational religious periodicals were included either because of their influence upon all American Protestants or because they were of special significance to a segment of American Protestants (such as the mainstream Protestants or the fundamentalists) or because they were special-interest periodicals devoted to a single purpose (such as missionary work among the Jews in America) from a Protestant-Christian stance. *The Christian Century* and *The Christian Herald* would be examples of the first; *The King's Business*, *The Moody Bible Institute Monthly*, *The Gospel Herald*, and *The Sunday School Times* of the second; and *The Hebrew Christian Alliance Quarterly*, *The Friend of Zion*, and *The Hebrew Lutheran* of the third.

Sermons of note were published in *Current Religious Thought* and *The Pulpit*, and the Federal Council of Churches of Christ in America, the premier "ecumenical" Protestant organization, published the *Bulletin* monthly and later took over a quarterly, *Christendom*, from Charles Clayton Morrison, its founder and the editor of *The Christian Century*. Insofar as a religious periodical did not represent a Protestant denomination as such but was undenominational, it would be classified as one of the above periodicals or as one similarly identified.

As for the general subject itself, any attempt to come to grips with or "understand" or "find the meaning for" the treatment of the Jews under Hitler and the Nazis yields no easy answers. Quite the opposite is the case. Imponderable, awful questions arose to defy my imagination, frustrate my earnest concern for the effort, and ultimately leave me speechless. The terror and the horror reach down through the years to the present as the dead march to the gas chambers through one's memory and the living (the survivors) tell of horrors beyond human comprehension. Richard L. Rubinstein, in the foreword to Davies's work stated the situation for the Christian most explicitly: "When I wrote *After Auschwitz*, I was convinced that the problem of God and Auschwitz presents as many theological difficulties for Christianity as it does for Judaism."[7]

Rubenstein also clearly pointed out another and perhaps central problem to which this study must address itself.

> As Dr. Davies points out, even contemporary Christian interpretations of Judaism which attempt to alleviate the burden of anti-Semitism are often compelled to see the Jews as the people who, by rejecting Jesus as the Christ, rejected God's covenant and brought upon themselves their sorrowful history. Implicit in every normative Christian interpretation of Jewish experience is the conviction that Jewish misfortunes have been God's chastisement against his people for rejecting

Jesus. After Auschwitz this position can only be maintained by asserting that Adolf Hitler's death camps were the instruments utilized by the just, loving and righteous God to punish his wayward people.[8]

A study of the American Protestant press in relation to the Jews in Hitler's Germany is a frightening confirmation of Rubenstein's statement. The Jews are seen as a "deicide people," and only rarely does an American Protestant periodical dare to challenge this assumption, the blackest of all calumnies against the Jews, in the context of reporting on events in Nazi Germany. Yet, this is what subscribers to this Protestant press read, and what they read is part of the larger whole that makes up Holocaust studies. What is found in these periodicals cannot be avoided, even though it too often confirms the lower concerns of the Church, rather than the higher Christian ideals of love, grace, forgiveness, caring for, and suffering with one's fellow humans. To use Roy Eckardt's phrase, the younger brother too often stood aside, or worse "passed on the other side," and was not only *not* a Good Samaritan but condemned the elder brother for not understanding why he was suffering and dying.[9]

And yet Franklin H. Littell was correct when he stated that interreligious cooperation is essential to Holocaust studies. Jews and Christian need each other.

> Both foci, the Christian experience and the Jewish experience, are essential to Jewish reflections on the Holocaust. There were some Christians who stood up to the Nazis. There were even some martyrs, their witness as glorious as any in the annals of the church (Father Delp, Helmuth von Moltke, Probst Lichtenberg, Dietrich Bonhoeffer, Franz Jagerstadter, Max Josef Metzger, Julius Leber, Paul Schneider, Karl Koch, Adam Trott du Solz come immediately to mind . . .). Jewish youth and students are entitled to know of this record, along with the general record of mass betrayal and apostasy. Without that dimension the Holocaust easily recedes into mere internal history, another rubric in the long list of persecutions by the gentiles (without uniqueness), exquisitely precious.[10]

Insofar as this study contributes both to reflection on the Holocaust by Jews and Christians and to knowledge about the part that American Protestant periodicals played in reporting and interpreting what was happening to the Jews in Germany under Hitler, the goal of the study will be achieved.

Innumerable people have played a part in bringing about this study, both directly by encouragement and support and indirectly by the intangible of their own commitment to Holocaust studies. Of the latter at this writing, some I have never met except through their written works. The list is long: Richard L. Rubenstein, Emil Fackenheim, Eliezer Berkovits, Elie Wiesel, Alexander Donat, Alfred Friedlander, Nora Levin, Raul Hilberg, Lucy S. Dawidowicz, Saul S. Friedman, Alan T. Davies, and Arthur Morse to name only a few. Those whom I have met comprise the contributors to two major collective works on the Holocaust, Franklin H. Littell and Hubert G. Locke (editors of *The German Church Struggle and the Holocaust*, Detroit, Wayne State University Press, 1974) and Eva Fleischner (editor of *Auschwitz: Beginning of a New Era, Reflections on the Holocaust*, New York, KTAV Publishing House, 1977). Of this company of scholars, Franklin H. Littell of Temple University, Michael D. Ryan of Drew Seminary, and F. Burton Nelson of North Park Theological Seminary have given me special encouragement and assistance. Franklin H. Littell is everywhere and his energy knows no bounds in relation to studies of the Holocaust and the Church Struggle.

Finally, Timothy L. Smith was absolutely right when he wrote in reference to his own study, *Revivalism and Social Reform*:

Especially must we go beyond the solemn quarterlies published for clergymen and sift the literature which their parishioners read. Vast collections of devotional and biographical tracts, popular histories of revival and reform movements, and files of weekly denominational newspapers remain almost unexplored. Here lie the records of events as contemporaries actually saw them, interpreted in the light of their own doctrines, hopes and prejudices. The only problem is to avoid spending the flower of one's youth [and manhood] in those dark and dusty areas where university [and seminary] librarians shelve religious books [and religious periodicals].[11]

So, the persecution of the Jews in Germany under Hitler and the Nazis was interpreted in the American Protestant press "in the light of their own doctrines, hopes and prejudices," from 1933 through 1945 and beyond. Now this reporting is to be interpreted in its turn as another small part of the larger effort to tell the story of the most tragic period in the long history of world Jewry, the Holocaust.

SO IT WAS TRUE

PART I

The Years of Persecution

CHAPTER 1

1933—Hitler, the Jews, and the Early Warnings

Germany's treatment of the Jews is an offense against humanity, a violation of the most basic human instincts, a revival of sadism on a wide scale, and from a Christian point of view, a denial of all that we hold most sacred.

ROBERT A. ASHWORTH
The Reformed Church Messenger

KEY EVENTS

1933, General: January 30, Hitler became chancellor; January 31, Hitler's Appeal to the German People; February 27, Reichstag fire; February 28, Decree for the Protection of People and State, article 48 of the Weimar Constitution used to decree the loss of freedom; March 5, general elections, appearance of concentration camps; March 21, Potsdam ceremony, Garrison Church; March 22, 24, enabling law dissolving Reichstag; April 7, loss of autonomy of all states, Law for Reenactment of the Professional Civil Service; July 8, concordat with Roman Catholic church; July 14, 15, Germany became a one-party nation; September 10, concordat signed; December 1, Law to Ensure the Unity of the States.

1933, Relating to the Jews: March 28, boycott order against Jewish shops, goods, doctors, and lawyers; April 1, 2, boycott throughout Germany; April 7, article 3, "Aryan paragraph," in Law for the Reestablishment of the Professional Civil Service; April 11, decree defining "non-Aryan"; April 21, banning of ritual slaughter of animals; April 25, Law against Overcrowding of German Schools; July 14, Naturalization and Citizenship Revocation Law; September 29, Hereditary Farm Law; October 4, National Press Law. By the end of 1933, all laws restricting or excluding Jews from public life, education, government, the arts, and the professions were in place.

On January 30, 1933, Adolf Hitler became the chancellor of Germany. Twelve years and three months later to the day, Adolf Hitler took his own life in a bunker under the chancellery in Berlin.[1] One week later, on May 7, 1945, Admiral Karl Doenitz, acting as the head of the German government, agreed to an unconditional surrender. The Third Reich had come to an end.[2] From the official beginning of the Hitler era on January 30, 1933, to the death of Hitler on April 30, 1945, one part of the Hitler program remained constant—the persecution of the Jews. In appendix A ("The Fate of the Jews in Hitler's Europe: By Country") of her book *The War against the Jews, 1933–1945*, Lucy Dawidowicz questioned the role of the Christian religions of Europe (Roman Catholic, Protestant, and Orthodox) in relation to Hitler's policies. She asked, "How was it possible for the world to stand by without halting this destruction?"[3]

An equally important question also needs to be raised about the impact of the persecution and destruction of the Jews of Europe on the predominantly Protestant Christian churches in the United States of America. Did American Protestant Christians know what was happening to the Jews in Germany from 1933 through 1945? One way to attempt to answer this question is to turn to the American Protestant press to see how it reported events in Germany during the Hitler era. The use of religious periodicals to answer the question is based on two assumptions. The first is that, if this press did systematically report during the entire period what was happening to Jews in Nazi Germany, then Protestant Christians had this information before them. They could not later claim that they had not been told. The second is that, if such reporting was not done, then Protestant Christians could later claim that they had not been told about the plight of the Jews in Nazi Germany.

Usually American Protestants have been served by two types of religious periodicals. One is the denominational paper sponsored by a Protestant denomination and edited by a member of the denomination in good standing, often a clergyman who is considered one of its central officers. In the instance of the Southern Baptists, the denominational membership is typically served by a state paper, for example, *The Baptist Standard* (in Texas), *The Arkansas Baptist*, *The Baptist and Reflector* (in Tennessee), and *The Christian Index* (in Georgia). In many denominations, one church magazine published weekly, biweekly, or monthly serves the entire national membership.

These denominational papers typically publish editorials, sermons, topical articles on selected subjects, Sunday school lesson materials, devotional pages, youth pages, women's auxiliary pages, and news of the congregations and their activities. News about the clergy (their deaths, transfers, honorary degrees, illnesses, and accidents) are included, as are book reviews, letters to the editor, and advertising (in various amounts).

The second type of Protestant church paper is described as undenominational or nondenominational. These papers are owned privately by parent corporations or groups of individuals (not belonging to a specific religious denomination), and the papers have their own subscription lists. They are intended for national circulation across denominational lines. Three such papers published during the years 1933–1936 were *The Christian Century, An Undenominational Journal of Religion* which was owned and controlled by Charles Clayton Morrison, its highly respected editor during those years, and which was perhaps the best-known religious periodical in America; *The Christian Herald*, owned by the Christian Herald Association and edited by Daniel A. Poling, who was also an active pastor and the president of the World Christian Endeavor during the 1930s; and *Church Management and Record of Christian Work*, published by the Church World Press of Cleveland, Ohio, but a paper closely identified with its editor and publisher, William H. Leach. *Church Management* did not limit itself to the areas suggested by its title. William H. Leach regularly wrote lively editorials with broad-based commentary (as did Morrison and his staff and Poling). It is probably accurate to say that *The Christian Century* was acknowledged as the premier Protestant religious periodical during the 1930s and 1940s; this is indicated by other editors' comments and frequent quotations from the *Century*. Morrison was not always agreed with. Yet, he was certainly read broadly and his paper exercised a considerable influence in religious publishing, though it did not have the largest circulation among such periodicals. Articles of interest on just about any subject were presented to the readers by writers from across the spectrum of American Protestantism by Leach, Morrison, and Poling. All three papers depended on advertising to help keep the papers going.

Examples of periodicals more conservative or fundamentalist in purpose and content were *The Gospel Herald* (Cleveland, Ohio), *The Moody Bible Institute Monthly* (later *Moody Monthly*, The Moody Bible Institute, Chicago, Illinois), *The King's Business* (the Bible Institute of Los Angeles), and *The Sunday School Times* (Philadelphia, Pennsylvania). All were circulated nationally.

Occasionally, a quarterly journal aimed at the popular denominational level (the church members) was published, usually without much success. The entire American Protestant press had been severely affected by the Great Depression, with a number of prominent denominational and nondenominational papers either closing up or merging in order to keep publishing.

The Early Warnings Begin

One common feature of Protestant periodicals was their news digest. Usually one page in length (but sometimes much longer), the news digest was devoted to reporting selected world news. In some periodicals, a single person was identified as the editor for such a page; in others, no such person was indicated, leaving the reader to assume that the editorial staff prepared the digest. Did the news digests, editorials, articles, lesson pages, youth pages, and printed sermons pay much attention to the situation of Jews in Germany in 1933? What information on this subject did they present to the Protestant audience? In fact, as early as 1933, the press was reporting a great deal about the Nazi treatment of Jews. Throughout the Hitler era, the Protestant press continued to write about what was happening to Jews in Europe. A news digest item from February 13, 1933, included the following warning:

> Besides economic ruin, the Jews of Europe are suffering increasingly from anti-Semitic atrocities. . . . [The universities in Poland were then mentioned as being partial to anti-Semites.]
>   Terrorization of Jews through economic boycott has also been on the increase. The atrocities have assumed a new form. Tear-gas bombs have been thrown into Jewish stores and cinemas in several cities in Germany, in Romania and in Poland. In Vienna, property damage estimated at 200,000 schillings [sic], and incalculable boycott damage, was wrought by Nazis in their terrorization campaign to prevent Christmas shoppers from trading with Jews. Tear-gas bombs were thrown into Jewish department stores compelling them to close.
>   From Germany also came reports of tear-gas bombing of warehouses and other places of Jewish business, in Giessen, Mainz, Darmstadt, Worms, and other towns—all attacks believed to be part of a prearranged programme worked out by Nazi leaders.[4]

This paragraph, without attribution, appeared in "Comments and Items of Interest" in *The Evangelical Visitor*. On the same page, again without attribution, the following paragraph also appeared.

Hitler, a leader of what is known as the Nazi political group in Germany, is finally made chancellor. He is granted certain honors without a great deal of power. He is trying to do in Germany what Mussolini did in Italy. Hitler is also a very devout Roman Catholic so wherever you go there is a feeling of unrest and at the least provocation men are liable to throw off all the forces of restraint and allow the spirit of communism which has pervaded the mind of many individuals to have full sway.[5]

The very early reports were somewhat mixed. Hitler was still relatively unknown, and neither his policies toward Jews nor his attitude toward Jews was as yet known. The first reports have about them a certain tentativeness, as though their writers were waiting for things to become more clear. Some items seem even a bit strange; this was apparent in the following item. *The Brethren Evangelist*, "official organ of the Brethren Church" (Ashland, Ohio), in its issue of January 28, 1933, reprinted a lengthy article from *The Christian Index*, the Southern Baptist periodical for the state of Georgia, titled "Paganizing Propaganda." The article included a "hymn to Hitler," which had been printed earlier in Germany by the *Catholic Augsburger Post* and reprinted in the *Frankfurter Zeitung* and about which *The Christian Index* had commented, "It is after such collective prayers as this, preferable after all to the obnoxious hymn type, such as 'When Jewish gore from sword-blade drips' that political murders are committed." There was no further comment from the editor of *The Brethren Evangelist*. No direct reference to persecution of the Jews or its potential for happening was reported in this very early article in 1933.

The Christian Century for February 8, 1933, reported the appointment of Hitler to the chancellor's position in a paragraph entitled, "How Much of a Menace Is Hitler?" but did not mention anything about the persecution of Jews.[6]

March 5, 1933, was the date set by Hitler for new elections for the Reichstag. The events leading up to this election were thoroughly reported in the secular press, including the Reichstag fire of February 27, 1933.[7] For the most part, however, little news was reported in the Protestant church papers about events in Germany from January through March 1933, though some of this press did take note of these events. *The Sunday School Times* of March 11, 1933, in a regularly published section entitled, "A Survey of Religious Life and Thought," edited by Ernest Gordon, reported in an article, "Encouragement and Warnings from All the World," that the Jews of Germany were sending their money to banks in Palestine because "there have been no bank failures there, and the Jews of Germany, alarmed at the threat of Hitlerism and its sinister implications, are sending their money to these banks for safe keeping."[8]

An editorial in *The Christian Century*, March 13, 1933, discussed the March fifth elections in Germany. Suspicious of the Reichstag fire, the *Century* judged it to be either a stupid act by "some half-witted anarchist" or an act "staged by the Nazis themselves" and questioned whether the Third Reich could be successfully established by Hitler. Calling Hitler a "demagogue and a great political orator," the editorial predicted that "the third reich will certainly come, but Hitler is not likely to go down in history as its founder."[9] The subsequent years, 1933–1945, proved that this prediction by Charles Clayton Morrison and his editorial staff missed the mark.

In *The Christian Century* for March 29, 1933, the first article on what was to become a major theme in the American Protestant press during the next twelve years appeared. E. G. Homrighausen wrote an article, "Hitler and German Religion," in which he attempted to assess the religious situation in Germany. In the article, he predicted that Hitler would last and that democracy would disappear in Germany and be replaced by "Hitlerism" and absolute autocracy. Becoming metaphorical, he foresaw an ultimate struggle between Christ and caesar in Germany at a time when "the age of Caesars is upon us." In his general discussion of Hitlerism, only once did Homrighausen refer to the Jews, and then he did so only indirectly. "There must come again that absolute national life in which every person will be forced to enlist with participative zeal as though he were a soldier fighting for the glory that once shone around the German people. Therefore the anti-Semitic spirit."[10] The main theme of this article was the impending Church Struggle, a subject that would dominate all other subjects in the Protestant press during the entire Hitler era and continuing into the immediate postwar years.[11]

The First Planned Attack on the Jews

On March 28, 1933, Hitler ordered a boycott of Jewish professionals and businesses to begin on April 1, 1933. In fact, it was a more serious matter than that. Karl Stern, a Rockefeller fellow at the German Research Institute for Psychiatry, observed events in Munich in 1933. He wrote:

> Right after that ominous first of April, 1933, the day of the
> anti-Jewish boycott, all my Jewish friends, all those who had
> graduated with me, in fact all Jewish professional people "ex-

cept for world war veterans" lost their jobs. The clause " . . . except for world war veterans" was intended to give the impression of a just and humane decision, and one could see that this was the psychological effect it had on our professors, technicians, dishwashers, janitors and charwomen, all except for Herr Eisinger and a few other people. A few months later the Jewish veterans lost their jobs too, but without anyone hearing about it.[12]

Dawidowicz documented the events leading up to the April first boycott of the Jews. She pointed out that Jewish department stores and Jewish judges, lawyers, and professional people were already being attacked in various parts of Germany, with official sanction and support. To mute world reaction an effort was made by Goering to have German Jewish leaders deny the stories of atrocities against the Jews being published in the world press.[13] The enactment of the first racial laws followed immediately upon the boycott on April 1, 1933, in Germany.[14]

These events did not escape the attention of the Protestant press in America. From April of 1933 through the remainder of the year, attention was paid to the treatment of the Jews in Germany under the new Nazi government of Adolph Hitler. The sources of information for articles, editorials, news items, and comments in the Protestant press came from secular newspapers, Jewish agencies in Europe, and German propaganda. Questions about the accuracy or possible exaggeration of conflicting reports of the persecution of Jews, the boycott, and the atrocities committed against them appeared often in Protestant publications. The Protestant press discussed observations made by visitors to Europe who had returned and competent eyewitness reports from respected professional journalists such as Edgar Russel Mowrer, chief of the Berlin Bureau of the *Chicago Daily News*.[15] Letters to relatives in America were cited as they became available to establish that the stories of persecution were not exaggerated. One such letter was mentioned in "Comments and Items of Interest" in *The Evangelical Visitor* (November 6, 1933) under the heading "Germany Still Much Upset."

It is whispered among those who know, that the world does not know half of the indignities practiced upon the Jews in Germany. One Jew has written relatives in New York City, that Hitler is a fine man, and that everything was going good if you agreed with him. His brother Isadore did not agree with the chancellor and they had just buried him.[16]

Those religious periodicals with direct ties to Jewish agencies in Europe reported from these sources as they were able to. They also reported on activities and speakers presented by the National Conference of Christians and Jews and the International Committee for Goodwill and Justice of the Federal Council of Churches of Christ in America. Statements made by the committee and by any other agency of the Federal Council were reported on in varying lengths.[17] The activities of the American Jewish Congress were reported, as well as the activities of other Jewish groups in America. Petitions and statements drawn up and signed by clergymen (Protestant, Roman Catholic, and Jewish), such as the statement by the Chicago Church Federation, were reported and protest rallies (regardless of their sponsorship) were covered, some extensively.[18]

Some of the more theologically conservative religious periodicals reported what was happening to the Jews in Germany as news items but frequently accompanied the news reports with comments related to their concern for the teaching of prophecy as they interpreted such teaching from the Bible. The Jews as the Chosen People and the persecution of the Jews that would force Jews to return to Palestine to live were two common themes in conservative and fundamentalist papers.[19] Another was the "comment" that Hitler was making a great mistake in persecuting the Jews because they were God's Chosen People and the biblical record was clear; anyone who undertook such a program against the Jews was sealing his own doom.[20]

Some articles and commentaries picked up statements that Hitler had made about the Jews either in *Mein Kampf* or in a political tract written in 1919 during the same month in which he had joined the National Socialist party. Also noted were the promises made by Hitler in his book, in his early statements, and in the party platform of 1920, which were in 1933 being carried out.[21]

Some discussion centered around whether the persecution of the Jews was an officially sanctioned party policy or whether the perpetrators were "Nazi thugs" somehow out of control or beyond party or governmental discipline. Some observers argued that a "revolution" was occurring in Germany and that, as in all revolutions, some blood must be shed. That such a revolution had happened was the view stated by Dr. R. C. Schiedt in *The Reformed Church Messenger*.

> The result was a thorough going revolution that completely overthrew the socialistic regime and restored without bloodshed the old order of things in government, school and home-life, seasoned by experience, but still based on the solid foun-

dation of faith in God and the blessings of a redemptive religion. Thus Germany saved once more the civilized world from
the spread of materialistic communism. Unfortunately among
the socialists and communists unceremoniously ousted from
office, there were many Jews who all along have supported the
Marxism doctrine through their press as well as through international finance, largely in the hands of Jewish bankers.[22]

This is a strange article. Through specifically denying his own anti-
Semitism, Schiedt repeated one anti-Semitic charge after another;
that is, that there was an international Jewish conspiracy, that all
Jews were Marxists and Communists, that Jewish bankers controlled
world finance, that German doctors and lawyers were predominantly
Jewish, that persecution and atrocity stories were largely exaggerated
or false, that antiracial measures were fully justified in light of "the
discovery of the gigantically planned communistic plot, largely fi-
nanced by Jewish capital," and that Hitler and the National Socialists
were to be praised, rather than blamed, for the rescue of the German
people from all of this.[23]

The Christian Century focused only on the persecution of Jews. Its
leading editorial for April 5, 1933, reported that "the apparent shock
suffered by the new government of Germany at the storm of indignation in other lands aroused by the Nazi persecution of Jews, justi-
fies raising that question in all seriousness." The "outcry" was based
on "violent attacks on Jews by bands of Nazi ruffians, who instituted
a reign of terror in the days immediately following the recent election."[24]

Through the spring of 1933 considerable attention was focused in
editorials, news reports, and articles on the persecution of the Jews.
What was really happening? Which reports were accurate? Could
they be trusted? The one-day boycott of April 1, 1933, was extensively covered, and there were reports about Jewish professionals
losing their positions and the general distress of the Jews in Germany. Where documentation was judged accurate, reports of the persecution of Jews (of beatings and shootings and disappearances)
were cited by some of the Protestant publications.

Citing respected, trusted, prominent authorities was considered of
vital importance for the sake of credibility. An editorial in *The Presbyterian Banner*, "Hitler Pursuing His Relentless Course," told of the
visit to Germany by Michael Williams, editor of *The Commonweal* and
a member of an American committee on religious rights and minorities.

He confirms the worst that has been reported as to the Nazi persecution of the Jews. More than 300 of them suffered physical violence, and 30 of them were killed and worst still is the relentless persecution and driving from their positions of the Jews in general.[25]

Samuel McCrea Cavert, the highly respected general secretary of the Federal Council of Churches of Christ in America, wrote an article, "Behind the Scenes in Germany," that was reprinted widely in the Protestant press. Cavert reported that a "distinguished German Christian, well-known in American circles (whose name must not be mentioned lest it arouse the wrath of the Nazis against him) . . . told me that he had knowledge of eight well authenticated instances of Jews being beaten to death."[26]

The Christian Century waited until one of its own editors, Paul Hutchinson, could visit Europe personally. The *Century* (August 16, 1933) published Hutchinson's editorial correspondence from Austria, entitled "Germany Welcomes New Messiah" (July 28, 1933), in which he mentioned the reluctance of Germans to talk about the persecution of the Jews and referred to their remarks about bloodshed in a revolution. Hutchinson wrote:

I am convinced, on the strength of evidence which for obvious reasons I cannot quote but which has satisfied me as to its reliability, that the actual brutalities inflicted on Jews, socialists, communists and pacifists have been even more severe than the responsible American press has published.[27]

In November 1933, this same periodical reported in its correspondence from Toronto that Francis Parkes of Geneva, secretary of the International Student Service, described as "an Oxford man, [who] embodies the fine judicial temper which is supposed to characterize the graduates of that seat of Christian culture," was confident that the reports of Nazi atrocities against Jews in Germany had not been exaggerated.[28]

The American Protestant press continued to be cautious in its reports about Germany's persecution of the Jews. When rumors of the existence of the death camps began to come out of Europe in 1942 and 1943, it sought confirmation. When the existence of the death camps had been confirmed by the Russian discovery of Majdanek in July 1944, eyewitness verification by persons of credibility was still being sought by the Protestant press. The fear of being proved victims of false propaganda about atrocities as had happened after

World War I lingered on in the memories of the editors from the beginning to the end of Hitler's years in power.

The Church Struggle, the "Aryan Clause," and the Jews

Dominating the concern of American Protestant editors and writers was their interest in the emerging struggle between their coreligionists in Germany and the Nazis. Political exigencies led almost immediately to the concordat between Hitler's representatives and those of Pope Pius XI.[29] It became clear very quickly that Hitler and the Nazis had definite plans as to how the Church in Germany, Protestant and Roman Catholic, was to participate in the New Germany. A concept called "positive Christianity" was presented to the leaders of the two major communions.

As the struggle developed, "positive Christianity" clearly involved making the Church, particularly the Protestant church, in Germany an instrument of the state and of Nazi politics and purposes. The story of the resistance, acquiescence, too, or neutrality of the Protestant leaders and clergy was watched intently by American religious leaders and editors. No other subject about Germany received so much attention from the Protestant press as did the struggle in Germany between the Protestant church and the Nazis, from 1933 to the end of the war. When the war in Europe ended in May 1945, the story of the reestablishment of contact with German Protestant church leaders and the concern for restoring the churches of Germany, along with the concern for feeding, clothing, and housing the millions of refugees and war victims throughout Europe, were the major, constant news stories and the subjects of editorials in the Protestant press about Germany and postwar Europe. (In a later chapter, it will be shown that the concern for what was happening to the German churches at the end of the war in Europe almost totally overwhelmed the news about Jews who were still alive, except as they were a part of the general question of refugees, or displaced persons.)

In 1933, Protestant periodicals often discussed the treatment of the Jews as a central issue in the developing Church Struggle in Germany. Paul F. Douglas included a chapter entitled, "The Christian Jews in the Third Reich," in his book *God among the Germans*. The chapter described in great detail what came to be called the "Aryan paragraph" or the "Aryan clause." Briefly described, the "Aryan clause" denied to professing or confessional Christians of Jewish or part-Jewish descent any active role in the local churches.[30] This included serving as a pastor or a church officer or being retained as a member or receiving baptism in the churches. The "Aryan clause" was one of the earliest direct applications of racial laws to be promulgated as official action within an institutional setting in Germany after Hitler came to power.[31] The origins of the "Aryan clause" are to be found in Hitler's own racial philosophy set forth in *Mein Kampf*, the Law for Reestablishment of a Professional Civil Service, the new Prussian Student Law of April 1933, and the subsequent laws establishing the racial basis for acceptable professional public service. In these laws, the identity of the grandparents, racially interpreted, was the key. If one had one grandparent who had been Jewish, even though one was a baptized, confessional Christian, this meant one's exclusion based on race from religious affiliations. Marriage to a Jew was also a basis for applying racial laws to the churches. More severe applications of racial laws were to be realized in the later Nuremberg laws announced formally by action of the Reichstag on September 15, 1935.

In many instances in 1933, the only reports of the persecution of the Jews in Germany came in the context of the "Aryan clause," most often as a paragraph or statement within a much longer article or editorial on the problems of the Church in Germany. Adoph Keller, Samuel McCrea Cavert, Henry Smith Leiper, E. G. Homrighausen, W. A. Visser't Hooft, and Reinhold Niebuhr, among others, discussed at length the problems of churches in Germany from differing perspectives. These highly respected churchmen were presumed to be thoroughly familiar with the situation in Germany.

Often, but not always, a very small part of a larger article on the Church Struggle would be devoted to either information about or discussion of the "Aryan clause." As early as March 9, 1933, E. G. Homrighausen, writing in *The Christian Century*, spoke of the known anti-Semitism of Hitler in relation to "that absolute national life in which every person will be forced to enlist with participative zeal as though he were a soldier fighting for the glory that once shown around the German people." Homrighausen went on to discuss the problems that the Protestants would have with Hitler, concluding that German Protestants were disunified, prone to yield under pressure, and without "unity of thought and action." "Besides," he concluded, "the church's relation to culture has always caused it to capitulate to the powers that be in a crisis."[32]

One week later, in the same periodical, Reinhold Niebuhr stated flatly "that the Protestant church in Germany has on the whole fallen under the spell of Hitler."[33] For the plight of Jews, Niebuhr warned, American Protestants could not be anything but disturbed, and for baptized Christians of Jewish ancestry (often referred to as Hebrew Christians or Jewish Christians in the American Protestant press) their concern had to be very great. (The terms non-Aryan Christian, Jewish Christian, and Hebrew Christian were used in the American Protestant press to describe two groups. The first group were Jews who were baptized Christians or who had converted to Christianity in Germany, thus they were non-Aryan Christians. The second group included the first category but in addition included Jews anywhere who had converted to Christianity or were baptized Christians, generally referred to as Hebrew Christians or Jewish Christians. Where the terms are used, they will be in the context of common use in the Protestant press. It must be further noted that, commonly, Jews consider Jews who convert to Christianity no longer to be Jews.) Developments were watched carefully. A long editorial, "Jews and Jesus," in *The Christian Century* pointed out that the Jews were the first "victims" of the program of nationalism introduced by Hitler.

> Through all the Christian centuries nationalism has been the
> Jews' chief enemy, shutting them out from the equalities and
> esteem of their fellows, condemning them to a place apart
> from the main community and subjecting them to ever recur-
> ring brutalities and cruelties.[34]

On May 3, 1933, W. A. Visser't Hooft included a section on the "Jewish question" in his article, "Christ or Caesar in Germany?" also in *The Christian Century*.[35] The Protestant press was concerned about what was happening to the Jews and also about what might happen as Hitler consolidated his position in Germany.[36]

In the summer of 1933, the "Aryan clause" frequently became the subject of discussion.

> In dealing with anti-semitism the church has, again, been so
> busy preserving its own moral integrity that it has nothing to
> say to the state. The degree of anti-semitism in Germany can
> be gauged by the fact that the German Christians[37] have in-
> sisted that converted Jews shall be dismissed from member-
> ship in the church. Against this the groups supporting Bodel-
> schwingh have protested vigorously. But in their very protest
> against anti-semitism in the church they have by implication
> allowed it in the state. They say in their protest, "The state
> must judge but the church must save," from which one can
> only draw the conclusion that they regard the anti-semitic poli-

cies of the government as justified. They are at least not criticized. Surely the church must know that a Christian attitude toward the very small groups of Jews who have become Christian has little influence upon the total tragic problem.[38]

German Christians (deutsche Christen) were sympathetic with the aims of the Nazis and accepted the principle that the Church ought to be an arm of the state. They were loyal to Hitler and to the Nazi party and were pro-Nazi, though they were never fully part of the Nazi hierarchy. At this point, they were little understood in America. The Lutheran Companion of July 1, 1933, in a regular department "With Lutherans in Other Lands," reported on the ten propositions of the German Christians. The third proposition read: "The National Evangelical Church is the church of the 'German Christians', of the Christians of the Arian race." The report concluded with a long paragraph taken from the Allgemeine Evangelish-Luth. Kirchenzeitung speaking favorably of the ten propositions as showing "so much understanding of Lutherdom."

> In regard to point 3, however, [we must say] that if it contemplates the exclusion of all non-Arians [sic] from the church the impossible has been asked for. Non-Arians [sic] are not only the Jews but the Slavs, Czechs, Japanese, Samoans, Negroes, etc. A church, however, cannot exclude unless it wishes to exclude itself from all that is known as the church on earth."[39]

From June-July 1933 through the remainder of the year, the progress of the German Christians in Germany was watched carefully by the American Protestant press, including the problem of the Jews and the "Aryan clause." In October 1933, the Federal Council Bulletin reported that a minority within the German churches was actively resisting the action of the Prussian Synod, where the "Aryan clause" had been adopted on September 5, 1933. A statement of opposition was drawn up by "leading ministers in Berlin."

> The very substance of the church is endangered. . . . The exclusion of Jewish Christians from our communion of worship would mean that the excluding church is erecting a racial law as a prerequisite of Christian communion. But in so doing it loses Christ itself. . . . Right doctrine, Christian conduct and spiritual endowments alone qualify for the ministry. It is therefore an ecclesiastical impossibility to exclude, as a matter of principle, Jewish Christian members from any office of the Church. . . . On a church whose essential nature has been violated the blessing of God can no longer rest.[40]

The Reformed Church Messenger, November 16, 1933, published an article by Henry Smith Leiper, secretary of the Department of Relations with Churches Abroad of the Federal Council of Churches of Christ in America. The article described what was happening among Protestant churches in Germany, including the exclusion of non-Aryans from the ministry, "thus setting up official race discrimination within the body of Christ." This action and other decisions made by the German Christians Leiper judged as actions that "clearly violate the spirit of Christ."[41]

The Christian Century in an editorial, "The Nazification of German Protestantism Continues," September 16, 1933, reported in a similar vein about a growing opposition to these actions from a minority of German pastors and church leaders.[42] In "News of the Christian World" in the same periodical, the correspondent to *The Christian Century* from Germany filed the following report.

> No storm has upset the church life of Germany in recent years comparable to that aroused by the passing of the famous Aryan paragraph forbidding pastors with Jewish ancestry the right to hold office. This also applies to church executives. Pastors and officials having wives with Jewish blood are also excluded. Will it be enforced? So far the German Christian movement has not stood unitedly for its enforcement. The eyes of the world are on Germany. Daily letters are received in Berlin asking if it really be true that a persecution of Christians has begun in the land of the reformation.[43]

The Mennonite also noted what was happening to non-Aryan Christians in an editorial on the situation in Germany.[44] But regardless of which American Protestant periodical discussed the "Aryan clause" and regardless of how long or how short the article or editorial or news report or the status and credibility of the commentator or writer, the matter was presented in a Christian context and from a Christian perspective.[45] The "Aryan clause" and its possible adoption by the German Christian, or Nazi-supported, church group gave to the American Protestant press a reason and a context for discussing the continued evidence of persecution of Jews in Germany. Persecution of Jews did not cease to be an item of concern, but the greater interest was in, and therefore the great emphasis was on, non-Aryan Christians whose exclusion from the Church in Germany for racial reasons was reported on as demonstrating the general continuation of persecution of the Jews and the continuation of the racial restrictions for Jews in Germany.

For American journalism, from June-July 1933 through December 1933, the nazification of the Protestant church in Germany was news, and the "Aryan clause" as a part of the larger story was also news for American Protestant periodicals. In the sense that the issue of the "Aryan clause" often included references to the continuing persecution of the Jews in Germany generally, this aspect of the news side of these events was included in the reports, editorials, and articles. But news was not the only reason nor perhaps even the primary reason or reporting events concerning the emerging Church Struggle. Editors, writers, and reporters expressed a genuine distress over what was happening to the Church in Germany, and even those American Protestant groups most tied ethnically to Germany, Lutherans and members of the Reformed churches, spoke unhesitatingly against exclusion of non-Aryan Christians from the churches.[46]

The fact that Jews who were baptized, confessional Christians had become the victims of the nazification program of the Protestant church in Germany was also abhorrent to writers, editors, and correspondents alike. Using racial laws as the bases for religious decisions was criticized in the American Protestant press. Pressure from denominational leaders, the Federal Council of Churches of Christ in America, and European-based church organizations and what the religious press called "world opinion" was cited as mounting protests against the persecution of Jews in Germany through the use of the "Aryan clause." Their cause was just; their concern, genuine and vocal; and their reporting of the events and decisions, accurate and timely in relation to the information made available to them.

But it must be stated once again that the events were seen from a Christian perspective; that is, the press protested the treatment of ethnic Jews as non-Aryan Christians who were being persecuted and excluded from the churches by Nazi decree. Concern for the Jews qua Jews was secondary. When Jews did not fall into the category of non-Aryan Christians less attention was given to them, although references to persecution of the Jews apart from a Christian context can be found in the Protestant press for all of 1933.

Book Reviews and the Persecution of the Jews

The portent that the persecution of the Jews in Germany under Hitler would be more serious than at first thought appeared not in editorials and articles, but in the departments found in some of the Protestant publications that published book reviews and to letters to the editor. Book reviews were published in two such periodicals when the translated version of Hitler's *Mein Kampf* appeared in the fall of 1933. *The Reformed Church Messenger* published a review of Hitler's book in its "One Book a Week" page, "Hitler Tells His Own Story." Frederick Lynch, the reviewer, explained that the translated version was only 300 pages long, less than half of the original. "It was evidently thought wise, either by the publishers, or by Hitler himself, to leave out many pages where his hatred of the Jews found virulent expression." Lynch then, in a later paragraph, spoke of Hitler and the Jews.

> Hitler gives vent to his hatred of the Jews in many vitriolic passages of this translation, . . . the worst passages in the original are omitted. . . . His hatred of the Jews seems to have come from his identification of Jews with Communism. To be sure, most leaders of Communism are Jews—in New York practically the rank and file are also Jews—but all Jews are not Communists. Then he became convinced that the Jews were tied up with all sorts of vice, indecency in the theatres and elsewhere, and with shyster practices in the professions and business, and that they held to a philosophy of materialism, having no Gods but money and pleasure. Some of the utterances on these subjects are really the most terrible things that have been said against the Jews. But one gathers . . . that at present his determination to rid Germany of the Jews is simply part of his scheme to make a nation of only one blood, one race, one religion and one family.

In the same review, Lynch also referred briefly to *The Brown Book of the Hitler Terror*, published by Knopf. Lynch dismissed the book as aimed at proving that the Hitlerites burned the Reichstag. "The book contains a long list of atrocities committed against the Jews. Unfortunately the book is so evidently propaganda for Communism that it loses much of its worth as evidence." Both in the main review and in the second review, Lynch had quite clearly succumbed to the Nazi propaganda that Hitler had saved Germany from communism and to the anti-Semitic slur that *Communist* meant *Jew*.[47]

The Lynch review was used as the basis for an editorial in *The Brethren Evangelist* for December 2, 1933, in which most of the review of *Mein Kampf* was quoted. The general subject of the editorial was, however, the threat to Christianity posed by Adolf Hitler, and the Lynch review (without attribution other than quotation marks) was one of several citations given to support the editorial comments.[48]

Other book reviewers were more blunt. James Waterman Wise, the son of Rabbi Stephen S. Wise and editor of *Opinion: A Journal of Jewish*

Life and Letters, wrote *Swastika: The Nazi Terror.* It was reviewed in "Books in Brief" in *The Christian Century,* July 12, 1933. The reviewer asked a series of rhetorical questions (for example, are the reports exaggerated? distorted? can the reports be compared with treatment of Negroes and Japanese in America? what can be done? what ought to be done?) and then concluded that "such questions are faced and answered in this book. The greater part of it consists of a sufficiently detailed and documented presentation of the facts, of which enough are given to demonstrate that the case has been understated rather than overstated in the press."[49] Other reviews of books on Germany published in *The Christian Century, Church Management, The Churchman,* and the *Federal Council Bulletin* did not mention the problems of the Jews. Rather they discussed the rise of the Nazis, the nature of the state under national socialism, and, in the one instance in which Jews were discussed, the accuracy of the charge that the Jews were responsible for crucifying Jesus.[50] No direct reference to the Jews in Germany and their plight was made in these books or by their reviewers.

Letters to the Editor and the Persecution of the Jews

Letters to the Editor as a department or an editorial responsibility did not exist for many of the papers examined in this study. Sometimes a letter received by an editor would be referred to in an editorial in a periodical where no letters to the editor were published. Some periodicals published letters to the editor as a separate page or section, but initially few contained letters about the Jews or the persecution of the Jews in Germany. Two of the periodicals examined that did publish letters to the editor regularly, as the year 1933 progressed, however, did include letters that referred to the persecution of Jews in Germany.

The letters tended to reflect several divergent points of view. There were letters that maintained that the persecutions were much worse than the editorials or articles indicated; letters that addressed the "Jewish question," which included references to the persecution of the Jews in Germany; letters that were prophetic interpretations of events that "proved" some sort of "end times" theory; letters that were anti-Semitic or Jew baiting, which stated that the stories of persecution were untrue or that the Jews deserved it and which included the common accusations that the Jews were Communists, responsible for the death of Jesus, an apostate people, money hungry, controllers of international finance and the entertainment industry, ad

infinitum (one is tempted to say ad nauseum); and letters that suggested that Palestine or the United States be made a refugee home
for persecuted Jews. This last suggestion, in turn, aroused another
controversy, and the editors received letters of strong opinion both
favoring and opposing such a suggestions, regardless of the country
named. As they published such opinions from readers through the
Hitler years, the editors indicated that they were plagued by the re-
curring question of "more atrocity stories." They remembered the
atrocity stories published during World War I that after the war were
proven to have been false or propagandistic. Correspondents were
also quick to warn that the reports of Nazi atrocities might be untrue.
In fact, this question was never really put to rest in the American
Protestant press even after the death camps were discovered (a matter discussed in detail in the chapters on the death camps).

The minister of the Brighton Park Congregational Church in Chicago wrote to *The Christian Century* in response to two editorials, one
of which was entitled "A Need for Light, Not Heat," April 5, 1933.[51]
In publishing the letter, the editors of *The Christian Century* used the
caption, "We Repeat: Light Not Heat."[52] The letter writer accused *The
Christian Century* of writing for "very immature minds." He went on
to write:

> We had race riots in Chicago and elsewhere and lynchings and
> the most impossible conditions in the mining districts of our
> state and other places and the German people had decency
> enough to mind their own business. You, and many who are
> once more stampeded into the wiles of European propaganda,
> would outdo or out-Hitler Hitler himself, were you living in
> distracted Germany.
> This is a fine time to divert tourists from visiting the Father-
> land to see once more the battlefields of our illustrious allies—
> some spell it all-lies, and perhaps it is just that and no more.[53]

Frank Hartl, the letter's author, then indicated that he would no
longer continue to subscribe to *The Christian Century.*

On May 3, 1933, the liberal-minded *Christian Century*, as noted earlier, published a long editorial article, "Jews and Jesus."[54] The article
forthrightly attacked anti-Semitism, the "apostate people" and "deicide people" arguments, and the fundamentalist analysis "still ob-
sessed with the so-called prophecies of scripture." It also spoke of the
problems of the Christian interpretation of the Jews' part in the Crucifixion and anti-Jewish bias "embodied in the sacred scriptures of
the Christian church—notably in the Gospel of John." The editorial

further stated that the churches in the United States, England, and Canada had given sermons and offered prayers "on behalf of the stricken Jews in Germany." Regarding the persecution of the Jews in Germany, the sympathy of Christians generally was "on the side of persecuted Jews and against the Hitlers," wrote the *Century*.

> [In] Hitlerized Germany . . . the principles of nationalism are being carried to an apotheosis higher than any nation has attempted since the days of ancient Israel, and the Jews themselves are made the first victims of it! But this is *Christian* [emphasis theirs] nationalism! Alas, it is even so! It is those nations which bear high the banner of Christ who are guilty of this evil. Thus the ironic circle is complete: Jewish nationalism crucified Christ, and Christian nationalism is now, and for centuries has been, engaged in crucifying the Jews![55]

The response to the editorial was immediate, and seven letters to the editor were published, five of which were from rabbis (one from Chicago, one from St. Louis, two from New York City, and one from Buffalo, New York). One was "from a Hebrew Christian" and one "from a Christian Clergyman."[56]

Rabbi Samuel Schwartz of Washington Boulevard Temple in Chicago wrote, "I have read your editorial in the last issue—'Jews and Jesus' three times. . . . I consider it a most courageous utterance by a truly great Christian on the age-old, unjust attitude of Christians toward Jews." He then devoted the remainder of the letter to the central themes of the scriptural origins of anti-Semitism in the Gospel of John. No mention was made in this letter of the reason for the editorial in the first place—the persecution of the Jews in Germany.

Rabbi Ferdinand M. Isserman of Temple Israel in St. Louis, in a very long response to the editorial, did mention the issue of the persecution of the Jews in Germany, commending the courage of the editors for centering anti-Semitic teaching in the Christian church in the teaching that the Jews crucified Jesus and for their concern about Germany's Jews. He then took exception to the main argument of the editorial in order to state another basis for the responsibility for the death of Jesus.

> If Christian civilization is at the present moment characterized by social injustice, by the threat of war, by race prejudice, it is not because but in spite of the Christian message. Christianity is no more responsible for the machinations of Hitler than Judaism is responsible for a few exploiters who happen to be Jews.

Rabbi Isserman argued that "Jesus was crucified, not by the nationalism of the Jew but by the *imperialism* [emphasis his] of Rome."[57]

Both Rabbi Isserman and Rabbi Alexander Lyons of the Eighth Avenue Temple in Brooklyn, New York, criticized the argument of the editorial when it had stated that "Israel needs Jesus to complete its own life" as "imperialism concealed in the philosophy of the missionary." As a response the editorial's question, "Why should not the Jew take Jesus into the synagogue?" Lyons stated, "This question exposes your protestation and plea to the suspicion of a missionary purpose." The only statement in the letter from Rabbi Lyons regarding Germany's persecution of Jews was a generalized one. "On the other hand, we Jews can cite an endless panorama of persecution ending in Hitlerism . . . of our people under the inspiration of a religion named after Jesus that we are urged to accept."[58]

Rabbi D. deSola Pool of the Spanish and Portuguese Synagogue, New York City, chose to comment only on the central themes of the editorial, with no mention of the persecution of the Jews in Germany. Rabbi Joseph L. Fink of Temple Beth Zion, Buffalo, New York, wrote at length, including a long statement on the subject of Germany's persecution of the Jews. He also contradicted the assertion in the editorial that Christian churches in the United States, England, and Canada had spoken out on behalf of the persecuted Jews. The paragraph, though lengthy, bears repeating.

> Sirs: *The Christian Century* has written the word for which we waited. It has fearlessly pronounced the Christian attitude toward the Jew and Jewish sufferings to an ununderstanding and callous world. It is a timely word, for the cruel hand of persecution is again upon the Jew. The argument of *The Christian Century* is sincere, eloquent and unanswerable. I regret, however, that I cannot share the encouragement that *The Christian Century* feels over the Christian reaction to present day persecution of the Jews in Germany. I failed to hear an emphatic and unanimous voice of protest from Christian pulpits over our land. Isolated, individual, notable ministers came forward nobly and courageously. The vast majority were painfully and complacently silent. . . . Here was a phenomenon with which every preacher and editor had to deal if he were at all humane and courageous. . . . The editors of our country responded nobly, unequivocally and almost unanimously. I had fondly hoped that the Christian pulpits would take the Easter season as the most appropriate time to preach emphatic sermons on the subject. How impressively they might have

stressed the thought that although Good Friday marks the crucifixion of a Jew centuries ago, we still go on crucifying *the* Jew
today [emphasis his]. The vast majority of Christian preachers
used the Easter season as a convenient excuse not to preach on
the subject of Christian persecution of the Jew in Germany.
When they were asked to speak on the subject, they replied
that it would be an intrusion of an alien theme into the holy-
day season.[59]

With minor changes, this paragraph could have been written in 1945,
at the end of the Hitler era. Rabbi Fink's letter, focusing as it does on
the predominant silence of Christian preachers about the persecution
(and later the extermination) of the Jews in Germany, spoke to the
issue that has dominated studies of the relationships of Christianity
to the persecution of Jews in Germany. This was the Silence. (The
Silence refers to the feeling among some Jews that Christians did not
speak out on behalf of persecuted Jews during the Hitler era and
specifically that Christians were strangely silent when the death
camps were discovered. A full discussion of the Silence will be found
in chapter 8.) He noted that only a few among preachers and churchmen did speak and act during that first year of the Nazi era. The
remainder of Fink's letter concerned the subjects of Jewish-Christian
relationships, brotherhood, humaneness, and peace and a response
to the question of Jewish conversion to Christianity.

"From a Hebrew Christian," a letter from Frederick Alfred Ashton
of New York City, called into question the accuracy of the editorial as
a reading of certain passages in the New Testament. No mention was
made of the persecution of Jews. "From a Christian Clergyman,"
signed by Cecil G. Osborne of the Larimer Memorial Baptist Church
in Chicago, challenged the editorial's statement about fundamentalists.

I challenge you to name so-called fundamentalist ministers
who rejoice at the treatment accorded Jews by the Nazi party
in Germany. That there are cranks who call themselves fundamentalists I have no doubt, . . . but surely you must know that
there are many millions of Christians who, while clinging to
the sneered-at fundamentals such as the atonement and the
doctrine of the inspired book, are as capable of human pity
and sympathy as our most liberal thinkers. When did liberalism corner the market on human sympathy?[60]

Another charge found in editorials was that Jews, especially German Jews, were Communists. John Ray Ewer, correspondent to *The*

Christan Century from Pittsburgh, had raised this question in his report, "Mass Meeting Protests Hitler's Anti-Jewish Program."

> May we ask if Hitler's attitude may be somewhat governed by
> the fact that too many Jews, at least in Germany, are radical,
> too many communists? May that have an bearing on the situa-
> tion? There must be some reason other than race or creed—
> just what is that reason? It is always well to try to
> understand.[61]

These questions elicited a quick response. Israel Gerstein from
Shreveport, Louisiana, in a letter to the editor, wrote:

> Anyone familiar with the German situation with special refer-
> ence to its Jewish citizenship could easily demonstrate that
> your contributor's assumption is not founded on fact. The con-
> trary impression is gained from Mr. Asher's article in a pre-
> vious issue of your magazine. He blames the Jews for having
> been too conspicuous in the parties that championed the exist-
> ing order and strove for the preservation of the status quo.
> Moreover, Hitler would have been the first one to make most
> of the existence of Jewish communists in order to justify his
> crusade against German Jewry, if the assumption of your corre-
> spondent had only a semblance of truth. The silence of the
> Nazi propaganda machine on this point is automatic refuta-
> tion.[62]

The article referred to by Mr. Gerstein in his letter was "A Jew Protests against the Protestors," in which Robert E. Asher, a German-
American Jew, specifically stated that the Jews in Germany, especially
the well-to-do Jews, tended to support the reactionary parties in an
attempt to prove how German they were. Also, Asher stated that the
Germans' anti-Semitism had been ignored by Jews even though it
had been growing "ever since the war, Hitler or no Hitler." Later in
the article, he wrote:

> But to the Nazis it is a problem of race. They consider the Jews
> a foreign group who persist in maintaining their foreign-ness.
> They have no objection, for example, to Catholics, because
> they still regard the Catholic as a German, but they do point,
> with considerable evidence to substantiate their contention, to
> the orthodox Jew as an alien.[63]

The accusation that Jews were Communists, which the Gerstein
letter argued against, was a common charge usually made in the context of anti-Semitic slurs. Horst Von Maltitz discussed this phenom-

enon with reference specifically to the period in late 1918 and early 1919, when Jews did take part in the revolution of the left that occurred just prior to the Weimar Republic. He pointed out that Hitler regularly referred to those Jews who had led this attempted revolution as the "November criminals" and that the *Dolchstosslegende* ("stab in the back theory") for the loss of World War I was also a favorite theme of Hitler's.[64] That the charge that Jews were Communists and Communist plotters or Jew-Bolsheviks should reappear in the context of the persecution of the Jews in Germany by the Nazis in 1933 should not be surprising. This theme had been developed by Hitler since his earliest politically active days just after World War I.

Letters to the Editor and Anti-Semitism in America

Anti-Semitic, anti-Jewish letters sometimes followed the editorials and articles that were published in *The Christian Century*. One, under the caption "Our 'Humanism' Runs Away!" was from G. F. Hedstrand from the Covenant Book Concern in Chicago.

> Sir: Your humanism is running away with you. This is evident from your attitude to the "persecution" of the Jews of Germany. It was very much surprised to see that Mr. Hutchinson [Paul Hutchinson, an editor for *The Christian Century*] was one of the sponsors for the mass meeting here in Chicago protesting against the "persecution" before the world really knew what was going on in Germany. The Jews can squeal much without meaning much by it, and he does not need to be hurt much in order to squeal much. And it seems to me that *The Christian Century* should know it and think before it runs to the defense of the "defenseless and persecuted Jew". Your editorial in the issue of May 3 is very disgusting. Even the Jew will laugh at you when he reads it.
>
> The Jews are not persecuted in Germany because of their religion, but because of their political and economic activity. They are communists many of them, and "persecuted" the nationalists before the latter came to power. Read in this month's *Moody Monthly* an article written by a person in Germany about the matter.

The writer continued to make racial slurs while he said, "As a Christian I do not hate the Jews. In fact, I have rented a flat from Jewish people the last two years, and have had ample time to make my observation." He concluded his letter:

They are children—reminding one of the colored race—in their mental makeup. They must be spoken to with authority, or they will not believe you. That is just what the nationalsts are doing. They are not persecuting the Jews—they are talking to them in the only language they know.[65]

On June 28, *The Christian Century* published a letter, "Nothing Will Save Us But a Pogrom," written by Richard F. Nelson of Mount Vernon, New York. The letter was a diatribe of accusations, racial slurs, and anti-Semitic charges. *The Christian Century* was accused of launching an "hysterical campaign of nauseous bathos which would be credit to a Hearst paper," of seeking Jewish circulation and the Jew dollar and of selling out Christians. "If you want Jew circulation say so and give up the Christian. If you serve the Jews, get your living from him." He then wrote:

I have studied this question for about ten years. During that time I have never found a Christian (minister or otherwise) who was friendly to the Jews who did not sooner or later show a looseness of conduct, ideas or practice.

After more in the same vein aimed at "Jew lovers," he concluded:

Before we see this Hitler flare-up end, it would not surprise me to have it reach America and have the blessing of the very men who have been damning Hitler now. . . . And it is only a question of time until the ever-recurring pogrom becomes necessary, for the Protestant never knows where the train is going until it arrives, neither does he heed warnings. He is too much immersed in his own ideas. And the Jew backs up before violence only. He will not change, or control himself, without it.[66]

And what of those interested in looking at the Jews only in relation to the study of prophecy and the "signs" to be found in the Bible? "Adolph Hitler, Alias '666'," was the caption over a letter from Earl H. Pendell of Cleveland, Ohio. Referring to the prophet Daniel in the context of "Adolph Hitler proposes to abolish the Old Testament," the writer asked the question, "Is Herr Hitler the person referred to in the book of Daniel as the 'Little Horn', the great persecutor of the Jews who is to be overthrown at the appearance of the Jewish Messiah?" Using an elaborate system of assigning numbers of the letters of the Greek alphabet, the writer concluded, "In other words, Adolph Hitler, or Herr Hitler, as he is commonly called, is identified by the Bible as the 'Little Horn' of Daniel, the 'antichrist' of the New Testament, 'The Beast' of the Apocalypse."[67] An article on the same theme, "A New Antichrist," was published in *Church Management* but only to point out that every generation had its antichrist and it was then Hitler's turn. "It's an old trick and really does not deserve all this space but some people seem to fall for it whenever it is used."[68]

On June 21, under the caption, "Yes, Where *Are* You?" (emphasis theirs), I. B. LeClaire of Los Angeles answered the earlier letter in *The Christian Century*, "You say Adolph is alias '666' according to Rev. 13:18. My dear brother, you are wrong on this. This refers to the Pope. . . ." The writer uses his number system to prove this, concluding, "I have the words of God on my side. Where are you?"[69]

A plea had been made in an editorial entitled, "Maintain the American Tradition," in *The Christian Century* suggesting that immigration restrictions be relaxed to admit German refugees to the United States and urging President Roosevelt to take such an action immediately. Walter J. Hogue of the First Presbyterian Church, York, Pennsylvania, responded to this plea. "It is the most discouraging editorial note I have seen in twenty years." The main thrust of his response was that further immigration would "mongrelize" American stock even more than it had been "mongrelized" already.

> And now when our national life is assuming the color of the second and third generation of immigrant stocks, with bootlegging, repeal of the 18th amendment, shrinking of the Protestant churches, corruption in our large cities, decadence of our American stock, because "the Canaanite would dwell in that land"—after all this, you use the empty phrases about "a land of refuge", "maintain the American tradition".

He then went on to state that, if immigration were permitted, the "ideals" of the Puritans, the English and German and northern people who settled America, would be destroyed "for a thousand years of mongrel civilization" and the good things inherent in the Protestant faith and Protestant civilization would be mere talk.[70]

E. G. Homighausen wrote a number of articles on Germany in 1933 published mainly in *The Christian Century* and *The Reformed Church Messenger*. Correspondents to the two periodicals did not always agree with him. And, from a perspective on his articles at the time of this writing forty-five years later, Homrighausen, especially early in 1933, does seem to have been more optimistic than others writing at the same time about what was happening to the Church and the Jews in Germany. His optimism then, and now, seemed misplaced.

Under the caption, "German Church Situation," *The Christian Century* published a letter from Paul L. Lehmann of Elmhurst, Illinois, which took exception to a number of things in Homrighausen's article, "Barth Resists Hitler," of July 26, 1933, also in *The Christian Century*. Lehmann's corrections were based on the fact that Homrighausen had heard a lecture by Barth during a just-concluded summer session in Germany and Lehmann had been a student of Barth's for that entire session. Lehmann suggested that Homrighausen either misheard or misstated himself on some key issues regarding Barth's stand on the Church in Germany. Karl Barth had written a manifesto basically opposing the emerging German Christian movement and the absorption of the Church by the state. Homrighausen, referring to the manifesto, said that it was soon to be released and that it had been sent to Hitler. Lehmann pointed out that it had already been publicly released and that it had been sent to the minister of education, not to Hitler. Lehmann also took exception to the statement that many Roman Catholics had become ardent supporters of Hitler, as leaving a false impression. He noted that Roman Catholic opposition to Hitler had appeared early, that it continued, and that the proposed concordat gave Roman Catholics little or no advantage as Homrighausen had intimated that it would in his article. Finally, Lehmann pointed out that Barth was not "one man" acting courageously but that he had consulted with a group of Reformed clergymen in preparing his manifesto and that other Reformed clergymen had also spoken out against "the one voice now that dares to speak against the tremendous tide of national feeling." Lehmann called this a "misstatement" [sic].[71]

Robert A. Ashworth, identified as "the former distinguished editor of *The Baptist*," wrote a letter to the editor of *The Reformed Church Messenger*. It was published in its entirety. Specifically, he took exception to Homrighausen's article "Behind the German Jewish Problem" in the *Messenger*, August 24, 1933. The original article had suggested that "a few protesting Jews in and around New York" were blinding Americans to the events in Germany and, therefore, what was really happening to the Jews in Germany was being distorted by the American Jews. So thought some Germans whom Homrighausen had talked with in Germany. Ashworth took him to task for this assertion, stating that

> the protest against the gospel of hatred against the Jews and
> the discriminations, indignities and cruelties of which the Jew
> in Germany has been made the object has been vigorously

voiced by very many non-Jewish elements in our country, athletic, literary, academic, legal and religious.

Challenging Homrighausen's tendency to ameliorate by such statements as "The persecution of the Jews has been magnified out of all proportions in the United States" quoted in the letter, Ashworth began a series of refutations of statements made by Homrighausen with the sentence, "And that the Jews are being disgracefully maltreated there can be no possible question." Several paragraphs later, Ashworth concluded:

> Germany's treatment of the Jews is an offense against humanity, a violation of the most basic human instincts, a revival of sadism on a wide scale, and from the Christian point of view, a denial of all that we hold most sacred.
>   As Hilaire Belloc says in the article from which we have quoted, "As it seems to me particular and flagrant injustice of this kind affects not only the individual who suffers from it, nor only the unhappy men who perpetrate this outrage, but also those who are silent in the presence of it. They themselves will be poisoned if they do not protest, for it is their duty to protest."[72]

A small paper published in Chicago, in a letter from Walter R. Mee, executive secretary of the Chicago Church Federation, reported that a decision had been made by the federation to issue a protest against the persecution of the Jews in Germany. The letter was sent to the federal government of the United States, asking that the information about such persecutions be substantiated and, if the persecutions were proven to be true, that strong protest be made immediately. At the heart of the Mee letter sent to Jacob Peltz, editor of *The Hebrew Christian Alliance Quarterly*, was a short paragraph that included the statement, "We as a Church of Jesus Christ cannot remain silent in the face of such wrongs or be indifferent to such conditions." The resolutions adopted at the federation meeting followed this statement.[73]

The Cautious and the Unconvinced

For some of the American Protestant press there was confusion and caution and in some instances there was outright disbelief and denial that anything adverse or unnecessary was happening to the Jews in Germany. Their experiences with false propaganda during World War I at least initially inclined some editors to urge that their readers wait and see.

Like all the rest of our readers, we have listened to radio broadcasts and noted articles in the secular press that report persecution of Jews in Germany by the National Socialist party. The assurance has been given by the American Department of State that the German government will not permit violence to continue.

The editor of *The Lutheran* stated that "irresponsible zealots" were to blame rather than "the Nazi party as such." He then wrote:

Time, the sure even though often slow divider of truth from partisan propaganda will also demonstrate the extent of exaggeration back of the reports. Could one forget experience with war propaganda and ignore evidence that the Germans are not naturally given to persecution, one could more easily yield to the clamor for wholesale condemnation and the radical demands for reprisals.

In a later paragraph, the editor stated:

We are the more inclined to urge caution in view of the present status of governmental affairs in Germany. . . . The situation is not one that remote amateur leaders, however earnest they may be, are competent to handle. Even the foreign correspondents of American papers can be unreliable guides. We have a good government: it is costing us a lot of money. Now is the time to make use of it.[74]

An even greater degree of caution and disbelief was expressed in an editorial in *The Moody Bible Institute Monthly* [later called *Moody Monthly*]. After a disclaimer, "No 'constant reader' of this periodical can ever doubt our love for Israel, the chosen people of God," with a generalized defense of this statement in the opening paragraph, the second paragraph began:

But after saying all this, and without qualification, we feel led to ask that Christian people suspend their judgment about Germany's present dealings with the Jews until both sides have an opportunity to be heard. We learn from private sources, more than one, and worthy of respect at least, that the Jews in Germany are not being persecuted as a race, but that communism organized by Russian Jews is being punished by Hitler.

The statement that there were too many Jews in government positions and that Jewish artists "always received the prizes" was followed in the editorial by a letter "dated at Berlin, March 22, in which the writer says:"

> Knowing how misinformed our American friends and Christians are by the latest revolution in Germany, I think it is my duty as a witness to give a true report, which you would oblige the German Christian world by publishing. All reports of bloody attacks, circulated in foreign papers, were inspired by a social-democratic or communistic press in order to depreciate Hitler. Ninety percent of all attacks were not made by the Nazis but by communistic elements which shot down Nazis wherever they could be found. Taking this into consideration, the world cannot expect Hitler to present those banner-bearers of Communism with a bouquet for their activity.

Who sent the letter from Berlin? The editorial did not say. But the editor closed the editorial with:

> There are times when all of us are in a quandary whom or what to believe, and only the grace of God in the heart can keep friends from becoming enemies. We pray for that grace in the editorial office of the *Monthly*, and we know that there are hundreds of our readers uniting with us in prayer continually.[75]

In June 1933, the editor of *The King's Business* wrote, "We heartily endorse the brief editorial in the *Moody Bible Institute Monthly* under the above caption."[76]

As late as December 1933, statements of the sort reported above were still being made. Ernest Gordon edited a section in *The Sunday School Times*, "A Survey of Religious Life and Thought," for many years. On December 9, 1933, he devoted an entire page to Germany. Using an article by a Pastor Ernst Modersohn, published in *The Evangelical Christian* (an undenominational periodical published in Toronto, Canada, Roland V. Bingham, president and editor), Gordon repeated the theme that "Hitler saved Germany from communism." Using other sources, some unidentified, some named, Gordon again suggested that the Jews really got only what they deserved, that the public book burnings rid Germany of "rotten literature," that Communism had been removed from the schools, and that the German Christian movement would actually revive the churches in Germany though there was an active and vigorous protest in the churches against "a national church on the basis of old Germanic myths."[77] That such an uncritical hodgepodge of an article based on news sources and readings should have been published that late in 1933 is, to say the least, surprising. *The Lutheran* editor continued, also, to be cautious:

> The present administration in Germany can complain that a minority segment of its citizens entered its borders from contiguous countries without permission during post-war years and that through political alliances and economic maneuvers these newcomers have obtained unearned and disproportionate authority. But justification for wholesale discrimination against Jewish citizens has not been produced. One hopes reports of it are exaggerated.[78]

An article in *The Lutheran Companion*, written by an Alf. Bergin who was otherwise unidentified, was published. The article opened with a long quotation from Hitler on the Jews, then there was the statement that the editor of the *Kansas City Star* was in Berlin to see and hear for himself. Then, Bergin wrote, "We know that the Jews control the movies, the newspapers and the money-market. It may not be out of place to find out where Hitler has received his strange ideas." He then referred to books he once received from Ford (Henry Ford) about the international Jewish conspiracy.[79] Presumably, the editor of the *Kansas City Star* was to serve as a credible witness regarding events in Germany, particularly with reference to the Jews.

In December 1933, the editor of *The Mennonite* was saying that, though the German people had clearly chosen Hitler, what was happening to Jews and German Christians should have been of concern to every Christian.

> We say this with the knowledge that press reports, such as come to us every day, are scarcely reliable and must be accepted with caution. Few, if any not intimately in touch with Germany from the inside, are in a position to give us a fair and intelligent picture of things as they are.[80]

One periodical, *The Reformed Church Messenger*, was on all sides of the issues, publishing articles and news notes that on the one hand spoke clearly to the issue of Jewish persecution in Germany while on the other hand publishing enough articles and news notes questioning whether these things were really happening that the reader could only be left in doubt. Of the latter sort was an article by a highly regarded international churchman identified by his full title, Prof. Dr. Adolph Keller (based in Geneva, Switzerland).[81] The title of the article by Keller is significant, "Facts and Meaning of the German Revo-

lution as Seen from a Neutral Point of View." In it, he included the
following:

> Public opinion in many countries has been roused first of all by
> the distorted news of atrocities committed against the Jews. We
> have no reason to doubt the official declaration of the Govern-
> ment and the Church that with a few exceptions no atrocities
> happened and that in general order and security were guaran-
> teed. . . . The attitude of the Government towards the Jews
> must, however, be considered as one aspect only of the aims
> and meaning of the German revolution. . . . As it cannot be
> denied that the Jewish element played an important role in
> Russian Bolshevism as well as in the growing of German Com-
> munism and atheism, a good deal of the blamed anti-Semitism
> and hatred finds its explanation in what is called the destruc-
> tive and morally disintegrating influence of the revolutionary
> Jewish mind. The hatred against Jews is therefore not only to
> be understood as a form of blind race antagonism, . . . but as a
> charge against a part of the foreign and recently immigrated
> Jewish element as being responsible for the lowering of moral
> standards in public life.

Or, what Hitler called the German revolution being premised on Hitler's concept of the "Total State," that

> the elmination of elements considered as dangerous . . . is
> considered as a necessary administrative measure. . . . This
> change is at least partly to be explained by the fact that in pub-
> lic life, such as the press, theatre, medicine, and law, the Jew-
> ish element is so preponderant . . . that it is in manifest con-
> tradiction to the proportion of the number of Jews in the whole
> nation.[82]

Words such as these from a person of the stature of Adolph Keller,
especially among Presbyterian and Reformed churches, would carry
a great deal of weight. In fact, they would be hard to refute because
Keller was thought by many to be the leading Christian expert on
European matters. He had served the international Christian community as their representative in Europe on refugee matters since
1922.

The article on May 4, 1933, by Dr. R. C. Schiedt, was even more
direct.

> All my letters and newspapers from home speak in the highest
> terms of Hitler and denounce the atrocity stories as pure prop-
> aganda fabrication. The "Hamburger Nachrichten" of April 5th

offers a reward of 2,000 Reichsmarks to anyone who can prove that a single Jew has been either tortured or killed.

He then repeated the familiar charges that Jews held professional positions far out of proportion to their numbers in Germany and that "since most of them were either socialists or communists it is easily understood why their far-reaching influence should be curbed, especially since the whole number of Jews is only 600,000 in a population of 65 million people."[83]

In "News of the Week," *The Reformed Church Messenger* reported that Secretary of State Hull had stated that mistreatment of Jews in Germany had virtually ceased. The editors stated their

> reports in the foreign press of atrocities suffered by German Jews at the hands of the Nazis were branded as "pure inventions" in a statement issued March 24 by the Central Union of German Citizens of the Jewish Faith. The Union has 60,000 members.[84]

No further comment was made, though other editors had treated this "report" from the Central Union with skepticism.

E. G. Homrighausen wrote two articles for *The Reformed Church Messenger* late in the summer of 1933. His articles were particularly significant because he wrote about Germany, which he had visited during that summer. Both articles bore the same title, "Behind the German Jewish Problem." They are particularly difficult to summarize because (though he ultimately made the points that the Jews were in fact being persecuted under continuing anti-Semitic practices in Germany and that Christians ought to have been greatly concerned because, as he finally said, "Our whole difficulty is that our dogmatism makes us oblivious to the fact that we are brothers already in God, but we will not acknowledge it") the fact is that he repeated every racial slur and anti-Semitic calumny that was being made in Germany. In a typical statement, he claimed of a Jew that

> he is a peculiar combination of a group loyalty and individualism. He delights in being exclusively a Jew, he looks upon Christianity with superior contempt, he has no capacity for individual imagination (he always thinks of his religion in terms of his race). He is a tyrant in business as well as a vociferous fellow in society.[85]

Homrighausen, whose sincerity cannot be questioned, made these charges with very little refutation. At one point in the first article, he did state that some Germans did not like the anti-Semitism they had witnessed, but his own early statement set the tone for his articles, regardless of his conclusion. "The persecution of the Jews has been magnified out of all proportions in the United States." He stated in two different places why he thought this to be so.

> Why is that? Is it because newspapers generally are so sensitive about their Jewish advertisers that they hesitate to state any other side of the problem favorably?[86] . . . [And] Germans generally, even the clergy, are vexed to think that Americans are allowing themselves to be blinded to the real German revolution by the vociferousness of a few protesting Jews in and around New York![87]

In retrospect, it must be said that the two articles by Homrighausen, in spite of his conclusion and plea for brotherhood under God, are anti-Semitic and anti-Jewish in tone and content in the context of his subject, the "German Jewish problem." His statement that reports of persecution were exaggerated out of all proportion to reality and that protesting New York Jews were to blame for these exaggerations did not square with the known, documented facts then or now. It is possible, though it would be extremely difficult to prove conclusively, that Homrighausen was placing his personal visit and interviews in Germany over against a 104-page release, *The Jews in Nazi Germany: The Factual Record of Their Persecution by the National Socialists*, published by the American Jewish Committee on June 9, 1933. The American Jewish Committee was based in New York City, at 171 Madison Avenue at 33rd Street. Its executive committee was made up of people from cities throughout the United States.[88]

The American Jewish Committee publication included laws discriminating against Jews publicly issued in Germany, reports of how these laws were enforced in Germany found in reputable newspapers and elsewhere, corroboration of persecution in statements made by Nazi leaders, personal letters from Germany, eyewitness accounts from refugees, excerpts from known anti-Semitic material used in Germany, addresses in the United States Congress on the subject of the persecution of the Jews in Germany, and extensive selections of editorial comment in American secular newspapers. Presumably, this publication was widely distributed.

The Protestant Press and the Jews, 1933: A Summary

The American Protestant press, then, did report to its readers what was happening to Jews in Germany in 1933. In twenty-nine representative periodicals, a total of 231 articles, editorials, news notes, letters to the editor and book reviews that referred to the persecution of the Jews in Germany were found. What was being done to German Jews was either the central topic being covered or it was mentioned in statements about Hitler and his rise to power, the establishment of the National Socialists' control of Germany, the emerging struggle of the Church, or in a discussion of the racial theories and laws promulgated by Hitler and the Nazis. Editors, writers, and commentators exercised considerable effort to keep up with the fast-moving events in Germany, though there was difference of opinion as to what it all meant.

Nine categories of themes in the periodicals' coverage of the issue can be identified.

1. Straight news reports, with or without accompanying commentary.
2. Notices of protest or statements of protest against the persecution of the Jews in Germany, including reports of protest rallies or mass meetings of protest.
3. Articles and notices of aid to refugees who were fleeing Germany.
4. Letters to the editor on all sides of the issue.
5. Discussions of the persecution of the Jews in Germany in relation to American anti-Semitism.
6. Discussion of the persecution of the Jews in Germany in relation to America's own racial problems, particularly those with Negroes and the Japanese.
7. Some suggestions of condemnation of the clergy in America for not speaking out more forcefully.
8. Particular subjects, such as the "Aryan clause," Palestine or the United States as a refugee haven, Hebrew-Christians and their dilemma, atrocity stories and exaggeration as a real possibility (and as an editor's concern), and the prophetic-millenial analysis of prophecy being fulfilled in anticipation of the "end times."
9. Comments about the Jews in Germany in relation to efforts to combat anti-Semitism actively in the United States.

Opinions expressed by editors and writers were in disagreement. Some were quite straightforward in their statements and condemnations; others were more cautious, presenting the information but with mild disclaimers. Some feared the charge that they were writing about "more atrocity stories" that would later be proven exaggerated or false. The two Protestant denominations with the most direct ties to Germany theologically, institutionally, and emotionally, the Lutherans and members of the Reformed churches, tended to be the most cautious, ameliorating or willing to speak favorably of events in Germany, especially in relation to questions involving the churches and the emerging Church Struggle. In several articles or statements in the Lutheran and Reformed periodicals, overt racial and anti-Semitic slurs and charges were made, in some at great length, even as the writer or commentator denied being personally anti-Semitic. Some of these articles more than hinted that the Jews were themselves to blame for their persecution.

Two types of analysis of the history of the anti-Jewish feelings and policies of the Nazis were attempted. One type of analysis was premised on the influx of Jews from Eastern Europe into Germany after World War I, the assimilation of Jews in Germany, and their advances in the professions of law, medicine, theater, filmmaking, publishing, banking, and merchandising. Frequent reference was made in a variety of articles and editorials to the fact that a disproportionate number of Jews held positions in the professions in Germany, where the Jewish population was generally set at 600,000 out of 65 million Germans, or about 0.92 percent of the total population. It was also claimed that many of the Jews were not really Germans but had come into Germany after World War I and prospered at the expense of Germans.

The other attempt to trace the anti-Jewish sentiment in Hitler's Germany was made in reviews of the English translation of *Mein Kampf*, though mention was made in the reviews that much of the more virulent anti-Jewish material had been left out of the shortened translated version. The reviewers pointed out, however, that enough of Hitler's hatred of the Jews remained in the translated version as to leave no doubt about how Hitler saw the Jews.

The more conservative-evangelical and fundamentalist periodicals discussed the persecution of Germany's Jews in a rather specialized way. In reading these articles, the feeling grows that the writers had no feeling for the Jews as persons, but only as a category or cohort called the Chosen People. References to the actual persecution of real people in Germany were included by some of the writers in these periodicals only to make the larger point that God was at work in the world in order that prophetic statements made in the Scriptures, as interpreted by these writers, could at last be fulfilled. Whether the writer was Alva J. McClain or Charles W. Mayes in *The Brethren Evangelist*[89] or that most prolific of such writers Louis S. Bauman in *The King's Business*,[90] or the editor of *The Presbyterian*[91] or *The Signs of the*

Times,[92] the theme was the same. The Jews were a "unique people," important most of all because they were the key to a fulfilled prophecy. A. C. Snead, writing in *The Alliance Weekly*, captured the whole concept in a single sentence. "The Jews are to return to Palestine in unbelief, and it may be that God is using the hatred of the Nazis against the Jews as a scourge to drive them in larger numbers into Palestine." A sentence or two later he wrote, "Surely during the last two decades it would seem that events in the world indicate the beginning of the fulfillment of prophecy."[93] Later in the same periodical, Joseph R. Lewak, superintendent of the New York Jewish Mission, wrote of the German Jews that "these Jews, who for so many years were sufficient unto themselves, have become quite humble and are now looking to God." Since the Jews were then ready to emigrate to Palestine, Lewak concluded, "the national restoration of the Jewish people is only a question of a short time. The fig tree is putting forth leaves."[94]

At least one periodical, *The Concordia Theological Monthly*, took strong exception to such prophetic-millenial interpretation. The articles being attacked were those of Louis S. Bauman in *The King's Business*, June and July 1933. The criticism of Bauman's articles, which were quoted at length, was summarized by the caption of the editorial, "Millenialism Running Wild." But, incidental to the criticism, the editors of this Missouri Synod Lutheran monthly themselves suggested that the descriptions of the persecution of the Jews in Germany used by Bauman were exaggerated.[95]

With regard to what do do about the persecution of the Jews in Germany, the prescriptive advice of the American Protestant press when it offered such advice generally ran along these lines in 1933: It is a German internal matter; therefore, let the Germans take care of it; "world opinion" will cause Hitler and the Nazis to cease their persecution of Jews; the American government through the Department of State is best able to handle these matters; we need more credible, responsible witnesses to confirm the rumors; we have little basis for criticism considering our own race problems in America; open Palestine for refugees and lift the immigration restrictions in the United States for refugees; boycott German goods; have the League of Nations intervene and investigate; hold protest rallies and send protest statements; and, that most American of all responses, form committees for protest, for refugees, for getting more reliable information, for organizing boycotts of German goods, for raising funds for assistance, and for whatever. And form committees they did.

But in the final analysis, with all the prescriptive suggestions, for the great majority of Christian adherents, clergy and laypersons alike, the accusation of Rabbi Joseph L. Fink in his letter to *The Christian Century* was the most accurate assessment made. There really was no "emphatic and unanimous voice of protest from Christian pulpits over our land. . . . The vast majority were painfully and complacently silent"[96] In this context, the editorial prologue to a reprinted article in *The Evangelical Visitor* may be the most typical response of all. The editor reported that he was giving his editorial space to the article, "Israel and Her Messiah," saying:

> Since its publication most of our readers know the things that have befallen the Jewish race in Germany, and the Anti-Semitic feeling there is growing everywhere. We agree with the writer of this article that little can be done for them at the present time except to pray and whenever possible to point them to the Messiah who we know has already come because here and there is one who will accept the Saviour.[97]

Christians were to either seek to convert Jews to the Christian faith or pray for them. To affirm the Jew as a Jew, religious or nonreligious, seems always to have been an unacceptable alternative.

1934–1935—Racialism as Reich Law: Toward the Nuremberg Laws

This arbitrary act [the enactment of the Nuremberg laws] . . . was, from the National Socialist viewpoint, a consistent ideological policy; not only did it furnish persecution and discrimination with a legal foundation, it also provided a loyalistic starting point for the later annihilation of the disenfranchised.

KARL DIETRICH BRACHER,
The German Dictatorship

KEY EVENTS

1934, General: January 30, Upper House of the Reichstag abolished, Law for the Reconstruction of the Reich (federal system abolished); April 24, law changing criminal law and procedure; June 1, Law for the Promotion of Marriage; June 30, purge of the SA (*Sturmabteilung*) by Hitler; July 1, 2, Hindenburg and the army approved of the purge; July 13, Hitler's report to the Reichstag on the purge; August 1, 2, offices of president and chancellor combined; August 2, death of Hindenburg; August 2, Oath of Loyalty changed to read loyalty to Adolf Hitler; August 7, funeral of Hindenburg; August 4–10, Baptist World Alliance Fifth World Congress, Berlin; August 20, all governmental power in Germany consolidated in the hands of Hitler and the NSDAP (National Socialist Workers' party, or Nazi party).

1934, Relating to the Jews: April, exclusion of Jews affecting hundreds of university teachers and approximately 4,000 lawyers, 3,000 physicians, 2,000 civil servants, and 2,000 actors and musicians; up to 60,-000 Jews had fled Germany by the end of 1934. There were no new

41

laws passed against Jews during the year, but their rights were severely limited.

1935, *General:* January 13, Saar plebiscite; March 16, Treaty of Versailles repudiated, compulsory military service announced; March,
seven concentration camps existing, with total population of around
10,000; September 15, Law for the Protection of German Blood and
Honor, Reich Citizenship Law, and the Nuremberg laws; November
14, first registration under the Reich Citizenship Law, the first of thirteen supplementary decrees under the Reich Citizenship Law defining the "meaning" of *Jew.*

1935, *Relating to the Jews:* March, Jews among the approximately
10,000 people held in seven concentration camps, boycotts and pogroms renewed against Jews throughout Germany; July, open attacks
on Jews, Jews restricted from theaters, recreational centers, swim-
ming pools, parks, and resorts, and attacks on small businesses of
Jews, Jewish newspapers forced to suspend publication; September
15, Law for the Protection of German Blood and Honor, Reich Citizenship Law, Nuremberg laws, disenfranchising all Jews in Germany; November 14, first supplementary decree under the Reich Citizenship Law defining who was to be classified as a Jew; in all,
thirteen supplementary decrees were issued by July 1, 1943.

The formal adoption of racial laws (the Nuremberg laws) by the
German Reichstag on September 15, 1935, institutionalized Nazi
racial theories. The "theory" of racial laws itself, however, had been
being applied throughout Germany, including the Church, through
the "Aryan paragraph," or "Aryan clause." In all areas of public,
professional, and ecclesiastical life, Jews suffered restrictions because
of their race. Systematic exclusion of the Jews from German professional life, boycotts, pogroms, and acts of violence were common
during 1933, 1934, and 1935. In 1934 and 1935, information about
these events was reported by the American Protestant press. Insofar
as the "Aryan clause" remained a part of the Nazi program for the
Church in Germany, it was also an issue discussed in the press, but
usually in the context of the Church Struggle, which continued to be
the news item of greatest interest in 1934 and 1935. In an examination
of thirty-two Protestant religious periodicals published in 1934, there
were eighty-six editorials, articles, letters to the editor, news items,
and book reviews that discussed the Church Struggle in Germany.
Within these various discussions, the racial law directly bearing on

the concerns of churchmen, the "Aryan clause," was mentioned in one form or another fourteen times.

Indirect Reference to the Persecution of the Jews, 1934

The second major item reported in the press about events in Germany concerned the persecution of the Jews. At least seventy-one items—news stories, editorials, articles, letters to the editor, book reviews, and in one instance, paid advertisements—mentioned the persecution of Jews in Germany. The direct references were statements or descriptions of the persecutions. Indirect references were usually more obscure statements within other articles or editorials, but their intent could not be mistaken. *The Arkansas Baptist* on March 22, 1934, published the following:

> As every one knows, the Hitler government in Germany is boycotting, persecuting, torturing and killing the 600,000 Jews, or the remnant of that number who remain in Germany. Just why a nation of 65,000,000 Germans should fear and hate and drive out a people which number only 600,000 is a profound mystery to the rest of the world. Is there such a thing as a national madness? It would seem so.[1]

In an earlier issue of the same periodical, a much more indirect statement had been included in a paragraph that had been taken from the *Baptist and Commoner*. The paragraph discussed the emergence of a number of dictators during 1933. One sentence in the paragraph read, "Adolph Hitler has banished the Jew from the commercial life in Germany and seeks an absolute control of all commercial, political and religious life."[2]

Another example of indirect reporting is the following discussion of the growing refugee problem from the *Federal Council Bulletin*:

> The plight of 60,000 refugees from Germany presents a peculiar challenge to the conscience of Christendom—a challenge which thoughtful Christians cannot escape. There are two reasons why we cannot say, "Let the Jews look out for these refugees". The first is that by no means all of the refugees are Jews. . . .
>
>   The second and more important reason why we cannot evade a responsibility for the refugees is the very fact that the great majority of them are Jews—who are suffering bitter injustice at the hands of those who call themselves Christians. It would be a standing reproach against Christendom if the true Christians of the world were callously indifferent when Jews

have been made the victims of unchristian policies perpetrated by nominal Christians.[3]

A plea for the involvement of Christians in positive ways, including suggestions made during a conference held earlier under the sponsorship of the Federal Council of Churches of Christ in America, concluded the editorial.

The editors of *The Alliance Weekly* used an even more indirect approach in early 1934 in reporting on the persecution of Jews in Germany. In the issue for April 14, 1934, "This Week's Comments" had three short articles listed under "Jewish Items." The first referred in part to laws protecting minorities in Holland brought about to try to curb anti-Semitic agitators and "propaganda from foreign political creeds." The second referred to a reawakened worldwide interest by Jews in "the characteristics that make for Jewishness." This interest was attributed in the article to Hitler's anti-Semitism. The third article referred to Jews in China and included no reference to Germany or Hitler at all.[4] In its October 13, 1934, issue, a small news item appeared from the Nazi magazine *Nordland*, which quoted from an article by a Hitler Youth Press representative addressed to Germany's youth. These youth were exhorted to throw off Jewish-Christian ideas such as sinfulness, pity, and love for enemies and raise high the symbol of the swastika. "We must be hard if we would conquer. A curse upon sympathy and mercy!" The editorial comment accompanying this selection from *Nordland* read, "Thus, as the movement develops, the origin of the attack on Judaism is seen to be but an offshoot of the larger hatred against Christianity."[5]

Direct References to the Persecution of the Jews, 1934

In the periodicals examined for 1934, the straight news of persecution of the Jews in Germany was reported in a variety of articles, including those devoted entirely to a prophetic analysis of Jewish persecution. Louis S. Bauman, pastor of the First Brethren Church of Long Beach, California, was a prolific writer on prophetic themes, always from a fundamentalist-literalist, premillenial, and dispensational perspective. He wrote most often for his own denominational paper, *The Brethren Evangelist*, and later, after a denominational struggle and division, *The Brethren Missionary Herald*. He also wrote frequently for *The King's Business* (the monthly magazine of the Bible Institute of Los Angeles) and *The Sunday School Times* and was considered an authority on prophetic matters by the fundamentalist Protestant press. That

Louis Bauman read all the current available news is unquestioned. His references to current happenings were up-to-date. This included direct reporting of persecution of Jews in Germany. His interpretation of these events, however, was always done in light of premillenial-dispensational "signs" that proved that the Scriptures were being fulfilled in "the latter days" and that the return to earth of Jesus as the "Bridegroom" to claim his "Bride," the Church (made up of true believers, those "born again" by faith and thus the "true church, or Bride of Christ"), was imminent. This approach to prophetic interpretation was not accepted by all who identified with the fundamentalist or evangelical-conservative wing of Protestantism. In fact, such interpretation of prophetic events was a hotly debated issue during the 1930s and beyond. Yet, all prophetic analysis, regardless of its origins and hermeneutical predispositions, considered the Jews to be the key to fulfillment of prophecy from the Scriptures. No analyst, however, consistently referred to how current happenings fulfilled prophecy to the degree that Louis S. Bauman did.

Bauman's articles were flawed consistently because, while discussing the plight of the Jews from a prophetic perspective, he very frequently repeated anti-Semitic and anti-Jewish propaganda. In 1934, he blamed the Jews for bringing anti-Semitism down on their own heads because "out of all proportion to the numbers, the Jews are the world's archtroubler." He stated, without attribution, that the nineteenth-century revolutions in Europe were caused by Jews. He further stated that the stage and the movies, "foremost of the Satanic agencies for the world-wide demoralization of youth, are wholly dominated by Jews" and that German Jews were probably (a careful hedging is characteristic) responsible for the breakdown of the gold standard. For Bauman, every "Bolshevik-Jew" was a Communist, antireligious and atheistic, and "a sworn enemy of his own believing brethren." In 1934, Bauman could write, "Even spiritistic Hitlerism is preferable to atheistic Sovietism." He concluded: "Anti-Semitism is to be the direct cause of Armageddon." He promised to discuss this theory more fully in his next article.[6]

In the next article, he spoke bluntly and directly about the persecution of the Jews in Germany. In the second through the seventh paragraphs, he described forthrightly the "Nazi program" of disestablishment, annihilation, extinction, sterilization, and "the death of all Germans marrying either Jews or Jewesses," the Jews for marrying Germans "to be slain." He described the elimination of Jews from educational institutions, the law, medicine, the arts, the theater, and journalism and the boycott of Jewish businesses, "in short . . . the literal extermination of all the Jews in Germany by banishment or by starvation or by violence." He supported his summary by references to statements by Dr. Franck, Reich minister of justice, made in an address to lawyers in Germany; to Jules Streicher in his *Der Stuermer*; to items from the *Quarterly Review* (July 1933), the London *Times* (July 26, 1933), the *Los Angeles Times* (whose columnist Harry Carr had just returned from Germany), the *Contemporary Review* (November 1933) and *Mein Kampf*. He concluded:

> Once, not so long ago, Germany was regarded as the most cul-
> tured nation on earth. One's education was not complete un-
> less it was climaxed in Germany. But, lo! How are the mighty
> fallen! Germany seems to have disposed of all the cerebrum
> stuff she once possessed—*shipped it to Palestine*! And what can
> be expected from the cerebrum she may have left! A change
> like this—an insane anti-Semitic outburst in that which was
> tooted [*sic*] to be man's most advanced culture—in light of the
> clear word of prophecy—how tremendously significant! After
> studying the situation on the ground the editor of the Catholic
> *Commonweal* (New York) exclaims: "A persecution of the Jews,
> which in its extent probably surpasses any recorded instance
> of persecution in Jewish history.!"[7]

The remainder of the second article was devoted to Bauman's analy-sis of "the clear word of prophecy," including a warning that Chris-tians might suffer the same fate as the Jews in Germany if Hitler should succeed and referring to a reported conversation between Dr. D. G. Barnhouse, editor of *Revelation* (January 1934), and Karl Barth in which Barth was said to have stated, among other things, that "the subtle spirit back of anti-Semitism is not merely anti-Jew. *It is anti-Christ!*" [emphasis Bauman's]. But finally, for Bauman, the purpose for all the persecution and turmoil was unmistakable: "*Anti-Semitism [was to be] the direct cause for Armageddon.*"

Bauman referred to a number of passages from the Bible to set forth his conclusions and make warnings of the "signs" of the im-pending "end of the age." In retrospect, what makes the prophetic analysis of a writer such as Louis S. Bauman more than a curiosity from a time when a large segment of Protestant Christianity was de-voted to such teaching of biblical prophecy is the observation that despite Bauman's invective more detailed and accurate reporting of the persecution of Jews in Germany often appeared in this type of article than in those of the more liberal Protestant press. If the seven paragraphs of Bauman's second article had been left to stand with only a brief conclusion, they would have constituted one of the best-documented statements on the persecution of the Jews in Germany in the Protestant press in America in 1934. The force of these statements was weakened, however, because they were subordinate to the larger purpose of the articles, discussing the purported prophetic significance of the events. In this context, the persecution of Germany's Jews was used only to illustrate and to lend support to the prophetic analysis of contemporary events. This had the effect of weakening or even of nullifying the terrible facts of the persecution of Jews for the reader.

More to the point, the approach of writers such as Bauman, who analyzed world events only for the purpose of prophetic interpretation, conditioned readers to look upon tragic happenings such as the persecution of the Jews in Germany only as illustrative of the terrible conditions in the world that required God's intervention. This left the readers free to choose to take the same point of view as the author, to read from a perspective of prophetic analysis, and to dismiss the illustrative material as something of no concern to them because it was somehow related to God's purposes in bringing about the fulfillment of prophecy. In this context, it was much easier for the reader to see the persecution of the Jews in Germany as part of what God was supposedly doing through the Chosen People to bring about the "end of the age" than to deal with the fact that individual Jews and Jewish families were suffering terribly under Hitler and the Nazis. The reader of this type of article assumed the role of the spectator, watching events unfold according to the scheme being set forth by the author. Franklin H. Littell called this premillenial-dispensational approach a "propositional abstraction rather than speaking of human persons."[8] That these records told of the real, immediate human suffering, humiliation, tragedy, and death of individual Jews was of little or no consequence. For these readers, the Jews of Germany were thus depersonalized. Collectively, they became objects to be manipulated as part of prophetic schemes, not persons to be helped or sympathized with in their hour of need. Yet, the facts about what was happening to Jews in Germany were clearly reported, in detail, in this type of article—a paradox that compounded the tragedy. This way of dealing with the Jews during the Nazi era might itself represent a sophisticated form of anti-Semitism related in kind to a commonly held view that Christians should only approach Jews for the purpose of persuading them to become Christians. Otherwise, Jews were to be dealt with only as an apostate people. This was a form of anti-Semitism all too familiar to Jews in Christian societies.

The Baptist World Alliance, Berlin, 1934

The third most frequently discussed event in 1934 was the meeting of the Baptist World Alliance in Berlin. The alliance had been scheduled originally to meet in Germany in 1933. Because of the depression and the economic problems and the unsettled political situation in Germany, a decision was made to postpone the meeting until 1934 and then, if it were feasible, to hold the meeting in Berlin. *The Baptist Herald* in January 1934 reported that the executive committee (presumably of the Baptist World Alliance) had met in New York on November 14, 1933, and had decided to announce that the meeting of the Baptist World Alliance would be held in Berlin, August 4–10, 1934. The fifth congress was definite; the German Baptists wanted the congress held, and the program proposed to the German government had been approved, with the promise of full freedom of discussion on all subjects (*volle Verhandlungsfreiheit*). Further, *The Baptist Herald* gave information about ship sailings, costs, and other travel arrangements as arranged by the transportation committee of the denomination, the German Baptists.[9]

On February 7, 1934, *The Christian Century* published an article by Conrad Henry Moehlman, "The Baptists Are Going to Berlin," that was sharply critical of the alliance's decision to hold its fifth congress in Berlin. Moehlman, a professor at Colgate Rochester Divinity School, was a Baptist and a highly regarded theologian and author. His article, which quoted *Mein Kampf* (the original, unexpurgated German edition) and Nazi laws, presented a devastating comparison between Nazi totalitarianism and traditional Baptist democratic practice, adherence to biblical faith and practice, emphasis on baptism by immersion, and emphasis on freedom in church-state relationships.

> The Baptist believes in free speech, a free press, a free pulpit, a free legislature, free schools, the absence of class distinctions. Naziism stands for tuned speech, a tuned press, a tuned pulpit, a tuned legislature, a tuned public school system, class distinctions, aristocracy and absolutism.

A few lines later, he stated:

> The Baptists of the world have reached Berlin. The three centuries' old ideal of the Baptists has also reached Berlin. It is in

direct conflict with the ten-year old platform of Naziism. Of
this there cannot be the slightest question. An explosion may
occur at almost any moment.

And finally:

> At Baptist conventions, a committee on findings is usually ap-
> pointed. The resolutions committee of this congress must sit
> upon either the soft horn or the sharp horn of the following
> dilemma. By remaining silent regarding Hitlerism, it would be
> accused the world over of endorsing the Hitler regime. By en-
> gaging in the criticism of Nazi ideals and practices it would
> merely increase the discomfort of fellow Baptists in
> Germany. . . .
>   When musicians, athletic societies, labor organizations, Bar-
> thians, Lutherans and Catholics are on record as critics of the
> practices of Naziism, the Baptists of the world cannot afford to
> accept the invitation of Hitler to meet in Berlin at the cost of
> impossible silence.

Moehlman drove home his arguments with direct references to persecution.

> Well, then, the Baptists must criticize both the philosophy and
> practices of the Nazis. Will they be bold enough to call atten-
> tion to Christianity's debt to Judaism and the shame of the
> ghetto, the inquisition and the pogrom? Will they dare to af-
> firm this faith in democracy, brotherhood and the kingdom of
> God and their opposition to propaganda, race hatred and war
> in Berlin in 1934?[10]

Conrad Moehlman was not the only one to raise questions about
the Baptists and their decision to meet in Berlin in 1934. G. B. Hopkins, in *The Watchman-Examiner*, also asked:

> If Baptists gather in Berlin will they not have to padlock their
> mouths . . . ? The present German government holds that the
> church must be subject to the state. . . . Will all the Baptists
> keep quiet on this subject?
>   Baptists have a comprehensive fellowship. . . . There are
> Baptist Negroes, Indians, Chinese, Japanese, Slovaks, and
> even Jews. . . . Can all these be free to meet in common fel-
> lowship? Will delegates be allowed to quote the Old Testa-
> ment? Suppose some one, forgetting his environment and the
> German law, should exclaim "Amen", would he be in danger
> of imprisonment? Perhaps our leaders have a special dispensa-

tion permitting liberty to Baptists. If so I would like to hear about it. If not it might be well to be sure the risk of meeting in Berlin is not too great.[11]

Reaction to both the Moehlman and Hopkins articles was immediate. A letter to *The Watchman-Examiner* came from F. W. Simoleit, chairman of the German Committee of Arrangements, and O. Nehring, secretary. In essence, they stated that no Baptist principles would be sacrificed, no parts of the Bible banned, and all races welcome. A good Baptist "Amen" was not unlawful because no such restrictive law existed, and the questions of Hopkins were regarded as "strange." "Our fellow Baptists must come and see how things really are! They need not have the least fear about full freedom for the congress. If we had not been certain that our government would allow that, we should not have sent our invitation."[12] Response to Moehlman also came from one of his fellow faculty members at Colgate Rochester Divinity School. F. W. C. Meyer did not disagree entirely with Moehlman but he suggested "another way open to us Baptists besides the one unalterably fixed by Dr. Moehlman in his recent article."[13] Meyer raised arguments based on his own study of the situation in Germany "for the past year," citing "all possible sources including conferences with German Baptist leaders." His letter suggested that Americans might be misguided, as they were in blaming World War I entirely on the kaiser. Germans (presumably including German Baptists), Meyer wrote, were "unanimous in their praise of the leadership principle in democracy. . . . It is not his personal but the people's interests the leader wishes to serve. Their enthusiasm for the totalitarian state seems to be unstinted." Meyer suggested that Moehlman and others see for themselves by going to Berlin and asked "whether our current opinion of Hitlerism demands revision."[14]

The Moehlman article apparently was published separately as a pamphlet; this was suggested in a letter to the editor of *The Christian Century* from a committee of a Baptist ministers' conference in Florida. The letter suggested that "a pamphlet" by Conrad Henry Moehlman contained erroneous statements, in opposition to which the conference in Florida adopted a series of resolutions. The issues raised all related to Moehlman's interpretation of Baptist history and origins. No mention of Berlin or the Fifth Congress of the Baptist World Alliance was contained in the letter. The headline over the letter seems, in retrospect, to be misleading.[15]

The most resounding criticism of Moehlman's article was published in *The Arkansas Baptist*, the Southern Baptist state paper for Arkansas. B. L. Bridges, general secretary of the Arkansas Baptist Convention, was the author. The signed article was quite long and anti-Semitic in point after point. Though discussing the planned Berlin congress and Moehlman, it was really an attack on Jews, which repeated virtually every anti-Jewish statement current in 1934. In summary, Bridges stated that the Baptists would go to Berlin, even though he personally thought they should not because of the expense involved and the indebtedness of Southern Baptists to creditors who would not understand such expenditures in light of the money owed to them. When in Germany, Baptists would have no cause to "flay Hitler for his attitude towards Jews in Germany." Further, the Baptists should not have been "a judge or divider in German affairs." Bridges attacked the "white book recently published by a committee of self-appointed New York Jews" (presumably *The Jews in Nazi Germany*, published by the American Jewish Committee in 1933). He then questioned that the Jews in Germany were being persecuted at all, and, if they were, Bridges asked, was it not for their political practices or as Bridges put it "not for righteousness' sake."

> I wonder if it ever occurred to Mr. Moehlman that Herr Hitler might be 99 44/100% [sic] right in his attitude and activity toward the Jews in Germany. The chances are that if there is any persecution at all it is not for righteousness' sake, but for political intrigue. The whole affair is a political question not a religious one.[16]

Bridges spoke favorably of the racial laws of Germany, which placed only "citizens" in public positions, and suggested parenthetically that America ought to adopt the same laws and practices. Bridges accused the Jews of being a "disturber of nations," a persecutor of others. He claimed that Communism was under Jewish domination and that "no one with the facts before him can doubt that Communism is Jewish." He referred to an article in *Time* (January 29, 1934) called "Jews Up" to support his statements; then, a bit further on, he stated that there had been a recent revelation that Roosevelt's brain trust had in it communistic Jews according to "Wm. A Wirt, Superintendent of Schools in Gary, Indiana, a man of unimpeachable character." Further, said Bridges, the Jew was an infidel but not an atheist, that is, a nonbeliever in the Christian faith; worse, Jews were enemies of Christianity. In support of the latter statement, he referred to the *New York World* concerning the death of a Mr. Lunacharsky, a "well-do-do Jew," who was quoted as saying that Jews hate Christianity and see it as an enemy.[17] He concluded:

> I hold no brief for Hitler. I have had no racial love for the Germans since the World War. All the love I can have for them is Christian love. I am not defending Hitlerism. I am only showing the utter folly and nonsense of Baptists raising their voices in condemnation of a nation's order against a group of that nation and, not only that nation, but seemingly at the throat of our own blessed America.

According to Bridges, the Baptists were more than ready to accept criticism and even the loss of the respect of the religious world if they came "from our refusal to criticize a nation for adopting a measure which after all may be necessary to its future safety."[18]

In April 1934, the leaders of the Baptist World Alliance felt obligated to respond to criticism for their decision to hold the congress in Berlin. A statement addressed to the editors of all Baptist publications was sent out over the signatures of John W. MacNeil (president of the Baptist World Alliance), J. H. Rushbrooke (general secretary), and Clifton D. Gray (honorary associate secretary) from the office of the president, Hamilton, Ontario, on March 27, 1934. According to the statement, extensive discussion by the Executive Committee of the Baptist World Alliance had resolved the issue as to whether, given all the known problems, Baptists had the courage to hold the meeting in Berlin as an opportunity to "witness to distinctive Baptist principles." After much debate, "the call to a venture of faith and courage was irresistible." Further, the German Baptists were most insistent in their invitation. "The German Baptists—who ought to understand their own conditions—repudiate the idea that our coming would imperil them." Further, all issues could be freely debated, including the nature of the Gospel, church-state relations, nationalism, racialism (the only hint of a reference to Jews and the persecution of Jews in Germany), world peace, et cetera. "Not one item of the program has been omitted or modified. . . . Nothing has been concealed from the Government—not even the fact that the free expression of our religious and ethical standpoint carries implications in the political realm."[19]

The correspondent to *The Christian Century* from the southeastern United States noted that Southern Baptists from Florida, Georgia, Alabama, and the Carolinas were planning to attend the congress in

Berlin in large numbers.[20] *The Alliance Weekly*, which was not a Baptist periodical, published an editorial on July 28, 1934, noting that the Baptists would be in Berlin and expressing an interest in the progress of the meetings in terms of "all friends of religious liberty" and also stating that "the present trend in Germany is the national tendency of the closing age."[21]

The first report on the meeting in Berlin during the congress itself appeared in *The Christian Century* as an editorial on August 15, 1934. It obviously had been sent by wire by an unidentified observer designated by the *Century* as its reporter. Essentially, the presidential speech was reported from the meeting of August 8, 1934. The editorial noted the courage of the speaker, President A. W. Beaven, in placing Christian conscience above all other claims, including those of the nation, school, or even family. This was seen as being particularly bold, considering where the congress was being held.[22]

One week later, again in an editorial, *The Christian Century* noted that free speech had, indeed, been fully in evidence during the congress. Maintaining free speech included listening to a speech by Reichsbishop Mueller in which he stated that Germany's internal troubles, "including presumably her religious difficulties, were no concern of outsiders" and to "an anti-Semitic Nazi Baptist's explanation that, while all races are equal in the sight of God, a government has to protect itself from a race that is 'destructive by nature'." The editorial continued, "Then it passed resolutions, as pointed and specific as though they had been formulated in Providence or Louisville, denouncing discrimination against the Jews, and denying the right of the state to interfere in the government of the church." Resolutions on war, armaments, and an end to nationalistic ambitions were also mentioned in the editorial, which concluded by stating that "press reports state that the German papers printed only those speeches and parts of resolutions which were favorable to the government's policies."[23]

Reports of delegates traveling to Berlin also began to appear by late August 1934. John W. Bradbury, of the Board of the American Baptist Foreign Mission Society, provided three articles for *The Watchman-Examiner* as its official reporter.[24] The first was an account of his travels, including his arrival and travels in Germany; the second, a day-by-day report of the congress; and the third, reflections and summation. He also was a speaker at the congress, as was Prof. Herman von Berge, the author of five articles published in *The Baptist Herald*, the German Baptist periodical. Frank W. Woyke, pastor of the Liberty

Street Baptist Church of Meriden, Connecticut, also contributed an article on his impressions while in Berlin to *The Baptist Herald*. John D. Freeman, editor of *The Baptist and Reflector* (the Southern Baptist paper for the state of Tennessee), and M. E. Dodd, president of the Southern Baptist Convention, supplied copy to the Southern Baptist state papers. One of Freeman's articles was reprinted in a number of them. Earle Eubank, a delegate to the Baptist World Alliance Fifth Congress, wrote a summation of the meetings for *The Christian Century*. Of all those written, Eubank's article was the most pessimistic. The officers of the Baptist World Alliance also released a brief summary statement about the Berlin congress in the fall of 1934.

John Bradbury traveled to Belgium and France before going to Germany, where he had visited in 1923. He expressed his misgivings about entering Germany.

> On to Berlin! The first stop was Strasbourg. I must confess that crossing the border was a dreaded experience. After all I had read in the American and foreign newspapers I was prepared for a tense atmosphere. The impression lingered around me that the police would be everywhere, spies would be listening to our talk; danger lurked around the corner; and many other similar kinds of bogies. Then, besides, it was the day following the assassination of Chancellor Dollfus in Vienna. Really, I dreaded a repetition of August, 1914.

He found his fears to be unfounded. The people of Germany were courteous; the public servants were exceedingly helpful; and everyone was cheerful, hopeful, confident, and in good spirits. As for the German people, "they do not know where they are going any more than the American people do, but, to borrow President Roosevelt's phrase, they are 'on the way'."[25] Prof. Herman von Berge in his articles for *The Baptist Herald* used these and other statements by Bradbury rather extensively.

Bradbury described his attendance at the Passion Play at Oberammergau, his attendance at a Wagnerian festival opera in Munich, his visit with a family of a New York friend in Leipzig, and his arrival in Berlin. He was taken to the Baptist headquarters and the Baptist mission house in Neuruppin, a suburb of Berlin. He then was taken to the Tagungshalle, the site of the Berlin congress, which he described, with brief references to the planned procedures, arrangements, and choice of German and English as the official languages of the congress. He closed his first article with a brief summary of Baptist history in Germany, of German mission work (including the "gospel wagons" [specially equipped automobiles] of the *Volksmission*, or "the mission of the people",) the Baptists in Berlin (who numbered around 9,000), and a greeting from the Rev. O. Nehring to Baptists in America. (Nehring was the secretary of the German Baptist Union and the chairman of the arrangements committee for the congress.)

Bradbury's second article was a day-by-day summary of the congress itself. It focused on the speakers, the music (outstanding and often moving), the business of the congress, the "scattering" of the delegates to the various Baptist churches on Sunday morning, August 5, and the "special observances" (for example, youth day, missions day [when representatives spoke of Baptist missionary work around the world]), the interruption of the congress on Tuesday, August 7, to hear the broadcast of the funeral of President von Hindenburg, and the official centennial celebration of modern Baptist work in Germany. Bradbury's closing comments stressed the openness of the meetings, the coverage of the congress in German newspapers, (also stressed in Eubank's article in *The Christian Century*), and the overall courtesy and cooperation the congress received from the people and the German authorities alike. He concluded:

> The land is full of people fanatically devoted to the new National Socialism. The world will have to reckon with this in treating with Germany. Baptists have witnessed these. God will give the fruit in due time and season. Reichsbishop Mueller has guaranteed that Baptists will not be forced into union with the Reich church. Meanwhile continue to pray for our German Baptists. They are a great people.[26]

Bradbury's third article was a series of short paragraphs about his impressions and memories of the Berlin congress. He mentioned the impact of the congress in Germany and Europe generally in terms of Baptist testimony: the coverage in the German and the European press; the "honor" in that Dr. George W. Truett of Dallas, Texas, had been elected president of the Baptist World Alliance; the meeting of a congress delegation of twenty-five Baptists with Reichsbishop Mueller; the absence of jazz, "sex literature," and "putrid motion pictures and gangster films"; the ever-present swastika flags and the apparent support of the people for Hitler; some unusual and humorous moments, an indirect reference to the new German "paganism." He also expressed the respect held for *The Watchman-Examiner* among readers in Europe and from around the world.

The only mention of Jews was in the context of his short paragraph on "sex literature" and films. "The new Germany has burned great masses of corrupting magazines and books along with its bonfires of Jewish and communistic libraries. It has reorganized its film industry and purged it of its sex rot."[27] The justappsition of *Jewish* and *communistic*, intentional or not, can hardly be judged as a comment favorable to Germany's Jews.

Prof. Herman von Berge was a member of the faculty of the German Baptist Seminary in Rochester, New York, and a delegate and speaker at the Berlin congress, representing the German Baptist churches of North America. *The Baptist Herald*, the German Baptist periodical, published five articles by von Berge, beginning in November 1934—"What Think Ye of Germany," "What Hitler Has Meant to Germany," "The Price of Hitlerism," "The Jew in Germany," and "Church and State in Germany." In the first article, von Berge claimed that the basic picture of Germany held by Americans was untrue. He cited the resolutions of the German Baptists meeting in their own caucus on Thursday afternoon, April 9, 1934, at the congress. Resolution one referred to the distorted picture of the New Germany found to be held by many delegates to the congress. Resolution two described "20 years of unspeakable suffering," from which "the assumption of power by Adolph Hitler has meant our salvation." Resolution three read, "We who live in the New Germany stand in confidence and loyalty on the side of our leader and imperial chancellor. We pray for our government. We rejoice in the New Germany." Resolution four asked for goodwill and understanding from fellow Baptists from other countries. Von Berge then gave his reasons for believing the German Baptist brethren to be "absolutely right" about the "altogether untrue picture of Germany and conditions there." He included a quotation from John W. Bradbury's article about Bradbury's timidity and what he had found upon entering Germany. "But why is that that we should get so untrue a picture of a great country here in our land? There are several reasons for that," von Berge continued. First, the reporting of the press, who concentrated only on the "exceptional." Second, the war psychosis left over from World War I, leaving Americans with a mental acceptance of atrocity stories even after they were proven untrue, so that the prejudice and hatred toward Germans remained in the heart. Third, certain groups carried on an organized campaign of propaganda. (Von Berge stated that "certain groups of people" was so well known a reference that it did not need to be named.) Fourth, he concluded, we do not understand what Germans have been through in the last twenty years. "And so for weal or woe, Germany is behind Hitler. They are convinced that it is for the welfare of Germany, and with gratitude they point to the things Hitler has done for them. But that is another story."[28]

The second article discussed Hitlerism in Germany. It was said to be a dictatorship. Americans did not like dictatorships. Yet, the German people liked their dictator, as evidenced by the resolutions passed by the German Baptists at the Berlin congress. Why? Von Berge stated that Hitler had "restored order and confidence in Germany," unified Germany, and "stopped communism."

> When communistic headquarters were raided in Germany it was discovered that many of the leaders of our Baptist brotherhood were marked to be shot. One of our pastors . . . told me that he had been secretly and confidentially told to secure civilian clothes for all his deaconesses, for they too had all been marked for purposes I must leave to the reader's guess. The resolution adopted by our German brethren at the Congress speaks of the salvation that God has brought through Hitler "in the eleventh hour". Some have said it was the eleventh hour and the fifty-ninth minute, for the communistic revolution was just about to be inaugurated and everything was ready for it, when Hitler stopped it.[29]

The economic benefits? They remained to be seen, von Berge wrote, but no one was hungry or homeless, with welfare and provision for the aged established.

> Our own brethren over there tell us that they believe God has given them Hitler in these difficult times, as God had given the rail-splitter Abe Lincoln to the American people when they needed him in the time of their emergency. History may well justify them in their conviction ere many years shall have gone by.[30]

But, wrote von Berge in his third article, there had been a price—dictatorship (which might be needed in times of emergency), ruthlessness (as in the Hitler purge of June 30, 1934, when seventy were "purged" at the orders of Hitler), and abolition of freedom of speech and press. About the June 30, 1934, "purge," von Berge wrote, "I confess that I was schocked when, after having voiced my own objection and protest against such action to one of our pastors in Germany, he quietly remarked, 'You may condemn that; we are glad he acted as he did'." Von Berge then suggested that his further inquiries led him to conclude that a plot or an uprising with a possible bloodbath was avoided by the "purge," ruthless as it seemed.[31]

As for limiting freedom of press and speech, von Berge, in a long paragraph, stated that America had limited both in times of emergency, such as during World War I. But the problems were for Germans to face and solve, free of hasty or "too harsh" criticism, von Berge concluded, so let us pray for them and be glad the problems are not ours. The fourth of the articles by Professor von Berge was on the subject of the Jews in Germany. He began by stating that the Jews may live in a nation but they can never be truly assimilated. The Jew may be patriotic, philanthropic, highly professional, "but he remains a Jew, marries Jewish, lives Jewish. This is not said by way of criticism but as a statement of fact." Jews had made great contributions to the world, and most of all to Christianity, von Berge said, but friction between Jews and gentiles had been constant for centuries. Christians were often to blame, but then so were Jews. Jews were said to have certain identifiable racial characteristics, were not known for meekness, and were often very aggressive, intelligent, and successful. For these and other reasons, Jews were often resented by others. This was not a problem peculiar to Germany, von Berge claimed.

He then traced Hitler's own anti-Semitism to Hitler's youth in Vienna, his supposed discovery at a time when he was interested in socialism that the leaders of socialism were Jews (for example, Karl Marx) and that socialism "leaned strongly toward communism, which he abhorred." Later, through von Ludendorff, Hitler's hatred of the Jews increased because, von Berge continued, von Ludendorff blamed the Jews (especially a Jew named Maximilian Harden) for spreading pacifist and defeatist propaganda behind the lines during World War I. "This broke down the morale behind the lines, and that was given as the chief reason for Germany's losing the war. Hitler's contact with von Ludendorff strengthened him in his anti-Jewish sentiments."[32]

As for Germans generally, von Berge claimed they resented Jews because they held "positions of power and influence in Germany altogether out of proportion to their numerical strength." Von Berge referred to Lord Rothermere, an English publisher, as his source for a paragraph and a half of percentage figures that demonstrated the disproportion of Jews who had purchased real estate, stores, homes, and businesses with their uninflated "foreign" currency as they came into Germany from Eastern Europe during the Weimar Republic. Physicians in all categories, hospital directors, dentists, medical faculties, directors of theaters, writers, and lawyers were all professional groups dominated by Jews in Berlin; generally more than 50 percent of those in the named professions were Jews while Jews made up only 1 percent of the total population.

Such a situation made it a simple matter for the German people to be won over to Hitler's anti-Semitic program, and put an
end to the domination by an aggressive minority-group which
was felt to be more or less alien.
Under the Hitler regime the status of the Jews has now been
completely changed. They are welcome to stay in Germany,
but they are not citizens; they are only "guest people".[33]

Von Berge then described the limitations on Jews in the professions, in government, and in business. "If Germany has ever been a paradise for the Jews, it is that no longer!"

The next section of his fourth article was headlined, "The So-called Jewish Atrocities." The headline well described the content. Said von Berge, Jews had suffered physical harm, but Germany had just gone through a revolution, and who could have controlled mobs in a revolution?

To take isolated cases which undoubtedly have occurred, and
to make them the basis of the propaganda of misrepresenta-
tion and hatred against an entire nation, which is now being
carried on by a certain group of people, is a contemptible
thing. It is worse than that. It is international criminality.[34]

Von Berge then stated, "All of my diligent inquiry while in Germany among our brethren and leaders brought the same answer, 'We per-
sonally know of no cases of atrocities against the Jews'."[35] He said that one person, the only exception to the above statement, had known of a Jew who had died from wounds inflicted by a mob. He concluded his section on atrocities to Jews by saying, "The government, however, is not behind any atrocities but rather deplores them where they have occurred and severely punishes those who may be guilty of them."[36] So much for von Berge on the Jews in the context of the Baptist World Alliance Fifth Congress in Berlin.

The remainder of von Berge's article discussed the Christian atti-
tude toward anti-Semitism (unchristian), the boycott of German goods (not all American Jews approved), and the source of anti-Ger-
man boycott efforts (the World Jewish Congress, Dr. Nahum Gold-
mann, Rabbi Stephen S. Wise, and Samuel Untermyer). According to von Berge, the implications were serious. If the Jews asserted their power in this way over one nation, what about another nation in the future? Further, said von Berge, the Jews were then 3 percent of

America's population and their numbers were growing. They were a powerful influence in industry and commerce. They were owners and managers of newspapers, theaters, jewelers, fur and clothing stores, and other businesses. "They furnish governors for three states, and mayors for ten cities. They are well represented in the state and national legislatures, and two Jews sit on the bench of the Supreme Court of the United States." Von Berge took this material from "The Jew in America: Home Missions Today and Tomorrow," *Missions* (October 1934).[37]

As used by von Berge and in the context of his larger discussion of the Jews in Germany, the implications of his remarks about Jews in America themselves constituted a veiled anti-Semitism. He did say that many in Germany felt that the anti-Jewish measures were too severe or that the "Jewish problem" had been badly handled, but, nonetheless, the general tone of his article left the reader feeling that von Berge believed the Jews in Germany to be a serious problem requiring the use of severe measures and that, by implication and context, America might have the same problem with its Jews. But, finally, he wrote, "We cannot settle it by rising in our righteous wrath and condemning Germany."[38]

In the last article of the five, Professor von Berge discussed the German Baptists' continued freedom and the promises given by Reichsbishop Mueller to the delegation from the Berlin congress that the freedoms of Baptists in Germany, including the work of the *Volksmission*, would not be limited. He did point out that the new "German Faith Movement" was strongly anti-Semitic, seeking removal of all Jewish traces for its "positive Christianity." The movement von Berge called "little more than the age-old atheistic movement under another name." He also described it as being very limited in Germany, but the struggle within the Protestant church in Germany, he wrote, was very real, and the protesting groups were people of courage, who had strong support. In January 1935, von Berge was optimistic. He felt that the evangelical protesters and their supporters would win in the Church Struggle. Von Berge believed that the Church in Germany should become a "free church," for in his view, "A state supported church becomes only too easily a state controlled church."[39]

Frank Woyke, the pastor of the German Baptist Church in Meriden, Connecticut, was content to describe "An Afternoon 'Unter den Linden'," at a sidewalk cafe. Von Hindenburg had just died, the people were somber, and a public meeting in the Lustgarten to commemorate the beginning of World War I was planned. He described the flags flying everywhere, the frequent marching in the streets by various groups (mentioned by all who wrote about their visits to Berlin for the congress), and his attendance at the memorial rally. He heard three speeches but could only ponder the significance of what he had heard about the New Germany. His only mention of Jews was incidental. He had observed several, as well as some Americans, at nearby tables in a sidewalk cafe.[40]

The statement released to the press after the congress had ended came over the signatures of Truett (president of the Baptist World Alliance), Rushbrooke (general secretary), and Gray (the associate secretary). It mentioned the fellowship, inspiration, and "sense of vast tasks to be accomplished." In the second paragraph, it stated "that there is no abiding solution to be expected of the international, racial, political, economic or social problems of the world save as we are faithful to the teachings of our Lord" and called the people to a sense of duty and strength in order to "exemplify the great law of love."[41]

Earle Eubank, who wrote his article for *The Christian Century* from his hotel in Berlin, mentioned that he had been a delegate to the Baptist World Congress and had attended all the sessions. He also noted that he had before him the Conrad H. Moehlman's article from February 7, 1934, that had raised so many questions about the Baptists' meeting in Berlin. Eubank had helped draft and represent on the floor of the congress the resolution on war and peace. He also consciously tried to answer some of the questions raised by Moehlman's article, "both in the formal pronouncements of the congress itself and in the numerous informal and written indicators open to any critical observer."

Eubank told about his conversation with J. H. Rushbrooke, the general secretary of the alliance, as to why the Baptists went to Berlin. The major reason given by Rushbrooke was that he believed the alliance should support the 70,000 Baptists in Germany during the trials through which Germany was going. The original decision was made at the world congress of 1928. In his conversation with Eubank, Rushbrooke had spoken of his trips to Germany, his meetings with German government officials, and the commitments made to an open and free meeting with no restrictions on the topics and issues that could be discussed. Eubank then affirmed that, in his opinion and in the opinion of the leaders of the congress, there had been no interference or constraint. He illustrated this by mentioning that the number of the audience for each session was around 10,000, the majority of whom were "plain citizens" of the German Baptist churches. The Germans were free to come and go, participated in the debates, voted on all issues (some judged as unfavorable to Nazi doctrines), and voted in open meetings by the uplifted hand, "which would definitely have put them on record before anyone who had been watching."[42] Also, the newspapers had given generous space coverage of the congress, especially in Berlin.

Eubank addressed one of Moehlman's questions directly, "What Baptists have *done* [emphasis his] with this freedom," expressing his own concern over having attended innumerable conventions that passed beautiful resolutions, "which are only pious wishes." Since Baptists emphasize evangelistic over social concerns, Eubank wrote, any statements in the social realm are more than welcome. He mentioned three points in the proceedings at which Nazi officials conceivably could have been disturbed by what was said by speakers or by the way the entire audience responded (for example, in the closing session, when loyalty to Christ was placed first, above all other loyalties, and when the entire audience lingered on after the official closing, clasping hands and singing the hymn, "Blest Be the Tie That Binds"). No interference or objection was voiced by Nazi officials.

In his article, Eubank included the full texts of the major resolutions on peace and war, nationalism and racialism. He noted that certain sentences he had underlined for emphasis. One sentence he had underlined condemned "narrow nationalism" as being at odds with the Christian spirit. Most of the underlined sentences, however, were in the resolution on racialism. The statements emphasized that racial differences should not be the basis for exploitation, oppression, or persecution. Race or color should bar no one from worship or fellowship in the Christian church, and anti-Semitism was said to be particularly abhorrent.

> With our fellow Christians in all the churches, *we deplore the long record of ill-usage of Jews on the part of professedly Christian nations, and declare such injustice to be a violation of the teaching and spirit of Christ.* We desire for ourselves, and for those we represent, to express to the Jews by word and act the spirit of Jesus Christ. . . .
> So! The Baptists have been to Berlin![43]

In his closing paragraphs, he noted the marching, brown-shirted men led by a band that passed his hotel on their way to a drill, something seen endlessly in Berlin. The people stopped and gave the Nazi salute as the flag corps passed. Eubank asked, "Will it eventually make any difference to them, I wonder—and to the rest of the world as well—that the Baptists have been to Berlin?"[44] Events in the next eleven years proved his pessimism to have been more than justified.

The report of the Baptists' Berlin meeting published in *The Concordia Theological Monthly* was almost entirely a reprint of the editorial published originally in *The Christian Century* of August 22, 1934, without additional comment. As for the Southern Baptists, they received their information primarily from John D. Freeman, editor of *The Baptist and Reflector* (Tennessee), and M. E. Dodd, president of the Southern Baptist Convention. It was characteristic of the Southern Baptist periodicals that the state papers reprinted each other's major articles, so the Freeman and Dodd reports were found in a number of them in 1934. Freeman's reports were more personal and anecdotal than those discussed earlier and, because he spoke no German, very different from those of Professor von Berge. Freeman mentioned the universal spirit of goodwill he felt with the delegates from different countries with whom he sat but could not converse and the "happy fellowship and Christian love" that he sensed. He stressed the openness of the meetings, the welcome extended by German officials, and, as with Eubank, he addressed questions about the expense of attending the congress and about what had been accomplished. He gave four answers to his questions, clearly designated as accomplishments, and added, "My estimate may not be very valuable, but at least it is my own."[45]

Freeman's first conclusion was this: the Baptists had become better known, particularly in Berlin and Germany. Second: the congress had greatly encouraged Baptists in Germany and throughout Europe. Third: international goodwill had been enhanced as people from many nations met together for a week. His fourth conclusion was negative; the Baptist World Alliance was controlled by a small group; "There was no chance for free discussion on the floor, even in the moments when it would have been possible. Every vote was a farce."[46] He then predicted that the alliance would eventually divide over the question of control versus freedom.

Freeman's second article was of a very different nature, focusing on Germany rather than on the Berlin congres. He mentioned that five questions had been asked most often since his return to America. In essence, he stated, as had von Berge, that Germany was badly misrepresented by the press, that Germany was one of three great

Protestant nations (therefore, as Freeman had heard, the Catholics opposed the Nazis in southern Germany, the "stronghold" of Roman Catholicism), and that Hitler had smashed Communism. Freeman wrote that Germany was surrounded by three "ambitious" powers— Russia, France, and Italy. Freeman said that he had heard nothing but praise for Hitler during his trip through Germany after the congress ended. The stores were full, there were no beggars on the streets, the trains ran on time, the harvests were plentiful and the farms beautiful. There were no shacks. Everything was utilized, even the pine needles. He saw no scrub stock. Flowers were everywhere, and there was "paint everywhere in Germany except on her women." The women from other countries who were "made up," he stated, were a problem for Germans because only "scarlet women" wore makeup in Germany.

He closed his article, the one most frequently reprinted in other Southern Baptist papers, by writing about the prejudices toward Germany he had had before his visit, but he (like others with whom he had conversed) had discovered that his prejudices had been unfounded. Germans were peace-loving, religious people, loyal to their country and to Hitler.[47]

M. E. Dodd's report was more formal, concerning itself with the business of the congress. His evaluations of the freedom of the congress were similar to those of the others, and he mentioned also that officials of the congress were interviewed on the radio without restrictions. Dodd also was quick to commend the leaders of the alliance for their decision to meet in Berlin, which had encouraged Baptists in Germany and Europe. He noted that the congress was unified on the issues brought before it, and especially in its resolution on racial prejudice, and stressed their commitment to understanding and goodwill both as Christians and as Baptists. He then devoted a portion of his report to the "Cause of German Antipathy to Jews."[48] He reported that the debate on racialism and anti-Semitism was the warmest, not in its principles, but in its methods of dealing with the subjects. Racialism and anti-Semitism were unanimously judged unchristian. But the Jews in Germany were a special problem, Dodd stated, and he repeated charges that Jews had taken over the arts, finance, professions, and the Institute of Science. Further, Dodd said, "Since the war some 200,000 Jews from Russia and other eastern places had come to Germany. Most of these were communist agitators against the government."[49] Dodd stated that the Germans came to resent this Jewish domination. "Naturally excesses occurred and irresponsible persons committed some atrocious deeds. But at the worst it was not one-tenth as bad as we have been led to believe. The new government became the agent of adjustment of positions proportionate to the population."[50] He went on to say that England and America were doing much the same thing through restrictive immigration laws and by limiting the number of Jews admitted to various fields and institutions (presumably universities, colleges, medical schools, and law schools). Dodd summarized the war and peace resolution, mentioning the continued missionary emphasis of the congress. He closed by noting that five Southern Baptists, including himself, had been elected to the executive committee. "The Berlin Congress was a great gathering of Baptists."

Dodd's article did not go unchallenged. Robert A. Ashworth, former editor of *The Baptist* and educational secretary of the National Conference of Jews and Christians (as it was called in 1934), sent Dodd an "Open Letter."[51] Ashworth concentrated on the section of Dodd's article, "Cause of German Antipathy to Jews." Ashworth noted that he had been a member of the Executive Committee of the Baptist World Alliance that met in New York, that he had opposed the Berlin decision, that he later acquiesced, and that he was glad that things had gone so well. He also wrote that Dodd's article said, "some things that cannot be substantiated by the facts and that may be a source of grave misunderstandings in this country." Ashworth noted that "so impartial and judicial a book as Calvin Hoover's 'Germany Enters the Third Reich' gives facts in abundance to controvert the impression that you received." He challenged Dodd's statement that the basis for German concern about the Jews was only political and economic, not religious. He quoted in its entirety the racial decree of the National Socialist party to point out that *non-Aryan* meant having a parent or grandparent who was "of the Jewish religion."

Ashworth challenged the figures used by Dodd, asking for the authority from which they were obtained. He then, point by point, refuted Dodd's figures as being exaggerated or incorrent. He particularly challenged the statement that there were 200,000 foreign-born Jews in Germany and that they were Communists. He said the number of foreign-born Jews in Germany was fewer than 60,000, and most of them had come from Poland, not Russia. These people had been specifically invited to come to Germany by General Ludendorff, Ashworth wrote. Furthermore, he continued, the German Communist party had a membership of 4,900,000; with only 600,000 Jews in Germany, suggesting a figure of 200,000 Communist Jews was just plain wrong.

Scarcely 200,000 [Jews] would have voted or been actually engaged in political affairs. It is well known that the vast majority of the German Jews were conservative in their attitude toward political and economic matters. The charge of communism is a mere red scare to win over unprejudiced people against the Jews.

Then, using the German statistical yearbook for 1931, he listed the number of Jews holding positions in all branches of government, including the federal railway, the Reichsbank, the Gold Discount Bank, and the nineteen cabinets formed during the Weimar Republic. Of the supposed Jewish officeholders, "Painstaking examination of these lists by impartial government employees proves that at least 70% of the names were spurious because the people named either do not exist at all or were neither Jews nor of Jewish descent." Of 500 officeholders, Ashworth stated, only 15 could be proved to have been of Jewish descent, and no Jew had held a cabinet position for at least six years.

It is hardly likely that these figures would bear out the assertion "that the Jews monopolized the majority of government, education and economic positions". Nor is it true that those few who were in positions of government service were using these positions, as you assert, "for self-aggrandizement, to the injury of the German people".

Ashworth then stated that there were many Jews in the medical profession but they were there as devoted scientists, not religious Jews. He questioned claims that Jews ran the Institute of Science. Which one, Ashworth asked; Germany had many. If such an institute was headed by a Jew and had only Jews on its staff, Ashworth suggested, perhaps they were there because it was the only place where they were welcome. "This is a perfectly natural process." He concluded his letter: "Your article makes me wonder whether some Baptists who went to Berlin were not 'taken in' by the hospitality and the congeniality which they met, just as some expressed the fear that they might be."[52] Ashworth did more than express the pessimism of Earle Eubank. He accused his fellow Baptists of having been hoodwinked by propaganda during their visit to Germany, although he used the gentle phrase "taken in." Again, the next eleven years proved that Ashworth was more than correct in his analysis.

Other Reports about Jews in Germany, 1934

The segment of the American Protestant press that did not mention the Baptist World Alliance in 1934, nevertheless, continued to publish articles, editorials, letters to the editor, and book reviews related to the persecution of the German Jews. Concern for what was happening to non-Aryan Christians was one topic of discussion. Non-Aryan Christians (more commonly called Hebrew Christians in the American Protestant press) in Germany, as reported in *Christian Faith and Life*, were officially being treated as Jews by the German government and as apostates by the Jews. Said to number 250,000, 400 of whom were ministers of the Gospel put out of their churches and desperate, they were unable to obtain employment.[53] *The Hebrew Christian Alliance Quarterly*, *The Hebrew Lutheran*, the *Federal Council Bulletin*, and *The Watchman-Examiner* printed similar reports.[54] Three periodicals reported the formation of a "ghetto church" in Berlin. Made up of Christians of Jewish origin, it was located near the Central Jewish Synagogue.[55] *The Moody Bible Institute Monthly*, however, published a letter from a German pastor, Ernst Modersohn, the editor of two German church periodicals, which specifically denied that Germans were treating Jewish Christians badly. Modersohn called reports of the prevention of Old Testament reading, the restriction of shopping in Jewish-owned stores, the forbidding of the use of "Amen" and "Hallelujah" "lies . . . circulated among the different nations in order to find fault with the new republic in which we live, and to arouse suspicions against its aims."[56]

The Question of Credibility, 1934

Faced with such counterclaims, the Protestant press kept questioning the credibility of reports on the persecution of Jews in Germany. John Haynes Holmes, pastor of the Community Church of New York, raised the question in an article, "How Do I Know about Hitler?" in *The Christian Century*. "I never denounce the Hitler horror but what sooner or later I am myself denounced for believing the current reports about Nazi Germany."[57] He then spoke of his training in sifting evidence, detecting propaganda, analyzing reports, and recognizing facts, saying that he had been mistaken before and might be again in the Hitler matter. "So I propose to begin over again, and judge this present situation on its own merits. How do I form judgments? What influences me? What are my reasons for finding that . . . Hitlerism is a reversion to barbarism, and a menace therefore to every precious thing in our civilization?" He cited six sources for his conclusions. First, the reports from the Geneva commission on refugees that German Jews, rich and poor, had been leaving Germany at the rate of 10,000 a month since Hitler had become chancellor. Second, his personal interviews with refugees from Germany. "I never belived the old 'atrocity stories' [referring to World War I]. . . . [But] I have seen with my own eyes and touched with my own hands some victims of Hitler's troopers, and I believe even as Thomas believed when he touched the wounds of Christ."[58] Third, Nazi books and literature (that is, laws, decrees, documents, official state papers, textbooks used in the schools, anti-Jewish pamphlets, and speeches) he had examined personally. Fourth, books by respected, established scholars and trained observers, (Edgar Mowrer, Charles Macfarland, and Prof. Calvin B. Hoover in particular).[59] Fifth, reliable journalists (for example, seven reporters posted to Berlin by American and British newspapers). And sixth, firsthand accounts of visitors, "not tourists who find hotels comfortable, streets quiet, and trains on time, not Germans, or German-Americans, or pro-Germans who think everything is right because it's 'made in Germany', not Jews or socialists or communists or intellectuals who have suffered and are therefore stricken and offended, but impartial spectators who are interested in the scene and know how to report it."[60] Of several, Holmes selected two for citation, Robert Dall of the *Nation* and Dr. Alice Hamilton of *Survey Graphic*. Holmes concluded that this provided evidence enough even if no other evidence existed.

> These are the sources of our information about Germany today. Let no one say we do not know or have been deceived about what is going on in the reich. We know with a certainty and a fullness which make the Hitler regime the most terrifying experience since the world war itself.[61]

In the same issue of *The Christian Century*, Ewart Edmund Turner, correspondent to the *Century* from Germany, while visiting in the United States, was asked about the credibility of the reports. His answer? He claimed that it depended on the newspaper. The United Press, the Associated Press, and the metropolitan dailies with their own reporters in Germany were very fair, said Turner, as were the reports from the American consulates. Needless brutalities did happen.[62]

The more conservative, fundamentalist *Moody Bible Institute Monthly* took a bit different approach in order "to be fair to the Jew whether in Germany, America or anywhere else." A December 1934 editorial cited a Dr. Otto H. F. Vollbehr, who had sent out "memoranda" setting forth Germany's side to American readers. Vollbehr's release number seven was a refutation of a pamphlet, "Chicago Committee for the Defense of Human Rights against Naziism," stating that Jews in Germany resented such pamphlets. The editorial note cited Vollbehr as the source for a statement about the suppression of a book published by the Jewish Printing House, "Atrocity Propaganda Is Based on Lies, Say the Jews of Germany Themselves," not available in America because of a conspiracy of silence. The German address for obtaining the book was given. The editorial comment was: "Of course, we are unable to pass judgment on the premises, although the objection sounds reasonable to us. We can only hope that the volume in the Jewish Printing House in Berlin may soon reach this country, if it will give us the facts."[63] The editors might have paid a bit more attention to an article in the same issue of their own magazine describing the report of Conrad Hoffman, Jr., director of the International Committee on the Christian Approach to the Jews, recently returned from an extensive trip to Europe and the Near East. Hoffman was quoted as saying:

> It would appear that the average German, or the casual visitor, is scarcely aware of any anti-Jewish discrimination, though it cannot be denied that acts of violence against Jews are committed. They are left in no doubt that they are being treated as inferiors and outcasts, and even little children are being hatefully tormented.

The article stated that Hoffman found Jews and non-Aryans being persecuted because of the "presumable guilt of certain individual Jews" and that Christians everywhere ought to protest such actions vehemently.[64] Was the editorial note about being fair aimed at having this article in the same issue? One can only wonder.

In 1934, articles on the "Jewish question" and anti-Semitism in America and significant book reviews on books about Germany (such as Charles S. Macfarland's *New Church and New Germany*, Cardinal Faulhaber's *Judaism, Christianity and Germany*, Adolph Keller's *Religion and Revolution*, and Everett R. Clinchy's *All in the Name of God*) appeared in a number of periodicals, with the book by Macfarland attracting the most attention. It concentrated on the Church Struggle but did refer to problems Jews in Germany were experiencing.[65]

Paid Advertisement about the Persecution of the Jews, 1934

A "new" item appeared in 1934, the paid advertisement on behalf of Jews, particularly in Germany. On the inside back cover of the February issue of *The Moody Bible Institute Monthly*, there was a full-page advertisement headed "Shout It from the Housetops, It's Time to Help the Jews." The advertisement included this one paragraph among many.

> In Germany, Hitlerism is bringing disaster to hundreds of thousands of innocent and helpless Jews, men, women and children. Jews are committing suicide by the hundreds, Jews are being robbed of their livelihood; nowhere to go, not allowed to leave Germany, and tortured if they stay. Even Christian Jews are not immune from this fiendish program of extermination. All this in the name of Christianity.[66]

The advertisement was placed by the American Board of Missions to the Jews of Brooklyn, New York, with the note that it was "paid for by a friend; for the sake of the Lord Jesus Christ." Such paid advertisements were published continuously from 1934 through 1945, their central theme being the persecution of the Jews in Europe.

Persecution, the Protocols of Zion, and
the "Jewish Question," 1934

The Protocols of Zion continued to require discussion and refutation in articles and editorials in 1934. The Protocols of Zion is the most reprinted of all anti-Semitic documents; they allege a "plot" by the "elders of Zion" to take over the world and establish Judaism as the only religion. In an effort to deal with the "Jewish question," the Protocols of Zion, the question of the persecution of the Jews in Germany, and the interest of its readers in a less spectacular prophetic analysis than that of Louis S. Bauman, *The Sunday School Times* published three articles by Will H. Houghton of Calvary Baptist Church in New York, who soon after the articles were published became president of the Moody Bible Institute in Chicago. Houghton had visited Europe and England in preparation for his articles. In a brief statement, he noted the rise of anti-Semitism throughout Western Europe, including England, and also noted the numbers of Jews said to have left Germany because of persecution. He obtained his information from reports in British newspapers and from the High Commission for Refugees from Germany. In his first article, he concentrated on Jews who were returning to Palestine and the interest in Palestine among Jews whom he had met in England.[67]

In the second article, "The Truth about Germany and the Jews," Houghton confirmed the basic facts about the persecution of the Jews in Germany. He obtained his information from friends and confidants in Germany who felt free to speak openly with him. Both he and they agreed that the German people did not know what was going on in Germany. Those who did obtained their information by subscribing to non-German newspapers and periodicals (apparently this was still possible in 1934). Houghton touched on some of the commonly accepted anti-Jewish propaganda but seemed innately suspicious about emphasizing that sort of information. He did note that more Jews seemed interested in their religion as a result of their persecution and also that small groups of Hebrew Christians met together. He had attended such a meeting. He then stated:

> The persecution has been very real to the Jews in Germany, however lightly the German Christians may esteem it. Tales of genuine suffering are heard everywhere. The separation of dear ones in the breaking up of families has occurred. Once again the Jew has become a wanderer.[68]

Houghton did not use the terms *Aryan* and *non-Aryan*, nor did he make reference to racial laws as such. He did, however, illustrate the effect of the German government's use of racial theories as he told of meeting a young woman twenty years old in Berlin. She was attending a Christian service. Her mother was a full German; her father half Jewish. She had been classed as a Jew and could not gain admittance to medical school because she was "outside the quota." The family had decided to emigrate to South Africa. Houghton's concern for the young women, who was the same age as his own daughter, was immediate. In the articles, though he did make prophetic references and some prophetic analyses, he seemed more interested in people than in prophecy.

From 1934 to 1935, Coverage of Anti-Nazi Movements

In the main, the themes of 1934 continued into and through 1935. The interest in the developing Church Struggle continued to dominate the American Protestant press. Two new aspects were added to the general discussion. The first was mention of Martin Niemoller, a leader of the growing opposition to the German Christian movement. *The Baptist Herald* for April 15, 1935, reported that Niemoller had been arrested after his reading of the manifesto of the Confessing Synod on March 7, 1935. The arrest of Niemoller, "the militant leader of the opposition of German pastors to Reichsbishop Ludwig Mueller and the Nazi policies of the German Christian party, had been expected for many months."[69]

In a letter to the editor, James M. Yard of the Committee for the Defense of Human Rights against Naziism, Chicago, described the rise of a second new dimension, an underground movement in opposition to Hitler centered in Prague, Czechoslovakia, and active inside Germany itself. Described as illegal and as using pamphlets and the "flysheet newspaper" and as plagued by a perpetual lack of money, newsprint, typewriters, and duplicating machines, it was nevertheless, publishing a newspaper, eight pages long and weighing only an eighth of an ounce, each fortnight. "During the first year two million copies were distributed. Not specifically religious, but primarily political, this underground effort was, to the writer, a brave effort by those opposed to Hitler."[70] In the thirty-two American Protestant periodicals examined for 1935, a total of eighty-six articles, letters to the editor, editorials, book reviews, and news items referring to the Church Struggle were found.

These periodicals contained eight discussions of the "Jewish question;" eight articles or notes concerning the Jews and prophecy; eight articles or references to the growing refugee problem, including Jews, and the raising of funds or the forming of committees to assist refugees; and four articles or references to non-Aryan or Hebrew Christians.

The Debate over Holding the Olympic Games in Berlin

The other major area of discussion in 1935 concerned the Olympic Games to be held in Germany in 1936. Thirty articles, editorials, and letters to the editor (mostly in *The Christian Century* but also in *The Federal Council Bulletin*, *The Reformed Church Messenger*, *The Concordia Theological Monthly*, and *The Friend*) expressed concern over holding the Olympics in Berlin. In general, the articles and editorials opposed going to Berlin; the letters to the editor reflected the division of opinion that such a stance engendered. On August 7, 1935, *The Christian Century* published a long editorial calling for the Olympic Games to be moved to another country. The reason?

> While the forces back of the new outrages against Catholics, Protestants and Jews are not clear, the facts are clear. Religious

persecution is being used as an official instrument of the Nazi government, and no person is safe in the enjoyment of the most elemental human rights.

The editorial suggested that, though the American government could not act directly in an internal matter of another nation, moving the Olympics would be a blow to Germany and especially to the Nazi government. "The proposal to move the Olympic Games away from Berlin offers the most dramatic, and, therefore, the most effective, opportunity which has so far occurred to tell Germany." And further:

> To let the Catholic, Protestant and Jewish youth of Germany know that the outside world is not indifferent to the persecution being inflicted upon them, and to let the Nazi leaders know of the horror with which their brutality is regarded, let the athletic authorities of America move to take the Olympics from Berlin! A move of this sort made in this country will be followed in other countries. It will have immediate moral effect inside Germany. It should, therefore, be made without delay. Germany must be told![71]

Ten letters to the editor were published in *The Christian Century* of August 21, 1935, responding to the editorial. They were, it seems, deliberately alternated, approving and disapproving. The five letters approving spoke to the subject of the Olympics; the five disapproving called the *Century* a Communist paper, unchristian, and an organization that had been "bamboozled, blackmailed or bribed" by communistic Jews who were trying to overpower America.[72]

Eight editorials in all were published by the *Century* in 1935, as well as four news items, all opposing the holding of the Olympic Games in Berlin. Thirteen letters to the editor were published also in 1935, six opposing holding the Olympics in Berlin and seven supporting the Olympics for Berlin. Only one of the opposing letters was courteous in that it did not attack *The Christian Century*.[73] Russell J. Clinchy (pastor of Mt. Pleasant Congregational Church in Washington, D.C., and brother of Everett R. Clinchy, president of the National Conference of Jews and Christians) suggested that, until the United States had solved its own racial problems, it was unwise to speak too loudly about racial practices in Germany.[74]

The *Federal Council Bulletin* directly linked the Olympics issue with the persecution of Jews in Germany.

> The fate of the Jews in Germany . . . is growing more and more tragic. The prospect is that the medieval ghetto will be

virtually reestablished in twentieth-century Germany. The world needs to be awakened to this fact.

One suggestion has been made which merits serious attention. It is the proposal that the Olympic Games . . . should be transferred elsewhere, or that Americans should decline to participate.[75]

The editorial went on to plead for assistance for those in Germany engaged in the Church Struggle and for sympathy and assistance for the refugees.

The Friend was more direct. In an editorial on August 15, 1935, the editor suggested that the Olympic Games probably should not be held at all, rather than moved as *The Christian Century* had proposed. On December 19, 1935, *The Friend* published a letter to the editor in which the writer suggested postponing any precipitate action and studying the matter. He further suggested that Germany might, in fact, profit from interaction with people from outside Germany, who would express to Germans directly how they felt about the situation' in Germany.[76] The editors of *The Concordia Theological Monthly*, on the other hand, were quite critical of *The Christian Century*, quoting from some of the letters to the editor of August 21, 1935, in the *Century* in support of the view that the situation in Germany was much different than what the *Century* editorials indicated. *The Concordia Theological Monthly* continued to be quite pro-German in its comments, not only on the Olympic Games, but generally.[77]

Reports of the Persecution of the Jews, 1935

The recording of incidents of the persecution of the Jews in Germany by the American Protestant press continued in 1935. Both in direct reports and in more indirect references, fifty-eight items appeared in the thirty-two periodicals examined for 1935. In an optimistic editorial on March 13, 1935, *The Christian Century* suggested that the policy toward Germany's Jews was apparently changing in their favor. "The world will require much more than the left-handed admission of February 28 to persuade it that the German persecution of the Jews is really at an end. But it hails with this evidence that controlling elements in Germany have awakened to the folly of the Nazi Jewish Policy."[78] The modified policy announced in Germany on February 28, 1935, was related to an attempt to have the boycott of German goods lifted.

By summer, such optimism was brought up short by events in Berlin. In editorials published July 31 and August 7, 1935, *The Christian*

Century reported open attacks on Jews and Catholics "reminiscent of the first days of the Hitler regime."

> On Monday night more than a week ago Jews in Berlin were attacked and beaten; Tuesday the anti-Jewish rioting spread; Wednesday the Catholic clergy were attacked in speeches by Nazi leaders; Thursday Catholic priests were warned to keep out of politics; Friday radical anti-Semitic and anti-Catholic Nazis were put into positions of power as fear spread among Catholics and Jews; Saturday the Catholic clergy were warned to guard their tongues in the Sunday services; and on Monday the drive against Hitler's opponents was pushed in all other quarters.[79]

References from the foreign press were cited that reported attacks on Jews occuring in open-air restaurants on the Kurfuerstendamn. Cars were stopped and pictures of persons seen entering Jewish shops and restaurants were taken. All of this was preceded by editorial attacks on Jews in Berlin newspapers through the late spring and early summer.

A second editorial in *The Christian Century* stated that, in spite of denials by the German government that attacks on Jews and Catholics in Berlin were not officially condoned or sanctioned, the policy of the Nazis was consistently anti-Jewish. "Back of the latter [policy] lies a definite social and political philosophy which the Nazi government has inculcated by every means within its power."[80] It is in the context of these new persecutions against Jews and Catholics in Berlin that the editors of the *Century* wrote their editorials about the Olympic Games.

H. R. Trauer, the London correspondent to *The Christian Century*, reported on the basis of his own personal verification the extent of the persecution of Jews in Berlin after a visit he made to the city in August 1935. He attended the speech of Julius Streicher at the Sportpalast in Berlin, spoke with individuals, and noted that many individual Germans "hate this 'Jew-baiting' yet have not the courage to stand against it, though all the time they realize that the ultimate harm will come to their children and to their children's children. Personal responsibility is at a very low ebb in the third reich." Trauer also pointed out that "there is no greater Jew-hater than Adolf Hitler; that it is his primary obsession, and that any of his followers who support him in this can do practically anything they please." To claim, said Trauer, that Hitler knew nothing of what was happening was to cling to a myth.[81] And there was no escape. The Jews were not welcome elsewhere and they could get neither money nor permission to leave Germany.

A. S. Eker, in his correspondence from Germany, fully confirmed Trauer's report of what he had seen.[82] *The Friend of Zion* reported these same events from Berlin and Breslau, in September and December.[83] *The Reformed Church Messenger* in August, September, and October of 1935 published two items in its "News of the Week" section, an editorial, and three articles detailing the events in Berlin and the situation in Germany.[84] Of the articles, one written by Samuel McCrea Cavert (general secretary of the Federal Council of Churches) was the most direct and explicit.

> The fate of the Jews in Germany, so far from being softened
> with the passing of time, is growing more and more tragic.
> The world needs to be awakened to this fact. The protest and
> appeals which arose spontaneously two years ago appear to be
> dying down. Can nothing be done now to show Germany that
> the rest of the world really cares?[85]

Cavert then spoke of the hope that the threat to the Olympic Games would help and of a statement released by the bishop of Chicester, who was chairman of the Administrative Committee of the University Christian Council, protesting the imprisonment of members of the clergy in Germany.

The Reich Law on Race, 1935

Only as the year advanced did the American Protestant press begin to pay serious attention to the developments that would lead to the adoption of the Reich law on race. Racial laws had usually been illustrated more by reference to persons restricted by such racial decisions than by reference to a binding law, adopted officially in Germany. An item in *The Sunday School Times* for January 5, 1935, for instance, noted that "in Germany the possession of one quarter Jewish blood is an occasion for penalization." The remainder of the paragraph discussed the failure of Jewish assimilation, originating with Moses Mendelssohn, an Enlightenment philosopher and a traditional exponent of Judaism who entered into dialogues with Christians. "Reform Judaism and conformity to Gentile citizenship and rational beliefs have received their death sentence."[86] But no mention was made of the official adoption of such racial determinations as a decision in law either by decree of the Nazi government or by some sort of parliamentary action by the Reichstag.

Indications of a change toward formal adoption of a race law as a basis for citizenship in Germany were announced to the readership of *The Christian Century* by the correspondent from Germany on May 29, 1935. J. Emlyn Williams, in a long paragraph, described the plan whereby the bestowal of Germany citizenship would be a formal ceremony granted to male Germans only after completion of military service. Dr. Wilhelm Frick, minister of the Interior, described the new laws as being in conformance with what had been described by Hitler in *Mein Kampf*. Citizens (*Staalsbürger*) would be different from subjects (*Untertanen*). Only Germans of Aryan origin could become citizens, "thus excluding all Jews even though they may have been residents here for generations."[87] Williams spoke of this planned action as legislation to be adopted but did not indicate when such legislation would be acted upon.

In August and September of 1935, *The Christian Century*, *The Friend of Zion*, and *The Watchman-Examiner* took note of the actions by which the new law was presented and adopted. In the *Century*, again, it was the German correspondent, then A. S. Eker, who conveyed the information. Referring to the radical elements in the National Socialist party and the increasing anti-Jewish and anti-Christian attitudes of the party leaders, Eker described the accelerated persecution of the Jews, which took the form of not so much public beatings as economic and political pressures. He described the problems of Aryans and non-Aryans who wanted to marry; "The marriage is not at the moment *legally* prohibited, but excuses are made by local registrars of marriages to prevent it taking place—until such time as a law can be made on the subject" [emphasis his]. The next paragraph described such a plan.

> Anti-Jewish action it is clear is now being led more and more into legalized channels. Well-informed observers expect that the coming party conference in Nuremberg (Sept. 10–17) will be marked by the sharpest measures against the Jews. . . . The introduction of the twentieth century ghetto should be expected. Jews will be given their own places of amusement, such as cafes, restaurants, and bathing pools, and their own schools; they will not be permitted to "contaminate" the rest of the racially-pure Teutons.[88]

He then pointed out that the Jew was being made the scapegoat, that the "official" reason for such action was to gain and to hold support of the workers, who were discontented with low wages, and that there really was no Reichstag anymore but in its place there was a party conference that would act as a Reichstag, this conference being more of a party rally than a legislative session.

The party's "Congress of Freedom" held in Nuremberg was reported in an editorial in *The Christian Century.*

> No new principle was enunciated, for Hitler had already gone the whole length in the statement of principles long before this. But the throne speech . . . and the decrees which followed immediately after it, all made it clearer than ever that the future holds in store only an increasingly rigorous application of Nazi principles of dictatorship, minority rule, rampant nationalism, drum-thumping militarism, ruthless anti-Semitism, and utter totalitarianism. All enemies of the dominant party are to be trampled underfoot.[89]

The "enemies" were Marxists, believers in democracy, churchmen, and "Catholic centrists. The Jews are to be excluded from the public schools."[90]

The Friend of Zion for September 1935 published a long article translated from Swedish by Victor Sternherz. The article, often referring to Hugo Valentin, "prominent Swedish author and journalist," traced the application of the racial theories of the Nazis from 1933 to 1935 and the first use of such designations as "quarter-Jew" and "half-Jew." In 1935, reported Valentin, these racial designations had been enacted into law. [Italics in the article] *"According to Nazi law, it is a crime in itself to have been born a Jew, a defamatory, dishonorable act to have a drop of 'Non-Aryan' blood flowing in one's veins!"* The original Swedish article was published in the *Gotesburg Stifts Tidning*, with no date given.[91]

The Watchman-Examiner, in two brief notes in "Men and Things," noted that Jewish children were being forced to attend Jewish schools and that Jews were being forced into "a twentieth century ghetto."[92]

The Lutheran, in an article "In the World's Eye" by Julius F. Seebach, included eight paragraphs on Germany. The first one began, "The Jews continue to hold a sorry place in the world's eye." The third paragraph read:

> The most recent Nazi action has been the denial of all citizenship rights to the Jew, with the probable intention of forcing him back into the Ghetto prison he inhabited during the Middle Ages. It is to be doubted whether even the absolutist

Nazi government can accomplish that feat of reversing the processes of time.[93]

The Alliance Weekly took note of the new racial decrees in Germany, referring to releases by *The Jewish Telegraph Agency* (London) and the *New York Sun* describing how a Jew was classified under the Nuremberg laws. A Jew was one who had one or more Jewish grandparents or an Aryan who was married to a Jew at the time the laws were passed.[94] A. S. Eker reporting from Germany to *The Christian Century* in December 1935 told of some confusion in applying the new Nuremberg decrees of September 15, 1935, largely due to foreign pressures. He mentioned that the Ministry of Justice in Germany seemed glad for the respite as it tried to "think clearly as to what shall be done with 'half-Jews' and 'quarter-Jews' as regards citizenship rights and property ownership." But the Jews knew what would be done. He reported that they "have been seeking to sell their businesses and property." They were receiving 30 to 35 percent of their value, receiving threatening letters, being told to be out by a certain date, and being advised that the German labor front had set up an "advisory office" with prospective buyers to assist in the sale of the businesses.[95]

The Nuremberg laws were in place. But no one reporting about these laws in the American Protestant press could foresee what the final result of the decrees was to mean for the Jews of Germany and, ultimately, of Europe. That the success of Hitler in his political and military objectives would one day lead to the mass extermination of Germany's and Europe's Jews could not be foreseen, even by the most prescient religious commentators. Certainly a sense of great concern was expressed on behalf of the Jews in Germany by Protestant Christians in a variety of ways in their press, but the sense of doom had yet to settle on the concerned Christians and for that matter on the Jews themselves.

Perhaps, of all the concerned groups, the American Jewish converts to Christianity sensed most clearly the coming terror. They continued to buy advertising to plead for funds to help the beleaguered Jews in Germany, victims of the Nazi hate. And yet even their appeals were cast into a prophetic mode, as the "eleventh hour" before the "trumpet blows" and before Christ's return. But, intentionally or not, the advertising copy did speak with some foresight, if not with prophetic intent.

"I Must Help the Jews!"
In the face of such a crisis the Church of God is silent!
What a reckoning will have to be given to Him in whose veins
flowed the blood of Abraham and Isaac and Jacob![96]

The Nuremberg laws and the silent churches—only time would reveal the fateful results of the one and the painful realization of the
other.

CHAPTER 3

1936–1938—No Doubt Left: Persecution, Humiliation and Kristallnacht

Relentlessly, the Jews and "non-Aryans" are excluded from all public offices, from the exercise of the liberal professions, and from any part in the cultural and intellectual life of Germany. . . . They are subjected to every kind of humiliation. Even the Jewish and "non-Aryan" children do not escape cruel forms of segregation and persecution.

JAMES G. MCDONALD
Letter of Resignation as High Commissioner for Refugees

KEY EVENTS

1936, General: March 7, German troops entered the Rhineland; March 12, League of Nations condemned Germany as a treaty breaker; March 29, 98.8 percent of German electorate in a plebiscite supported Hitler's move into the Rhineland; July 11, Austro-German agreement; July 16, Spanish civil war began; August 1–16, Olympic Games in Berlin; October 18, Decree on the Execution of the Four-Year Plan; October–November, Rome-Berlin axis formed; December 1, Law on Hitler Youth.

1936, Relating to the Jews: The four-year plan against the Jews included these points: (1) war against Bolshevism, that is, world Jewry, (2) all Jewish property to be expropriated if Germany goes to war, (3) crime by an individual Jew to be the responsibility of all Jews if against the German people or economy, (4) stepped up propaganda campaign against Jews; July–August, anti-Semitism severely modified for Olympic Games, death by suicide of Captain Forstner (a Jew, the designer and commandant of the Olympic Village, after he was removed from his position at the last minute), token participation by German Jews in the Olympic Games.

1937, General: January 30, Hitler's fourth anniversary speech to the Reichstag; September 13, Hitler's speech to National Socialist Party Congress; September, Mussolini's visit to Germany; November 5, select meeting during which the concept of *Lebensraum* and a timetable for conquest laid out; December, "Operation Green" military plan ordered, Schact resigned.

1937, Relating to the Jews: March–April, Hitler's Vogelsang Political Academy speech and veiled attacked on Jews; September 13, NSDAP Congress speech attacking Jewish Bolshevism, B'nai B'rith in Germany dissolved, further attacks on Jewish professional people and on garment workers, many small businesses owned by Jews liquidated.

1938, General: February 4, Hitler took over the army and the foreign office and became total dictator; March 12, Austria annexed; April 10, plebiscite on Austria won overwhelming support; March–September, Sudetan-German question; September 29, Munich conference and sacrifice of Czechoslovakia; October 1, German troops to Czechoslovakia; November 7, Ernst Vom Rath shot in Paris; November 9, Vom Rath's death; November 9–13, Kristallnacht (the Night of Broken Glass).

1938, Relating to the Jews: January, plan to expropriate Jewish businesses; January 5, Law Regarding Changes of Family Names and Given Names; March 26, Aryanization of Jewish businesses announced; March 28, Jewish religious communities lose status as legal public bodies; April 22, "camouflage" decree regarding hiding Jewish ownership of property; April 26, Decree Regarding Reporting of Jewish Property; June 14, Third Decree of Reich Citizenship Law, stating that a business was Jewish when the owner was a Jew; June 30, all property, domestic and foreign, held by Jews was to be reported; May–June, mass arrests of Jews begun under the expansion of "protective custody" and "antisocial" decree of January 25; July–August, Buchenwald, Sachsenhausen, and Dachau enlarged to hold anticipated increase of arrested Jews under "protective custody" decree, Jewish businesses and self-employment liquidated by decree, ending community services and barring doctors and lawyers from general practice; July, trustee administration was set up to take over Jewish businesses and property; July 23, identification cards of Jews required to be marked with "J"; August, Decree on Changing First Names, adding Sarah and Jacob to all Jewish names; October 5, all passports of Jews marked with "J"; November 9–13, Kristallnacht (nationwide attack on Jews, including those in Austria); November

12–December, a series of fines, assessments, penalties, and restrictions put on Jews, including decree removing Jews from all economic life, blocking of money, expulsion from public schools, forced sale and confiscation of property and wealth.

On November 7, 1938, Ernst Vom Rath, a third secretary in the German embassy in Paris, was shot by a seventeen-year-old Polish Jew, Hershl Grynszpan, a student in Paris. On November ninth, Vom Rath died of his wounds. From the ninth to the thirteenth, the Nazis reacted. These were days of terror, humiliation, violence, and destruction for the Jews of Germany. Synagogues were burned, Jewish businesses and homes were destroyed, and the sound of shattering windows in homes and plate-glass windows in stores was heard throughout Germany in large and small towns alike. The breaking of the glass gave to these November days the name Kristallnacht (Night of Broken Glass).

American Protestant Press Reports, 1936–1938

The terror and humiliation, the killing and mass arrests of Jews, the destruction that took place during Kristallnacht (November 9–13, 1938) demonstrated how badly the situation for Jews in Germany had deteriorated between 1936 and 1938. The American Protestant press continued to report quite accurately the plight of the Jews in Germany during these three years. James McDonald, high commissioner for refugees (Jewish and other) coming from Germany, who had been appointed by the Council of the League of Nations, in carefully documented statements (*The Christian Century*, January 15, 1936) had clearly intimated what could happen to the Jews in Germany as a result of the Nuremberg laws. Intimations, however well documented, are not events; the full force of McDonald's foresight had to await the events of the summer and fall of 1938, which proved him to have been correct. As for the years 1936 and 1937, specific incidents of persecution of Jews in Germany were less frequent; therefore, reports about them in the American Protestant press were also less evident. Other concerns dominated.

In 1936 and 1937, particularly, the continuing concern over the Church struggle dominated the American Protestant press's coverage of the events in Germany. In 1936, in the thirty-two periodicals examined, the Church Struggle was discussed sixty-eight times and the persecution of the Jews, forty-nine. (These figures would have been substantially different had the individual references to the persecution of the Jews in the supplement of James G. McDonald been counted, but for comparison the entire McDonald supplement was counted only once since the persecution of the Jews in Germany was its major subject.[1]) In 1937, in thirty-three periodicals, the difference in coverage was more evident: there were ninety-one references to the Church Struggle and only twenty-nine to the persecution of the Jews.

For 1938, there was a dramatic change. The total number of reports on the persecution of Jews in Germany and nearby countries (Austria, Czechoslovakia, Poland, Rumania, and Italy), with specific references to Kristallnacht categorized separately, was 206; the total number of references to the Church Struggle was 113. The year 1938 was the turning point in the Nazi program and its policies concerning the Jews in Germany and the nearby countries in Europe. Direct persecution increased in Poland, Austria, and Rumania. Anti-Semitic policies were announced in Italy, and anti-Semitic activity was reported in Belgium. With the invasion of Czechoslovakia, concern for Jews in that beleaguered, occupied country was heightened in light of known Nazi practices. Pressure to conform to the Nazi program for Jews increased in the countries bordering on Germany, on Germany's ally Italy, and on those countries adopting a Nazi-style dictatorship, as Rumania did. To say that 1938 was a bad year for German Jews, and for all European Jews, is to beg the question. The full meaning of the disenfranchisement of the Jews in Germany under the Nuremberg laws began to become a dread reality. This was the year in which Hitler and the Nazis set in motion the program that came to be known as the Solution for the "Jewish problem" in Germany and, by extension and conquest, in Europe. The last phase of this program was called the Final Solution for the "Jewish problem" in Germany, planned between 1939 and 1941 and instituted in 1942. Disenfranchisement became destruction.[2]

. It is the reporting of the American Protestant press for 1936, 1937, and 1938—in the time between McDonald's published resignation of January 15, 1936, and the close of 1938—that will be described in this chapter.

The Letter of Resignation and "Annex" of James G. McDonald

As originally published, McDonald's letter of resignation and supporting "Annex" were addressed to the secretary general of the League of Nations. In addition to being published as a supplement of *The Christian Century* for January 15, 1936, it was also made available in a pamphlet sold for fifteen cents a copy. It detailed, down to the finest points, what McDonald believed to be the major causes of the refugee problem in Germany. In addition, he cited the reasons for his resignation. First, his mandate as commissioner came from the Council of the League of Nations, not from the League of Nations itself. The commissioner, having independent status, had no power to deal with the causes of the refugee problem in Germany. Second, McDonald presented the argument that the League of Nations ought to replace his office with an office fully endorsed by the League of Nations and that the League of Nations should accept this responsibility because the issues were political, not, as originally thought, economic, financial, or social.[3] He supported these views in his full statement. Yet, the document was virtually ignored by the American Protestant press (except *The Christian Century*) even though it was the most detailed, thorough, well-documented record of Germany's actions and pronouncements regarding the Jews published in the American Protestant press up until January 1936, and probably afterward.

The formal letter of resignation was organized into seventeen points, some very short, others constituting several paragraphs. Twelve of the seventeen points included direct references to the persecution of the Jews in Germany, and two of the points made indirect reference to the persecution. In four of the seventeen points, three direct references to the Nuremberg laws and one indirect reference were made. Two points contained references to the problems of Protestants and Roman Catholics who wanted to remain loyal to their faiths, though no direct reference to the Church Struggle was made. Reference was also made to the distribution of official hate literature by the National Socialist party, the teaching of Jew-hatred in the schools, and the ghettoization of Jews, as well as to the inability of Jews to hold government positions, keep their own businesses, find employment, or care for themselves. McDonald's statement was a description of the systematic and increased exclusion of Jews from all aspects of German life. One long statement concerned the proven loyalty of Germany's Jews as patriots, public servants, cultural and philanthropic leaders, and as true Germans.

As for the "right" of the League of Nations to intervene in the internal affairs of Germany on the issue of individual protection and rights, McDonald cited law and custom in Europe from the Congress of Vienna and the Congress of Berlin of 1878, to the Upper Silesia

Convention of May, 1922, to the agreements protecting minority rights in the Treaty of Versailles and the actions of the League of Nations in 1922 and again in 1933 as a legitimate basis for intervention. He stated that the League of Nations, its member-states, and private, philanthropic, and religious organizations should join in "friendly but firm intercession with the German government, by all pacific means. . . ."[4] McDonald placed the full burden of intervention on the League of Nations within its covenant powers as "affecting the peace of the world."

The seventeenth and final point of the letter stated, "I feel bound to conclude this letter on a personal note." McDonald referred to his former work for the German people before he became high commissioner. He then wrote:

> But convinced as I am that desperate suffering in the countries adjacent to Germany, and even more terrible human calamity within the German frontiers, are inevitable unless present tendencies in the Reich are checked or reversed, I cannot remain silent. I am convinced that it is the duty of the High Commissioner for German Refugees, in tendering his resignation, to express an opinion on the essential elements of the task with which the Council of the League entrusted him. When domestic policies threaten the demoralization and exile of hundreds of thousands of human beings, considerations of diplomatic correctness must yield to those of common humanity. I should be recreant if I did not call attention to the actual situation, and plead that world opinion, acting through the League and its Member-States and other countries, move to avert the existing and impending tragedies.
>
> I have the honour to be, Sir, your obedient servant,
>
> James G. McDonald.[5]

The "Annex" followed. Its first chapter covered discriminatory legislation and the "Aryan" decrees in relation to government service, the professions, educational and cultural areas, industry, agriculture, and commerce, and the "exceptions" (that is, certain Jewish war veterans, physicians, et cetera, most of which were no longer in force by 1936). The second chapter of the "Annex" covered the administrative measures and party activity and touched on the law and the justice system, medicine, education, labor, commerce, industry, the boycott, and non-Aryans. The third chapter concerned the racial law and the courts in an applied sense, discussing racial inequality, judges as party functionaries, elimination of "fair trial" practices, marriage, divorce, children, lawyers and the legal profession, business, and commerce. The "Annex's" fourth chapter described "unwelcome" guests, deprivation of citizenship, denationalization, the "intent of government," and the refugee problem.[6]

These twenty-two pages represent a thorough, detailed, and comprehensive analysis of the situation in Germany at the time they were prepared late in 1935. Commissioner McDonald most certainly exercised his intimate knowledge of Germany, its politics, procedures, decrees, laws, and practices. Not only did the document describe, by implication and analysis it indicted. The introductory, explanatory, and narrative paragraphs left no doubt as to what was happening to Jews in Germany under law, decree, and Nazi-party practice. His statements were fully documented both within the body of the "Annex" and by extensive footnotes. In presenting the material, an editorial in *The Christian Century* stated that it "gives the fullest particulars so far made public concerning the treatment of Jews in Germany" and that readers can judge for themselves what McDonald faces "and even more what those who are the objects of Nazi hatred and harrying are up against." The editorial then supported the call from McDonald for action, as he proposed, by the League of Nations and its member-states.[7]

The American Protestant Press's Response to McDonald's Resignation

Most curious of all was the Protestant press's almost complete failure to notice (except for the *Century*) McDonald's resignation and his detailed analysis of conditions in Germany for Jews. The major Lutheran, Presbyterian, Congregational, Baptist, and nondenominational periodicals contained no reference or comment. The smaller Protestant denominations also did not comment or refer to the statement. *The Reformed Church Messenger*, in an item under "News of the Week," reported that McDonald had announced his resignation "as High Commissioner of the League of Nations for Refugees (Jewish and Other) Coming from Germany."[8] The item went on to report that he had served in the post for just over two years and that he had urged the League of Nations to intervene with Germany to protect the refugees. There was no comment on the substantive documents, either the letter of resignation or the "Annex."

One letter to the editor was published in *The Christian Century*, which was an attack on the *Century*, not on McDonald. The letter seems to have been a reaction to an editorial rather than to the full supplement by McDonald. The tone of the letter was not so much anti-Semitic as it was condemning of the failure of the *Century* to be concerned about racial problems in America, particularly in Chicago. "In Germany they do things strictly legally, in Chicago and the United States we simply disregard law according to personal interest." The writer continued:

> You fail to harp upon the wrong the Jewish bankers did in Germany during and after the war. . . . More than that, reliable American reporters say (and you know it) that Jews who mind their own business are not molested as much in Germany as men who advocate a change of government in the United States even by legal means. If you were "Christian" you would try to right the wrongs of our own citizens instead of muckraking Europe.[9]

The writer signed himself John G. Geiser, Yakima, Washington.

Only *The Friend of Zion*, a periodical distributed by the Zion Society of Israel (a Lutheran organization supporting missionary work among Jews in America, with headquarters in Minneapolis), published an article, a release from Our Jewish Neighbors News Service. It was a full description and summary of James G. McDonald's actions and recommendations, as well as his reasons for submitting his resignation. The title of the article, "I Cannot Remain Silent," was taken from the last paragraph of the letter of resignation, and the subtitle was a summary description, "The High Commissioner Voices the Wrongs of German Jewry."[10] Having described conditions in Germany as reported by McDonald, the article commented:

> Why do not Jews seek to escape from these intolerable conditions? About one hundred thousand have already done so. . . . Most of the remaining 500,000 would gladly follow their example. But Nazi inhumanity has ordained that Jews may not take their money out of the country. Besides, to what lands can Jews go? Not to America, except in limited numbers. Nor to any other land, not even to their ancient homeland in Palestine, except within a carefully restricted quota. . . . This unhappy people, hounded and harassed, unable to find a way of deliverance from their "house of bondage," are compelled to face starvation and the lot of pariahs.[11]

The article then posed questions for Christians and for the Church and in doing so indirectly referred to the Church Struggle in Germany.

Has all this no meaning for Christians? Can we stand idly by while half a million members of the race of Jesus are ruthlessly degraded, pillaged and treated as the off-scouring of the earth? Have we Christians no responsibility when we see the dearly-won liberties of the Jewish people being destroyed before our eyes? Is the voice of the Church so feeble that it cannot be heard about the clash of national self-interests and political chicanery? Has Christian compassion become so enervated that it can no longer respond to the cry of persecuted humanity? The Jewish problem is a Christian problem. In a country like Germany, nominally Christian, which has defied its own race and fostered hatred of others, Christianity has to fight for its life. This is what is actually going on in Germany. Many German Christians have revolted [revolved, in the article, clearly a misprint] against the anti-Semitic policies of Hitler's regime. The spirit of Luther is not dead in the Fatherland.[12]

Little was done either as a result of McDonald's appeal or in response to *The Friend of Zion's* article. In March 1936, the war to come, World War II, was still a shadow hovering in the distant background, not yet a reality. Neither was there a full comprehension of the meaning of Adolph Hitler's anti-Semitic policies, and opposition to these policies by Christians in Germany would have little or no impact despite the hopeful note in the article in *The Friend of Zion*.

The "Jewish Problem and the American Protestant Press

In 1936 and 1937, the situation for Jews in Germany continued to deteriorate but, relatively, less rapidly than it would in 1938. This was reflected, in part, by the American Protestant press in that the press turned to discussions of the role and place of Jews in America. Articles, editorials, and letters to the editor on the "Jewish problem" appeared.

In 1936, forty-four articles, book reviews, and letters to the editor were devoted to this subject; in 1937, five items on this theme were noted. In 1936, *The Christian Century*, initiated a series of articles on the "Jewish problem"; responses and letters to the editor followed. The editors first published an article by Joseph Ernest McAfee, "An Open Letter to Rabbi Weisfeld," on April 29, 1936, and an editorial in the same issue, "The Jewish Problem."[13] The editorial and the article were two parts, stated the editors of the *Century*, of their desire to discuss the root of the problem in the relationship of Jews and Christians, particularly in America. The reason for presenting the discus-

sion referred to the persecution of the Jews in Germany, which was
to "forestall, if possible, any like development here." The intention
was to support the efforts of groups engaged in fostering better understanding between Jews and Christians, such as the National Conference of Jews and Christians.[14]

In a word, the editorial and the article voiced a certain apprehen-
sion about a new note of Jewish "exclusivism" being set forth in the
writings of Jewish scholars in America. The editorial referred to a
book by Prof. Mordecai M. Kaplan, *Judaism in Transition*; and the article, to Rabbi Weisfeld's *The Message of Israel*. McAfee accused Weisfeld of excluding non-Jews while at the same time enticing them.
"You would open the door to the sanctuary so that those without
may catch glimpses of the effulgence within, thus making more glar-
ing and obnoxious the no-admittance sign which this portal bears."[15]
Both the editorial and the article argued that such exclusivism was
contrary to the American spirit, since it came across as conscious
propaganda by leading Jews to be not Jewish Americans or American
Jews but Jews in America who, in one significant area, remained unassimilated.

> I feel that you should know how disturbed are many who
> cherish the sincerest good will toward their Jewish fellow-citi-
> zens by the widespread zeal in Jewry to cultivate national aspi-
> rations and develop a national life independently of the com-
> munity of which American Jews are assumed to be loyal
> citizens. And it only deepens the concern for the peace and
> harmony of our common life to have the graphic evidence
> which your volume displays that the best brains of Jewry and
> the sanctions of religion are being invoked in pursuance of this
> policy.[16]

The unstated premise of both the editorial and the article was clear.
The Jews in America were making the same mistake made by the
Jews in Germany that had led, in part, to their persecution; that is,
the Jews were stressing in too strident language their differences.
Because of this tack, Jews would be seen as being unassimilated into
the mainstream of American life, just as had been the case in Germany, and it was implied the result might be similar—persecution.

> You should not be surprised, therefore, if many of the readers
> of your volume shall devoutly hope that its announced pur-
> pose shall not be fulfilled. . . . In hoping and believing that
> your effort will fail, these readers will rather hope and believe
> that the inconsistent and hazardous position in which rabbini-

cal Jewry thus places itself shall become apparent, to you as to others, and a policy so pregnant with bane to our Jewish fellow-citizens and so menaceful to our American community shall be abandoned.[17]

In retrospect, what the article and the editorial revealed is that neither the editors of *The Christian Century* nor McAfee as yet understood that the Jews were not being persecuted in Germany for their exclusivity, or as a people unassimilated, but on a racial basis, as Jews qua Jews. The racial theories of the Nazis, of Hitler, of Rosenberg, and in the statements in *Mein Kampf* and the Nuremberg laws of September 1935 had either been missed or misinterpreted. Perhaps they had not carefully read James G. McDonald.

The American Protestant press in general and *The Christian Century* in particular at this point never seemed to fully comprehend what basis the Nazi policies toward the Jews were formulated upon. Such persecution seemed to be seen in light of the more familiar historical precedents of ghettoization and pogroms and not as a policy of total extermination (to settle the "Jewish problem" in Germany and Europe), as ultimately proved to be the case.

Responses to the editorial and the article, predictably, were mixed. *The Christian Century* editors thought some readers had so misinterpreted the editorial that a second editorial explaining and defending the first one was published on May 13, 1936.[18] This, in turn, resulted in more letters to the editor, and a responding article by a rabbi was published, adding to the controversy.[19] The names and groups arrayed against the position espoused by *The Christian Century* was impressive. Reinhold Niebuhr wrote a long letter to the editor in disagreement; individual rabbis in El Paso, Texas, in Chicago and Glencoe, Illinois, and other individuals also sent letters of criticism or support.[20] These letters and the second editorial set off another round of letters, most of which continued to be critical. Nine leading reconstructionists, including Mordecai M. Kaplan, signed a long letter. Kaplan's book had been mentioned as being part of the basis for the original editorial. Other letters, five in all, were also published, with the editors of *The Christian Century* noting that the response had been so heavy that yet another editorial would be published at a later date.[21] A letter signed by four Orthodox rabbis, including the president of the Union of Orthodox Jewish Congregations in America, and a letter from Joseph Ernest McAfee specifically responding to Reinhold Niebuhr appeared on June 10, 1936.[22]

The third (and last) editorial on the "Jewish problem" was published on July 1, 1936, essentially reiterating and attempting to clarify the position of the editor of *The Christian Century* in response to the critics.[23] A second letter from McAfee was also included in this issue. Predictably, more letters followed; three were published July 15, 1936, and two on July 29, 1936. Then, editorially, the subject of the "Jewish problem" was dropped for the remainder of 1936.[24]

As the controversy over *The Christian Century's* discussion of the "Jewish problem" developed from the initial editorial and article to the last published letters, the subject of the persecution of the Jews in Germany virtually disappeared, except referentially. From April 29 to July 29, 1936, the editorials, articles, and letters to the editor in the *Century* centered almost entirely on Jews in America. Thus, in reality, the whole discussion might retrospectively be correctly identified as the *Century's* views on the "Jewish problem" in America. When respondents to the editorials or articles did refer to Germany, it was only to point out that assimilation of Jews into the total life of Germany was perhaps the most complete of any European country and yet it had not saved the Jews of Germany from persecution. The subject was brought up, editorially, once more in *The Christian Century* in 1937. This time there was no mistaking the intention. The editorial, "Jewry and Democracy," was an attack on Jewish exclusivism based on the Jewish claim of being a covenant people, or a Chosen People, which the editorial called "an illusion, the illusion that his race, his people, are the object of the special favor of God, who requires the maintenance of their racial integrity and separateness as the medium through which, soon or late, will be performed some mighty act involving human destiny."[25]

The tone and content of the editorial can hardly be said to be friendly to American Jews, generally. Specifically, it seemed uncomplimentary.

> Their idea of an integral race, with its own exclusive culture, hallowed and kept unified by a racial religion, is itself the prototype of Nazism. The Jewish problem in American democracy may be visualized in principle, by imagining five million Germans, held together in racial and cultural unity by the Hitler doctrine of the Folkic soul, transported to America, established in our democratic land as the Jews now are, and determined to maintain their racial doctrine and their racial separateness.[26]

Such an analogy or comparison with nazism was at least unnecessary, if not unwise.

Two responses followed, one by the editor of *The Christian Century* in yet another editorial, "Why Is Anti-Semitism?" and a letter to the editor from Rabbi Morris S. Lazaron of Baltimore, Maryland, who was well known and respected nationally.[27] Lazaron had been the rabbi who had traveled in the first nationwide tour sponsored by the National Conference of Jews and Christians (NCJC) with Everett R. Clinchy, the first director of that organization and a Presbyterian minister, and Father John Elliot Ross, a Roman Catholic priest.[28] The publishing of the Lazaron letter was a deliberate choice by the editor of the *Century*. The editorial on anti-Semitism opened with an acknowledgement by Charles Clayton Morrison that his desk was piled high with letters and manuscripts in response to the editorial "Jewry and Democracy" but that he had decided that only the Lazaron letter would be published. "The others fail to discuss the issue raised, or they raise so many false issues that the publication would only darken the question upon which our sole desire is to throw light."[29] In neither the last editorial nor in Lazaron's letter was there any reference to the persecution of Jews in Germany. The series of editorials, articles, and responses beginning with the initial editorial of April 29, 1936, and continuing to the July 7, 1937, editorial had thus moved from the initial referent in the first editorial, the persecution of Jews in Germany, to the single, complex issue of Jews in America.

The "Jewish Problem" and Jews in America

Louis Minsky may have best described some of the conditions that formed a context for these discussions. In 1936, an election year, American Jews, according to Minsky, had been bombarded in their press with warnings about extreme anti-Semitism and even a threatened pogrom against American Jewry. The pogrom did not happen, and the elections in November effectively silenced the hate groups and the anti-Semites in that none was elected to office.

> Despite an unparalleled campaign of villification in which anti-Semitic groups brought in the Jewish issue, the American people refused to be taken in. Jews hailed the results as a vindication of American principles of freedom and tolerance and voices were lifted to call a halt to the jittery tendency which was developing among American Jews.[30]

Minsky went on to state that as a result American Jews were also more calm about the situation of the Jews in Germany. "The mood of

shock and bitter protest over the barbaric anti-Jewish policy of the
Nazis has been followed by a feeling that nothing can be done about
Hitler. Protests and boycotts have failed to improve the Jewish situation."[31] Also, Minsky added, the Jews in America had come to realize
that nazism was not only anti-Jewish but anti-Christian as well and a
danger to all of Western civilization. As for persecution, he noted that
the assimilated Jews of Germany were severely persecuted but then
the unassimilated Polish Jews were being as severely persecuted,
also, a situation that American Jews had failed to note. Minsky made
this latter observation in explaining the sudden attractiveness of
Zionism to American Jews and to American Jewish leaders, in part
because of the number of German Jewish refugees who had settled
in Palestine.

In other words, if Minsky was correct in his analysis, the failure of
the threatened pogrom to develop in America, the defeat of anti-
Semites in the 1936 election, and the more realistic approach to Hitler
and the Nazis in regard to changing things in Germany for the Jews
apparently worked to quiet partially the fears of American Jews, thus
enabling them to shift their attention from Germany to America.
They could enter into an extensive dialogue with the editors of *The
Christian Century* because they felt less threatened or more at ease
with reality than they had earlier under the press of anti-Semitic
propaganda before the election of 1936.

Louis Minsky's commentary was credible. He was the founder,
with Everett R. Clinchy, of what is now called the Religious News
Service and its first managing editor. He had been a free-lance writer
in the religious field. He was of Russian Jewish descent, was born in
England, and was actively interested in American Jewry. As managing editor of the Religious News Service (formerly the NCJC News
Service for the National Conference of Jews and Christians), Minsky
had access to worldwide religious news. By 1936, the RNS was the
best known news service devoted exclusively to the religious field,
serving both the secular and religious press.[32] Minsky's credentials
and his known ability as an experienced correspondent gave him his
credibility.[33]

Anti-Semitism in the
American Protestant Press, 1936–1938

Though *The Christian Century* carried on the most lively debate on the
"Jewish problem" and reported on anti-Semitism in America and in

the world, by no means was it the only Protestant periodical presenting these themes in 1936, 1937, and 1938.

In 1936, readers of *Advance* (Congregational), *Christendom* (a quarterly published by Charles Clayton Morrison and later by the Federal
Council of Churches of Christ in America), *The Friend* (Quaker), *The
Gospel Herald* (nondenominational), *The Gospel Messenger* (Church of
the Brethren), *The Lutheran* (United Lutheran Church), *The Reformed
Church Messenger*, *The Presbyterian* (Presbyterian, U.S.A.) and *The
Watchman-Examiner* (Baptist) had access to paragraphs, short news
items, editorials, and articles on anti-Semitism in America. The activities of the Silver Shirts, the Black Legion, the Ku Klux Klan, William
Pelley, and other anti-Semitic groups were regularly reported, almost
without exception unfavorably.[34]

In 1937, *The Churchman* (Protestant Episcopal) launched its first series of articles on fascism in America, examining particularly anti-
Semitic groups that had become or were becoming active. The same
periodical continued the series in 1938 and again in 1939. No other
Protestant religious periodical examined anti-Semitism in the United
States as thoroughly and persistently as did *The Churchman*. The series was introduced by an editorial on February 1, 1937, with the first
article appearing in the same issue, written by Guy Emery Shipler,
Jr., the son of the editor of *The Churchman*. In this article, Germany
was identified clearly and specifically as the source of a considerable
amount of the anti-Semitic propaganda in America. The second article noted that the organizations and their publications followed "the
Nazi type" in the content of their publications. The third focused on
a group being organized to oppose such anti-Semitic organizations in
America actively and aggressively.[35]

On January 1, 1938, *The Churchman* reported that the twenty-four
denominations composing the membership of the Home Missions
Council had issued an official statement "opposed to the vice of anti-
Semitism."[36] From time to time, it noted statements of other groups
opposing anti-Semitism, and, in an editorial published on September
15, 1938, it warned its readers about Father Charles Coughlin, who
had reissued the Protocols of Zion while admitting that he could not
vouch for their authenticity. *The Churchman* accused Coughlin of "following the pattern so skillfully used by Hitler."[37] The aggressive attack on anti-Semitism was continued through the publication of an
article called, "Manners and Morals of Anti-Semitism," which analyzed the causes of anti-Semitism and suggested remedies for dealing
with those causes.[38] In 1939, anti-Semitism in America was one of the

major themes carried throughout the entire year in *The Churchman*, and there was yet another series of articles on fascism in America prepared by the staff (these will be discussed more fully at a later point).

The Hebrew Lutheran reported the action of representatives of five Lutheran bodies, the Norwegian Lutheran church of North America, the Augustana Swedish Lutheran Synod, the Danish United Lutheran church, the American Lutheran church, and the Norwegian Lutheran Free church, condemning anti-Semitism. The statement called for a "firm stand against slander and falsehood" against American Jews, "augmented by many so-called Fundamentalist leaders in our free country, a persistent propaganda of Jew hatred." The background for the statement made direct reference to Hitler, Germany, the Nazis, the flow of propaganda from Germany in books, pamphlets, and periodicals and reissuing of the Protocols of Zion. It further urged Lutherans to oppose actively anti-Semitism and the "bearing of false witness which according to the Bible is a sin and condemned by the Word of God."[39]

The editor of *The Hebrew Christian Alliance Quarterly* reported a letter exchange that resulted from the protest sent by him to the editor of the *Citizen Times* of Asheville, North Carolina. He was protesting remarks made by Gerald B. Winrod, founder of the Defenders of the Christian Faith and a well-known anti-Semite.[40] A. J. Kligerman, a Hebrew Christian and the editor of the *Quarterly*, included in his letter to the Asheville paper a direct charge about Winrod. Referring to the presence of several Christian leaders in Asheville, he then wrote:

> Among these I note the presence of Dr. Gerald B. Winrod, a "Christian" divine who hates the Jews much more than he loves the Christ whose cause he pretends to serve. This Dr. Winrod sees nothing but red, red in everything he touches, and of course he blames the Jews for his optical illusions.[41]

Kligerman reported a sympathetic response to his letter to the *Citizen Times* from many Christian leaders in the Asheville area. Then, he published in full a letter from F. C. Miller, who identified himself as a Presbyterian elder. Miller's letter was strongly anti-Semitic in tone and content, excoriating Kligerman and defending Winrod in his accusations that the Jews were Communists because Winrod "knows more about this question than you ever knew about anything." Miller, at one point, called the Jews "enemies of Jesus Christ" who were actively engaged in a campaign to "destroy the things of Christ." If there is such a thing as a classic anti-Semitic statement, that of F. C. Miller, the Presbyterian elder, would be it.[42] Kligerman did not attack Miller but let the letter stand as its own commentary. Rather, he pled for Christian tolerance and for respect for the Jew.

Christendom, in the summer of 1938, published a book review of a book by Rabbi Morris S. Lazaron, *Common Ground: A Plea for Intelligent Americanism*, which included a chapter that grew out of Rabbi Lazaron's disagreements with the editor of *The Christian Century* (see above p. 93) on the origins of anti-Semitism in America.[43] *The Evangelical Visitor* confronted anti-Semitism directly in an article, "Three Big Questions for Jew Haters," which, as did the statement of the five Lutheran denominations, laid part of the blame on the fundamentalists. "'Down with the Jew' is the cry that is sounding out, not only from Nations, but from circles of so-called Fundamentalist Christendom and we hear the echo taken up by voices who profess the Non-resistant faith." The three big questions were (1) "Is Communism as we know it, identical with Judaism?", (2) "Is the present day spirit of Anti-Semitism Christian?" and (3) "How can you curse the Jew when God has not cursed him?"[44]

The Lutheran Companion (Augustana Swedish Lutheran) published a statement on anti-Semitism by Samuel McCrea Cavert, which was subtitled "Anti-Semitism Leads to Anti-Christianity," in which Cavert reminded Christians of their indebtedness to "the spiritual heritage of the Hebrews."[45] *The Mennonite* published an article by Al Segal, identified in a footnote as "a well-known columnist of the *Cincinnati Enquirer*, and a writer in the English Jewish press." The article began, "Sometimes I wish I were a Gentile," and then it continued:

> To be sure you have your troubles, too. You are worried about your children, and wonder fearfully at tomorrow and suffer unemployment and tread timorously on an insecure world. All this is the pain of Jews as well.
>
> Yet you have only your own pain as individuals to suffer. Tomorrow morning you will not be searching the newspapers anxiously (as Jews do): "What are they saying about us today? What new reproaches are being heaped upon us this morning? What new outrages?"
>
> I dislike even hypothetically to put any people in the unhappy place of Jews! But in order that you may understand Jews, let us imagine that some hidden fate has done to Gentiles as Jews have been done by for a long time.

Segal then went on, substituting the word *Gentile* for *Jew*, to describe suspecting that one's neighbors are "anti-Gentile;" suffering job discrimination, "We don't employ 'Gentiles' here;" having apartment rental denied; hearing about lawless "Gentiles" and that therefore all Gentiles are lawless; reading hideous reports about "Gentiles" in the newspapers and seeing what falsehoods do to the minds of people; reminding oneself of the great "Gentiles" and their contributions to the world and of the millions of less-distinguished good people, "Gentiles," who live among you. Segal concluded:

> Your diffidence restrained you. You raised your head proudly above the accusing headlines. If some of these eyes were lifted from the newspapers to turn with reproach against you they must see that you are not a scourged culprit but a righteous man who takes with dignity the lash that falls upon him unjustly.

As a postscript Segal added:

> I have written this in response to a letter from E. F. S. of Brooklyn who writes in part: "It seems to me that the case of the Jews has not been presented properly to the non-Jews. Why don't you try?"
> Well, I tried.[46]

The American Protestant Press and Jews in America, 1936–1938

The Christian Century had dealt with the "Jewish problem" in America and the relationship between American Jews and Christians extensively in 1936 and 1937. So had other Protestant periodicals, but with more modest or different emphases. *Christendom* discussed the problems of Jews in America through book reviews, four in number, under the general heading, "Jews in American Life." Two books were related to the National Conference of Jews and Christians (NCJC); two were by Mordecai M. Kaplan on Judaism, primarily in an American context.[47]

The Friend of Zion, The Moody Bible Institute Monthly, The Gospel Herald, The Presbyterian, The Sunday School Times, The Messenger (formerly *The Reformed Church Messenger*), and *The Watchman-Examiner* tended to discuss the "Jewish problem" and the relationship between Jews and Christians either in terms of Jewish-Christian goodwill, instruction in the form of information about Jews from the perspective of the Bible, or prophetic analysis and interpretation or from the perspective of Christian witness or mission to the Jews in America. Their approach was both more typical in terms of their own commitments and interests and less theoretical, as in *The Christian Century* editorials and articles. Of mainline Protestant or conservative and evangelical cast, these periodicals reflected their stance in the manner in which they discussed the Jews generally, as well as the Jews in America. *The Presbyterian* announced that it was going to publish a series on the Jews. The writer of part of the series was to be Arno C. Gaebelein, editor of *Our Hope*. The title of his two-part series, "The Future Fulfillment of the Promises of Israel," indicated the thrust of the articles as prophetic, biblical, millenial, and interpretive. Albertus Pieters contributed a third article in the same vein.[48]

Later in 1936, *The Presbyterian* published an article by John Stuart Conning, of the Office of Jewish Evangelization, Board of National Missions, Presbyterian church, U.S.A. Conning served for many years as the secretary of that office. In his article, he reviewed general information about the Jewish presence in America and listed the cities that had large Jewish populations and then centered his article on what he saw as an unparalleled opportunity for Christian missionary work among Jews in America. His purpose was twofold: (1) to encourage a parish-based missionary effort (which had a formal title, the Christian Approach to the Jews) and (2) to take advantage of the opportunity not only to oppose anti-Semitism and racial prejudice but to "create Christian attitudes toward the Jewish people."[49] Calling anti-Semitism a challenge to the Church, he then stated:

> Hitherto, America has been singularly free from organized anti-Jewish movements. . . . Now, however, anti-Semitism has become a menace, not only to Jews, but to American ideals and the peace and harmony of our people. Jew hatred that has spread its blight over Germany, Poland, and other European countries has made its appearance in our own land. Nazi propaganda has planted its cells in many American cities. Other anti-Semitic movements bear the brand "Made in America." It is said that no fewer than six hundred centers of anti-Jewish propaganda exist to foster prejudice against the Jews and impose on them racial disabilities. It is the old, old way of meeting the Jewish problem, the way of Pharoah and Haman, of Torquemada and Pobiedonosteff. But it is not the Christian way.[50]

The article by Conning stressing anti-Semitism and the problems of Jews in America as a challenge and opportunity for the Church provides an interesting contrast to the more extended earlier series by Gaebelein and Pieters, which had a prophetic and millenial cast.

Instruction was the intent of the writer of the youth page of *The Gospel Herald*. Susie H. Keen, basing her lesson on the Scriptures, wrote of "Appreciation of the Jews," referring at one point to "an increasing Anti-Semitic feeling abroad in the world today and even some who profess to be the followers of the Christ." She then stressed the need for Christian witness to Jews.[51] *The Presbyterian* in 1937 reported on a conference held at Princeton Seminary, September 13–15, 1937, on the problem of Christians and Jews in America.[52] *The Watchman-Examiner* also briefly noted contact between Presbyterians and Jews in its "editorial Notes and Comments."[53] Its own effort to enter the discussion was undertaken in the publication of an article, topical in nature, concerning one of the charges often made against Jews, that Jews are "a race of usurious shopkeepers, . . . loaning money at usurious rates of interest and exacting the same even to the pound of flesh." B. A. M. Schapiro traced the history of usury from biblical teaching, through Roman practice, to the medieval period when Jews became moneylenders largely because of strictures enforced by the Roman Catholic church against Christians participating in moneylending activities. Now, said Schapiro, Jews were blamed for a practice learned from Christendom and they are subject to slanders as a result. "Therefore we conclude that usury is not of Jewish origin."[54]

The American Protestant press in 1936 and 1937 did reflect, then, an awareness of Jews in a new dimension. The concerns reflected in discussions of the "Jewish problem," Jews in America, and anti-Semitism were clearly brought about by events occuring in Nazi Germany. But more than that, the growth of Nazi influence, fascist organizations, and what Conning had called "Made in America" organizations of Jew-haters seemed to have awakened the Protestant church to the extent that some effort to counteract these forces was necessary. The stance of the periodical (in the commonly accepted descriptions of the 1930s, liberal, evangelical-conservative, and fundamentalist) was reflected in its editorials, articles, lesson pages, book reviews, and letters to the editor. Some Protestant periodicals addressed the problem directly, some from a biblical perspective as a lesson to be taught, some from a topical perspective, and some from the prophetic, millenial point of view. In the latter context, the continuing interest in Palestine and the number of Jews returning to Palestine as refugees was important. One approach was to support the opening of Palestine as a refuge for Jews from Germany and Europe; such support resulted in part, from the reluctance of most countries to accept large numbers of refugees, particularly Jews.

The Protestant Press, Palestine, Prophecy, and the Jews

Those more interested in the prophetic, millenial importance of Palestine and the Jews saw the return of Jewish refugees to Palestine as a key "sign" of fulfilled biblical prophecy. Louis S. Bauman continued to write articles in this vein.[55] Those of Arno C. Gaebelein in *The Presbyterian* also followed this theme. In 1937, *The Sunday School Times* presented two series centering on Palestine and the Jews. A. G. Fegert wrote "Zionism's Stupendous Failure to Acknowledge God" and "The Light of Prophecy at a Zionist Meeting."[56] George T. B. Davis wrote four articles as a series entitled, "Seeing Prophecy Fulfilled in Palestine." Davis had spent the summer of 1936 in Palestine, was particularly interested in doing missionary work among Jews, and was considered an authority on the subject. The editorial introduction to the last of the four articles captured the purpose for the series.

> Like the faint gray light that hovers over in the East before the sunrise, the events of Palestine presage a new day for the Jew and for the world. But before the day breaks for Israel the terrific storm of the tribulation will come upon them. Yet there is a new day beyond, and it is not the creature of mere sentiment or of the false optimism that expects man to usher in a golden age. It is a hope founded on "the sure word of prophecy", which has been shining through all the long night of this world's history, and whose light is ever more welcome to the true Church in these dark hours before the dawn.
>
> In this concluding article of his series, Mr. Davis traces through the Scriptures the prophecies concerning the Jews, and describes the blessings that will be poured out upon them in their own land.[57]

A sobering note in such interpretive analyses grew out of the reports in 1936 and 1937 of direct confrontations between Arabs and Jews in Palestine. An editorial, "Renewed Rioting in Palestine," *The Christian Century*, May 6, 1936, reported riots in Palestine involving Arabs and Jews.[58] *The Lutheran Companion* reprinted the editorial without comment ten days later on May 16, 1936.[59] The conflict was reported directly to *The Friend* by two Arab educators. Khalil Totah sent his report, dated May 30, 1936, and published as "Palestine Again." Wadi R. Tarazi and Khalil Totah wrote later, longer articles on the Arab-Jewish conflict, and, at the end of the year, Daniel Oliver described at length his role in mediating the conflict and in settling the strike by Arab merchants and tradesmen that lasted six months.[60]

In June, September, and November of 1936, *The Friend of Zion* reported on the Arab-Jewish troubles in Palestine, usually in its "Jewish World News" column. The June report mentioned 30 deaths and 190 injuries, with 18 Jews and 12 Arabs having been killed in rioting attributed to Arab nationalism. And that the rioting was continuing. Subsequent reports contained further descriptions of the conflict, the numbers of deaths, and the hoped-for end of the strike.[61] In light of Arab opposition, optimism about a ready acceptance of Jews in Palestine certainly was unwarranted by even those who were most committed to this process as a part of God's plan for the end of the age.

The Olympic Games in Germany, 1936

The expressed opposition to holding the Olympic Games in Berlin first voiced in 1935 continued into 1936, but with considerably less enthusiasm. The American Olympic Committee had resisted pressure to boycott the games, and the winter games had been held without incident. Only *Advance* and *The Friend of Zion* reported a continuing opposition. *Advance* reported the division within the American committee; *The Friend of Zion*, opposition by a group calling itself the German-American League for Culture, supported by others also opposed, mainly educators.[62] The editorials and news items from the correspondents in Berlin during the Olympic Games tended only to report that things were going well, that Germany was preparing itself for the coming event, and that some direct steps were being taken to minimize evidence of anti-Semitism throughout Germany, such as the removal of the "No Jews Allowed" signs in towns.[63] The late-summer reports tended to be about the Olympic Games in a descriptive sense. An editorial did report the refusal of the American athletes to dip the American flag during the opening ceremonies, the subsequent success of American Negro athletes, and Hitler's refusal to meet them.[64] Only one article was published about Jews. Sherwood Eddy, in fact, did not discuss the Olympics so much as conditions in Germany and Europe, noting only that Germany had tried to make the best possible impression on visitors to the games. Eddy found and reported on ample evidence of the enforcement of racial policies and persecution of Jews and the continued troubles of the pastors of the Confessing Church in Germany. He reported also that all of his personal papers were searched by German police and plain-clothesmen as he left Germany.[65] In his correspondence from Germany dated August 18, 1936, A. S. Eker reported that the Germans were pleased with the management of the games, the success of German participants, the propaganda campaign promoting German culture, and the extended effort at promoting German nationalism and "unification" among Germans who attended the games.

Eker also reported that the Nazi party congress was about to meet again at Nuremberg, referring to the passage of the "notorious anti-Jewish laws . . . published to the world, of the impotent reichstag having been summoned to raise their right hands in approval." Eker also despaired of the continual German penchant for not only believing the propaganda about the Russian danger, but also in believing that Adolf Hitler was Germany's savior from the Communists. He included a jarring note that the threat of war was pressed daily on the German people through the state-controlled press.[66]

An editorial commending the selection of Frau Anna Klara Fischer, president of the Women's Christian Temperance Union, as hostess for the sports women's residences was published in *The Gospel Messenger*. She and 100 German WCTU volunteers, said the editorial, gave clear evidence of "moral purpose and judgment, and an assurance that proper care and goodwill" were the concern of the Olympic Games Committee.[67] And so the Olympic Games of 1936 passed into history. The early protests over German racial policies had failed to halt the games, and Germany, temporarily, made the most of its opportunity to influence its own people and the foreign visitors. But, by the summer and fall of 1938, the German success in hosting the Olympics was largely forgotten.

Paid Advertising and the Persecution of Jews in Germany

One persistent warning and record of what was happening to Jews in Germany and Europe continued to be published in several fundamentalist periodicals through paid advertising. In all three of the advertisements placed in 1936 and in those of 1937, the stress was on continuing Jew-hatred in Germany, Poland, Austria, and Rumania and on the need to assist Jewish refugees. These paid advertisements were placed by the American Board of Missions to the Jews of Brooklyn, New York.[68] To some readers, the statements in this advertising might have seemed overwritten and exaggerated, even strident. Only later could they be judged as having been too true and accurate in their description of conditions for Jews in Europe and Germany. As the Board of Missions sounded the warning through its advertising, the deteriorating situation for Jews became evident in the increased number of requests for refugee assistance, both Jewish and Christian.

In 1937, such references to the need of refugees, the work of assistance organizations, and appeals for funds, homes, and volunteers to help in refugee programs became more urgent. In the thirty-two American Protestant religious periodicals examined for 1937, twenty in a total of thirty-three items including paid advertisements, news notes, articles, and editorials referred to the growing problem of refugees (Jews, Christians and non-Aryan Christians from Germany). Possible sites for relocation, such as Madagascar, Costa Rica, Santo Domingo, and Palestine, were mentioned. Problems of relocation of Jews to Australia and South Africa were discussed, and appeals for monetary aid and for volunteers for committees were included.

In this context, two refugee-related matters drew particular attention. Harry Emerson Fosdick and the American Christian Committee for German Refugees sponsored and showed a film, *Modern Christian-German Martyrs*, at the Riverside Church in New York City on April 12, 1937. The film received unexpected publicity because the German government lodged a strong, formal protest to Washington D.C., and the film was attacked in the German press as a "film of hate." It was, in fact, a well-documented film designed to help raise $400,000 for the Committee for Refugee Assistance.[69] Churches and religious groups were urged to show the film, which was available without charge from the committee that sponsored it.

The second refugee-related item that received significant coverage was an official appeal by the Federal Council of Churches of Christ in America for assistance to refugees. Labeled a Christmas appeal, it asked for funds to be used to assist Chinese refugees driven from their homes by the Japanese invasion, Spanish children on "both sides" of the Spanish civil war, and "the Christian German refugees who are victims of the cruel laws against all 'non-Aryans' and who are classified as 'non-Aryans' if they have even a Jewish grandfather's blood in their veins."[70] A number of Protestant religious periodicals brought this appeal to the attention of their readers.[71] That this appeal and the film and other statements about the needs of refugees from Germany were timely can best be measured by what happened in 1938.

The Accelerated Persecution of the Jews, 1938

That the situation for Jews in Germany worsened in 1938 is a well-documented fact. Had no other event occurred in 1938 than Kristall-nacht (November 9–13, 1938), there would have been enough evidence. Unfortunately, Kristallnacht was only the most blatant instance of the persecution of Jews in Germany in 1938. From 1933 through 1937, references to the German Church Struggle outnumbered references (indirect and direct) to the persecution of the Jews in Germany in the American Protestant press. In 1938, this was no longer the case. In examining thirty-seven such periodicals for 1938, references to the Church Struggle numbered 113; references to the persecution of the Jews, including Kristallnacht, 206. What is more significant, *without* reference specifically to Kristallnacht, reference to persecution of the Jews in Germany, Poland, Austria, Rumania, Czechoslovakia, and Italy totaled 165; thus, for the first time, the press cited more references to the persecution of the Jews than to the Church Struggle. Nazi Germany's plan for settling the "Jewish problem" unquestionably had changed dramatically in 1938.

The American Protestant press reported this changed attitude soon after the new year (1938) began. Notice was taken of the persecution of Jews in Poland and Rumania in January 1938 and of the continued if not increased persecution of Jews in Germany and Poland in February 1938. News from Austria and the threat to Jews in Vienna began to appear in March 1938 after the capitulation of Austria to Hitler between March 10 and 14, 1938. The concern for Austrian Jews became very great. *The Presbyterian* (March 3, 1938) reported as a part of its report on the discussions between Hitler and Schuschnigg that the "Jews in Austria are terribly alarmed, afraid of new persecutions as Nazi anti-Semitism comes to the fore."[72] In April, May, and June of 1938, the persecution of the Jews in Austria was added to the news of persecution of the Jews in Poland and Rumania and to the continuing persecution of the Jews in Germany. The Protestant press particularly noted the number of suicides of Jews in Austria. *The Presbyterian* and other periodicals reported the warning given by Goering to the Jews of Vienna, which was to become a German city.[73] Within three weeks, on April 28, *The Presbyterian* carried the following statement:

As a result of the German seizure of Austria, the most deplorable conditions have been precipitated among the large Jewish

population, particularly in the city of Vienna. This information
is furnished by the World Dominion Press:

"The scourge of the Jews has begun and the average of Jewish suicides is now well over one hundred a day. The 1934 census gave 176,000 Jews in Vienna and 10,000 in the provinces. It
is estimated that about one half of Vienna's population of
nearly two million have some Jewish blood. About 470,000 [ob-
viously, this is a misprint] of Vienna's 176,000 Jews are reduced
to poverty and are receiving assistance from the Jewish Central
Union.[74]

During the following months, *The Christian Herald* questioned whether
the Nuremberg laws would be enforced in Austria since no such laws
existed in Austria apart from German occupation. In the second report, the answer was given as *The Christian Herald* reported the Nazi
takeover of Austria.

So "death of Austria." Troops took possession of Vienna, and
began a ruthless enforcement of the new decrees. Jews, especially, had a foretaste of what they might expect from the new
regime. Professional men were ordered to sweep streets and
clean buildings; one Jewish General appeared for that menial
work in full uniform as an Austrian General, and others came
to work in top hats and synagogue garments. Thousands are
leaving the country.[75]

The Alliance Weekly commented, not on the humiliation of Vienna's
Jews, but on the suicides. "Many hundreds took their own lives, and
in some cases those of their families, in despair as to the future of
their country. . . . Both Jews and Gentiles were included in the list,
the former especially being the objects of the cruel and unreasoning
persecution of the authorities."[76]

As the increased Jewish persecution in Rumania, Poland, and Austria was reported, Germany was not forgotten. Several periodicals
published a request for prayer for Jews prepared by Jacob Gertenhaus, himself a Jew and a Christian convert, who was a minister of
the Southern Baptist church appointed to work among Jews in America. German, Rumanian, Polish, Austrian, and Palestinian Jews were
identified by him as under persecution, committing suicide and
starving.[77] *The Christian Century* reported a renewed, direct persecution of Jews in Germany beginning in December 1937 and continuing
into the winter of 1938. Jewish doctors were not allowed to treat pa-
tients in insurance companies, and Jews were ordered out of the entire textile business, especially ready-made clothing. The homes of

Jews were being confiscated, and the attempts of German Jews to leave Germany were being thwarted by the confiscation of their passports.[78] The confiscation of the Jews' possessions in excess of 5,000 marks by decree of Marshall Goering was reported in full. As given in *The Christian Century*, the report was ominous. Pointing out that the disposition of German Jewish wealth was an undecided matter, the *Century* commented:

> The 400,000 Jews remaining in Germany are first to be robbed of what they still possess, and then starved. Then, according to the *Schwarze Korps*, organ of the elite Nazi S.S. corps, those who persist in clinging to life will be deported either to Palestine or to Madagascar. Soon after Hitler came to power a spokesman for the German foreign office, while addressing a group of Americans in Berlin, defined the Jewish policy of the National Socialist Party as "benevolent extermination." There was some question as to the meaning of the term at the time. Marshall Goering now makes it entirely clear. *This* is "benevolent extermination." Don't shoot your victim to put him out of his misery; simply rob him and then let him starve [emphasis theirs].[79]

Only the fall of Czechoslovakia and the announcement of racial policies restricting Jews in Italy remained for the full European persecution of the Jews to fall into place in 1938.

Italian policy changes were first reported in *The Hebrew Christian Alliance Quarterly* in the winter of 1938 and in one of a series of articles by Louis S. Bauman in *The Brethren Evangelist* in the early spring of 1938. The Rev. M. Zeidman of Toronto, Canada, wrote, "An Italian paper recently declared that Fascism has three foes, namely, 'Judaism, Masonry and English Protestantism.'"[80] Bauman was explicit. He cited *Giornalissimo* and *Il Papolo Italia*, Mussolini's newspaper, as having openly attacked Italy's Jews, 50,000 to 60,000 in number. He also included a statement from *Informazione Diplomatica*, the Italian foreign office's paper, which called for the settlement of the "Jewish problem" through establishing a Jewish state, but not one in Palestine. He also used material from the United Press and the Jewish Telegraph Agency (London) in his article. As in his other articles in previous years, Bauman gave complete, extended information but his purpose was to support his prophetic, millenial, dispensational interpretation of events, particularly those relating to Jews and the Second Coming of Jesus Christ.[81]

By the summer and through the fall and winter of 1938, *The Friend*,

The Brethren Evangelist, The Christian Century, The Christian Herald, The Friend of Zion, The King's Business, The Lutheran, The Lutheran Companion, The Messenger, and *The Presbyterian* had all reported in some manner the change of policy toward the Jews in Italy.[82] Some reports blamed Hitler's influence on Mussolini for the Italian policy; others blamed fascism. Regardless, Italy had adopted anti-Jewish racial laws.

The Munich meeting of September 29–30, 1938, to settle the Czechoslovakian crisis was an historic moment for Germany and Hitler's policy of *Lebensraum*, and Chamberlain's "peace in our time" statement was heralded around the world.[83] The journalistic-historical account of these events in Shirer's *The Rise and Fall of the Third Reich* is a reasonable summary account of the events of 1938 and 1939 concerning Czechoslovakia.[84] Typically, of all the American Protestant press, *The Christian Century* gave the most coverage to the Czechoslovakian crisis, Munich, and its immediate aftermath. Between July 6, 1938, and December 28, 1938, of 790 published pages in the *Century*, 93 pages were all or in part devoted to discussing Czechoslovakia, Munich, and the assessment of the effects of the Munich pact. The discussions took the form of articles, editorials, correspondence, and letters to the editor, a total of 63 discrete items from short paragraphs to several 3-page articles, such as Sherwood Eddy's "The Critical Hour."[85] Twenty-one letters to the editor were published in the *Century* in response to the various articles and editorials on Munich and Czechoslovakia.[86]

Concern for minorities in Czechoslovakia, including Jews, was expressed early in the periodicals. A reference to the cabinet in Prague and its commitment to protect the minorities, including Jews, was made by Brackett Lewis in an article in *The Christian Century*, published on August 3, 1938.[87] "Tortured Minorities in Sudentanland" was the headline of an editorial on November 2, 1938.[88] An announcement in the *Federal Council Bulletin* called for "A Day of Prayer for Victims of Racial and Religious Oppression," specifically calling attention to the Jews.

> We would direct special attention, however, to the plight of those of Jewish blood in Europe, whether Jewish or Christian in faith. The inclusion of Austria and parts of Czechoslovakia in the German Reich has greatly added to the number of "non-Aryans" who suffer grievous civic and vocational disabilities and have to endure all kinds of public ignominy. Deprived of their opportunity for a livelihood, hundreds of thousands have

no alternative except to become voluntary exiles and when they do so they are forced to go in an almost penniless condition.[89]

The appeal was signed by the heads of seventeen Protestant church bodies in the United States.

The Presbyterian followed the Czechoslovakia crisis in its news pages and on September 22, 1938, published a letter from the faculty of theology in Prague and the Czech Brethren Evangelical church.[90] By October 20, persecution of the Jews in Czechoslovakia was being reported.[91] Sherwood Eddy, in analyzing the Czechoslovakian crisis, wrote:

> This victory by threat of force speeds the military and imperial advance of a ruthless dictatorship that will now . . . consolidate the 68,000,000 population and the resources of the Danubian and Balkan peninsula clear to Constantinople. And it is a fascist reich founded on a false racialism, an exclusive nationalism, an aggressive militarism and imperialism and neopaganism which will continue to persecute Jews, Social Democrats and free Christians like Niemoeller. From this new area also the Jew will flee lest they be robbed, impoverished and forced to put on their sacred phylacteries and clean lavatories with their bare hands. Here, as in Vienna, sadistic anti-Semitic museums will be opened and cards prepared for infants to instill hatred of the Jews in the children of all the expanding reich.[92]

The November 15, 1938, issue of *The Churchman*, over a paragraph requesting aid to refugees, printed the headline, "Refugees: 400,000 Christians, 30,000 Jews Flee Sudetanland."[93]

Kristallnacht (Night of Broken Glass)

Even as *The Churchman* reported the needs of the refugees, the dark sorrow of Kristallnacht (Night of Broken Glass), November 9–13, 1938, fell on Germany. The American Protestant press reported and reacted. At opposite poles in the Protestant community in the United States, *Advance* (Congregationalist) and *The Sunday School Times* (nondenominational fundamentalist) gave major editorial space to the events of November 9–13, 1938, in Germany. The editor of *Advance* wrote:

> The thoughtless deed of a young Jew in Paris, crazed by the suffering of his parents and his people, has led to reprisals against Jewish people in Germany that have shocked the

world by their calculated group brutality and betrayal of every element of justice, humanity, and government. What the world has witnessed is not government, but the unrestraint of moral and political perverts. It is incredible that the German people as a whole should approve of what was done, though one is sadly forced to conclude that Germany has gone far in decadence and degradation as a nation.

An accompanying editorial on the same page described the reaction from "the Christian churches in America, both Protestant and Roman Catholic," the Federal Council of Churches, the radio broadcast of Bishop E. E. Hughes, ex-president Hoover, Harold Ickes, and the later statement of protest made by President Roosevelt.[94]

The editor of *The Sunday School Times* devoted the two pages regularly assigned for the lead editorial to the events in Germany. Consistent with the theological commitment of his periodical, the editorial headline read, "Germany Brutally Fulfills Prophecy."

The shot that rang out at Sarajevo, Yugoslavia, in 1914, when Archduke Ferdinand of Austria was assassinated, was heard around the world, for it precipitated the Great War. Another shot is reverberating through the world today, for on November 7 Herschel Grynszpan, seventeen year old Polish Jew, wounded Ernest Vom Rath, Third Secretary of the German Embassy at Paris, and two days later the German attaché died. The echoes of that shot might have been shortlived if Nazi Germany had not turned upon the Jews in brutal reprisals that have outraged the civilized world.

Propaganda Minister Goebbels in a speech in Berlin before 70,000 listeners blamed German Jews for the Paris slaying, and asserted that the shooting was a plot to stir up trouble between Germany and the Western powers.

The editorial then described the collective assessment to the Jews of $400 million and up to $60,000 individually as the penalty for the murder and to repair the damage "done by Aryan window-smashers and store-wreckers seeking revenge."

A cartoon published in Hitler's newspaper was then described, and the *Philadelphia Inquirer* was quoted as speaking of "Godless Nazis" and "mad dogs running amuck." A long paragraph from a letter to a Jewish friend by Dorothy Thompson was included also, and then the remainder of the editorial turned to what the editor saw as the prophetic significance of these events. The greater part of the editorial was devoted to this prophetic analysis.[95]

The Sunday School Times carried a paid advertisement from the American Board of Missions to the Jews on the inside front cover of the last issue for 1938. The advertisement described the cause for Kristallnacht and the reprisals against Jews "in all parts of Germany" and claimed that it was a reign of terror, that Jews were beaten, their stores looted and wrecked, and that "Jewish families were committing suicide. These suicides were by Jews high in banking, law, manufacturing." The advertisement also reported that the largest German-language newspaper in America, the *Staats-Zeitung*, in an editorial entitled, "Cold Terror," had repudiated and condemned the Nazis in Germany. Two paragraphs of the editorial were included as copy in the ad. Money was then requested to assist Jews, mostly Christian Jews, in Europe.[96]

The Lutherans, often reluctant to be condemnatory of events in Germany and as aware as any denomination in America of the Church Struggle and church affairs in Germany because of historic Lutheran ties to Germany, spoke forcefully and quickly. In a editorial entitled, "It Is Hard to Believe," *The Lutheran Companion* said:

> The recent brutal attacks on Jewish lives and property in Germany were described by Dr. Goebbels as "typical, spontaneous, popular demonstrations." We do not believe it. They bear the earmarks of offical Nazi planning and constitute a deliberate act of government policy. They do not reflect the spirit of the German people.

The editor of *The Lutheran Companion* (Augustana Swedish Lutheran Synod), having written so bluntly, in the next issue included a report of President Roosevelt's "stinging rebuke to Germany because of its treatment of the Jews."[97] "Across the Desk," the editorial page of *The Lutheran* (United Lutheran church), carried an editorial on November 23, 1938, that read in part:

> People in the United States and no doubt elsewhere who did not approve the terms of the Treaty of Versailles imposed upon Germany, are now concerned by the reports of anti-Semitic orgies of mob destruction and by announcements that further punitive discrimination against Jews has been authorized by the National Socialist Government.

Referring to the incident in Paris, and the exorbitant sums demanded of Jews, the editorial moved to a more general, but ever cautious, discussion which contained this minor caveat, "After making due allowances for some exaggeration in the reports of the anti-Semitism of the present National Socialist authorities in Germany," as though the editors were still reluctant to acknowledge that the reports were true.[98]

The Lutheran Herald (Norwegian Lutheran church of America) published four editorials on Germany on November 29, 1938. One was on anti-Semitism, specifically in relation to persecution of Jews in Europe; the second was reprints of President Roosevelt's press conference statement concerning persecution of German Jews and the statement of protest of the Minneapolis Church Federation. The last two were excerpts from a letter written by the Rev. Elias Newman, Lutheran missionary to the Jews, on the situation in Austria and Germany. The first excerpts were about Jews; the second, about persecuted Christians. Using words such as "brutality," "savagery," and "hunted beast," Newman told of his personal conversations with Jews. He also mentioned the "protective custody" of the concentration camps. "And what a custody! It is better, I think, to pull down the curtain and not even attempt to tell of what went on and what is continuing to go on in these unspeakable places of filth, torture, and licentiousness."[99]

The Brethren Evangelist, more often dealing with the Jews and their persecution in articles on prophetic analysis and interpretation, published four paragraphs in "The Editor's Box" page for November 26, 1938. The first paragraph spoke of the arrests of Jews in Vienna and Munich and of the fine assessed on Jews in Germany "simply because one unfortunate member of Jacob's race committed a crime."[100] *The Federal Council Bulletin* issued another call for prayer and contributions.[101] *The Calvin Forum* published an editorial using the Vom Rath shooting as a basis for a larger discussion of the "Jewish problem."[102] On December 1, 1938, *The Churchman* published several items related to Kristallnacht in its "People-Opinion-Events" section. A radio address by the Rev. Elmore M. McKee on persecution of the Jews in Germany broadcast over station WMCA, New York City, on November 11, 1938, was reported in full. "While we abhor and repudiate the spirit of short-sighted revenge now at work; while we brand its sub-human and sub-personal savagery as anti-Christ as a reversion to the Dark Ages, let us remember that the doers of iniquity are those really who in the long run suffer most." The request for assistance funds to aid the persecuted was reported, with the figure of 1 million given as the number of those requiring such assistance, including Jews, Catholics, and Protestants. The protest statement of the Church League for Industrial Democracy was published, as was a prayer sent to all parish churches in Pittsburgh written by Bishop Mann on behalf of persecuted Germans.[103]

In the same issue, in response to a request from *The Churchman* "for expressions of opinion on the Nazi outrage against the Jews," ten letters were published from bishops and clergymen of the Protestant Episcopal church. The theme in all of them was similar. The German people were not to blame for the outrages; rather, it was the Nazi party that was to blame, both as the party in power and in its capacity as the government of Germany. All condemned the persecution of the Jews, one only slightly, preferring to point out that Abyssinians, Spaniards, American slum children, and Chinese were also suffering. Some charged that America was complicitously involved because of its cooperation in international inequities and in its failure to clear up its own domestic evils.[104] The statement of the House of Bishops on persecution was the last item published by *The Churchman* on the subject of Kristallnacht.[105]

The Friend (a Quaker publication) published a cautious editorial, whose perspective was a bit different than most of the other editorials.

> The news which comes out of Germany can hardly fail to spread the deepest gloom. It is possible, of course, that the newspaper stories are exaggerations of the truth, but they are accompanied by photographs that are most convincing. Perhaps the most distressing was the picture of destroyed and looted buildings, with the faces of the passers-by wreathed in smiles. It is a terrible thing for a power-mad dictator to seek to ruin thousands of innocent persons, but it is a far more terrible thing for a great people to give wholehearted assent to such efforts, and to find brutality amusing. The smiles on those faces haunt us.[106]

As though to compensate for the slight doubt expressed about the accuracy of the reports in the newspapers, the same issue of *The Friend* included a report from the American Friends' Committee, which was sent to all monthly meetings in the United States and Canada.

> Dear Friend:
> Abundant evidence has come to the office of the American Friends' Service Committee during the past few days revealing a profound shock to our spiritual life by the Jewish and non-Aryan persecutions in Germany. Cables from Germany indi-

cate that American newspaper reports have not exaggerated
the tragedy.

The report then went on to describe the involvement of the Service
Committee Centers in Vienna and Berlin in assisting refugees. The
report was signed by the highly respected Quaker leader Rufus M.
Jones, chairman, and Clarence E. Pickett, executive secretary for the
committee.[107] The efforts to assist refugees were described in each of
the two remaining issues of *The Friend* for 1938.

The Friend of Zion in its issue of December 1938 published a brief,
descriptive news item about the events in Germany, dated November
10, Berlin, from the Associated Press. It then reported, again from
the AP news service, protests from various groups in the United
States and concluded with its own brief summary of Jewish world
news, including some items referring to Kristallnacht.[108] *The Messenger*, a periodical representing members of the Reformed church, who,
like the Lutherans, had close ties to Germany, began its editorial:

> The recent anti-Jewish outbreaks in Germany have been so in-
> human, so coldly calculating, so insanely ruthless that it is dif-
> ficult to use restrained language in discussing a campaign of
> intolerance that has disgraced the Nazi government and put a
> sickening strain upon the honored German name.

It then described briefly the events, the protest statement of President Roosevelt, and the emptiness of the "man's inhumanity to man"
denuciations and closed by citing the remarks of Rabbi F. M. Isserman of St. Louis, who had called for restoration, reconciliation, and
forgiveness "that the minds and hearts of the persecutors may be
changed," as a most "Christ-like" statement.[109]

The Presbyterian, through Arthur Byrd McCormick's "The World as
I See It," followed the events of Kristallnacht. McCormick regularly
blended reporting and commentary in his short reports on the world
scene. In commenting on Kristallnacht, McCormick said that the Nazis lacked imagination in that they should have known that an attack
on Jews because of the actions of a crazed youth would turn the
world against Germany. A week later, he concluded that the whole
thing had been carefully planned and carried out, awaiting only the
right event to institute the plan, and that the sentiments of mankind
had turned against Germany because of its action against the Jews.
He reported the German reprisal and penalty plans two weeks later,
concluding his report with the statement that a Nazi leader had
stated that Jews were to be impoverished so they would turn to crime

"and that would give the Government an excuse for killing them off."[110]

On December 29, 1938, McCormick included in his commentary a brief statement attributed to a correspondent who had visited many German people in their homes. "All over Germany and even in the ranks of the Nazis he found many who were shocked and shamed by what had been done in the name of the German people. There is deep regret over the persecution of the Jews."[111]

The brief editorial in *The Watchman-Examiner* for December 8, 1938, placed its emphasis on Christian sympathy because of the persecution of Germany's Jews during Kristallnacht. No direct report of the incident was given in the editorial.[112] The statement of the Pastors' Conference in Knoxville, Tennessee, adopted on November 20, 1938, was reported. It was called a statement of "strong resolutions against the atrocities committed against the Jews" but it also included a call for Jews to turn to Christ as their Messiah. Also, the actions of a Negro congregation of Baptists in New Rochelle, New York, were reported. The congregation stood in silent prayer, adopted a resolution denouncing the persecution of Germany's Jews, and began to raise funds to assist Jewish refugees.[113] The latter incident was also reported in full in a letter to *The Christian Century*, signed by Pastor J. Henderson Brown, the chairman of the deacons, W. J. Brown, and the chairman of the trustees, J. B. Bullock of the New Rochelle church.[114]

The Christian Century published the most comprehensive and continuous coverage of the events in Germany from the shooting of Vom Rath on November 7, 1938, to November 13, 1938, when the looting and burning and the arrests and persecutions of Jews slowed, through the remainder of 1938. Accurately, the *Century* had noted that Kristallnacht had taken place on the fifteenth anniversary of the beerhall putsch and that Hitler was in Munich to give a speech.[115] That the speech was never given on that November-ninth evening is now known. After a hurried conference with Goebbels, Hitler left early.[116]

The reporting of Kristallnacht itself began in *The Christian Century* with a long editorial article published on November 23, 1938, and entitled, "Terror in Germany."

> Type will not carry the sense of horror and consternation with which the world reacts to the latest outburst of Nazi violence against the Jews. The murder of the third secretary of the German embassy by a half-crazed young Jew was the hook on

which were hung (1) a simulated popular rising against the Jews in Berlin (in reality an officially stimulated and planned pogrom), in which Jewish shops and places of worship were stormed, burned and looted until Goebbels gave the signal to cease; (2) the imposition of a "fine" of one billion marks upon German Jews as an indemnity for the murder; (3) a new and drastic series of edicts completely eliminating Jews from every gainful occupation by which a decent living can be made; and (4) the arrest of something like fifty thousand Jews.

If the rioting and violence had been the spontaneous act of an indignant and undisciplined people, it would have been bad. But this is worse. The Germans are not an undisciplined people. They riot only when they are instructed to riot. The damage to property—which the owners have been ordered to repair at their own expense, besides being forbidden to occupy it hereafter and robbed of their resources—was as much the act of the Nazi government as though it had been done by troops in uniform and under the direct command of their officers.

The editorial continued, condemning the actions against the Jews as unwarranted by the crime and stating that the action was fully consistent with Nazi ideology and policy, that the New Germany was "a power . . . potent and unscrupulous," that the Church had to take a stand, that the potential for total massacre of Jews was very real, that the promise of further reprisals against the Jews would result if foreign nations intervened was no empty threat, that the world seemed paralyzed and unable or unwilling to act, and that at the very least the response to these events should be wholesale condemnation of Germany's treatment of the Jews by governments and churches.[117]

In the same issue, an article noting that all Jews in Germany were required to take Semitic names was published. Was this a deliberate editorial choice, given the propitious moment, or was it included by the mere accident of printing and publishing schedules? No indication of the reason the article was published was given elsewhere in the issue.[118] The correspondents that comprised the network that regularly supplied copy for the "News of the Christian World" feature of *The Christian Century* reported the outrage, the statements of leading clergymen and churches, and the protest rallies and appeals to the United States government to take direct, strong action. The article from the New York correspondent typified these reports. It was headlined, "New York Aghast at New Pogroms: Protestants, Catholics and Jews Unite to Protest German Persecution—Urge U.S. to Act Officially."[119] The plea for justice and mercy on behalf of Germany by Rabbi F. M. Isserman of St. Louis was cited as an unusual instance of broad tolerance toward Germany.[120]

A second, long editorial article was published on November 30, 1938. Essentially, it condemned Germany and its Nazi leadership for rejecting out of hand the accumulated protest from around the world against the actions taken against the Jews in Kristallnacht. It then moved to a long discussion of the Jewish refugee problem and reluctantly concluded that either the majority of Germans supported their government or they themselves were without power to bring about change in Germany. Military intervention, then, seemed to be out of the question.

> With respect to the specific Jewish problem created by German inhumanity, this editorial, therefore, seems to end in a blind alley. We make no attempt to disguise our bafflement. . . . Meantime the solution of the deeper and universal problem of anti-Semitism rests, we hold, with the Christian Church, and with the Jewish people themselves. Democracy cannot solve this deeper problem. Perhaps religion can.[121]

On December 7, 1938, a short editorial, quoted from *Schwarze Korps*, reported that further retaliatory measures were to be taken against the Jews.[122] The correspondent from North Carolina reported the strong protest statement from the Southern Baptists, meeting in Durham, North Carolina.[123] A similar protest from Memphis was also noted, including the fact that a Negro pastor had spoken at the protest meeting.[124] The correspondents from Chicago, Detroit, and England reported similar protest meetings and statements.[125] Yet another editorial, on December 14, 1938, reported further reprisals, particularly pointing out that ghettoization of Jews seemed imminent in Germany as a result of these new restrictions.[126] Direct defiance of Goebbels's "advice" to England was reported in the correspondence from England, in a report of the growing demand of the British people for aid to Jewish refugees from Germany.[127]

A formal meeting in Albert Hall, London, was reported on December 21, 1938, by the English correspondent; a mass meeting of protest, from the correspondent in Los Angeles.[128] The correspondent from Cleveland reported that Cleveland's German-language newspaper, *Wachter und Anzeiger*, had "forcefully denounced the Nazi persecution of Jews as a great shame in soiling the German name because law and irresponsible baiters are stirring up vile and mean instincts of the rabble against defenseless human beings." Called a courageous statement, the correspondent noted that Cleveland had an unusually large German population.[129]

Letters to the editor followed. One offered suggestions for havens for Jews, either in Africa or in one state in the United States turned over to Jews, who would undoubtedly make that state prosper. One enclosed a letter from St. John's Evangelical and Reformed Church, Florence, Missouri, sent to President Roosevelt as a protest against German actions toward Jews. The church identified itself as having a congregation largely of German descent; another letter writer accused the *Century* of being a socialistic and communistic weekly and asked to be removed from its subscription list.[130]

The year 1938 was the watershed for Jews in Germany and Europe as the spread of the persecution of Jews, the policies of racial ideology, and the Nazi pressure on Jews increased. Poland, Rumania, Austria, and Czechoslovakia actively increased their direct persecution of Jews, Austria and Czechoslovakia as the result of German occupation and the application of the anti-Jewish decrees, the Nuremberg laws. Jew baiting and direct, immediate persecution accompanied the German occupation of both countries. Italy adopted anti-Semitic ideology and initiated restrictive measures for Italian Jews.

James G. McDonald, in his letter of resignation and its accompanying "Annex," had spelled out in detail the perilous situation for German Jews in January 1936. Citing, with extensive documentation, the Nuremberg laws and the application of those laws into every aspect of business, judicial, educational, social, economic, and religious life in Germany, McDonald's evidence, in retrospect, ought to have been compelling. It was not, at least as indicated by the response his letter and "Annex" received in the American Protestant press. Both his substantive, documented evidence and his plea for intervention by the League of Nations and the supporting member-states and interested religious, private, and philanthropic organizations went unheeded. His arguments, though accurate, proved to have been unpersuasive.

Without intending to be, however, McDonand was prophetic. Citing the Nuremberg laws, McDonald wrote, "Indirectly, through this new law, a constitutional basis was laid for unrestricted discriminations against all whom the Party may wish to penalize." He could then write, "I cannot remain silent. . . . When domestic policies threaten the demoralization and exile of hundreds of thousands of human beings, considerations of diplomatic correctness must yield to those of common humanity."[131] Had McDonald discussed the humiliation and dehumanization of the Jews and others and had he noted the imminent possibility of mass arrests and concentration camps, he would have fully described the situation in Germany, but his accuracy and prescience would have been frightening. He did not foresee these aspects of the persecutions, or at least he did not include them in his letter and statement. The events of 1936, 1937, and 1938 would tell that story to the world.

As indicated by the increase in the number of items found in the American Protestant press for 1938, clearly in Germany and in the German-occupied or influenced countries of Europe, there took place a sharply accelerated program of direct persecution of Jews in 1938. As Lucy S. Dawidowicz clearly described it:

> The plans for war and for the expropriation of the Jews, the directives providing for their identification, the rash of police arrests, and the explosion of violence all converged that summer of 1938 in a tidal wave of terror. . . . The plan for war had, for the time being, misfired and with it the opportunity for taking drastic, but less visible, action against the Jews. But an unexpected opportunity for dealing with the Jews opened up with the assassination on November 7, 1938, of Ernst Vom Rath, a third secretary in the German embassy in Paris, by a seventeen-year-old Polish Jewish student, Herschel Grynszpan.[132]

That was Kristallnacht!

The American Protestant press did record the events of Kristallnacht, and they did report the reaction of almost every conceivable group, denominational and individual. Shock, revulsion, condemnation, and protest statements and actions were noted. Accelerated efforts to assist refugees from the humiliation and terror of Kristallnacht were also noted. These periodicals, in part, also reported that the actions against the Jews in Germany in Kristallnacht had turned world opinion against Germany and that, as the news of the continuing program of reprisals against the Jews came out of Germany through the remainder of 1938, the situation for the Jews in Germany was becoming worse.

Yet, with all the reporting, Kristallnacht and the prior increase of persecution of the Jews in late 1937 and in 1938 was reported as a contemporary event or as news. No one in the American Protestant press, even while reporting, commenting upon, or analyzing these events from any and every perspective, fully comprehended their

meaning for the future of the Jews in Germany, not even the immediate future encompassed in the years 1939–1941.

The public record was there to be read. Jews were not only removed from their businesses; they were denied the right to reopen
them. Jewish children were officially barred from the schools, curfew
restrictions were imposed on Jews, and by the end of 1938 they were
denied all access to public places. Finally, economic sanctions were
imposed on all Jews by Goering, as he and Reinhard Heydrich began
to assume the full responsibility for settling the "Jewish question" in
Germany. The camps at Dachau, Sachsenhausen, Buchenwald, and
Mauthausen were being filled by thousands of newly arrested Jews.
Adolph Eichmann had already been noticed for his work in transporting Jews out of Austria and would shortly be moved to the offices
of Heydrich to assume the same responsibilities for German Jews.

Most directly, Adolph Hitler made a public statement in his address to the Reichstag on the anniversary date of his assumption of
power, January 30, 1939. The address was well reported as general
news. In it were two paragraphs on the Jews. Hitler referred to himself as a prophet who had been laughed at in his struggle for power
by the Jews. "I suppose that meanwhile the then resounding laugh-
ter of Jewry in Germany is now choking in their throats." Hitler then
went on to say:

> Today, I will be a prophet again: If international finance Jewry
> within Europe and abroad should succeed once more in plung-
> ing the peoples into a world war, then the consequence will
> not be the Bolshevization of the world and therewith a victory
> of Jewry, but on the contrary, the destruction of the Jewish race
> in Europe.[133]

Of the thirty-six Protestant periodicals examined for 1939, only in
one, *The Presbyterian*, was the speech even mentioned. Arthur Byrd
McCormick included a paragraph, "Hitler's Speech," in his weekly
commentary, "The World as I See It," for February 9, 1939. Two sentences were devoted to the Jews. Neither sentence mentions a word
from or about the above paragraph.[134]

Editors, writers, and commentators in the American Protestant
press seem to have been reporting the persecution of the Jews in
Germany and Europe by the familiar rules of earlier pogroms and
acts of anti-Semitism. They did not yet know that these rules had not
only been changed, they had been abolished. For Hitler and his
henchmen there were no rules, only "expulsion" and then "extermi-

nation." Hitler had not been believed in his statements about the Jews in *Mein Kampf*, in his speeches after 1933; he was not believed in his speech of January 30, 1939, in the very shadow of the Final Solution.

CHAPTER 4

1939–1942—Toward
the Final Solution:
Who in America Knew?

The word "final" . . . has a double meaning. . . . The destruction process had now been clarified. During the concentration stage it was still conceivable to shove the Jews out of Europe. . . . But the phrase "final solution" has a wider, more significant meaning. In Himmler's words, it meant the Jewish problem would never have to be solved again. Definitions, expropriations and concentrations can be undone. Killings cannot.

RAUL HILBERG
The Destruction of the European Jews

KEY EVENTS

1939, General: January 30, Hitler's Reichstag speech; March, invasion and occupation of Czechoslovakia; May, German-Italian military alliance; September 1, invasion of Poland, World War II begun as Britain and France declared war on Germany.

1939, Relating to the Jews: January 30, Hitler's Reichstag speech reiterating threat to destroy Jews; January, Reich Central Office for Jewish Emigration established under Heydrich; March, Jews taken to forced labor battalions; July 4, central organization for Jews in Germany taken over by security police; September 1, terror for Jews in Poland begun; October 9, ghettoization and resettlement of Jews begun; September 1939 through 1942, mobile killing squads (*Einsatzgruppen*) accompanied the German army in the invasion of Russia (approximately 2 million Jews were killed by these squads); October, general government under Hans Frank established in Poland, eastern Poland (Lublin district) designated a Jewish preserve.

1940, General: April 9, invasion of Denmark and Norway; May

9–10, Belgium and Holland invaded; May 26–June 4, "miracle of Dunkirk"; June 5–16, defeat and occupation of France; July 10, Battle of Britain begun; September 7, massive bombing of London.

1940, Relating to the Jews: Deportation of Jews accelerated, all Jews in Poland forced into ghettos; May–June, 500,000 Jews in Western Europe come under German control; October, French Jews deprived of citizenship, Saar Jews deported.

1941, General: January–March, war in North Africa; April, German invasion of Yugoslavia and Greece; June 22, invasion of Russia; November 15, German assault on Moscow; December 7, Pearl Harbor attacked; December 8, United States entered World War II.

1941, Relating to the Jews: Deportation and resettlement of Jews in German-held territories, reduction of food ration to Jews, adding starvation and disease to killing techniques, thus accounting for the deaths of 20 percent of Polish Jews; July, order to Heydrich from Goering beginning the planning of the Final Solution of the "Jewish question"; November, letter from Heydrich calling for a conference on the Final Solution (which was postponed until January 20, 1942); September, "star decree" requiring that a yellow star was to be worn by all Jews; September–December, Jewish property confiscated.

1942, General: Germany stalemated in Russia, beginning of Allied turnaround in North Africa and beginning of Allied shift from defense to offense in Europe; November 7–8, Allied armies land in North Africa; November 19–22, Russian counteroffensive at Stalingrad.

1942, Relating to the Jews: Six "killing centers" established in Poland at Kulmhof (Chelmno), Belzec, Sobibor, Majdanek (Lublin), Treblinka, and Auschwitz; January 20, Final Solution conference held at Am Grossen Wannsee, near Berlin, leading to the formation of the death camps and the speeding up of the extermination process; March 27, first Slovakian Jews sent to Auschwitz; July 22, first Warsaw Jews sent to Treblinka; July–August, first Jews from France, Holland, and Belgium sent to Auschwitz; August, first Jews from Lvov sent to Belzec; September, first Croatian and Dutch Jews sent to Auschwitz; November, first Norwegian Jews sent to Auschwitz.

W ith Kristallnacht (the Night of Broken Glass), the policies and actions that linked together the events of November 9–13, 1938, and the Final Solution of the "Jewish problem" were begun. After Kristallnacht, deportations of Jews were continued, with Jews being arrested and sent to Buchenwald.[1] The word *deportation* during the ensuing years was to have an ever more ominous meaning as form of the Final Solution began to take shape from 1938–1939 to January 20, 1942, when the formal plan for the Final Solution was approved at a meeting called under an order from Reichsmarshal Hermann Goering.[2] Reinhard Heydrich was the chairman of the meeting, held at Am Grossen Wannsee, near Berlin, and commonly called the Wannsee Conference. Fourteen representatives of the state and Nazi-party apparatus, including Heydrich, were present at the Wannsee Conference, including SS-Lt. Colonel Adolph Eichmann, who was officially acting as secretary for the meeting.[3]

The Jews as Hostages: The High Price for Emigration

As Gerald Reitlinger described it, planned deportation of Jews was carried out in 1939 and in 1940 and again in 1941, before the Wannsee Conference.[4] During this same period, the vocabulary of the Final Solution began to develop. *Emigration* and *evacuation* were terms used to describe what was happening to Jews in Germany and in Nazi-occupied Europe in 1939, 1940, and 1941. Emigration was forced; evacuations, planned and executed carefully. During the early phase in 1939, the question was, how much were the Jews worth? Could they be ransomed, either for their own assets or as guarantors for a loan from outside Germany that could be used to improve the foreign exchange rate and provide needed foreign currency? The Jews were to be held hostage, rich Jews as ransom for poor Jews within the Third Reich and then all Jews in an attempt to improve the German foreign exchange rate through the promise of Jewish emigration, but at a price. *The Christian Century* took note of the idea that the Jews were to be held as ransom.

> As to the money, it is asked that Great Britain and the United States make governmental loans of $25,000,000 each. Private benevolence must supply the rest. What it boils down to is . . . that the principle of robbing the German Jews of most of their wealth before allowing them to escape is unchanged, that the plan of compelling the nations which are shocked by German inhumanity to the Jews to meet most of the cost of their resettlement and . . . to make room for them is unchanged, and that the hope of cashing in on the Jews for the relief of Germany's unhealthy foreign trade situation is unchanged. Meanwhile, . . . the Jews remaining in Germany will not be mur-

dered until their foreign brothers and their international
friends have had a chance to buy them out.

An earlier sentence read, in part, "The implication is that the other
three-fourths of the property of the Jews in Germany (one-fourth was
to be reserved to aid in financing Jewish emigration) will be confiscated, and that the resources of the well-to-do will be applied to finance the emigration of those without funds. It remains to find the
rest of the money (which will be most of it)."[5] The mechanics of the
Final Solution of the "Jewish problem" began to take shape. As Lucy
S. Dawidowicz wrote, "In 1938, 'emigration' was a euphemism for
'expulsion.' Once war began, 'evacuation' became a euphemism for
'deportation,' which, in turn, signified transportation to a place of
death." Hitler's speech on January 30, 1939, both confirmed the inevitable and sealed the doom of Germany's Jews and the Jews of Europe. He promised a solution to the "Jewish problem" consistent
with his plans (and his patience) and embodied in his Four-Year Plan
whereby, by means of war and *Lebensraum*, he would accomplish his
promised destruction of the Jews of Europe.[6]

In brief, oblique references, *The Christian Century* took note of the
events summarized above. "There are signs that the German states-
men are not entirely steeled against the judgment of the world upon
their Jewish pogrom. But at the moment it looks as if they were ex-
ploiting the generous desire to help the refugees for their financial
enrichment."[7] On January 18, 1939, the correspondence from Philadelphia reported the return of three Quaker representatives—Rufus
M. Jones, George A. Walton, and Robert Yarnell—from a trip to Germany on behalf of the American Friends' Service Committee. While
in Germany, they were permitted to investigate conditions "and report that tentative plans have been worked out which may prove of
tremendous importance in caring for the Jews of the Reich." The correspondent from Philadelphia then mentioned that a plan for emigration of able-bodied Jews had been discussed. One hundred and fifty
thousand Jews, a figure confirmed in the discussions of the ultimately rejected Schacht plan discussed in Reitlinger's *The Final Solution: The Attempt to Exterminate the Jews of Europe, 1939–1945*, were to
comprise the first pool of Jewish emigrants. A chilling sentence was
included by the Philadelphia correspondent. "The plan is to set up
large transit camps outside Germany, where emigrants could be kept
and fed and trained, while the doors in the country of their destination were opened."[8] Those "large transit camps" bore the names Da-

chau, Sachsenhausen, and Buchenwald and were already being enlarged in the summer of 1938 to accommodate the forced emigration
of Jews, with a new camp being opened at Mauthausen. Adolph
Eichmann was the administrator of the plan, which he began in Austria, as head of the Central Office for Jewish Emigration. In an exchange described by Dawidowicz as "'emigration' as an alternative
to terror," Eichmann supervised the forced emigration of 45,000 Jews
from Austria in just six months.[9] By October 1939, Eichmann was
moved in the political structure to the Office of Emigration and Eval-
uation, coded IV-B-4, of the political police. This office would then
be transferred intact when the war came, and Eichmann with it.
Thus, he moved from a bureaucrat's desk (political), to a police desk
(political police), to a military desk in the Reichs Ministry Security
Office, but the numbers did not change. He became an SS-major,
then an SS-lt. colonel assigned as chief of IV-B-4 (Jews) under Heydrich.[10] Eichmann, hidden in the bureaucratic structure, was unknown to the Quaker visitors Jones, Yarnell, and Walton.

The Friend, in which the American Friends' Service Committee regularly published reports of its activities, also took note of the return
of Jones, Walton, and Yarnell in an optimistic editorial on their return
from Germany, "with something to show for their mission." The editorial spoke about the apparent sincerity of the German government
about getting "the able-bodied Jew out of Germany" and also about
the responsibility of the Friends for accomplishing the task of reliev-
ing human suffering.[11] In the same issue, a letter-article from Rufus
M. Jones was published. In it, he spoke of "results . . . of an intangible sort. They cannot be put down in black and white and summed
up or cashed in." He then wrote:

> We carried by our presence at this crisis in their lives a silent
> message of good-will, and we made those, who needed help
> most understand that there was someone who cared and who
> sympathized and who suffered with them, and who were ea-
> ger to help. From that point of view the journey was worth
> making and it reached its goal. We felt and found each other.

In the next paragraph, Jones gave a concise, accurate description of
Kristallnacht, using the descriptive phrase, "the 'glass breaking
day'—November 10th." He described the destruction of every synagogue in Germany, "nearly every Jewish shop," and "many private
homes" that had "all the glass on the street front smashed and much
of the property destroyed." He reported that 35,000 Jewish men had

been sent to concentration camps and that a veritable reign of terror had been launched against the Jews in Germany.

He asked for funds to be given to the Jewish Central Relief Committee, reporting that the Service Committee would send two workers, one to Berlin and one to Vienna. Every effort, he continued, would be made to accelerate the emigration of Jews from Germany and the work would be coordinated through the Intergovernmental Refugee Commission in London. He then told of meeting the German finance minister, Dr. Schacht, "who told us in confidence of the way in which plans for a vast emigration of Jews from Germany is being worked out. This plan, of course, is not our Quaker plan, but if it can accomplish the purpose we shall rejoice."

Jones's closing paragraph tells of meeting cordially with the "heads of most of the important departments of the Governments." The closing sentences were cautiously hopeful, without being overly optimistic.[12] Jones could not have known that shortly after his article was published Hitler would dismiss Schacht and that the Schacht plan would be abandoned, and with it the hope that large numbers of Jews could leave Germany.[13]

Kristallnacht: Early 1939 Reports in the Protestant Press

The context of the Jones-Walton-Yarnell visit to Germany had been the events of Kristallnacht. Some American Protestant periodicals continued to comment on Kristallnacht in 1939, mostly in January, February, and March. The editors of *The Christian Herald* put the shooting of Vom Rath in an optimistic context, stating that world opinion would condemn the Nazis. Describing the incident as "the perfect excuse for which the Nazis had been waiting," the editors wrote that "the new purge of the Jew was on." From this point on, the editorial declared that the incident had aroused the world, generally, against Germany, that it was not the doing of the German people, but that "the German people are in the hands of a murderous gang; the gang-leader is not even German himself." The editorial continued:

> Now the hope in the situation is that these hospitable and representative Germans will be aroused by the purge which followed the shooting in Paris. It has happened before. . . .
> There is every reason to believe that it will happen again.
> There comes a time when any human heart draws the line at more frightfulness.

When that happens, Hitler will go, and the fear of a world-war will go with him.[14]

If only Daniel Poling had been right. In fact, events of the immediate future would prove him wrong. Hitler would not go and a world war would come. More to the point, there was little evidence that the German people did anything, openly, to voice their opposition to the purging of the Jews or the penalties exacted from them over Kristallnacht.

The editor of *The Evangelical Visitor* published a long, two-column editorial based on a report in *Collier's* magazine about Kristallnacht, by Quentin Reynolds. Reynolds had been sent to Europe specifically to obtain firsthand, accurate information about what had happened to the Jews in Germany. The editor, in using the *Collier's* story, stated that he believed Reynolds to be a reliable reporter whose story could be trusted. The editor recounted the restrictions on Jews in Germany under German law, the reaction of German Jewish children in England when they were told they could walk on the lawns without being punished, and then some specific details of the events on November 10, 1938, especially citing the burning of the synagogue on Princeregent Street. This fire had been seen by an American living in Berlin.

Streicher's remarks to newspapermen were noted, as were incidents of persecution in Vienna and Leipzig and at an orphanage for Jewish children near Berlin. The persecution of Catholics in Sudetanland was also described, with the notice that the Germans officially said the Catholics had been imprisoned as enemies of the state, not because they were Roman Catholics. Attempts to obtain visas to leave Germany were also described, noting that it was next to impossible and that the American restriction on immigration was among the most severe among nations. The closing paragraph was taken entirely from the *Collier's* article, describing the Jew as a "hunted, tortured soul" who had lost everything and was unwanted. "Sometimes he must think that even the Supreme Being he has worshiped has deserted him. He must wonder whether when he reaches the celestial gates he will see a sign crying out 'Juden unerwuenscht' (Jews unwanted)."[15]

The Friend of Zion stressed the billion-mark fine assessed as an indemnity against the Jews of Germany to pay for the damage of Kristallnacht, and then went on to describe further economic penalties in the form of a 20 percent levy on all Jewish property as a capital tax, which, added to the assessed value, amounted to a forced sale at a net of nothing to the Jewish owner. This, said the news note, exceeded the seven circles of hell of Dante.[16]

The Gospel Herald, without direct reference to Kristallnacht but in the context of the ensuing events, reported the offer made to London for the emigration of Jews from Germany. As in the Quaker report of Rufus M. Jones, the figure used was 150,000 (or up to 200,000) Jews who would be permitted to leave Germany, if indemnified in foreign currency. The report also mentioned that the United States reported that its quota for Germans had been completely filled for two years and for two years in advance and that Jews were being given temporary permits to remain in the United States.[17]

The organizations doing work among the Jews did not hesitate. Using paid advertisements as they had in the past, they placed ads in *The King's Business* and *The Sunday School Times*. In a full-page ad, the American Board of Missions to the Jews continued to refer directly to the events and consequences of Kristallnacht, in January 1939.[18] The Friends of Israel, a Christian missionary organization from Philadelphia, ran quarter-page and half-page ads asking for an increase in donations because the situation for Jews had deteriorated so badly.[19]

1939–1942: The Major Subjects Reported in the Protestant Press

Beyond Kristallnacht as a specific event, the American Protestant press reported the persecution of the Jews in 1939, 1940, 1941, and 1942 more than it reported on anything it had reported of events in Germany and Europe since 1933. The Church Struggle continued as the second most reported item of continuing concern, and refugee problems and aid to refugees became the third most reported item for these years. In a discussion of this reporting, one specific exclusion must be noted. The question of the Final Solution of the "Jewish problem," as a distinct reported item, was isolated and recorded as a separate, specific subject beginning in 1942. The questions one must ask at this point are: What evidence, if any, was reported in the American Protestant press regarding the significant change in the persecution of the Jews in Germany and German-held territories that indicated a knowledge about the mass deportations of Jews to camps, however described, in Poland or to the east? What references, if any, began to appear in this press that indicated that these camps were not labor camps only, but were there to serve some other more sinister and terrible purpose? What references, if any, began to appear in this press in 1942 or earlier that indicated a knowledge of mass killings, other than in the camps, by shootings, by firing squads or death squads?

During the four years between 1939 and 1942, the persecution of the Jews, exclusive of discussions of the Final Solution, was extensively reported. A total of 616 direct and indirect references to the persecution of the Jews (which by that time had expanded to include Poland, Hungary, Czechoslovakia, Bulgaria, Rumania, the Baltic countries, Yugoslavia, France, Belgium, Holland, and Italy as well as Germany) were reported, exclusive of references to the Final Solution. Thirty-eight periodicals were examined for 1939; thirty-three, for 1940; thirty-five, for 1941; and thirty, for 1942.

On the Church Struggle, including a significant increase in the reporting of the Norwegian Church Struggle under Nazi occupation and including the struggle of churches in France, Belgium, Italy, and Holland, a total of 476 references were noted. As the German occupation of France, Belgium, Norway, Poland, the Baltics, and Holland, as well as Austria, Czechoslovakia, Bulgaria, Hungary, and Yugoslavia, solidified under the realities of the expanding advances of German troops, news about the Church Struggle often included a note that the Church and church leaders were being punished for their support or assistance to Jews who were being persecuted or deported. (When such dual references were found in the same article, editorial, or news report, the Church Struggle reference was noted by date and periodical as a separate item and the reference to the persecution of the Jews was noted as a separate item, also, by date and periodical. This was done in order to isolate and note all references in these two separate categories.)

Also, in recording the Church Struggle references, two other isolated items were noted. With reference to the Church Struggle in Germany, all references to Martin Niemoeller were recorded as a separate item, as were all references specifically to Roman Catholics and their problems, both in Germany and in the occupied countries. As the reporting for 1939 through 1942 was done, there is no question but that Martin Niemoeller emerged as an authentic hero for the American Protestant press. He had defied the Nazis; he was in a concentration camp after having been arrested, released, and rearrested; and he had been a prisoner since 1937. News came out of Germany about him intermittently, sometimes in the form of rumors, such as that he had converted to Roman Catholicism and that he had volunteered for service in the submarine service of the German navy. A book written by Leo Stein, whose credentials were that he had been a fellow prisoner with Niemoeller, became popular. Niemoeller's own writings appeared. However, Niemoeller was a hero mostly because he succeeded in staying alive when the deaths of other prominent church leaders were being reported from the German concentration camps.[20]

It also became more and more clear that priests, church officials, and Roman Catholics generally were subject to direct persecution, imprisonment, and death. Polish priests, German Roman Catholic church leaders, and the church generally suffered heavily as resistance to the Nazis grew and as church leaders spoke out in opposition to Nazi measures against the Jews. In France and Holland, many Roman Catholic church and lay leaders joined their Protestant counterparts in statements of opposition to the Nazis and to the persecution and deportation of Jews. In continuing to carry out forbidden activities in the churches or by supporting the growing resistance, Roman Catholics, too, eventually paid the price as enemies of the state.

As the active persecution of Jews and others increased during the years 1939 through 1942, so did the concern of the American Protestant press about recording any assistance to refugees. These efforts were usually reported in three separate categories. The first was aid to refugees; the second, the refugees' problems apart from direct references to aid and assistance; and the third, refugee havens or refugee sites (Palestine continued to be identified as the most logical but not the only place where refugees, particularly Jews, could go if they could escape Germany and Europe). Costa Rica, Mindanao in the Philippines, the Dominican Republic, Madagascar, Australia, sites in Africa and South America, Alaska, and India were among the places put forward as possible sites for refugee relocation. The ability of England, Canada, and the United States to take more refugees, especially children, was discussed, and the hostility of the Arabs toward increased immigration of Jews to Palestine was an item of some concern. In discussing Jewish immigration to a "national home" in Palestine and Arab opposition, those periodicals of a more conservative bent viewed these events, generally, from the context of their interest in prophetic interpretation and the prophetic significance of the Jews and their return to Palestine as refugees. Though they did express concern and distress over what was happening to Jews in

Germany and Europe, their major interest continued to be in prophetic "signs" in relation to the Second Coming of Jesus Christ as the Messiah. They remained consistent with themselves, continuing their messianic or prophetic analysis, though some evidence began to appear that even those interested in the prophetic emphasis were questioning some of the preoccupation with this form of prophetic interpretation.[21]

Anti-Semitism in America

The question of anti-Semitism continued to be a major topic of discussion in the American Protestant press. In the religious periodicals examined for 1939–1942, 176 references to anti-Semitism were noted. The categories were references to anti-Semitism as a general topic, anti-Semitism in America, and the Jews and anti-Semitism; there was also a group of articles that discussed fascism in America, Father Coughlin, nazism in America, the Christian Front and the Ku Klux Klan, and the threat of a fifth column (that is, Nazi spies coming with refugees to America). The activities of the Christian Front and the Coughlin followers in New York and other eastern cities were followed closely, particularly by The Churchman. In 1939, the Episcopal periodical published its second long series of articles on fascism in America. No American Protestant religious periodical of those examined exceeded The Churchman in its coverage of all aspects of anti-Semitism in America in terms of groups or individuals who were actively promoting anti-Semitic propaganda or pro-Nazi activities.[22]

In 1940, The Churchman continued to discuss these critical topics, but to a somewhat lesser degree. One news article referred to Coughlin; several editorials were written by Guy Emery Shipler, the editor, and one article was published on anti-Semitism. The article and the editorials were all written to defend the actions of clergymen who opposed anti-Semitism and who were under attack, often by laypersons in their own denominations or churches, for their stand against anti-Semitic movements in America.[23]

In 1941, The Churchman again became more aggressive and outspoken in its campaign against anti-Semitism. In editorials naming names, specific instances of direct condemnation of anti-Semitic actions or statements were made. Father Coughlin, Henry Ford, Charles Lindbergh, and William Ward Ayer (pastor of the Calvary Baptist Church of New York City) were mentioned specifically. In his parish paper, Calvary Pulpit, Ayer, from his well-known conservative-fundamentalist church, had attacked refugees as being dangerous to the United States and as being "radical, ungodly trouble-makers." *The Churchman* accused Ayer of aligning himself "with the American Nazis and Coughlinites in adding his contempt to theirs for the refugees who have come from totalitarian lands." An editorial, "Anti-Semitism Goes into High Gear," which specifically noted Lindbergh's attack on the Jews, also took note of the attempt of anti-Semitic groups to join together in a common effort and of the implied support for such groups given by Senator Nye in a speech made in Washington, D.C. The editorial concluded:

> Strangely enough, many otherwise decent citizens, even members of Christian churches, have fostered the Nazi-directed efforts by indulging in anti-Semitic talk. When Lindbergh came out in the open with his anti-Semitic brutality large members of such cooperators began to see the ultimate meaning and danger of such talk. It is a pity that many Christians, whose anti-Semitism has denied their right to the name Christian, had to be awakened.[24]

Then came the war. In 1942, *The Churchman* published only two articles and no editorials on anti-Semitism. The first article discussed the closing down of the Nazi Bund by the federal government and wondered why, if the Bund was seen to be so dangerous, Father Coughlin was still allowed the freedom to speak and write. The second article was a discussion of anti-Semitism written by a prominent member of the Anti-Defamation League of B'nai B'rith.[25]

The Federal Council of Churches also became actively concerned about anti-Semitism in America, especially in 1939. This is apparent from the number of notices about council statements in the American Protestant press. The *Federal Council Bulletin* in 1939 published its own direct warnings. In January, its report of the thirtieth anniversary meeting of the previous December was published, including a statement condemning anti-Semitism in America. A long editorial was published in the February issue of the *Bulletin*, warning Christians that anti-Semitism was in fact an attack on Christianity, whether in Germany or in the United States. In the June issue, the *Bulletin* took note of a World Council of Churches statement condemning racial ideologies as the basis for denying people access to the Christian churches, particularly in Germany; and, in September, it announced a program by the Race and Relations Department and the Church Women's Committee to actively combat anti-Semitism.[26] In 1941, the *Bulletin* noted that an official statement of condemnation of anti-Semitism was reported as having been adopted on September 19, 1941.[27] In 1940 and 1942, anti-Semitism was not mentioned in the *Federal Council Bulletin*.

Jews and Christians in America

As during previous years, the "Jewish question" and articles about Jews, the relationship between Jews and Christians, the problems of the Jews as refugees, the tension between Arabs and Jews in Palestine, the Jews and prophetic interpretations of what was happening to them, and Zionism continued to be discussed in articles and editorials. In most instances, these articles did not focus so much upon persecution as upon Jews themselves. In this context, the subject of the most interest and concern was the relationship between Jews and Christians, given the times and the events that were taking place between 1939 and 1942. On this one subject, for the four years, a total of eighty-three articles, editorials, and news items were noted. Sub-themes included the problems of Jews who had become Christians, non-Aryan Christian refugees, interfaith activities such as Jews and Christians worshipping together or in dialogue, brotherhood week activities, what continued to be referred to as the "Jewish question," the emphasis among the more conservative and evangelical churches on missions to the Jews, and the discussions in articles and youth lesson materials on the Jew in the world or the prophetic significance of Jews in terms of biblical interpretations.

The number of such articles, editorials, news items, and references was greatest in 1939. They were also typical of what was published during the following three years. No new themes were introduced through 1942 in the general references to Jews. Examples of the continuing interest in the Jews for 1939 could be taken from some twenty-three periodicals. *The Brethren Evangelist*, conservative and evangelical, published eight items directly about Jews and articles and editorials basically along three themes. Prophetic interpretation was one emphasis, missionary work and Christian witness to Jews was the second, and editorial commentary on Jews as refugees was the third. One article was a reprint of the article by Alfred Segal, "How It Feels to Be a Jew," which had been published in a number of religious periodicals earlier with attribution to the Presbyterian Board of Missions.[28]

Arthur Acy Rouner wrote an article on interfaith activity in New England for *Advance*.[29] Pieter Smit, in *The Baptist Herald* (a German

Baptist periodical), wrote "The Remarkable Jew," and the same issue carried an article by Ina Corinne Brown, "Who Are the Jews." *The Christian Advocate*, in one of its regular features, published "The Thoughts of Justis Timberline: The Healing Jew" and several editorials on the plight of Jewish refugees.[30] Jacque Maritain's book on the "Jewish question" was reviewed in *The Churchman*, and *The Christian Century* continued its publication of articles, editorials, and letters to the editor on Jews, the "Jewish question," and Jews as refugees— twenty-three in all for 1939, apart from those articles and editorials on the persecution of the Jews.[31] It also published, among other things, an article by Morris S. Lazaron, "Judaism a Universal Religion," as one of a series on religious belief.[32]

The *Mennonite* published "What Is a Jew," by a Jewish author; *The Messenger*, a news item on the committee formed after the Evian Conference and its attempt to raise money and a reprint of the Justis Timberline article from *The Christian Advocate*: it also published, among other items, editorials on aid to the refugees.[33] *The Presbyterian*, in 1939, published editorials on the refugee problem and aid to Jewish refugees and several articles on the responsibility of Christians to witness or minister to Jews in America. Three articles specifically highlighted such efforts being made at the local church level.[34]

The S.S. St. Louis and Jews as Refugees

It is interesting to note that the ill-fated journey of Jewish refugees on the Hamburg-American ship S.S. *St. Louis* did not receive much coverage in the American Protestant press. Neither did they report about other ships with Jewish refugees aboard that also failed to find landing points in North and South America and in the Caribbean.[35] An editorial in *The Lutheran Companion* reported the incident of the S.S. *St. Louis*, describing the refusal of Cuba to admit the over 900 passengers, even though they had tourist visas for a stay of up to ninety days.

> As the *St. Louis* steamed out of Havana harbor, presumably to return to Hamburg, its decks were described as scenes of abject despair. Mass suicide among the passengers was predicted. Later the vessel was reported to have cast anchor three miles off shore at Miami Beach, Florida, where it was marking time while further negotiations were being conducted with the Cuban authorities in the hope that the latter might relent.

The editorial then went on to describe other efforts to find havens for Jewish refugees and then said:

Whatever blame may attach to the Jews themselves, Christians must feel a sense of pity for this unfortunate people. Their own Palestine closed to them by an English decree, their age-long dream of a national home has again been shattered, and they know not where to go. No other nation wants them. A ship-load of dejected refugees sailing the high seas with no port willing to receive them—what a tragic picture of a people without a country.

The editorial called for prayer for these unfortunate Jews and for renewed efforts to solve the Jewish problem, and it concluded that "there is no better way to win the Jews for Christ than by revealing to them a spirit of Christian love and compassion in their day of need."

In the thirty-eight American Protestant periodicals examined for 1939, only two other references to the S.S. *St. Louis* were found. In a letter to the editor of *The Christian Advocate*, which addressed itself to the admission of Jewish refugees to the United States, the writer (H. R. Hibner, of Lawrence, Kansas) concluded his letter by saying:

I rejoice that the Jewish refugees aboard the liner *St. Louis*, compelled to return with its passengers to Europe, have been received into the Christian countries of England, France, Belgium, and Holland, and I hope and believe that if ever again a shipload of those suffering persecution enter our waters, they will not again be turned back but be wholeheartedly received by a Christian people.

Little could Mr. Hibner even conceive of the possibility that those refugee Jews on the S.S. *St. Louis* who returned to Belgium, France, and Holland would once again become victims of the Nazis and that the majority of them would perish in the death camps. An indirect reference to the S.S. *St. Louis*, not by name, was made in an editorial in *The Brethren Evangelist* of June 24, 1939; it referred to "900 Jewish refugees from Europe who have been cruising from one continent to another looking for a place to land."[36] Equally curious, it seems strange that most of the major Protestant periodicals, including *The Christian Century*, made no mention of the S.S. *St. Louis* and that a Lutheran periodical of the Augustana, or Swedish, Lutherans devoted a lengthy editorial to the matter without reference to any other religious periodical. The editorial in *The Lutheran Companion*, in other words, was not a reprint.

The Jews and Prophecy

In 1940, 1941, and 1942, interest in Jewish-Christian relations, mission and witness to Jews by Christians, the "Jewish question," and interfaith activities continued to be reported and discussed, much as in the articles, editorials, news items, and letters to the editor cited for 1939. Aid to refugees and the refugee problem continued to be the dominant concern, but, as the realities of the war settled in, fewer items appeared; and, by 1942, discussions of aid and assistance to refugees diminished dramatically. The world was at war. The one subject that was discussed still, however, was the Jew and prophecy. *The Gospel Herald* published two articles on Jews and prophecy in 1942. A. J. Kligerman published "Israel's Position in Romans 11," and Hyman Appelman, a Jewish convert to Christianity and an evangelist, published "Can Hitler Win the War? Examining His Three Great Mistakes in the Light of Scripture" in *The Sunday School Times*. According to Appelman, Hitler's third mistake was that "he has persecuted my people, the Jews, with a heavier hand than that of any other tyrant the Jews have faced in all their bloody and bitter history."[37] The interest in the prophetic interpretation of world events and of the Jews in relation to prophetic interpretation of these events among fundamentalist and conservative, evangelical groups never seemed to wane. Some concern was expressed, however, by one respected fundamentalist leader, Roy L. Laurin, who was associated with the Bible Institute of Los Angeles. Writing in *The King's Business* in 1939, Laurin questioned the wisdom of dealing disproportionately with "the prophetic aspect of the Scriptures . . . , particularly in preaching." He called for a balance between what he called "timely" and "timeless" themes and then wrote, "If Daniel is in the canon of Scripture—so is John. If Antichrist is a menace—Christ is the panacea. If totalitarianism threatens—regeneration is still our greatest hope."[38] Earlier in the same year and in the same magazine, Louis S. Bauman had published yet another prophetic series of three articles, the second of which specifically centered on the Jews and prophecy. He also wrote an extensive series on prophetic themes in *The Sunday School Times* in 1940.[39] Among the more conservative-evangelical and fundamentalist papers, interest in such prophetic analysis remained high, apparently.

What Was Happening to Jews in Europe?

But what of the increasingly desperate situation for Jews in Germany and Europe? Did the American Protestant press report their deteriorating situation? Did the press recognize, even to a small degree, the implications of what they were reporting? As described by Raul Hilberg, Lucy S. Dawidowicz, Nora Levin, and Gerald Reitlinger, among others, the machinery for the destruction of the Jews in Europe was then being set up in Germany. Dawidowicz made a persuasive case, based on extensive documentation, that, in 1938 and after, Adolph Hitler would carry out his plans regarding Jews. These plans he had formulated in his speeches, and he had stated them in *Mein Kampf* for all to read. She argued that Hitler, ever patient, never deviated from his intentions; he simply waited until he felt the timing was right. With the task to be the responsibility of the National Socialist party (rather than the army or officials less loyal to Hitler) and with Himmler, Goering, and Heydrich as the persons assigned to find the means of implementing the Final Solution to the "Jewish problem," 1939 and the years after were to be the crucial years. The chilling details of the plan were laid out in full by Dawidowicz, first from the German documents and the records of the National Socialist party and then from the Jewish perspective in a long essay, "Between Freedom and Ghetto: The Jews in Germany, 1933–1938."[40] The cold, impersonal record (which includes all the euphemisms used to disguise what was happening, thereby hiding the truth from the Jews and from the world and making the realities of killing Jews, Poles, Gypsies, and enemies of the state at least possible for the Germans and others actually employed in the task), was told in full in Raul Hilberg's two books.[41] In the documents assembled by Hilberg, the word *efficiency* takes on a new and terrible meaning: The killing process must be efficient; the trains for transporting the people must be available and they must run on time; the warehouses for gathering and sorting the clothing, shoes, eyeglasses, teeth, luggage, and all the rest must be well organized; the money collected or obtained from the sale of the goods in the warehouses must be banked and accounted for; the record itself must bear witness to the *efficiency* of the killing operations.

Did the American Protestant churches know? The lesson topic in the *Adult Class and Adult Leader* for March 1939 was "Peter Preaches to Gentiles: Or a Faith That Breaks Down Racial Barriers." One of the discussion questions asked under "Practical Questions for Class Discussion" was, "Do you try to account for the persecution of the Jews in Germany? A breakdown of the Christian religion there? Yet for a thousand years the Germans had been a Bible-reading, Christ-worshipping people. What then?"[42] Indeed, "what then?"

An editorial in *Advance* began, "Nothing can compensate to individuals for the tragedy of the loss and suffering that they have sustained by persecution in Germany and elsewhere, or for the insecurity and peril with which their lives are still menaced." It is the word *elsewhere* that would become significant in that, as the conquest of Europe by Hitler and the Nazis became a reality in 1939, 1940, and 1941, the persecution of the Jews intensified to become the terrible destruction of European Jews. The Final Solution was no longer confined to German Jews; it included all the Jews in Europe.[43]

In early 1939, the concern was still the persecution of the Jews in Germany in the aftermath of Kristallnacht. Henry Smith Leiper in his regularly published feature in *Advance*, "The State of the Church," referred directly to the continuing persecution of Jews in Germany in January and February of 1939. In April 1939, he wrote about apologists for Germany and their comparisons with American racial problems, particularly the treatment of Negroes. He flatly stated that there was, in reality, no comparison, wrong as America's treatment of Negroes was. He then wrote:

> What Germany is doing to the Jews and to other minorities or liberals is being done with the provocation and under the leadership of Hitler and those associated with him in the government of the country. Even if one assumes . . . that the whole course of persecution is repugnant to the minds of many Germans, protest against such action would itself be very quickly suppressed and would land the protestors in a prison or in concentration camps.[44]

In March 1939, *The Alliance Weekly* published an editorial referring to an appeal "for the multitudes of Jews who are suffering great privations in Europe," signed by twenty-eight prominent evangelical and conservative ministers and laypersons. Those identified as needing assistance were "the Jews and . . . Jewish Christians of Central Europe."[45] No longer were the German Jews the only victims. In September 1939, *The Alliance Weekly* was describing the expanded persecution of the Jews, naming Slovakia, Bohemia, Moravia, Czechoslovakia, Bulgaria, Rumania, Danzig, Memel, Poland, Hungary, Italy, and "even far-off Turkey." The report, taken from a British publication (the London *Christian*), described the burning of synagogues, the public humiliation of Jews, their loss of civil rights, their suicides, the homeless refugees, the deportations and expulsions, the expulsion of foreign Jews from Turkey, and the return of German Jews to Germany from Italy, where they had fled earlier.[46]

J. Hoffman Cohn, general secretary of the American Board of Missions to the Jews of Brooklyn, New York, and himself a Jewish convert to Christianity, wrote an article for *The Brethren Evangelist* about his trip to Europe. He began his article:

> "In five years, one half of the Jews in Europe will be exterminated; some by natural death, the rest by starvation, disease, drownings, suicides, massacres."
>
> So a prominent Jew told me a few weeks ago as we were crossing the Atlantic, I am on my way back from one of the saddest journeys I have ever made. For awhile, I had thought of preparing an address on my experiences, and entitling it "To Hell and Back." But it sounded too startling, and so I gave up the idea.

Cohn then discussed the persecution of the Jews in Central Europe, primarily in Austria and Germany. He described suicides, loss of all rights, loss of jobs, and deportation to concentration camps. He referred to a letter he wrote to a friend about what he saw and heard, in which he had written that the Jews of Central Europe were "facing extermination within the next five years." He also wrote later in the article that "the Evian Conference on Jewish refugees proved to be only blares of trumpets." Cohn must have written this sentence at the time negotiations were arising from the Evian Conference since his article was published on March 25, 1939. This early insight into the failure of Evian was, to say the least, surprising. But, again, the emphasis of his article was on the persecution of Jews in Central Europe, and not just in Germany.[47]

In the following issue of *The Brethren Evangelist*, a long report on Kristallnacht was given.[48] In this report, the restrictions on Jews in Italy was reported, but not the expulsions, and the persecution of Jews in Czechoslovakia was mentioned briefly. In the April 8, 1939, issue of *The Brethren Evangelist*, the persecution of Jews in Austria, Italy, and Danzig was specifically noted.[49] In July, an editorial reported from a letter of a missionary to Polish Jews, which described the need to work rapidly among Poland's Jews "before the war starts in Europe, either in August or September." It continued, "if you knew what we know of the things, awful things going on, you would not wonder that we are in a hurry." The same issue contained two other editorial paragraphs on the hatred of the Jews. Louis S. Bauman was an editor of *The Brethren Evangelist* in 1939.[50]

Reports of the persecution of the Jews in *The Christian Advocate* centered on Germany in January and February of 1939. By March, Austria had been added and then Bulgaria, Moravia, and Slovakia.

In the latest additions to the rapidly growing German Empire secret police and Storm Troopers are busy suppressing civil liberties, just as they have done in Germany, Austria and Sudetanland. In the newly acquired territory, Jews are being persecuted and they are trying to get away, just as they have done in older sections of the Reich.

The remainder of the short article discussed *Lebensraum*, the policy followed by Hitler for his expansion into new areas of Eastern Europe; the article also noted that Poles, Rumanians, and Yugoslavs were worried. References to the direct persecution of Jews in Austria were made in an article by George Mecklenburg, a Methodist minister who had visited Germany and Austria during the summer of 1938, where he had clandestinely interviewed Jews in Vienna.[51]

In July, *The Christian Advocate* told of the search by Jews for places to emigrate and reported that "Jewish leaders are warning the tardy, 'It's later than you think.'" Specifically, it mentioned that refugee havens were being sought for German, Polish, and Rumanian Jews.[52] By November, *The Christian Advocate* was reporting that Polish Jews were fleeing for their lives but that they were not welcome anywhere and that they had no place to go. Polish Jews who had reached Rumania in an effort to reach Palestine ultimately were sent back to Poland because they could not obtain entry permits to Palestine from the British Colonial Office.[53]

Like the other Protestant periodicals already discussed, *The Christian Century* reported the persecution of the Jews in early 1939 primarily in Germany and primarily in relation to the negotiations for possible emigration of Jews to selected refugee sites. In one editorial comment, the suggestion was offered that, if German Jews could be ransomed for Germany's financial benefit, then the Jews of Europe might also become hostage for financial profit.[54] The persecution of the Jews in Hungary was reported, and it was noted that Prime Minister Imredy had resigned because it had been discovered that one of his grandparents was Jewish; even so, he had fully supported the program for the persecution of Hungarian Jews.[55] In March, the *Century* reported the expulsion of Jews from Italy, many of whom were reported to be walking on foot through the Alps. The *Century* called it an expulsion without any sense and "merely a cheap imitation of the Nazi fanaticism without even the excuse of a fanatic's crazed sincerity."[56] Albert Viton published an article on Memel, in which he made direct reference both to the Nazi terror and to the persecution of Jews, in April 1939.[57] At this point, direct reporting or discussion of persecution of the Jews in Germany and Europe disappeared from the pages of the *Century* through the spring and summer of 1939. This did not continue in the fall. In September, the persecution of the Jews in Poland was reported; another such report was made in November 1939.[58] Generally, in 1939, reports on incidents of the direct persecution of Jews appeared less frequently in the *Century* than in previous years. No reason for the lack of reporting was given.

In September 1939, the *Century* did report one curious action of the Nazis.

> Dr. George Mecklenberg of Wesley Methodist Church [Minneapolis, Minnesota] was barred from Germany while conducting a travel tour. It is believed that his spoken and written attacks upon totalitarianism were responsible for his being banned. The topic he has chosen for his first lectures in America is: "Why Hitler Slammed the Door in My Face."[59]

Certainly, Mecklenberg's reporting in the *Christian Advocate* of the persecution of Jews in Germany and Vienna must have played a significant part in the Nazi decision to bar him from Germany.

The pattern of reporting the persecution of the Jews in the American Protestant press for 1939, as described, was consistent for all those periodicals examined. The persecution of Jews in Germany was reported early in the year; in other parts of Europe, late in the year. In October 1939, *The Churchman* reported the persecution of the Jews in Austria, Sudetanland, and Poland.[60] *The Hebrew Christian Alliance Quarterly* reprinted an article from a British periodical, in which Slovakia, Ruthenia, Bulgaria, Rumania, Danzig, Memel, Poland, and Hungary were mentioned as places where persecution of the Jews had either increased or begun.[61]

The *Moody Monthly* followed the pattern. So did *The Presbyterian*, *The Presbyterian Guardian*, *The Signs of the Times*, *The Sunday School*

Times, and *The Watchman-Examiner.* In the latter, in an editorial entitled, "Suffering of the Jews," Poland, Austria, Bohemia-Moravia, and Lithuania were mentioned specifically, including the statement that "several hundred thousand were subsequently reported to have fled into Soviet areas to escape Nazi terrorism." These thousands were Polish Jews. The editorial went on:

> Thus about 2,300,000 Jews are now under Nazi rule. Indications are that they are not reported as desirable citizens by either country. [Germany and Russia are the countries referred to in the editorial.] Hitler's Reichstag address of October 6 had in it a proposal for the "regulation of the Jewish problem." Persistent reports give the impression that a special region for Jews is being established around Lublin in the southeastern part of Poland. Thousands of Jews from Vienna and the Bohemia-Moravia Protectorates have already been sent there.[62]

The long shadow of the death camps thus appeared in the American Protestant press at the end of 1939, as a "persistent report" of a special region in Poland, near Lublin, where Jews were already being sent. This region, in fact, was made up of Treblinka and Majdanek, which had been first established as labor camps in 1939, but, as Dawidowicz pointed out, soon were to become annihilation camps.[63]

A Summary of What Was Known in 1939

The reporting of the persecution of the Jews for 1939 in the American Protestant press thus conformed to the events in Europe, events that were being determined in significant degree by Adolph Hitler and the Nazis. Kristallnacht and its aftermath focused world attention on the plight of the Jews. The attempt to negotiate a planned emigration of Jews from Germany in January and February of 1939 kept concern for the Jews in the forefront of the news. As Henry Feingold pointed out, these negotiations and their modified form in the amendments carried to Berlin by George Rublee and Robert Pell were an absurdity. Rublee and Pell were both Americans who represented the Intergovernmental Committee on Political Refugees, jointly headed by Rublee and Earl Winterton, an Englishman. This committee was formed as a result of the Evian Conference, but it was not successful in its attempts to negotiate a refugee plan with the Nazis.[64] The Intergovernmental Committee for Political Refugees, though it was a failure, was maintained at the insistence of President Roosevelt.[65]

The Quaker's plan, described with cautious optimism by Rufus M. Jones, failed. When J. Hoffman Cohn, writing in *The Brethren Evangelist*, said that the Evian Conference was also a failure, he was right. His judgment was expressed in March 1939, almost at the same time the negotiations were taking place.[66]

Within Germany itself, a brief respite for persecuted Jews came about because the spring and summer of 1939 was the period in which plans were being made by Hitler for the next phase of the Nazi program. Hitler was coordinating his plans for the invasion of Poland, Herman Goering was beginning his assigned task of implementing Hitler's Four-Year Plan preparing Germany for war, and Reinhard Heydrich was at work on the plans for the Final Solution of the "Jewish problem." The successful work of Adolph Eichmann in expelling Jews from Vienna became a model. Both Eichmann and his methods did not go unnoticed.[67] Those incidents of persecution of the Jews reported in the American Protestant press in Memel and Danzig fit into the general timetable of events as the fate of Lithuania and Poland was being determined by Hitler.

Reports of the persecution of the Jews in the already-occupied areas of Sudetanland and Austria were evidence of the continuing concern of Jews in a situation in which the German occupation and the Nazi terror were an established fact. Bohemia, Moravia, and Slovakia were the first names to appear, as Hitler's concept of *Lebensraum* began to become a reality. The fate of Jews in these newly occupied and Nazi-controlled areas would confirm again that, when the Nazis occupied a territory, the Jews suffered severe persecution beginning with loss of civil rights and ending with deportation, expulsion, and, ultimately, death.

Early in 1939, Rufus M. Jones had mentioned the planned transit camps in his report of negotiations for the emigration of large numbers of Jews, camps where Jews would be held prior to emigration. The editorial in *The Watchman-Examiner* at the end of 1939 reported the rumor of a different sort of camp for Jews in southeastern Poland, where Jews from Vienna and Bohemia-Moravia had been sent already in 1939. Neither Jones nor the editor of *The Watchman-Examiner* knew it, but they were describing, very early, an aspect of the Final Solution of the "Jewish Problem," the transportation of large numbers of Jews from Germany and Central Europe (and soon Eastern Europe) to concentration camps in southeastern Poland, which at first were designated labor camps but soon were to be turned into annihilation camps.[68]

The Jews of Europe, 1940–1942

The reporting of the persecution of the Jews in Europe, 1940–1942, followed the course of the war. World War II began on September 1, 1939, with the invasion of Poland. The next phase of World War II involved the invasion of Denmark and Norway in April 1940 and the invasion of Western Europe beginning on May 10, 1940. By June 22, 1940, this phase of World War II had concluded with the surrender of France. Ten countries were under the rule of Hitler and the Nazis: Germany, Austria, Czechoslovakia, Poland, Luxembourg, Belgium, Holland, Norway, Denmark, and France.[69] What had happened to the Jews in Germany, Austria, and Czechoslovakia was already known. What would happen to the Jews in the seven newly conquered countries of Europe would constitute the basis for the reporting of the persecution of the Jews in 1940, 1941, and 1942 in the American Protestant press.

In 1940, the reports of the persecution of the Jews began with Poland and ended with the countries in Western Europe—Belgium, Holland, and France. In an examination of thirty-three periodicals for 1940, two rather curious things became evident that had not been the case in the years prior to 1940. The first was that the most frequent and direct reporting of the persecution of the Jews was found in the conservative-evangelical-fundamentalist religious periodicals, more than in the more liberal and mainline Protestant press. The second was the marked increase in the number of advertisements paid for, again, by conservative-fundamentalist denominational and interdenominational Christian organizations doing missionary work among Jews. These paid advertisements reported "hard news" (that is, specific instances or conditions of persecution by country and city), rather than merely generalized accounts. Direct reporting of the persecution of Jews also appeared in the religious periodicals published by such missionary organizations. By and large, however, the general impression gained in a review of the American Protestant periodicals examined for 1940 is that they were overwhelmed or at least preoccupied with the coming of the war in Europe, with America's confused stance and response, and with the continuing problem of refugees and aid to refugees, rather than with what was happening to Jews and others under Nazi rule.

In an early issue of *The Brethren Missionary Herald* (a magazine published by those who had recently left the Brethren Church [Ashland, Ohio]), in an internal dispute over doctrinal differences and management policies, Louis S. Bauman (one of the editors) wrote an editorial, "Israel's Day of Sorrow." Actually, the editorial was based on a letter from Poland that had been sent to the Hebrew Christian Alliance of America, dated December 12, 1939.

> The misery of our Jewish people in Central Europe cannot be described. The bestial inhumanity that they suffer at the hands of the demoniacal persecutors cannot be put down on paper. It is unmentionable. Apart from wanton persecutions, they suffer from the ravages of war. Think of 450,000 in the city of Warsaw! Think of 3,000 Jews, brethren in Christ, according to the flesh—men, women and children wandering in fields and forests in the wintry dawns in Poland, dressed in rags and half-naked, sick, starving, desperate, half-crazed people. As one eye witness says, "The living envying those who are dead."

Bauman's comment? "And Poland is not the only place in which the Jews are suffering all the horrors of earthly hell these days." After a few other remarks he concluded, "We cannot help but believe that the hope of Israel cometh quickly! Come, Lion of the Tribe of Judah, come!"[70]

Transportation of Jews was reported in the same magazine in March 1940, in another editorial. Speaking of Jewish refugees and "countless thousands of destitute Jews along the German-Jewish [sic, Polish] border; . . . homeless, friendless . . . with nothing to eat . . . and no one in Poland or Germany caring whether they live or die; like hunted animals they seek shelter behind clusters of bushes and trees . . . and dream of the home they used to have." The editorial continued:

> Now comes the report of tens of thousands of Jews being forcibly ejected from their homes in Germany and hauled to an all but barren section of Poland. From London we learn that two thousand Jews are stranded in barges in the Danube River where they were stopped trying to escape from the terrors of Hitlers hate. Other thousands are reported trying to cross the mountains from the Balkan countries where Jewish hatred is
> · so fierce and unrelenting, hoping that they will succeed in slipping across the borders into Palestine under cover of night.[71]

Deportation, deprivation, migration—major and massive turmoil befell the Jews of Central Europe. Of the 3 million Jews in Poland, 1 million were beggars, said *The Brethren Missionary Herald*, reporting from the International News Service.[72]

"Germans Bring 'Jim Crow' Cars to Warsaw," announced headline over an editorial in *The Christian Century* in January 1940, describing forced segregation, with Germans in the front of streetcars, Poles and Jews in the rear, with hygiene and fear of epidemic cited as the official reason for this decision.[73] At a conference in Indiana, Conrad J. Hoffman, Jr., reported that, "if the 600,000 Jews still in Germany are pushed into Poland, . . . we are likely to witness a situation as bad as the Armenian massacres after the World War."[74]

By March 1940, conditions in Warsaw and all of Poland were being reported directly. Devere Allen, Western European correspondent to the *Century*, reported that organized bands of Hitler youths were being sent to Warsaw, "where the windowless houses, the humiliated Jews, the torn streets and the desolate scene" were pointed out as proof of Nazi strength and superiority. In the same report, he told of Jewish women who carried rags in their purses because they were subject to being forced to enter homes and scrub floors without warning and, when they had no rags, they had to use their coats. Fleeing Jews were harassed at border towns, forced to pay exorbitant exit fees, and not told in advance of such fees so that local refugee committees had to be formed to aid them. Occasionally, but very rarely, the Germans showed kindness. Allen cited two instances, one of a Christian family who entertained a fleeing Jew until his exit fee could be obtained and one of a "'Nazi' soldier who was seen to give 20 zlotys to a needy Jewish woman, and say to her quietly, 'All Germans are not swine' and then shout loudly at her to square himself with the orders of the day and his near-by fellow troopers, 'Get on with you, you Jewish pig!'"[75]

By April 1940, the Jewish population in Germany was reported by the *Century* to have dropped to 185,000, from 550,000 in 1933; in Austria to 66,000 from 180,000.[76]

News Reports and Conservative-Evangelical and Fundamentalist Response, 1940–1942

Organizations doing missionary work among Jews reported direct information about the persecution of the Jews in 1940 in their periodicals and by purchasing advertisements mainly in the conservative-evangelical and fundamentalist periodicals. *The Friend of Zion* carried a series of reports on Jews in Poland. Using the White Book of the World Jewish Congress as its source, it reported that a quarter of a million Jews had been exterminated in Poland.

It is said that German sources admit the Jewish death toll was 120,000. If the figure of the White Book is correct, the loss represents one of the major casualties in Jewish history, and ranks in horror with the destruction of Jerusalem, with the expulsion from Spain, the murders during the Crusades, the massacres of Chmielnitzni and the outrages in the Ukraine under Petlura.[77]

In a leading article in the March issue, a mission worker for *The Friend of Zion*, Elias Newman, wrote:

Seven million Jews, men, women and children of all ages; strong, weak, healthy and sick, in full flight, where flight is possible, but in most cases they are being driven by the merciless agents of states lacking the least consideration for the laws of God or the decencies of men.

In Nazi Germany thousands have been robbed of wealth and every human right, homes destroyed and synagogues burnt, humiliated, driven like cattle from place to place, or crowded into loathsome pesthouses called concentration camps, where violent death or suicide has abruptly ended the earthly pilgrimage of many.

In Poland the Jews . . . are being haunted by the thundering cannon, the whizzing aeroplane, the shrieking bombs or the persistent rattle of machine guns as they leave the pillaged cities, the devastated homes, the wasted roads, shell-torn streets, marshy fields, bogs and desolated forests: hunted, tortured, persecuted, disorganized, brutalized, terrorized abandoning land, stock, food, clothes, all the cords of home, loved ones, parents, and children, in the attempt to escape. . . .

After the last World War 3,000,000 Jews became beggars. Before this war ends 7,000,000 will be corpses.[78]

The same issue reported that only 185,000 Jews remained in Germany, half of them in Berlin and most of them reduced to poverty and charity in order to survive.[79]

In April, *The Friend of Zion* was reporting further restrictions on Jews in Germany in an article quoting from Oswald G. Villard, former editor of the *Nation*, who, on a tour in Europe, wrote for the London *Spectator* that

"the public is not being kept informed of the incredibly brutal and cruel tragedy which Hitler is inflicting on the Jews."

Mr. Villard says, "With practically no publication of the plan in the German newspapers, Adolph Hitler is going ahead with

the creation of a so-called Jewish State located in Poland, near
Nisko, on the San, southwest of Lublin. A stretch of land,
about 50 to 60 miles in area, has been set aside. It is enclosed
by a barbed-wire fence, and only Jews are to be allowed to live
therein. Into this small territory are to be crammed no fewer
than 1,945,000 Jews. . . .

"Whether it is poor or rich, this mass-migration by force has
been begun now, in the dead of winter, and in a manner that
cannot be interpreted as anything else than a determination to
create, not a Jewish State, but a most horrible concentration
camp, which can certainly become nothing else than a habita-
tion of death!"

The article then described the deportation process, with the Jews
being deported forced to carry only hand luggage, taking no more
than 300 marks, with all other possessions being confiscated "in the
usual custom of the men who declare that they belong to the purest
and noblest strain of humanity the world has yet seen." Villard stated
further that they "are simply dumped in and left to shift themselves."
Then he wrote:

"It is impossible to conceive of any more barbarous cruelty—
and it is deliberately calculated. Behind the barbed-wire fences
the Jews are to live or die in circumstances which would not be
permitted in any civilized country if the victims were dogs or
cattle."

Villard concluded his article by describing the Jews of Germany as
waiting for the knock on the door telling them to prepare for deportation to Poland "and what they consider certain death."[80]

The remarks of Dr. Nahum Goldmann, chairman of the World Jewish Congress, in a speech in Los Angeles were reported in *The Friend
of Zion.*

"Of the more than 9,000,000 Jews in Europe less than 1,000,000
are still living normal lives."

He described the Jews under Nazi rule as "living in a big
concentration camp. . . .

"The full story of the tragedy of Poland has not yet been
learned," he said, "because Poland has been hermetically
sealed to foreign observers. Only after the war is over will the
truth be known.

"Day after day, thousands of Jews are being massacred
there, and tens of thousands more are sent out of the commu-

nities into the wilderness to begin life anew where now there is nothing but desolation.

"And through the streets of Polish cities run thousands of hungry Jewish children looking for their parents from whom they have been separated."

Dr. Goldmann predicted that if conditions continue as they have half of Poland's 2,000,000 Jews will be exterminated within a year.[81]

The Hebrew Christian Alliance Quarterly for the spring and summer of 1940 reported persecution of the Jews in Poland also, but with much less specific information. The Lutheran Companion reported the ghettoization of Jews in Warsaw, citing the creation of the Warsaw ghetto as ostensibly for health reasons. The brief statement then went on, "However that may be, the fact remains that, more cruelly than by masonry, the Jews have been walled about, and walled out in Europe."[82]

Three conservative-evangelical and fundamentalist publications, in articles and by accepting paid advertising, also reported as specifically as had The Friend of Zion about what had been happening to Jews in Europe since 1940. In The King's Business and The Sunday School Times, Louis S. Bauman published a series of articles, characteristically prophetic, dispensational, and premillenial in emphasis but in which he reported specific acts of the persecution of Jews. In January 1940, he mentioned denial to the remaining Jews in Germany of clothing and wool to mend old clothes.

Remember that the expression, "Jews in Germany," now means not only those in the Germany of a year ago, but the millions that a year ago were in Austria, Czechoslovakia, and Poland. The slow tortured-to-death methods now being used by the Nazi government may not seem so bloody, but are infinitely more cruel than the quick death by the sword. Antiochus Epiphanes was far more kind than Adolph Hitler.[83]

In all, during a two-year period (1939–1940), Bauman wrote twenty-one articles for The Sunday School Times under the general title, "Light from Bible Prophecy on the European War and Its Results." In the February 3, 1940, issue of The Sunday School Times, the editor fully endorsed the articles and viewpoints of Bauman, apparently in response to criticism of the premillenial and dispensational interpretation of the war and Bauman's interpretation of the "signs" of the Second Coming of Christ in relation to events. At the completion of the series, the editor again included a statement of endorsement and support.[84]

As for references to the persecution of the Jews, Bauman's articles in February, June, July, and August contained statements about Poland, Finland, Holland, Norway, and Belgium; about "Jewphobia," the Jews as scapegoats, the sterilizing of Jews, their extermination, the "hate of Jews"; and about Hitler, Goering, and Goebbels, described as "three rabid Jew-baiters."[85] Two brief editorials on the prophetic interpretation of the persecution of the Jews and an article by Joseph Taylor Britan, "Continued Persecution of the Jews in Europe," were also published in *The Sunday School Times* in 1940. In the latter article, Britan mentioned the persecution of the Jews in Poland, Germany, Czechoslovakia, Austria, Slovakia, Bulgaria, and Rumania. He also told of the concentration of Jews near Lublin, of individual deaths of Jews in the camps by shooting, and of other brutalities against individual Jews.[86]

By June 1940, Holland, Belgium, and France were the countries in which the persecution of the Jews was being described.

> News filtering out of the military screen now surrounding Holland and Belgium indicates that native Jews in those countries and the large number of refugees, some of them in transit, will receive no better treatment than in Germany or Poland. It is reported that the Lublin (Poland)—ghetto plan is to be installed near Amsterdam and 160,000 Jews are to be moved there. Jews are also being seized for forced labor in cleaning up the wreckage wrought by Nazi bombers.[87]

Still reactions were mixed. *The Brethren Missionary Herald* for October 26, 1940, reprinted a number of items regarding the persecution of the Jews in Europe from *The B'nai B'rith Messenger*. Six items were selected, in which Rumania, Spain, Italy, Berlin, France (unoccupied), and Palestine were mentioned, all citing persecution. The lead line of the editorial, however, is disturbing. "The treatment of the Jewish race upon the earth today does not just happen. It is in the plan and purpose of God." Scripture was then quoted, passage by passage, to sustain this point of view that God was using Hitler to punish the Jews because of their unbelief.[88]

The Churchman published an article on France by a writer identified as an editor for the Inter-Continental Press. He reported that the institution of racial laws in France was imperiling native French Jews and Jewish refugees who had fled to France. "This state of affairs is approved by Hitler, and furthered by his agents, the Gestapo. 'Gentle Heinrich' Himler [sic] is working very hard in the little building on the Avenue Foch, Paris, cooperating with Chiappe, the traitor."[89]

Douglas V. Steere wrote a long article about his trip to Portugal, Italy, Spain, unoccupied France, Geneva, and Zurich in *The Friend*. He was representing the American Friends' Service Committee. The article is valuable largely because it described the immense dislocations caused by the German occupation of most of Western Europe, referring to Jews specifically as refugees in Switzerland.[90]

November 28, 1940, saw the publication in *The Friend* of a telegram sent to the offices of the World Council of Churches in New York City. It had been sent by Karl Barth, Emil Brunner, and Alphons Koechlin, distinguished European theologians.

DESPERATE MISERY NON ARYAN REFUGEES FROM BELGIUM BADEN PALITINATE ETC. DEPORTED TO CAMP DE GURS PYRENEES IMPERIOUSLY CALLS OUR COMMON HELP STOP FINANCIAL HELP MEANS GREAT RELIEF STOP OUR EFFORTS INSUFFICIENT PIECE [sic] APPEAL STRONGLY TO CHURCHES AND CHRISTIANS FOR IMMEDIATE SUPPORT.

Gurs was the largest concentration-refugee camp in France. It was filled with Jews and others and was under the Vichy government. The conditions at Gurs were and remained terrible throughout World War II.[91]

The Jews in Occupied Europe, 1941

The American Protestant press reported the increasingly precarious position of Jews in all Nazi-occupied countries in 1941 but seemed to concentrate somewhat on Holland, Belgium, and France. The awareness that the Nazi persecution of the Jews was virtually a Europewide phenomenon was frequently noted. *The Alliance Weekly* wrote, "Steadily throughout Europe the conditions of the Jews grows worse. In each subject country, there is gradually being put into force the restrictions that have prevailed in Germany." France, Holland, and Denmark were especially mentioned. Particularly noted was the fact that both native Jews and refugee Jews were equally restricted by the laws and decrees.[92] In a later issue, the editors suggested that the pressures of the war had worked to the advantage of Jews; this also had been noted in the *Contemporary Jewish Record*. Less persecution took place in the winter and spring of 1941, at least according to this editorial report.[93]

Several Protestant periodicals reported the heroic action of Henri Bergson, the distinguished philosopher and Nobel Prize winner, who as the final act of a distinguished career resigned from his honorary professorship in the College of France, even though he had been offered an exemption. He chose to obey the law forbidding Jews to hold educational posts, one of many laws restricting Jews passed in France as a Nazi-occupied country.[94] *The Baptist and Reflector*, reprinting a few paragraphs from the *Western Recorder*, stated that, when the Nazis entered Paris "to begin their dread work, over 300 Jews committed suicide in twenty-four hours." The opening sentences of the paragraphs were "Nazism is out to exterminate the Jews. Untold horrors have overtaken multitudes of Jews in European countries."[95]

Slowly but persistently the news of the relocation of large numbers of Jews came out of Europe. In the same issue of *The Churchman* that reported a seeming moderation in the persecution of the Jews in Germany and a marked sympathy toward the Jews by some German citizens, it was also reported that Jews in Germany were living in unheated houses, had no telephones or radios, and were subject to severe food rationing restrictions; it reported that trainloads of Jews (some of which were turned back) had been sent to Poland and that Jews in large numbers were being sent to France. The deteriorating situation for Jews in Lodz was also mentioned.[96] In describing the work of a French Protestant pastor in the camp at Gurs in southern France, the report mentioned observing the unloading of a truckload of elderly women, identified as non-Aryan Christians, from homes for the aged in Germany. They had come from Mannheim and had traveled for two days. Two of the women were over 100 years of age, several of the women had died during the trip, and they had been afraid because they thought they were being sent to Lublin in Poland. "They were wonderfully relieved when they learned that it was to France that they were going."[97] A small point, but a significant one. These non-Aryan Christian women—residents of homes for the aged, senile, and the incurably ill—knew about Lublin and what it meant for Jews to be transported to that region of Poland. This happened in the winter of 1941.

Jews in Poland, Rumania, and Eastern Europe, 1941

The Friend of Zion, continuing to monitor and report from as many reliable sources as possible, reported that *The Jewish Missionary Magazine* told of the continuing annihilation of Jews in Poland.

> The constant massacre, which seems to be the Nazi boast, according to their Press, is accounting for 200 Jews per day. In addition to deaths by starvation, exhaustion from forced labor in stone quarries, the homeless roaming in fields are perishing by their [sic] thousands. Deaths from epidemics and disease are enormous. It is said by an observer who toured Nazi occupied Polish territory, that unless a miracle happens, the whole of Polish Jewry in this area, estimated at two and a half million, will be annihilated in a short time.[98]

By June 1941, *The Friend of Zion* was reporting that Julius Streicher was going to Denmark to supervise the anti-Jewish campaign; that Hans Frank (governor-general of Nazi-occupied Poland) was issuing new food-rationing cards that were to be given only to those working on labor gangs and that those without the new cards in all occupied countries were to be put in slave-labor camps; that the 400,000 Jews in Yugoslavia and Greece were then threatened by the Nazi blitzkrieg in those countries; and that 400,000 Belgian Jews were to be transported from Antwerp, with Ostend to come next; and that 125,000 Jews from Paris and 175,000 Jews from France outside of Paris were also to be transported. It also published the following:

> Oppressive anti-Jewish measures increased during the month of March. In the Reich, Jews between the ages of 18 and 65 were being herded into forced labor camps. . . . From Nazi-ruled France came the announcement [that] the government was beginning to enforce Nuremberg decrees, while from Slovakia, cables revealed confiscation of 1,800 business establishments. From Poland, Holland, Austria, Bulgaria, and Norway, mass expulsions and deportations of Jews were announced. In Holland twelve Jews last month paid with their lives and twenty-four were wounded in riots between Nazis and anti-Nazis. In Poland, Hitlerite rulers avenged a mass escape from a Polish prison by executing one hundred Jews whom they had held as hostages. In Paris, Nazi vandals demolished tombstone of the great Heinrich Heine. (OPINION, April, 1941).[99]

The news sources used by *The Friend of Zion* were identified as mainly Swedish, thus establishing Sweden and Geneva and, to some extent,

Lisbon, Portugal, as the primary sources for news from occupied Europe, particularly news about Jews.

The news in the second half of 1941 expanded the concern for European Jews after Germany attacked Russia on June 22, 1941. Jews in Eastern Europe were then, more than ever, in peril for their lives. What they did not know was that the planned annihilation of the Jews had proceeded to the point that trained death squads were accompanying the German troops as they advanced eastward into Russia. These death squads (*Einsatzgruppen*), four units of 3,000 men each, had been specifically ordered to kill Jews under a directive issued by Fieldmarshal Keitel on March 13, 1941. Members of these death squads were not soldiers of the Wehrmacht, or regular troops, but loyal, committed members of the National Socialist party, who had been totally indoctrinated about the necessity of eliminating the "Jew-Bolsheviks." Their operation was directly under the command of Reinhard Heydrich. As described by Otto Ohlendorf at the Nuremberg trials, Jews were to be called together by their elders in each towns and village "for the purpose of resettlement." Instead, they were robbed of their valuables and marched to places of execution, usually two to three miles outside of the town or village, where a ditch had been dug, and there they were ordered to undress. "Then they were shot, kneeling or standing, and the corpses thrown into the ditch."[100]

By December 1941, *The Friend of Zion* had included a report about the planned extermination of Rumanian Jews announced by Premier Antonescu and continued reports of deaths in the concentration camps in Poland (still being attributed mainly to starvation and disease) and deaths in the Warsaw ghetto at an increasing rate (with unburied corpses left lying in the streets because there were so many that the collecting of them was a nearly impossible task). And it published this report:

> The Jewish Telegraphic Agency which is not given to atrocity stories, reports from "a German frontier" that tens of thousands of Soviet Jews are now being held "practically foodless" in barbed-wire concentration camps established by the Nazis under the open sky in occupied Russian territory where the houses of the victims have been wiped out by Russian and German artillery fire. Jews: men, women, children, exposed to the elements, and dying in veritable droves. Open-air camps for Jews in Minsk, Chernichov, Uman, Revel, Riga and other Nazi-occupied cities, are crowded with suffering victims. From

Bratislava comes the report likewise through the Jewish Telegraph Agency, that the mass expulsion of 10,000 Jews into so-
called Jewish centers has begun. Slovak authorities estimate
that by the end of the year Bratislava will have been "purged"
of at least 70 percent of its Jewish population. The remainder
will be shunted into a ghetto.[101]

In the fall of the year, *The Hebrew Christian Alliance Quarterly* was
also reporting deportations of Jews from Rumania, Hungary, Tran-
sylvania, and Russia and from within Poland. Most ominous, however, though it seems not yet to have been fully comprehended, was
the following:

> In view of the "hostile attitude of international Jewry," says the
> German Press, Germany has decided to take measures for a
> radical solution of the Jewish question in all conquered coun-
> tries, and possibly in Allied countries also. This is understood
> to mean that ghettoes will be instituted in all countries under
> German control or influence.[102]

Ghettoes, indeed. If only this had been true, but the "radical solution
of the Jewish question" announced in the German press was far more
radical than anyone seems to have guessed or imagined, though the
evidence seems already to have been available and to some extent
known. The shape of the Final Solution of the "Jewish problem" was
evident in 1941. What could have been added in 1942?

The Final Solution of the "Jewish Question,"
Wannsee, 1942

The United States was itself at war with Germany and Japan and the
Axis powers in 1942. This placed the nation on a war footing, both in
terms of men and matériel, and in terms of the reporting of events.
Neutrality, even a belligerent neutrality, was no longer a factor. The
Protestant churches and denominations had to be mobilized, and the
nation's production and distribution systems had to be regeared toward the total war effort.

But the American Protestant press did not lose sight of the persecuted Jews and the conditions faced by Jews under the Nazis. Without being aware of what they were reporting, they were in fact telling
the story of the last phase of the Final Solution, that is, the death
camps. This was being done in a context of conflict, however, for as

the news of the death factories began to be reported in the latter part of 1942, so was caution about "more atrocity stories" like those from World War I voiced, particularly about the more terrible details about the camps, which were not fully confirmed until the end of the war.

An almost classic example of this conflict appeared in an editorial in *The Christian Century* of December 9, 1942. At the time, editor Charles Clayton Morrison either refused to believe or discounted what he was discussing. His approach to reporting even the factual material was tentative.

> Beyond doubt, horrible things are happening to the Jews in Poland. It is even probable that the Nazis are herding all the Jews of Europe, so far as they can capture them, into Poland with the deliberate intention of exterminating them there. A responsible official of the Nazi foreign office once told an editor of this paper that Hitler's policy called for the "humane extermination" of the Jews. He was speaking in perfect English, and knew exactly what he was saying. There is probably little humaneness about what is going on in Poland, but plenty of extermination. The Nazis are loading upon themselves in that country a weight of guilt for which Christian Germany will, we hope, one day hold them to account. We question, however, whether any good purpose is served by the publication of such charges as Dr. Stephen S. Wise gave to the press last week. In the first place, although Rabbi Wise went out of his way to place the responsibility for his charges on the state department, that branch of the government has conspicuously refrained from issuing any confirmation. In the second place Dr. Wise's figures on the numbers of Jews killed differ radically from those given out on the same day by the Polish government in exile. Whereas Dr. Wise says that Hitler has ordered all Jews in Nazi-ruled Europe killed by the end of this year, the exiled Polish government claims only that the orders have been issued for the extermination of half the Jews of Poland by the end of this year and that 250,000 had been killed up to the end of September. In the third place, Dr. Strasburger, whose "underground" figures are used to support Rabbi Wise's charges is the same Polish leader who is campaigning in this country for the complete destruction of Germany. And in the fourth place, Dr. Wise's allegation that Hitler is paying $20 each for Jewish corpses to be "processed into soap fats and fertilizer" is unpleasantly reminiscent of the "cadaver factory" lie which was one of the propaganda triumphs of the First World War.[103]

In retrospect, whether Rabbi Wise's figures were exact or not or whether Dr. Strasburger's agitation was an irritant or not were almost meaningless. What was important is that the editor of the *Century* bore reluctant witness to the mass murders of Jews in Poland, as a planned and official action of the Nazi government of Germany. He also bore reluctant, even skeptical witness to what has since become an established fact, that soap and fertilizer were manufactured from the bodies of Jews killed in the death camps. That such a possibility existed, even as an unsubstantiated rumor, in December of 1942 is astonishing. The churches in the United States were thought not to know much about such things prior to the discovery of the death camps at the end of World War II. Such was not the case. Here, tentative as it was, is recorded the evidence of the mass extermination of Jews and of the horrible ends to which modern technology was being put.

By December 30, 1942, even Charles Clayton Morrison had become convinced. In the lead editorial of the *Century* for that date, he reported that a joint declaration by eleven governments, the Allied nations, had been released on December 17, 1942. In the declaration, the "essential facts" concerning the mass murders of the Jews in Poland were established as true, "though without other statistical estimates than that 'the number of victims of these bloody cruelties is reckoned in many hundreds of thousands.'" Morrison wrote that the statement served two purposes, to express the horror and revulsion of the conscience of the world and to enter the facts into the record so that the perpetrators of those crimes could be settled with later. He then stated that the primary effort should be put into winning the war so "that this gigantic crime can be stopped and the criminals punished." No longer was he tentative or equivocal. The facts were known, authenticated by an official statement having the sanction of all the Allied nations. He wrote, "Extermination of a race has seldom, if ever, been so systematically practiced on a grand scale as in the present mass murder of Polish Jews by the Nazi power." The essential, central fact of the Holocaust was stated, there had been an extermination of a race or a people, the Jews.[104]

Other evidence was being reported in 1942, though not so directly as in the editorials of the *Century* in December. Persecution of the Jews in Europe and, in particular, deportation of Jews into Poland was noted. *The Christian Century*, in January of 1942, in noting the protest statement of Prof. Emil Brunner on anti-Semitism prepared for Swiss Protestants, mentioned the deportation of Jews.[105] In May, the *Century* noted that Rosenberg had spoken of the Nazi sterilization program "in the interests of race selection and social hygiene" in an editorial in a German newspaper.[106] By September, the *Century* was writing editorials about the deportation of French Jews and about the protest from within France, both occupied and unoccupied, to this action, which was described as revolting and fiendish, and it was speaking of the Jews being sent to Poland and Germany as "doomed victims."[107] By October, it was Dutch Jews whose deportation brought protests from Dutch Catholic and Protestant church leaders.

"In reality, the policy of deportation has already been in effect for some time, and thousands of Jews have been rounded up and shipped out of the country—generally on midnight trains to avoid popular demonstrations, says the Basle *National Zeitung*—to concentration camps in Germany pending distribution for permanent settlement in the worst places that can be found for them."[108]

The Churchman, in an editorial in October 1942, wrote of the protest of the Roman Catholic leaders in France made to Pierre Laval over deportation of French Jews and of Laval's published rejection of their protest.[109] In the same issue, an article was published that cited the persecution of Jews in Belgium, Poland, Czechoslovakia, and Bohemia-Moravia and cited *The Black Book of Poland*, published by the Polish Information Center in New York City, as a source of information.

It is the story of Nazi atrocity in Poland based on maps, eye-witness accounts, pictures and official papers. . . . The material in this book is crude, something like raw material, but if you look into it I think you will find something on every page to give you the shudders—persecution, murders, mass slaughters, tortures of prisoners, brutal treatment of women.
These atrocities in Poland are the work of hate which is the driving force of Nazism.[110]

Several periodicals published the report by Samuel McCrea Cavert, general secretary of the Federal Council of Churches, who had traveled in France, Switzerland, Spain, and Portugal for six weeks during the late summer and fall of 1942. Cavert wrote specifically about the deportation of French Jews.

According to the reports of eye-witnesses the Jews were herded into box-cars like cattle, about thirty to a car, with no equipment for the journey of a fortnight except a bit of straw on the floor and an iron pail for toilet purposes. The destination, though unannounced, was presumably the Jewish reservation in Nazi-occupied Poland where they would be put at forced labor. Included in the group were some Christians, both Protestant and Catholic. Their future existence will almost certainly be a process of slow death from exhaustion and semi-starvation—unless actual extermination comes sooner.

Cavert's figures included 10,000 to 15,000 who had been deported, but he also mentioned that 5,000 children, presumably the children of those deported, had been left behind.[111]

The Gospel Messenger summarized an article from the London *Daily Telegraph*, which in turn was a summary of a 10,000-word statement by the Inter-Allied Information Center. The subject was religious persecution. The situation in ten European countries and China was described. The persecution, deportation, and shooting of Jews and the use of Jews as hostages in Poland, France, and the Netherlands, in particular, were mentioned.[112] Later news notes in the same periodical mentioned the deportation of French Jewish children, the mass arrests of Jews, and the persecution of Jews in Greece and Norway.

The Signs of the Times, saying that it felt free to discuss only a fragment of the "terrible record," told of the experience of William Bayles, a war correspondent in Europe. Bayles told of Poles shot, Czech families executed, French hostages shot. He told of friends in Prague who would not meet with him or talk to him, of the silence of the people in Bromberg, Poland, and in Vienna and Amsterdam. "'Europe stinks with hate and fear,' a Dutch professor remarked to me. 'He was right.'"[113] *The Watchman-Examiner*, in January, published an editorial on the plight of Europe's Jews. It mentioned the concentrating of Jews in eastern Poland and the deplorable conditions there, the shooting of Jewish hostages in France and the terror of Jews in Holland, and then it said, "Firing squads eliminating Jews are the daily order in certain Balkan countries."[114] The *Einsatzgruppen*? In October, as a news item, the same magazine reported that

the British section of the World Jewish Congress reports that more than 1,000,000 Jews have been killed or died as the result of ill treatment in countries dominated by the Nazis. No one knows how many people of other faiths, or how many Norwegians, Danes, Belgians, Frenchmen, Netherlanders, Poles, Czechs, Serbs, and Greeks have perished.[115]

Paid Advertisements, 1940–1942

Paid advertisements were placed in *The King's Business, Moody Monthly, The Presbyterian, The Sunday School Times,* and *The Watchman-Examiner* in 1940. The sponsors were the American Committee for Christian Refugees, the Friends of Israel Refugee Relief Committee, the Million Testament Campaigns, and the International Hebrew Christian Alliance. The headlines of the full-page ads read, typically, "It's Suicide or Christ"; "These Are Christian Victims of Nazism, and Being Sorry Is Not Enough"; "Jewry's Darkest Hour"; "The Agony of Israel in War-Torn Lands: A Report of the Appalling Sufferings of Jews and Jewish Christians"; "Refugees Seek Haven in Stricken England"; "Highways for Christ, Jews of Europe Are Starving to Death" and "The Jew—A Christian Test"; "The Tragedy of Israel"; and "A Christmas Appeal on Behalf of Hebrew Christians." The ads appealed for funds to aid Jews and Jewish converts to Christianity. Some concentrated only on describing the needs for funds to aid refugees in England, Scotland, and Palestine; others referred directly to persecution throughout Europe.

The paid advertisements of the International Hebrew Christian Alliance regularly contained the most specific references to the persecution of the Jews and of Jewish converts to Christianity, listing countries and referring to concentration camps, individual persecutions, and conditions in specific cities. In November 1940, for instance, the full-page ad in *The King's Business* contained phrases about "unparalleled suffering," "harrowing tales of Jewish mothers whose husbands had been murdered and whose sons have been tortured in concentration camps," and the "terror of the Gestapo by day and by night." Increasingly, in headings and in content, these ads became more explicit in describing conditions under the Nazis.[116] By November 1941, the paid advertisements were reporting disease and death, famine and starvation in the ghettos of Poland; hunger among French Jews in Paris; and the killing of 8,000 Jews in Rumania. "In Sarajevo Nazis murdered Jews in labor camps, charging they worked 'too slowly.'"[117]

The paid advertisement of the Friends of Israel Refugee Relief Committee in *The Presbyterian* for December 11, 1941, read, in part:

FOR NINE MILLION JEWS LIFE APPEARS HOPELESS. . . .
LIFE FOR THE JEW IS IMPOSSIBLE under the NAZI regime.
Thousands of Jews are in Concentration Camps dying inch by inch. One Hundred Thousand Committed Suicide. Over

200,000 Have Been Murdered or Died.
THE TRAGEDY OF HEBREW CHRISTIANS IN POLAND.[118]

In 1942, the paid advertisements of the International Hebrew Christian Alliance, the American Board of Missions to the Jews, and the Friends of Israel Refugee Relief Committee repeated the details of Jewish suffering as they sought to raise funds to do what they could to relieve the suffering of Jews and Jewish Christians in Europe.

The Friend of Zion gave the same details of massacres and killings of Jews, deportations, and the Nazi plan for a "Jew-free" Europe by the end of 1942 in a column, "Jewish World News." Deaths by starvation and disease in the ghettos of Poland were reported, as were massacres by shooting such as that in Kiev, where 52,000 Jews reportedly were shot. In the September issue, the story of a Jewish refugee woman who had managed to escape from Kaluszyn, Poland, to Warsaw and then to Palestine was told. The 2,000 Jews of Kaluszyn were driven out of the town at night. The women and children were allowed to return to their homes, but the next morning the bodies of the men were found on the roads surrounding the town.[119] By November of 1942, The Friend of Zion, quoting from the Sentinel, was saying that no one really knew how many of Europe's 6 million Jews under Nazi domination were dead, having been shot, hanged, buried alive, or beaten to death in Poland, Russia, and the Balkans.

Whether articles or paid advertisements, the specter of "more atrocity stories" hung over these reports. In an effort to establish the credibility of the reports, Dr. J. H. Rushbrooke (president of the Baptist World Alliance) wrote a letter to Dr. J. H. Hertz (chief rabbi of England). In effect, Rushbrooke was asking for information while at the same time expressing the sympathy and concern of Baptists for the persecuted Jews. A part of the reply by Rabbi Hertz was published, with Rushbrooke's letter, by The Watchman-Examiner in December 1942. Hertz wrote:

Destruction, total and irretrievable, is overhanging Israel in Europe. A sentence of death has been pronounced upon the entire Jewish population on the Continent, and—by machine gun and poison chamber, by torture and famine—millions of my brethren have already fallen victims to the Nazi fury. In such a time, when multitudes of my brethren are daily consigned to slaughter, the sympathy and prayers of our countrymen strengthen our faith in humanity, and cause us hopefully to look forward to the victorious peace.[120]

Who in America Knew?

Who in America knew about the Final Solution? The reports in the American Protestant press clearly establish that, as early as 1939 and through the subsequent three years until the end of 1942, the record of the Final Solution for the "Jewish question" was being written for the readers of that press. To be sure, the editors, writers, and composers of copy for the paid advertisements did not have a full understanding of what they were reporting. They did not know that a formal set of directives and orders had been issued that were, in fact, designed to eliminate all Jews by annihilation in Nazi-occupied Europe. They did not know of the dedication of Heydrich, Himmler, Eichmann, Hans Frank, and the Nazi bureaucracy as they set about to accomplish the task of exterminating the Jews. They did know that Hitler, Goering, Goebbels, Himmler, and members of the Nazi party hated Jews, that nothing was done by the Nazis to halt the extermination of the Jews, and that one of the first actions of the Nazis upon their conquest of a country was to initiate the persecution of Jews, establish the Nuremberg decrees as law, and soon after begin to deport Jews to Germany and Poland.

The American Protestant press from 1939 through 1942 did report the establishment of a "Jewish reservation" in eastern Poland, concentration camps in Poland, Holland, and France, and labor camps in Germany and Poland. The press also reported the ghettoization of Jews in Poland and the Baltic countries and the subsequent planned deprivation of the Jews in these ghettos, leading to death by disease and starvation.

As the Nazis attacked Russia, moving eastward through the Balkan countries, the Protestant press did report the mass killings of Jews by firing squads and mobile killing units (*Einsatzgruppen*) and the massacre of Jews in towns, cities, and villages in Eastern Europe. They also reported the untold desperation of the Jews who were forced to flee for their lives and who were wandering throughout Poland and Eastern Europe, homeless, unwelcome, and dying. In 1941 and 1942, the press was reporting the deportation of Jews numbering in the thousands from Belgium, Holland, and France, Jews being transported to German and Poland. As the elderly women who rejoiced at finding themselves in France knew, being transported to the east meant death.

American Protestants knew. They gave money, offered prayers, wrote words of sympathy, and passed resolutions condemning Hitler, the Nazis, and anti-Semitism of the extreme form practiced by the Nazis. But, even in knowing, Protestant Christians in America did not seem to understand or grasp fully the enormity of the crime being committed against the Jews and those designated as "enemies of the Reich," those judged to be racially or medically inferior, to use the Nazi nomenclature. But the cumulative evidence had been written. Deportation, labor camps, hostages, Nuremberg decrees, sterilization, disease. Food cards and work permits, the lack of which meant deportation, destitution, hunger, massacre, extermination, mass murder, and finally "poison chambers." American Protestant Christians knew!

CHAPTER 5

1943–1944—Ear to Destruction: What Was Known, What Was Heard

Prominent guests from Berlin were present at the inauguration of the first crematorium in March, 1943. The "program" consisted of the gassing and burning of 8,000 Cracow Jews. The guests, both officers and civilians, were extremely satisfied with the results and the special peephole fitted into the door of the gas chamber was in constant use. They were lavish in their praise of the newly erected installation.

"Auschwitz Observed: Report of
Two Escaped Eyewitnesses"
In Lucy S. Dawidowicz, A Holocaust Reader

KEY EVENTS

1943, General: January–May, victory of Allies in North Africa; February 2, Russia took offensive against German army; July 9–10, invasion of Sicily; July 19, Rome bombed; July 25, Mussolini replaced; September 3, Italy invaded; September 8, Italy surrenders; September 10, Germans occupied Rome; November 6, Kiev recaptured; November 28–December 1, Teheran meeting of Roosevelt, Stalin, and Churchill.

1943, Relating to the Jews: January 18, resistance in Warsaw ghetto begun; January 20–26, deportations from Theresienstadt to Auschwitz; February 5–12, Bialystok Jews "resettled"; February 27, Berlin Jews (armaments workers) deported to Auschwitz; March–May, Jews from Croatia, Salonika, Thrace, Macedonia deported, Jews from Holland, Vienna, Luxembourg, Prague deported to Treblinka; May 9, Berlin *Judenrein* ("Jew free"); April 19–May 16, Warsaw ghetto liquidated; August 19–27, Bialystok ghetto liquidated; September 11–14,

Minsk and Lida ghettos liquidated, "family transports" from Theresienstadt to Auschwitz; September 23, Vilna ghetto liquidated; October 18, Rome Jews to Auschwitz; November 3, Riga ghetto liquidated; fall 1943, beginning of dismantling of death camps (Treblinka, Sobibor, Belzec).

1944, General: January 22, Allied landing at Anzio; January–May, Russians advanced into eastern Poland; April, Black Sea ports retaken by Russians; June, Russian summer offensive launched; June 4, Rome captured by Allies; June 6, D day, Normandy invasion; July 20, ill-fated attempt on Hitler's life; August 25, Allies liberate Paris; September 3, Brussels liberated; September 14, Allies at German border; December 16, Battle of the Bulge opened, Russians in central Poland.

1944, Relating to the Jews: April 14, Athens Jews to Auschwitz; May 15–June 27, Hungarian Jews transported to Auschwitz; July 24, Majdanek-Lublin death camp captured by Russians; August, Lodz Jews liquidated; September–October, Slovakian and Theresienstadt transports to Auschwitz; fall 1944, Auschwitz then the only death camp still in operation; November, crematoria at Auschwitz dismantled by order of Himmler.

When the United States entered World War II, the American Protestant press represented by its periodicals and denominational publications "went to war," also. This did not mean that all of the editors and writers of these periodicals fully supported the war effort or that the peace movements and the traditionally pacifist churches ceased to voice their concerns and opposition to war; it did mean that the concerns of the war (including limitations on supplies of paper for publishing; restrictions on travel; mobilization of men and matériel; war-accelerated work schedules; limitations on national conferences, conventions, and denominational meetings; provision of manpower for the military chaplaincy, which resulted in the depletion of the number of clergymen available for work in local churches and denominational leadership; and accommodations to a wartime economy and to the exigencies of war) had a direct and immediate effect on Protestant periodicals.

For members of the traditionally pacifist churches—the Quakers, the Mennonites, the Brethren, and some of the Methodists and members of the other mainline denominations sincerely devoted to peace, or at least committed to noncombatant alternatives—the problems

involved in conscientious objection, alternative service, draft eva-
sion, and the organization and maintenance of the CPS camps (Civilian Public Service) were of primary concern. Counseling and direct-
ing young men to forms of alternative service were the major
concerns of the pacifist groups. Reported in the peace church periodicals were constant appeals for financial assistance, reports of efforts to resolve disagreements with the federal government over
problems in the CPS program, letters from young men in the CPS
camps (describing their work and asking for books, games, et cetera,
for their free-time use), and frequent expressions of concern over the
relative uselessness of CPS work and of the boredom of the camp
environment. Along with the traditional, respected commitment to
aid for refugees and the concern for refugee workers of the American
Friends' Service Committee and the Mennonite relief agencies still in
Europe and often in concentration camps, the CPS reports and the
refugee-related items and the occasional reports on the progress of
the war constituted the involvement of the peace denominations in
the war years. Apart from war-related items and discussions of the
peace movement and its problems during wartime, as with most
other Protestant periodicals, the major effort of these periodicals was
concentrated on carrying on as normally as possible, given the prevailing conditions.

The Protestant Press and War-Related Reporting

Most of the denominational and nondenominational Protestant press
simply added war news and war-related activities to their regular
publishing task. Letters from servicemen and women were published. Items from local churches of a war-related nature, such as
efforts to accommodate military populations in communities near
major military bases, were reported. Special programs and ministries
for service personnel and war-factory personnel were also reported.
Most denominational periodicals began to report regularly news both
from and about the members of the clergy serving as military chaplains. As the war progressed, this often meant reporting the wound-
ing or death of a military chaplain or the capture of a chaplain who
then became a prisoner of war.

Two domestic items were of concern to some Protestant press writers and editors. Early in the war, the concentration of Japanese Americans into camps by the federal government was opposed by most
Protestant writers and editors who spoke or wrote about the problem

at all. And with the opposition came a genuine concern over ministering to the Japanese Americans who were in these camps and over assisting them in any way possible. A great deal of discussion about the wisdom and justice of the internments took place in the Protestant press, and, when most of the Japanese Americans had been released from these camps, calls for full restitution of status and property to them were voiced in the press.

The second matter of concern became the presence of, and ministry to, German prisoners of war confined in prisoner-of-war camps in various parts of the United States. Reports of the use of pastors from communities near these camps for conducting religious services appeared from time to time, often involving clergymen who could speak German or Italian. The benefits and limitations of such involvement were usually described rather completely, as were the reactions of the prisoners who participated. In some instances, prisoners of war were permitted to attend religious services in churches close to their camps; this was almost always reported as being of mutual benefit to the prisoners and to the congregations visited. Such attendance usually came about only after a relationship between the local minister and the chaplain or officers in charge of the prisoner-of-war camp and a regular congregation of prisoners of war had been established.

In a variety of ways (through news notes, editorials, articles, and letters from chaplains and service personnel), the progress of the war itself was reported. At this point, one of the wartime limitations of the Protestant press must be noted. The printing and publishing deadlines of these periodicals were such that current reporting of war news had to be limited. As the Allied Forces assumed more dominance in taking control of the prosecution of the war from 1942 on, things happened so quickly that the Protestant press, by and large, did not try to maintain an extensive, current war-news reporting apparatus. This press was not the place to go for day-to-day war news. This task, apparently, was left largely to the secular press and the broadcast media. Much of the war-related publishing, then, was of a different nature. Commentary and stories on human interest, bravery, and tragedy were more commonly the themes. Even the letters sent by service personnel and chaplains, particularly those from overseas, tended to appear weeks after the fact, and therefore they focused on ministry, human interest, and personal relationships rather than on battles won and lost, command strategy, or purely military matters.

Reporting the Persecution of the Jews during Wartime

In this general context then, it is imperative to ask: What about the themes that the American Protestant press had so assiduously followed since 1933, when the Nazis came to power in Germany, what of the Church Struggle and the Nazi persecution of the Jews? Would wartime restrictions, the relative sparsity of accurate, verifiable information, and the general limitations on news from the Axis-controlled countries in Europe make reporting of the Church Struggle and the plight of the Jews virtually disappear from these periodicals? The answer is an emphatic no! In 1943, 1944, and 1945, these periodicals continued to report, as they had since 1933, items related to the Church Struggle, to the Nazi persecution of the Jews (including news of the extermination of Jews in Nazi-held territories), refugee-related items (including news of Jewish refugees), and most of the related topics that have been discussed in previous chapters.

Given the limitations, restrictions, and difficulties—the censorship of news both at home and abroad, the restrictions on paper supplies imposed by the United States government in 1943 and 1944, and all of the other problems inherent in keeping Protestant periodicals alive, including publishing fewer and smaller issues—the press continued to report actively both on the Church Struggle and on the Nazi persecution of the Jews. Sources for what was reported were often mentioned. News came out of Nazi-occupied Europe by way of Switzerland, Portugal, and Sweden, through the Balkan states by way of Turkey and the Arab countries, and through the underground and resistance contacts maintained by the various "free" governments of occupied nations functioning in London. The Polish, Norwegian, Dutch, and French organizations in London received information from clandestine and resistance groups in their occupied countries. Those refugees who did manage to escape carried with them not only the news of what was happening, but often the compelling admonition from those left behind to "tell the world what is happening to us" in the concentration camps and the death camps.

The World Council of Churches in Geneva, the International Red Cross, and the relief and refugee aid groups in Switzerland and Lisbon, Portugal, tried by every means possible to obtain as much news as possible about what was happening to Jews and Christians, particularly pastors in the Confessing Church in Germany and throughout occupied Europe.

For 1943, in the thirty-one American Protestant periodicals examined, there were well over 100 direct references to the Nazi persecution of the Jews, including what was reported in paid advertisements. The information was explicit, identifying the Nazi intention to exterminate the Jews in Nazi-occupied Europe, citing Hitler's speeches and a variety of other sources to establish credibility for such a statement, and then giving explicit details of the methods used, including planned starvation. The death camps in Poland were described, though not always by name; their use of poison gas chambers was described, as were specifics about the firing squads and the massacres of Jews, when details were known.

The Brethren Missionary Herald, The Hebrew Christian Alliance Quarterly, and the paid advertisements of the International Hebrew Christian Alliance were the most complete in detail of those 1943 reports, with the advertisements describing what was to become fully known when the formal plan for the Final Solution was discovered in the postwar documents and through the inquiries and testimony at the Nuremberg trials. Virtually no detail discovered in 1945 had not been already reported in the American Protestant press by 1943, with the one exception of the total number of death camps and perhaps some of the more refined methods used in the death camps, such as the crematoria and the brutality of the SS guards and the Kapo system. Through all of these reports of terror and persecution, the American Protestant press continued to express its admiration for the tenacious and heroic survival of Martin Niemoeller. He was still a prisoner; he was still alive.

The Problems of Verification, Propaganda, and "More Atrocity Stories"

As with all reports that cannot easily be verified, reports of the Nazi persecution of Jews were often cautious, restrained, and hesitant, even skeptical, but the information was published nonetheless. News from the occupied countries and the military fronts was subject to censorship by the military and by the governments involved. At times when news reports were available, even from highly credible sources, efforts to verify the accuracy of the reports through governmental or military agencies proved futile; such agencies simply did not respond or responded neutrally for reasons known only to themselves. At times, news was released by the Axis powers for propaganda purposes. Nazi Germany had long been a master of this process. Adolf Hitler had explained the role of propaganda explicitly in

Mein Kampf. Joseph Goebbels had developed Nazi propaganda techniques to such a high level of efficiency that he still stands as the epitome of the skilled propagandist. Given, then, the conditions of war and censorship and the resulting inability to verify fully the propaganda techniques of both sides in the conflict, the need to use printing space economically with less paper available, and the need to continue to serve the denominational constituency, editors could hardly be blamed or criticized for their failure to publish more than they did about what was being done in Eastern Europe under Nazi policy.

Reporting Persecutions of Jews and Christians in Europe

But the word did creep out, in ghastly, almost unbelievable detail. Even the cautious Protestant press could not dismiss it out of hand. But the specter of "more atrocity stories" also had to be faced. At times, as reports were published, the reminders were strong that the atrocity stories of World War I had been proven false. Would this be the case again? It was a possibility. Therefore, editors tried their very best to give attribution to reliable sources whenever possible. In two news items published in *Advance*, the issues of concern to editors and commentators and the problems of reporting them were illustrated. In the first report, the Church Struggle and the Nazi persecution of the Jews were both presented to the reader. The headline of the report carried the central message, "exiled German Lutheran pastors ask prayers for suffering Jews." German pastors, exiles from Nazi Germany who were serving in German Lutheran congregations in England, appealed to all Christians, particularly those in England, in a formal statement. In part, it read:

It was anti-Jewish legislation applied to the ministry which brought the Lutheran Church in Germany to its first witness against idolatry and barbarism and caused it to become a confessing church. Some of us wish that the protest had been stronger, but it is not for us who now live in safety to criticize those who under fire have done their best not to bow to Baal. While they are silenced by the terrors of persecution we know that they would want and expect us to speak on their behalf. . . . In fellowship with them and in solidarity with the people of whom Christ our Lord was born, we recall, in solemn protest and deep repentence, the words of the Old Testament—Proverbs 31:8–9—" Open thy mouth for the dumb in the cause of all such as are left desolate. Open thy mouth, judge righteously and minister justice to the poor and needy."

The comment of the editor at the beginning of this report was significant. "Far more vividly aware than apparently are Americans of any church group concerning the unspeakable massacre of Jews which is going on on the Continent under Hitler's direct orders, the German Lutheran congregations have asked for prayers for suffering Jews." This is particularly pointed language, since the editor of the page on which the report was given was Henry Smith Leiper, the highly respected and credible churchman. Associated with the Federal Council of Churches and the World Council of Churches, Leiper had direct, personal contact with the church leaders in Europe and worldwide. His page, "The State of the Church," was a regular feature in the Congregational church periodical *Advance*.[1]

Two months later, Leiper included among his brief news items a report of the mass killings of the Jews in Poland. The headline read, "Six Thousand Jews Executed Daily in Poland." Immediately, Leiper attempted to establish the credibility of the item.

A message recently received directly from *a very responsible and well-informed friend* in Europe indicates that the tales that come out of unhappy Poland *are not mere rumors or atrocity stories.* [Emphasis mine.] An average of six thousand Jews a *day* [emphasis his] are being killed by the henchman of Hitler who has recently reaffirmed his intention of wiping out all the members of the household of Israel on the Continent. What this means in horror staggers the imagination and many Americans simply take refuge in their refusal to believe it. There is cumulative evidence to show that probably 2,000,000 Jews have already died at the hands of the murderous Nazis; yet I had a letter from a Christian minister only a few days ago in this country saying that Churchill was, he thought, worse than Hitler![2]

On the same page, four brief articles or reports on the Church Struggle and the execution of clergy in Belgium were included. Norway, Denmark, and Holland were the countries mentioned, where the Church and church leaders were being persecuted, restricted, and held as prisoners or hostages or where minor but significant victories had been won by the Church.[3]

The reporting, with as much factual basis as possible, of the Nazi persecution of the Jews and the persecution and martyrdom of church leaders and clergy in 1943 focused on all the occupied countries. During the war, these events continued to be followed in reports, news items, articles, and editorials; but, with the added urgency of the mass killings of Jews, as Leiper said, "under Hitler's direct orders," Henry Smith Leiper's frustration was evident. The American church, he argued, did not understand the seriousness of the situation, not only for Jews but for European Christians in occupied countries. By implication, Leiper indicated that, if his sources were not reliable and fully responsible persons, he would not risk his own journalistic and editorial credibility by publishing a report of the killing of six thousand Jews a day by the Nazis. In this, Leiper was representative of a good many editors of Protestant periodicals, who sincerely sought to report responsibly and accurately and who, at the same time, sought to break through to their readers the fact that the situation for the Jews under the Nazis was more than desperate, it was tragic. All of the Jews in Europe were to be liquidated, or, in Leiper's words, Hitler "has recently reaffirmed his intention of wiping out all the members of the household of Israel on the Continent."[4]

The number of news reports increased concerning arrests of Christians, clergy, and laypersons, whose crime was aiding the Jews. This was further evidence that Protestant journalists were seeing the relationship between the Church Struggle and the Nazi persecution of Jews. From Holland, Belgium, Norway, Denmark, and France, such reports became increasingly frequent.

> With curious inconsistency, . . . the Nazi-controlled French government has freed the pastors in Chambon who were arrested because of the aid they had given to Jewish victims of the wholesale deportations; while at the same time arresting pastors and laymen in other areas for rendering assistance to other Jews. Inevitably all of the work for refugees in France has been seriously curtailed, although workers in many areas have continued to carry on their activities at great personal risk. They probably know of the terrific sentences meted out to Belgian women for adopting Jewish babies; and they have seen the dissolution in France of the Salvation Army because of its refugee aid program.[5]

The Problems of Accuracy, The Christian Century, and Rabbi Stephen S. Wise

The problem of achieving accurate reporting in the face of the possibility of believing false "atrocity stories" also plagued the editors of

The Christian Century. A sharp, personal difference of opinion involving Rabbi Stephen S. Wise and the *Century* editors developed late in 1942 and in early 1943.

Early in December 1942, Rabbi Wise released figures and other evidence concerning the tragic extermination of the Jews by the Nazis. In an editorial, "Horror Stories from Poland," published December 9, 1942, *The Christian Century* questioned the figures used by Rabbi Wise and also his statement that his information could be verified by the State Department of the United States. Citing other sources, the editorial suggested that Rabbi Wise was at least exaggerating, and it took particular exception to the Wise's statement that corpses were being bought by Hitler for $20 for processing into soap and fertilizer. The closing sentence of the editorial then suggested that this declaration by Rabbi Wise sounded much like the false "cadaver factory" atrocity stories of World War I, which were later proved to have been propaganda.

Rabbi Wise took exception to the editorial in *The Christian Century* of December 9, 1942, in a strongly worded letter published in the *Century* on January 13, 1943. The letter read in part:

> It would appear that you are more interested in seeking to prove that figures which I gave out in the name of five important Jewish organizations of America are inaccurate in respect to Jewish mass massacres in the Hitler-occupied countries than you are in making clear to American Christians how unspeakable has been the conduct of Hitlerism against the Jewish people.

Wise then stated that he took this charge as questioning his personal veracity. He also said that the editorial was consistent with the *Century's* attitude toward him as evidenced in past references and then reiterated that the State Department would verify his claims, if asked to. He also cited a statement by Anthony Eden, the British foreign secretary, made to the House of Commons, which "spoke for the United Nations, including our own country, the governments in exile and free France, and has made a permanent record of the Hitler infamy." Presumably, Eden's statement confirmed that of Rabbi Wise.

The letter closed with a long paragraph in which Wise attacked *The Christian Century*, accusing it of taking "a frankly or disguisedly anti-Jewish attitude whenever it deals with Jewish subjects." Then:

> Whether this is merely a reflection of a personal Judeophobia on the part of the editor, or whether it conveys the considera-

ble attitude of the editorial board of *The Christian Century* is not for me to say. Christian ministers with whom I have discussed the problem have felt your article reflected the subconscious desire not so much to express compassion for the victims of Hitlerism as to shield Hitler from the consequences of his crime. I confess that I cannot quite understand that you should seem to be spiritually unconcerned about the tragic fate of the people whose gift to the world you purport to revere and worship.

I take it for granted that the above letter will appear in the columns of *The Christian Century*, and for your sake I trust a deeply penitential word of your own may be added.

Strong words, to be sure, but the accompanying note by the editors of the *Century* centers on one issue only, that of verification by responsible sources. The editorial note stated that, on the same day that Rabbi Wise made his statements concerning corpses being bought for fat and Hitler's having ordered all Jews exterminated in German-occupied Europe, the *Century* had contacted its own sources in the State Department.

The state department promptly replied through an accredited officer. Unfortunately, it specified that its reply was "not for publication." We have that reply in our files; it does not support Dr. Wise's contentions. Our editorial comment on his charges was written in the light of the state department's reply to our question.—The Editors.

The controversy between Rabbi Wise and the editors of *The Christian Century* highlights the dilemma of the reporting about the Nazi persecution of the Jews, the mass murder of Jews, and the now-established (1942–1943) fact that something terrible was happening to Jews in Nazi-occupied Europe. Rabbi Wise wanted these facts known with the fullest possible impact on Americans generally but especially on American Christians. The editors of *The Christian Century*, mindful of the atrocity stories of World War I, wanted responsible, credible verification. Neither side was wrong, but the editors of *The Christian Century* were journalistically cautious. Rabbi Wise did not receive the "deeply penitential word" he had asked for but only indication that the *Century* took its position based on a check with its own sources. The disagreement remained unresolved. Rabbi Wise, in his autobiography, spoke of this whole incident under the chapter heading, "Death by Bureaucracy."[6]

In other editorials and reports received from the various corre-

spondents who sent in their news reports from strategic points in
Europe and the United States, *The Christian Century* showed, and
would continue to show through 1943 and 1944, that it did not disagree with Rabbi Wise's central contention that Jews were being systematically massacred in Nazi-occupied Europe. The correspondent
from Cincinnati had filed a report (dated December 26, 1942, and
published on January 6, 1943) that contained a resolution adopted at
the Hebrew Union College in a meeting called by the Central Conference of American Rabbis to discuss a just and durable peace. The
resolution adopted was reported under the headline, "Fear Extermination of the Jews." The preamble read:

> The American Institute on Judaism and a Just and Enduring
> Peace expresses its wholehearted approval of the warning is-
> sued by the United Nations to the Axis leadership to halt the
> extermination of Jews of occupied Europe. Hopeful as we may
> be that this warning will have a restraining effect, we assert
> that moral indignation and assurance of reprisal are not
> enough, and that additional measures must be taken to save as
> many Jews as possible from their impending doom.[7]

The resolution called for opening neutral countries and Palestine for
Jewish refugees, sending food to Jews in Europe, saving Jewish children, and defeating the Axis forces by the United Nations, at which
time discrimination against Jews would immediately cease.

On February 3, 1943, an editorial in *The Christian Century* was titled,
"The Return to Barbarism in Eastern Europe."

> Americans stand appalled to reports at the atrocities being per-
> petrated, mainly against Jews, in Eastern Europe. They feel
> that signing "protests" is too cheap and ineffectual a way to
> register their indignation; many are taking out their sense of
> frustration by registering their determination to see that pun-
> ishment is meted out after the war to those guilty of such bar-
> barities. Quite generally it is taken for granted that these
> monsters are German Nazis.

The editorial quoting from the *New Statesman and Nation of London*
then pointed out that Lithuanians, Latvians, and Russians were actively involved in the killing operation under the orders of the German Nazis. "But the horror of the situation in Eastern Europe, and
the magnitude of the problem involved in bringing peace and order
to this unhappy region, are laid bare by the discovery." In addition to
the *New Statesman and Nation*, the Polish government was cited as a

source for this information.[8] London was the location of both the Polish government in exile and the *New Statesman and Nation*.

Could the Jews Be Rescued? Reports of Extermination

Could Jews still have been rescued from parts of Europe in 1943? *The Christian Century*, citing the *New Republic*, which in its turn referred to events in London, told of the efforts of the chief rabbi of Great Britain to prod the United Nations into accepting Rumania's offer to save 70,000 Jews. Rabbi Joseph H. Hertz "wants to know why all that outburst has not led to some action." The outburst was the indignation expressed in the American and British press over "the nazis' despicable treatment of the Jews."

> And the United Nations so far have not lifted a finger! . . .
> More than a month has passed since Rumania offered not sim-
> ply to release that number of Jews—who have been pushed on
> her by the nazis—but to provide them with safe transportation
> to any haven the Allies might designate. Numbers of places of
> refuge, at least of a temporary nature, are available. Nothing
> yet has been done. Apparently it is a lot easier to make indig-
> nant speeches and sign resolutions and raise money for full-
> page newspaper advertisements than it is to get a little real hu-
> manitarian action out of governments. Rumania has blasted
> the alibi that the Jews are beyond the reach of rescue. . . . But
> Rumania's offer puts an entirely new face on the matter. The
> chief rabbi is fully justified in pressing home on the British,
> American and Russian governments his demand that some-
> thing shall be done.[9]

One week later, *The Christian Century* reported that the British government had agreed to admit 35,000 Jews, mostly children, to Palestine from the Balkans. "Transferring these children to Palestine is . . . only a start toward the full effort which will be required to save Europe's still surviving Jews from extermination."[10] The editorial then called for transporting the remainder of these Jews to other refugee havens, even to the United States temporarily, in order to save them. Implicit in the editorial was the realization that the remaining 35,000 Jews in Rumania would be exterminated if they were not rescued.

There is no question but that the American Protestant press knew by 1943 that these exterminations were being carried out and that special sites were used to accelerate the mass killing of Jews. The firing squads had been reported; so had those concentration camps involved in mass killings using "steam chambers" or "poison gas." Without knowing the exact details, for no one did, these periodicals were reporting the existence of the *Endlösung*, the Final Solution and the death camps.

The editor of *The Brethren Missionary Herald*, on January 16, 1943, wrote:

> How anyone can read the reliable reports coming from Europe regarding the Jewish tragedy on that continent and not have a broken heart for this sad people is a mystery. . . . Thousands of refined and cultured Jews and Jewesses are being forced out into bitter winter weather with almost no clothing. Both men and women are being herded into ghettos and concentration camps where they die of disease and exposure like flies.
>
> Men are forced to dig their own graves, then are tortured to death and thrown in. Young Jewesses by the thousands are shipped to Germany for use in brothels. The young men are moved to defense plants to slave under indescribable cruelty to make war equipment. In Poland alone 8,000 die of starvation daily and are buried like dogs. Hitler boasts, and not without reason, that no Jews will remain in Europe after 1943.[11]

He concluded his editorial with a plea for involvement with, and Christian witness to, the Jews in the hour of their greatest trial.

On July 3, 1943, in an editorial signed by Louis S. Bauman, part of a Hitler speech was given in which Hitler was quoted as blaming the Jews for Germany's situation. No date was given for the Hitler speech, but in it Hitler was quoted as referring to the "Jewish world coalition" and as saying, "I am entitled to believe that Providence slated me to fulfill this mission because without its grace I could not have started as the unknown man I was on my way from this hall." Presumably, this was taken from a speech given annually by Hitler in Munich to commemorate the beerhall putsch in Munich, Germany.

Bauman's comment was, "Now, if there is any such thing as a 'Jewish world coalition' will someone please tell us where its headquarters are? Who is its head? Wherein has it power? Millions of agonizing, dying Jews would like to know where they can go for a bit of help." Bauman went on to excoriate Hitler. "Were it not so sad, it would be downright funny to hear Adolf Hitler speaking of the existence of any 'Providence' beside his own ego." But, committed as Bauman was to biblical and premillenial-dispensational hermeneutics, he again stated that the real reason for Hitler's existence was to "chasten Jew and Gentile that are forgetting God and counting Christ out of their program." He then called for repentance from Great Britain and America or darker days would come, especially to America.[12]

Later in the same month, an editorial in *The Brethren Missionary Herald* reported that, as the end for Hitler seemed to be approaching, he seemed determined to "carry Israel down to extermination with him." The editorial continued:

> At the rate the Nazis are killing the Jews of Europe, there will be no Jews left at the end of the war. It is well known that the Nazis are now using poison gas in their continued efforts to destroy the Jews. . . . The Belgian Government-in-Exile has reported that the Nazis have been putting Jews to death in Dusseldorf through the use of poison gas. . . . A Swedish Jewish weekly in Geneva has reported that during the last eight months more than 10,000 Jews in Brest Litovsk alone have been exterminated by the Nazis in gas-filled rooms. A correspondent in the *London Times* reports that 50,000 Jews in Salonika, Greece, have disappeared. . . . Fifty thousand Jews are known to have been deported by the Nazis to Cracow, Poland, but they have "disappeared". . . . After Goebbels announced that no mercy would be shown to Jews, thousands of them disappeared from Latvia and Lithuania. . . . The Nazis have been endeavoring the make Holland completely *Judenrein* (free of Jews). They forbade any Jew to live anywhere in Holland except in the Ghetto at Amsterdam, and now the ones concentrated there are about to be deported to death in camps in Poland. . . . In Belgium more than 52,000 Jews have been expelled by the Nazis and are either dead or in Polish concentration camps, awaiting death; and Belgium is almost completely *Judenrein*.

The editorial went on to mention the rounding up of Jews in France and the report of the Jewish Telegraph Agency that 100 immigration certificates had been obtained for Jewish children in Vienna to go to Palestine. The "Jewish Consul" in Vienna replied that there were not 100 Jewish children left in Vienna. The editorial continued: "Those best acquainted with the world's situation with regard to the Jews are agreed that of all the efforts that hell has ever made to destroy the Jewish people, the present effort is the greatest and most tragic of them all."

The last three paragraphs of the editorial spoke of the prophetic significance of these events but mostly emphasized that anyone who fought against Israel, fought against God—the Christian version of the Chosen People theme.[13]

This long editorial is important for a number of reasons. It clearly points up the fact that by 1943 a great deal of specific information was available to the American Protestant press, for those periodicals that wanted to publish it. It also clearly referred to the concentration camps as sites for mass death for Jews and to the use of "poison gas" and "gas-filled rooms" for accomplishing the killings. It also established the fact of mass deportation of Jews from Nazi-occupied countries, not only in Belgium, Holland, France, Poland, Lithuania, and Latvia, but as far east in Europe as Greece.

Further, sources for the information reported were given as the London *Times*, the Belgian government in exile, a Jewish weekly published by Swedes in Geneva, the Jewish Telegraph Agency of London, and even Joseph Goebbels, the Nazi propaganda minister. Without knowing the term, this editorial described quite accurately the essential program of the Final Solution as adopted at the Wannsee Conference of January 20, 1942; mass deportation of Jews, ghettoization, concentration camps, and mass killing of Jews to the end that Europe, and not just Germany, would be *Judenrein*, free of Jews. In one brief reference to Jews in Holland, the editorial also noted that many of the Jews in Holland were being hidden by non-Jews since the Nazis had found only 130,000 of the 200,000 Dutch Jews. But Hitler would fail, wrote the editorial writer, just as others in other centuries had failed when they had set out to destroy the Jews. Hitler, "perhaps the greatest anti-semite of all time, is facing extermination today."[14]

In two later editorials, *The Brethren Missionary Herald* continued to report the mass killings of Jews in Europe in 1943. On August 14, 1943, it included the information that, "of the 6,000,000 Jews in Europe, more than a third have already been killed and butchered by the Germans, Rumanians and Hungarians." On September 4, 1943, under the title "Greatest Mass Murder in History." an editorial spoke of Hitler as the worst of the "archfiends" who had attempted to destroy the Jews. "In the few years he has ruled the German nation, he has succeeded in murdering two million defenseless Jews—men, women and children. Three million more face the same awful fate if Hitler continues on."[15]

On a page, "Concerning Israel," devoted to news about Jews throughout the world, *The Brethren Missionary Herald* included two news items in its September 25, 1943, issue. The first reported the liquidation of the Warsaw ghetto. "The last 14,000 were deported to the east after three weeks of desperate fighting in which 2,000 Jews were shot to death with machine guns and 3,000 perished in their flaming homes." The evacuation of the Wilno ghetto was also reported. The second item reported that thousands of Jews who were being deported by the Nazis to "unknown destinations" were, in fact, being exterminated "by suffocation in groups of 500 in special 'steam chambers' erected in several concentration camps." The information reported was contained in a sixty-three-page report published as a Black Paper. The report specifically mentioned Treblinka as a camp where 5,000 Jews were being exterminated daily in these "steam chambers" and that the facility at Treblinka was being enlarged. "It describes how the victims, before being driven into the steam chambers, are forced to take off their clothing and stand naked for hours in the open. Similar procedure is followed in other 'Jewish camps'."[16] The original news report was published in the *California Jewish Voice* as a release from the Jewish Telegraph Agency of London.

The final editorial of 1943 in *The Brethren Missionary Herald* referring to the extermination of the Jews actually was about the total number of war casualties worldwide. "But the staggering loss of this war is among the Jews. With a world population of not more than sixteen million, they have already been tortured to death and murdered to the extent of close to four million. This is practically twenty-five percent of all—the most tremendous loss of all the peoples of the world. And Israel is not at war with anybody!"[17]

The *Federal Council Bulletin* for January 1943, published the resolutions of the biennial meeting of the Federal Council of Churches in December 1942. Among the resolutions was one on anti-Semitism, the first paragraph of which reads:

> The reports which are reaching us concerning the incredible cruelties toward the Jews in Nazi-occupied countries, particularly Poland, stir the Christian people of America to the deepest sympathy and indignation. It is impossible to avoid a conclusion that something like a policy of extermination of the Jews in Europe is being carried out. The violence and inhumanity which Nazi leaders have publicly avowed toward all Jews are apparently now coming to a climax in a virtual massacre. We are resolved to do our full part in establishing conditions in which such treatment of the Jews shall end.

A later part of the larger resolution condemned continuing anti-Semitism in America and urged furthering friendly relations with Jews.[18]

The February *Bulletin* expressed "Christian Concern for the Suffering Jews" in an editorial headline, in describing a meeting with six representatives of Jewish organizations comprising the Synagogue Council of America. The reason for the meeting of these leaders and the Federal Council leadership was to discuss what Christian churches could do "to assist the Jews of Europe who are the victims of the Nazi terror." The report also contained this paragraph:

Many people of Europe—have suffered incredibly under the Nazi occupation, but the Jews have been singled out for the greatest cruelty of all. Others may be allowed to live as subject-peoples in the Nazi "new order," but the Jews apparently are not to be allowed to live at all, if the Nazi regime has its way.

The paragraph then closed with a partial quotation of the biennial meeting's resolution concerning the policy of extermination. As for how churches might assist Jews, refugee assistance, aid, and sites were mentioned, but the emphasis was on a full acceptance of the place of the Jews in the postwar world and on the "tangible evidence which was given to genuine concern of Christians to work with their Jewish fellow-citizens for justice to all the people of Israel."[19]

May 2, 1943, was designated a Day of Compassion by the Federal Council of Churches, which made the announcement in the April 1943 *Bulletin*. The same announcement, assigned the Federal Council's research department to examine what was happening to Europe's Jews and issue a report on its findings to the churches. The June issue of the *Federal Council Bulletin* reported that the research department had released its special study, "The Mass Murder of Jews in Europe." The Jews were described in the report as suffering "beyond anything the civilized imagination can picture." The editors of the *Bulletin* also noted that they thought the Day of Compassion to have been a success because proclamations by governors, statements by denominational leaders, et cetera, had supported the day.[20] Apparently, the New York correspondent for *The Christian Century* had reported on the Day of Compassion in a dispatch dated May 10, 1943, in which he suggested a broad support and participation in New York City churches. A letter to the editor from a resident of New York City took direct exception to the report of the New York correspondent and to the success of the Day of Compassion. He went so far as to call the day a "complete fiasco." He examined the metropolitan dailies, the church notices, and the reports of sermons in the New York City press following May 2, 1943, and concluded that a Jewish rabbi had occupied one pulpit in Manhattan and his own small Unitarian

Church in Brooklyn had held a service and that had been all he could find. The sermon that was mentioned was that of the rabbi. Basically, said the letter writer, the Day of Compassion was ignored, at least in New York City.[21]

Direct reports of the extermination of the Jews by the Nazis appeared in many Protestant periodicals in 1943 but none in as complete detail as *The Brethren Missionary Herald*. Presumably, the same sources of information were available to editors and writers of these periodicals as were available to *The Brethren Missionary Herald*, but, for the most part, the items reported tended to be shorter and more condensed. *The Alliance Weekly* in a very brief item on its news page, "This Week's Comments," for September 1943 included a brief paragraph from a speech by Cordell Hull, secretary of State, before the forty-sixth annual conference of the Zionist Organization of America, in which Hull spoke of "stupendous crimes which the Axis powers have perpetrated against the Jewish people." He then promised assistance by "every feasible step to ameliorate the wretched plight of Jews."[22] *The Baptist and Reflector*, on June 10, 1943, published in full a radio address given over station WEVD, New York City, on May 11, 1943, by William C. Kernan. The article's title, and presumably the radio address's as well, was "What about Nazi Atrocities Now?" It included the following:

> Nazi atrocities are real. . . . And they continue unabated to this hour. . . . The Yugoslav Government said that, since April, 1941, the Nazi record in Yugoslavia had been one of imprisonments, murders, shootings, hangings, concentration camps and the destruction of entire villages. . . . The Czecho- slovak Government declared that, by the end of 1941, 400,000 Czechoslovaks had been done to death. . . .
>
>   And yet, we shall never understand the scope or meaning of Nazi brutality until we realize that the chief victims of it are the Jewish people. . . . They have suffered most. There were only 7,000,000 Jews in all of Europe to begin with. Already, 2,000,- 000 of them have been shamefully put to torture and death. And Hitler has decreed that the remaining 5,000,000 be destroyed as rapidly as possible.

Kernan then went on to state that any and all measures should be taken by the United States for rescuing European Jews, many of whom could still be rescued, and that the United States should act independently in offering refuge. Unfilled quotas should be used, but, said Kernan, Congress should also act to change immigration laws to make the rescue of Jews possible. He then stated that no problems created by such an influx of people could possibly equal the "problem of conscience we shall have if we stand by and let these innocent people perish."[23]

The Calvin Forum, addressing itself to the "Jewish question," with an intentional eschatological emphasis (that is, the doctrine of the last things), asked the question, "Who Is Anti-Semitic?"

> Our first reply to the above question is: the Nazi. The Nazis have answered the Jewish problem by systematic extermination of the Jew. The mind finds its keenest relish in the most barbarous methods of eliminations. Nazism is mass butchery in the abattoir of a relentless philosophy.[24]

The remainder of the article discussed whether the Jew is the "key" to fulfilled prophecy, as the dispensationalists were teaching. The author concluded that the Jews were important for the fulfilling of prophecy, but not as the dispensationalists presented the matter. Curiously, however, he came to one conclusion that dispensational, premillenialists taught regularly. "Hitler has forced scholars to investigate the contributions of the Jewish race. He may be a rod in God's hand for Gentiles to know the Jew." Even a Reformed theologian opposed to dispensational, premillenial teaching could not escape the "Hitler as a rod of God to punish the Jew" theme.

Of those Protestant periodicals reporting on the topic in 1943, The Churchman and The Christian Century contained the largest number of items on the extermination of the Jews by the Nazis. William C. Kernan, whose radio address was reported in The Baptist and Reflector, wrote an article, "Lidice and the Jews: You, Christians, Are also Responsible," in The Churchman for January 1, 1943. After describing the destruction of the Czechoslovakian village of Lidice, the killing of all the men, the concentrating of all the women, and the dispersal of all the children to "appropriate centers of education," Kernan went on to write, "Yet, the destruction of Lidice is not the worst of the Nazi's crimes. . . . What they did to Lidice they first did to the Jews. . . . The Christian civilization which perished at Lidice received its first blow when the first Jew died at Nazi hands." Kernan then went on to cite William W. White's report in the New York Herald-Tribune concerning the machine-gunning of 25,000 Jews in Odessa and the burning of the barracks where the bodies were placed; the machine-gunning of Jews in East Galicia before open graves that the Jews had been forced to dig as reported in the New York Times; the killing of

children and the aged in the streets and the deportation of the remaining Jews; a report by Joseph W. Grigg of the United Press in the
New York World Telegram of the massacre of Jews in Latvia by firing
squads; and the report in *PM* of the existence of gas chambers and of
death by injection administered by physicians whereby 100 Jews per
hour could be killed. Finally, Kernan included a paragraph reported
in the *New York Times*, which was an exact description of the process
developed in the death camps for the mass extermination of Jews.
The location described was Belzec (Chelmno) in Poland and the
source for the story was given as the Polish government, presumably
the Polish government in exile. "'Deportees from Warsaw were
packed into a barracks and ordered to strip naked ostensibly to have
a bath—then they were pushed into a room with a metal floor. The
door was locked and current was passed. Death came instanta-
neously.'"[25]

Like other writers and editors in the American Protestant press,
Kernan was careful to substantiate the details he was reporting. The
specter of "more atrocity stories" was always in the background. In
his radio address, Kernan had stated flatly that the atrocity stories
were true and not propaganda. In the earlier article in *The Churchman*,
which cited responsible reporters or responsible American newspapers, Dr. Stephen S. Wise, the United States State Department, and
the Polish government in exile, Kernan documented his statements
carefully. This he did in an effort to prove to Christians that the Nazi
plan to exterminate the Jews was no fiction or propaganda piece
meant to incite hatred toward Germany.[26]

When an organization, Loyal Americans of German Descent, published a declaration calling for the overthrow of the Nazi regime for
victory by the Allied forces, *The Churchman* published the statement
in full. In commentary accompanying the statement, the content of
the first paragraph was highlighted because it "denounced the cold-
blooded extermination of the Jews of Europe and the barbarities committed by the Nazis against all innocent peoples under their sway."
Prominent German Americans from thirteen states signed the original statement and invited others of German descent to join them in
the declaration.[27] In March 1943, *The Churchman* reported on a speech
made by Bishop Tucker to a mass meeting in Madison Square Garden, in which the bishop called for total victory by the Allied forces
as the only means "of saving the Jewish people of Europe from the
brutal treatment which they are receiving."[28]

Dorothy Moulton Mayer's article came quickly to the point. Hitler did not invent anti-Semitism; he was the ultimate anti-Semite and nazism, according to its ideology, had to destroy the Jews.

> The coldblooded murder of 2,000,000 people and the systematic segregation of millions more calls for more than haphazard devices: trains have been set aside for deportation, men chosen and trained for their bloody work, even the slaughter houses must be built and equipped.

And later in the article:

> The only thing that can be done for the Jews imprisoned in Nazi Europe is to *get them out* [*emphasis hers*]. . . . These people are being exterminated; they must be destroyed if Nazism is to succeed. When they are gone it will be the turn of Christianity and Christian democracy [this is the major thesis of the article]. . . .
> But time is of the essence.[29]

The efforts of the Federal Council of Churches to initiate programs to rescue and support European Jews were also reported quite completely in *The Churchman*. The three-point program adopted at the March 16, 1943, meeting of the executive committee of the Federal Council was given in the April 1, 1943, issue. The three points were: (1) the department of research and education's documented study; (2) the announcement of the Day of Compassion; and (3) the planned support of a program by the governments of the United States and Great Britain for financial aid to Jews in neutral countries and for the provision of places of temporary refuge for Jews rescued from Nazi-controlled Europe.[30] In the only letter to the editor published in 1943 in *The Churchman* that made any reference to the massacre of Jews in Europe, the correspondent referred to a news item reported in *Time* magazine about the massacre of Jews in Poland and then moved on to discuss the problem of anti-Semitism in the United States and the need for the Christian churches to become more militant in the fight against sin.[31]

The bishop of Albany, the Rt. Rev. G. Ashton Oldham, addressed a meeting sponsored by the American Jewish Congress and the Albany Jewish Congress. In the report of his remarks, he was quoted as saying:

> The massacre of the Jews is unique in its horror. It is . . . a deliberate planned policy of extermination not only of a nation

but of a race. These people are doomed without trial, without crime, without possibility of defense, solely because they belong to the race which produced the prophets and of which our Lord and His apostles were members. Nothing in history can quite equal this abomination.[32]

The Churchman closed the year with a Christmas editorial paying tribute to the Jews as a people. One sentence in the editorial attributed to Rabbi Stephen S. Wise the statement that he estimated that 3 million noncombatant Jews had been murdered by the Nazis.[33]

In its annual review of religion for 1942–1943, *Church Management* included a paragraph on religion in Europe. In this paragraph was included a statement about the slaughter of the Jews of Europe, with some 2 million given as the number of Jews massacred by the Nazis.[34] Even *The Concordia Theological Monthly* left its parochialism long enough to include a small mention of the decimation of the Jewish population in European countries occupied by the Nazis, citing *The Christian Century* as its source of information.[35]

The two religious periodicals devoted to reprinting sermons, *Current Religious Thought* and *The Pulpit*, each included a sermon in which reference was made to the extermination of the Jews in Europe under the Nazis. The sermon of Rabbi Abba Hillel Silver, the well-known rabbi of the Temple, Cleveland, Ohio, was published in *Current Religious Thought*. More of an address than a sermon, the occasion was a meeting sponsored by the American Jewish Conference in New York City to support a national homeland for Jews in Palestine. In the course of his address in a section called "The Connecting Stout Black Cord," Rabbi Silver linked together the better-known incidents of overt anti-Semitism in Europe. "There is a stout Black cord which connects the era of Fichte in Germany with its feral cry of 'hep, hep,' and the era of Hitler with its cry of 'Jude Verrecke.'" Silver listed them, ending with "the Ukrainian blood baths after the last war and the human slaughter houses of Poland in this war." This was the only direct reference to Jewish extermination in the text, which was devoted to the central subject of a Jewish national home in Palestine.[36]

The Pulpit published a sermon by a Canadian clergyman, A. D., Cornett, not otherwise identified. The title of the sermon explained the subject, "Is This War a Judgment of God?" He stated, early in the sermon, that he believed in the affirmative, that the war was a judgment of God, and then he devoted the body of the sermon to his reasons for this conclusion. At one point, he developed a part of the sermon around "How Judgment Came to Germany." Here, he stated that Germany was under the judgment of God because the German people had accepted the Nazi doctrines of racial pride and racial supremacy, "and they catered to the lowest instincts of the mob by urging them to persecute the Jews. They encouraged the sadistic instincts of gangsters by allowing them to perpetrate unmentionable cruelties in concentration camps. In a word they accepted the motto of satan in Milton's 'Paradise Lost'—'Evil, by thou my Good!'" No further reference to the Jews was made in the remainder of the sermon.[37]

Periodicals published by those Christian missionary organizations devoted to the evangelization of Jews continued to report extensively on the Jews in Europe. *The Friend of Zion* in virtually every monthly issue for 1943, from a variety of sources in the United States and Europe, reported on the persecution and extermination of Jews by the Nazis. The January 1943 issue reported on the Nazi deportation of Jews from Slovakia, Greece, Vienna, and France and the threat to Jews in France who tried to evade the Nazi deportations, which was that they would be shot. Frenchmen who helped Jews would also be shot.[38] The February issue reported on the assistance given to Jews in Holland and in Denmark under the direct leadership of King Christian of Denmark.[39]

Two articles in *The Friend of Zion* for March 1943 were devoted to the persecution of Jews. The first pointed out that Christians and people other than Jews had also been victims of Nazi persecution. Cited were Poles, Russians, Czechs, Greeks, Belgians, French, Norwegians, Dutch, and Yugoslavs. "Thus in the struggle the Jews are not alone and not isolated. The fury of Nazism is directed not against us alone, but against the entire world. In this lies our salvation and our only hope." The subject of the second article was extermination. Citing the *Los Angeles Times*, it reported that "the Nazi savagery [was] undertaken in cold blood, and systematically organized against the Jews. No punishment could be devised which would adequately avenge the deaths of millions of innocents, whose only offense was their faith." The article went on, listing country by country, the planned deportation of Jews to begin December 1 as decreed by Hitler. One and a half million Jews had already been exterminated. The original article cited the American State Department and "well-authenticated documents" as the sources for its figures. The year to which the date December 1 was attached was not given.[40] Other, smaller news items were also included in the March 1943 issue.

Reports of Help to Jews throughout Occupied Europe

By April, *The Friend of Zion* was reporting on the Swedish protest against the deportation of Jews from Norway, the resistance of Norwegians themselves to this deportation, the continued defiance of Denmark to anti-Jewish measures, and the accelerated deportation of Jews from France, as well as the internment of many other Jews in France.[41] The reports in July 1943 included references to the British agreement to allow 35,000 Jewish children to be emigrated from the Balkans to Palestine, and the statement of Rabbi Stephen S. Wise that the bodies of exterminated Jews were being processed into soap fats and fertilizer.[42] In October and again in December of 1943 in the "Jewish World News" sections, further items were reported on the persecution of the Jews, the removal of the Nuremberg laws by Badoglio in Italy, and the report of a "balance sheet" that summarized the "devastation wrought by Hitler upon the Jews of Europe in the course of his ten year war on them." The Jewish population of 8,-300,000 had been reduced by 5,000,000 by Hitler, according to this report. The December issue reported Goebbels's attack on Sweden for accepting Jews escaping from Denmark.[43]

The editor of *The Hebrew Christian Alliance Quarterly*, in the Winter of 1943, came directly to the point. "Hilter Plans to Destroy European Jewry" was the title of the article. In two and one half pages and after several introductory paragraphs that included the identification of the article's sources, "the Record of German Atrocities of World War II that was recently submitted to President Roosevelt" was presented. Germany, Austria, Bohemia-Moravia, Poland, Belgium, Holland, Yugoslavia, Greece, France, Rumania, Bulgaria, Slovakia, Latvia, and Lithuania were the countries surveyed.

The opening paragraphs began:

> Is this the truth? Is it not the voice of another alarmist, trying to stir up hatred against the Germans? Let me tell you that the arch-enemy of mankind is not only planning to destroy the Jews of Europe, but that Hitler and his kind have actually been at work slaughtering them long before the Statesmen of Great Britain and America have been stirred into action. . . . Note the methods used to exterminate them and your heart will be as sick as mine, and you will cry out, How long, O Lord?

He continued, identifying Poland as the place where the Nazis were carrying out the extermination, saying, "they [the Nazis] have chosen Poland for their slaughterhouse." At this point a third source of information was identified, a Polish underground newspaper. Shootings, medical experiments, gas vans (an early experiment in the use of carbon monoxide), injections, massacres, death in the ghettos, slave-labor battalions, deportations, and death by suffocation in the transport trains were described.

> What do these revelations of German atrocities do to you? Are you sick at heart? Are you indignant? You should be. Too long have we Christians been silent. Our voices of protest should have been heard long before this had happened. We are our brother's keeper and we are duty bound to help the helpless, to pray for them, to feed and clothe them AND TO DEFEND THEM IF NECESSARY. We are not asking for revenge. We call for the defeat of Hitler and his philosophy.[44]

This indictment of the silence of Christians on the matter of the extermination of Europe's Jews was as strong or stronger than any other found (and there were very few) in the American Protestant press, even as late as 1945, after the death camps had actually been found.

The summer 1943 issue of the same periodical included "Notes by the General Secretary." His theme was "The Jewish Tragedy."

> The Jewish tragedy in Nazi occupied territories cannot be described in detail, because it sickens one to read in print the wanton cruelty, shame and persecution, oppression and wholesale massacre of human beings, men, women and children.

The central topics for discussion were the Warsaw ghetto and its complete destruction and the report in *Time* magazine of the death by suicide of Zygmunt Zygielbojm, a Jewish exile and escapee from Warsaw and a member of the Polish National Council. Upon receiving news of the destruction of the Warsaw ghetto through the Polish underground and from some who managed to escape, Zygielbojm, described as "only one man and a tired one," committed suicide in his room in London. His wife and children had already been victims of the Nazis.[45]

The reporting in *The Gospel Herald* tended to be within the interest of the periodical, that is, in the Jews and prophecy. One article contained the sentence, "The world has been shocked at the atrocious cruelty that is being meted out to Israel." That was all.[46] A later article, again prophetic in content, mentioned three significant things happening to Jews. The first was that there were more Jews then than at any other time in their history. The second was that they were under the "greatest world-wide persecution of the Jews every known. Cruel tortures, the firing squad, the concentration camps in many places. . . . Disease, suicide, famine, pestilence, etc." And the third was that the Jews were not fighting for Germany, Italy, or Japan. The only Jews engaged in the fighting were among the Allied forces. This latter fact was seen to be prophetically significant. "This fact alone will give victory to Britain and the United States."[47]

The Presbyterian published a news item in which the document referred to in the article "Hitler Plans to Destroy European Jews" (*The Hebrew Christian Alliance Quarterly*) as having been given to President Roosevelt was specifically identified. According to the report, on December 8, 1942, a committee representing several Jewish organizations had presented President Roosevelt with documented evidence of the planned extermination of Jews. Figures from this document were in turn released by the World Alliance for International Friendship through the Churches in its December newsletter. Two million Jews "have been put to death under the Nazi regime and . . . five million others face a similar fate through Hitler's edict calling for extermination of all Jews in subjugated lands."[48] On April 8, *The Presbyterian* reported on the Federal Council of Churches of Christ in America and its efforts to facilitate the rescue of Jews where possible and called for Christian support for such efforts.[49]

In November 1943, *The Presbyterian* published an article by Joseph T. Britan, who, as treasurer of the Interdenominational Friends of Israel Missionary and Relief Society of Philadelphia, wrote about the Apostle Paul's concern for the Jews and their salvation and then said:

> Today we are not only interested in saving the souls of the Hebrew race, but also their bodies. The "New Order" of Hitler is responsible for perhaps the greatest massacre of all history. About three million Jews and Jewish Christians in Europe have been done to the death by the order of Hitler. By slow starvation, by machine guns, by suffocation, by live steam, and by other means, the Jew has died by the millions under the diabolic hand of the Devil's man.

The remainder of the article told of the difficulty of maintaining any contact with conditions or persons in occupied Europe, of the nearly impossible task of rescue efforts for Jews, even when they could obtain passports, and of the work of the Friends of Israel Society to do what it could, where it could.[50]

The reports in *The Watchman-Examiner*, in the main, tended to be very similar to those of other large-circulation denominational papers, such as *The Presbyterian*. There were small news items from time to time about the Nazi persecution and extermination of the Jews.[51] Only toward the end of 1943 did two separate editorials discuss Jewish extermination. The first, "Russia and Jews," reported that, out of the original 8,300,000 European Jews, 3,000,000 remained alive, 1,800,000 in the Soviet Union. The plea was for freedom of worship in Russia and for Russian support for a Jewish homeland in Palestine.[52] The second editorial concerned the Jews in France, with attribution to a newspaper in Stockholm, Sweden, the *Aftonbladt*. Mass arrests of French Jews were reported in Marseilles, Toulouse, Perpignan, and Limoges, and the terrible conditions in the concentration camp of Drancy, from which Jews were being deported to Eastern Europe, were described.[53] Christian compassion and prayers were sought that God would intervene on behalf of these suffering Jews in France.

Even *The Christian Century* added little new information directly on the extermination of the Jews as the months passed in 1943. On May 5, 1943, an editorial's title read, "Two Million Jews Have Been Liquidated." It was essentially the release of the Information Service of the Federal Council of Churches of April 24, 1943, in an editorial form. The editorial contained the words "deliberately planned and ruthlessly executed program of annihilation." The same information appeared in a number of other Protestant periodicals during about the same time period.[54]

Later that month, a letter to the editor signed by Theodore N. Lewis of the Progressive Synagogue, Brooklyn, New York, was published. The letter commended the *Century* for the above-mentioned editorial, specifically for the editors' recognition of "the truth about the slaughter of Jews in Europe."[55] A later editorial appeared in the September 8, 1943, issue, "European Jews Are in a Desperate Plight." This editorial was based on the report of the Institute of Jewish Affairs which represented the American Jewish Congress and the World Jewish Congress. Again, this report had been widely circulated and was used in a number of Protestant periodicals as a basis for news items and editorials. The four-point call to action in the *Century* editorial listed as point four, "defeat the Axis."[56]

The Persecution of the Jews and the Church Struggle

What *The Christian Century* and a number of other protestant periodicals did in 1943 was to link directly the Church Struggle in Germany and in Nazi-occupied Europe with the persecution and extermination of the Jews. Articles, news items, and editorials stressed increasingly the growing open resistance to the Nazis and the heroic, often fatal efforts of Christians to speak out agains the Nazi extermination of the Jews, hide Jews, oppose deportation of Jews, and openly defy the Nazis by helping Jews to escape. It was not just the continued and growing resistance of the Church, Protestant and Roman Catholic, that was noted, but this fact was directly reported with reference to protecting, defending, and hiding Jews.

The January 1, 1943, issue of *Advance* reported the arrest of a Belgian priest for publicly praying for the Jews "who were being murdered and persecuted by the enemies of the Belgian people'" and the efforts of a Christian underground organization in Belgium to aid persecuted Jews. It also reported the firm anti-Nazi stand of the free churches of Sweden against anti-Semitism and the "outrages perpetrated by the Nazis," as well as the Swedish support of Norwegian Christian groups that helped persecuted Jews.[57] The arrests of Protestant and Roman Catholic clergymen some for aiding Jewish refugees, were reported in *Advance* in July 1943.[58]

William Ernst, who had been a prisoner in Dachau and Buchenwald wrote an article for *The Friend* describing the courageous lives of "Die Gesellschaft Jehova's," the Jehovah's Witnesses, among whom were three Jews who were members of the group. "These Jews bore their lot with the same humility as their Aryan fellow members." the members of the sect remained steadfast against Nazi threats and continued their witness as they worked together.[59] *The Messenger* was explicit in its issue of January 12, 1943. "One of the dominant features in the religious situation on the Continent continues to be the cooperation between Protestants and Roman Catholics in the face of the threat to their common heritage, and especially in the face of the inhuman cruelties to the Jews." Churchmen who were in the forefront of such a protest in France were then named, including the bishop of Beauvais. Because one of his ancestors had been Jewish, the bishop had to register with the Nazi authorities. He came to register "in full pontificals. In front of him walked an acolyte, carrying the cross." Other resistance in France, the Netherlands, and Switzerland; the work of the American Friends' Service Committee and French civilians in rescuing Jewish children; and the open resistance of the German Roman Catholic bishops, von Galen and Bornewasser, was also reported.[60] The issue of January 19, 1943, contained similar reports, as did that of January 26, 1943.

The arrest of Pastor Edouard Theis of the French Reformed church in Le-Chambon-Sur-Lignon for assisting Jewish refugees was reported in *The Watchman-Examiner* of April 1, 1943, with the added note that he was a graduate of Union Seminary of New York City and was well known in the United States.[61] *The Churchman* included a paragraph in its March 1, 1943, issue, describing measures taken in France and Slovakia by Christian groups to aid Jews, including hiding them and feeding them regularly. In France, an illegal, underground Christian magazine was circulated that contained the full text of a statement by church leaders who had spoken out against persecution of the Jews.[62]

No one gave a more direct report of such activity and its consequences than did *The Christian Century*. Two editorials published in consecutive weeks in July of 1943 and based on information supplied by the United Nations Information office and from the bulletin of the World Council of Churches gave extensive coverage to the European Christian churches and their growing resistance to the Nazis and their heroic efforts in behalf of Jews. Archbishop Damaskinos, metropolitan of Athens, was named for a number of actions in defiance of the Nazis, including saying that the Greek clergy should be shot by firing squads, rather than the Greek civilians, if the Nazis felt compelled to shoot Greeks. French cardinals were commended for a pastoral letter condemning Nazi policy and the archbishop of Lille for preaching against the Nazis. Seven Czech bishops were commended for a letter read in the churches condemning persecution. Other such actions in Belgium, Denmark, Norway, and Holland were also mentioned. In Holland, a letter was sent to the Reich commissar protesting the persecution and sterilization of Jews; the letter had been signed by the representatives of eight church groups, including members of the Reformed Church, Roman Catholics, Calvinists, Remonstrants, Baptists, and Evangelical Lutherans.

In the editorial of the next week, France, Holland, Yugoslavia, and Hungary were named as places where the resistance of the church was growing, and Skovakian Lutherans were commended for publicly opposing anti-Jewish decrees. The word out of Switzerland was that there were many reported instances of aid to Jews by churches and Christian people in France and elsewhere in Europe.[63] The *Century* commended Damaskinos of Athens again in its August 18, 1943, issue, mentioning his defence of the Jews.[64] The next week, it was reported that the pastoral letter of the Catholic bishops of Holland had been read in all Protestant churches, also, and that Protestants and Catholics alike "gave help to Jews fleeing from the lightning roundup by the French authorities last year."[65] The Danish commitment to helping Jews escape and interfering actively when arrests of Jews were made on the streets as well as the arrest of Danish fishermen who helped Jews reach Sweden and the assistance of their friends in helping the fishermen escape from jail were reported, also. "In the Danish churches, a pastoral letter was read on Sunday, Oct. 3, sharply condemning the anti-Jewish measures."[66]

Editors and writers would have liked to have had access to much more information. They reported what news they could obtain and almost always credited their source or sources to maintain their credibility. By 1943, even though it was much too late for the vast majority of Europe's Jews, it had been established that the churches and Christians of Europe were actively rescuing and hiding Jews from the Nazi authorities. That church leaders and laypersons were themselves arrested did not deter their growing efforts. This newest phase of the struggle of the church for its own perilous existence included assistance to Jews. These acts of heroism are remembered to this day, especially by those Jews who owe their lives to the Christian rescue effort.

The Continued Use of Paid Advertisements in 1943

The number of paid advertisements placed in Protestant periodicals in 1943 increased. The number of groups and agencies carrying on a missionary effort among the Jews increased also. The International Hebrew Christian Alliance, the Bethel Mission of Eastern Europe, the New York Jewish Evangelization Society, the New York Gospel Mission to the Jews, the Christian and Missionary Alliance's New York Mission to the Jews, the Friends of Israel Missionary and Relief Society, the Million Testaments Campaigns, and the American Board of Missions to the Jews were the sponsors of the paid advertisements. They used such phrases as "the most opportune time" and a "sorely harassed and distressed people" as well as more direct references to "Jewish persecutions" and "the starving Jews in Poland, many of whom are children." The ads also referred to "the Nazi oppression," "the mass murders of the Polish Ghettos and in the human slaughterhouses of the numerous concentration camps," and the conclusion that "out of six million Jews in Europe, four million have been done to death by methods which only Satan himself could have devised." But the most explicit ads were those produced by the International

Hebrew Christian Alliance. One example should suffice. The full half-page advertisement for the September 1943 issue of *The King's Business* carried the headline, "The Agony of Israel: Will the Jews of Europe Survive the Torment?" The copy read, in part:

> Poland has become the Nazi slaughter-house for the Jews of Europe. Already two million Jews have been exterminated, authenticated reports show. The firing squads and bayonets are too slow for the Nazis, so they have devised ingenious methods for the wholesale slaughter of the Jews.
>
> Jewish men and women are herded into pens and blown up by hand grenades. Freight cars, their floors inches deep in quicklime, are packed with Jews to the suffocation point and then locked and shunted off to some remote siding. Thousands of Jews have been driven like cattle into "gas chambers," and other thousands stripped naked, are herded into wired halls and electrocuted.
>
> The food allowance in Nazi occupied Poland is scarcely above the famine level. About 700 calories are allowed to Catholic Poles and less than 300 for Jews, as compared to a pre-war standard of 2,600 calories. As a result of the starvation diet additional thousands die of tuberculosis, dysentery, scarlet fever and spotted typhus.

The ad continued, stating the belief that some Jews would survive in spite of the Nazi plan to exterminate them. It asked for funds and offered a publication, "The Present Day Attempt to Destroy the Jews," that would be sent free upon request.[67] The Protestant periodicals accepting such advertisements tended to be on the more conservative-evangelical or fundamentalist side of the theological spectrum for the 1930s and 1940s.

The War Continues, 1944

In 1944, there was a war weariness, and, even though the advances and victories of the Allied forces were mounting up, a quick end to the war was not in sight. The American Protestant press felt the pressures of war-forced restrictions directly. Bans on travel for meetings and conventions forced some denominations to cancel their planned annual meetings. Subscription lists were trimmed and fewer copies of many of the periodicals were printed because of restrictions and cutbacks on paper allotments, and some periodicals used a poorer grade of paper. Many cut back to monthly issues with fewer pages in each issue in order to continue publishing at all.

The reporting of the Nazi persecution and extermination of the Jews continued, with little new information beyond that published in 1943. Of the thirty-three American Protestant periodicals examined for 1944, thirteen contained reports of the heroism of Christians in aiding Jews, including reports of pastors and laypersons who had helped Jews to escape, hidden Jews, fed them, or otherwise had come to their assistance. The countries from which the reports came in 1944 were the same as the sources of the 1943 reports: France, Holland, Belgium, Denmark, Sweden, Norway, Slovakia, Greece, Yugoslavia, and Germany itself.

The information reported also continued to come out of Europe from the same places: Sweden, Portugal (Lisbon), the Balkans, London, and Geneva and other cities in Switzerland and from the governments in exile and wherever the underground and resistance forces could make contact with the Allied forces or with the West. The news services, particularly the Jewish Telegraph Agency of London and the Religious News Service, as well as the major wire services were used as sources of information, as were the large newspapers and the news magazines. A credible, responsible report was still preferred to a rumor or a questionable source.

As the Allied forces gained control of previously occupied areas, first in North Africa and then on the Continent in Southern Europe, occasionally the report of the lifting of all restrictions pertaining to Jews would be published, but not often. Also, occasionally, the first reestablishment of contact with Jews still found alive in conquered territory would appear. A military chaplain, for instance, would report the joy of conducting religious services for his Jewish soldiers with Jews in the area attending and joining in the worship. Such a report appeared in *The Messenger*. It had been sent by a minister of the Evangelical and Reformed church who was serving in the United States Army as a military chaplain.

He reported his part in organizing two services in the Alsace-Lorraine and in a large French city. With the assistance of a Jewish medical captain and a Jewish private, the chaplain held a service for the Jewish men of all the units nearby during the Jewish High Holy days of September 17–26, 1944. The Kosher feast was prepared by a Jewish woman, who with her husband had been sheltered and hidden by a Roman Catholic priest who was a count and who owned a large chateau. The Jewish couple lived in a servant's house. The feast was prepared in the home of the village mayor from food supplied by the military. The service was held in the mayor's home.

I secured a medical captain and a private who read the prayers in Hebrew from our *Army Prayer Book;* I addressed the congregation; my organist played Jewish hymns. This first Jewish service in France, for our units, at least, was followed by a fine holiday feast for the 42 officers and enlisted men, the Jewish couple, and the town's mayor and his family.

The second service was held in the smaller of the two synagogues found standing in the French city. The chaplain gained permission for the synagogue to be emptied out and cleaned up. It had been used as a storage warehouse for medical supplies by the German army. An orthodox Jewish French couple was found, and an orthodox service was held, again with the medical captain and the private assisting. The service was held on the Day of Atonement. Word about the service had spread, and some 15 French civilians joined some 200 Jewish officers and enlisted men in the service. A French Huguenot pastor came and gave a short sermon in French; the chaplain gave a sermon in English. "Every man present felt, I am sure, the deep meaning of this historical occasion when the sons of Abraham became the pioneers of religious liberty in this long persecuted and oppressed land."[68] The chaplain's name was Stephen E. Balogh; he had been the pastor of an Evangelical and Reformed church on Chicago's south side before entering the military service in 1941.

Reports of the invasion of Europe at Normandy seemed somewhat subdued in the Protestant press. For most it was two or more weeks after the fact before they could report or comment. The response was hopeful rather than exuberant. Perhaps, no event more shocked the Protestant churches in America than the murder in Denmark of the highly regarded clergyman-playwright and anti-Nazi hero, Kaj Munk. The details of his murder were reported fully in a number of Protestant periodicals. Munk had been a man of national stature as well as a religious leader; his murder outraged the Danes, as it did Christians in America.[69]

The Continued Extermination of Jews, 1944

The existence of the "firing squads," a separate and specially trained unit of the Nazi apparatus, was first reported in 1944. "Vernichtungskommando" was the heading of an editorial in *The Brethren Missionary Herald* for March 4, 1944.

"Vernichtungskommando" is a German word meaning "annihilation squad." It refers to Nazi squads who have busied themselves with the Hitleric determination to destroy the in-destructible earthly nation Israel! There are twenty letters in this German word, and for every letter in it the *World Dominion* tells us that 137,000 Jews have been slaughtered in Poland alone. [This figure comes to 2,740,000.][70]

The plight of Jews in Hungary began to be reported. The World Council of Churches released a public protest against the reported deportation of 400,000 Jews from Hungary to Auschwitz. (Auschwitz was named in the statement; one of the first such mentions of Ausch-witz by name and designation as a death camp.)

> Trustworthy reports state that so far some 400,000 Hungarian Jews have been deported under inhuman conditions, and those who have not died enroute have been brought to a camp in Auschwitz, Upper Silesia, where, during the past two years, many hundreds of thousands of Jews have been systematically put to death.[71]

One month later the same periodical, *The Messenger*, printed in full the protest statement of Hungarian-American Christians presented at a service held in the First Magyar Evangelical and Reformed Church in New York City. News reporters from major New York dai-lies, as well as from the Hebrew- and Yiddish-language press, were present. The protest statement and a telegram from Hungarian Jews living in Palestine were read.[72]

Majdanek, First Discovery of the Death Camps

But even more significant news than the naming of Auschwitz and the plight of the Hungarian Jews appeared. *The Christian Century* and a number of other Protestant periodicals reported the discovery of Majdanek, near Lublin in Poland, by the Russian army in the sum-mer of 1944. *The Christian Century* report, however, was given with considerable caution and no little disbelief. Though it was long, it should be quoted in full.

> No atrocity story of the year is likely to top the latest concern-ing the alleged killing of 1,500,000 persons at the German con-centration camp near Lublin, Poland. W. H. Lawrence of the *New York Times* was a member of the party of thirty journalists who were taken on a tour of the camp by a body called the Soviet-Polish Atrocities Investigation Commission. He de-scribed it as "a veritable River Rouge for the production of

death." The victim's were shipped there from all over Europe, the correspondents were told, were asphyxiated in gas chambers and their bodies cremated in huge furnaces. Chief evidence for the charge that 1,500,000 persons were killed in this manner was a warehouse "about 150 feet long" containing clothing of people of all ages who were said to have been done to death in the camp. As many as 18,000 persons a day were said to have been killed in the camp, although the capacity of the cremating furnaces was estimated to have been 1,900 per day. Maurice Hindus, who was another of the thirty correspondents, also reported the 1,500,000 figure. He said the warehouse contained 820,000 pairs of shoes. Many newspapers gave the Lublin charge the big headline of the day, but the parallel between this story and the "corpse factory" atrocity tale of the First World War is too striking to be overlooked. The story started in 1917 and was not fully discredited until 1925. There may or may not be a relation between the fact that the Lublin account came out immediately after it was charged by London Poles that the Russians had stopped their advance within artillery range of Warsaw and waited until the Germans had killed 250,000 Poles within the city who had risen to fight for their freedom in response to the call of the Polish government-in-exile.

Clearly, Charles Clayton Morrison, editor of *The Christian Century*, was a hard man to convince, even though his own periodical had been reporting evidence of the existence of such death camps for some time.[73] He would reflect his inability to grasp the significance of the death camps even after more of them had been discovered in 1945.

The editorial in *The Churchman* attacked Nazi racial theories and Hitler for advocating these beliefs, but it ended:

He has proved only how stupid is the leader who leaves out of account the values which decent men cherish and which lie outside the realm of the mechanical. Perhaps the ghastly horrors of Majdanek for which he is responsible will haunt his muddled brain until some-day even he may recognize the truth.[74]

The Living Church labeled its editorial "The Tragedy of Germany" and began, "The unfolding of the hideous barbarities of Nazi Germany, climaxed by the horrors of the Majdanek murder factory at Lublin, has sickened and disheartened those who hope against hope that a place may be found for Germany in the family of nations." Referring to Berdayaev's term "bestialism" as "refined, conscious, rationalized, developed through reflection and through civilization," the editorial continued, "Majdanek might even be said to be the logical extreme of civilization—efficient organization utterly unaware of the significance of human life. It is the end product of the dehumanization of man."[75] In this editorial and in a brief article published one week later, a new question was raised. Were these actions of the past eleven years the actions of Hitler and the Nazis only, or was the entire German people somehow to blame? Karl Barth was quoted as saying that the whole German people was responsible and must be prepared to accept its guilt.[76]

"Murder, Inc." was the title of the editorial on the subject in *The Messenger*. Referring to Richard Lauterbach, Moscow correspondent for *Time* magazine, as its source, the editorial told essentially the same story as that in *The Christian Century* (Lauterbach was one of the thirty correspondents who had visited Majdanek). The only additional information concerned a "cabbage field fertilized by a 'layer of human bones, a layer of human ashes, and a layer of manure.'" The editor of *The Messenger* also chose to be cautious, also remembering the atrocity stories from World War I, but he wrote, "This terrible story of Majdanek may be true" and warned against an "orgy of hate with its resultant mass cry for vengeance."[77]

A second editorial followed in the same issue of *The Messenger*, "We Shall Not Stoop." The editor, again warning against an overreaction and an assumption about who had been guilty, suggested that the perpetrators should be punished "befitting their crime." The rest of the editorial was taken from *The Christian Advocate's* editor, Dr. Roy Smith, who warned that, "'to match mass murders with more mass murders will be to stoop to Nazi levels, and nothing could be more tragic.'"[78] *The Friend of Zion*, taking a paragraph from the *Pentecostal Evangel*, reported that there could no longer be any doubt about "Jewish atrocities in Nazi-held Europe, . . . now that Lubin [*sic*] has been recaptured and newspaper correspondents have visited this Polish city for themselves."[79]

Paid advertisements were still being placed in some periodicals. In five Protestant periodicals for 1944, a total of twenty-nine paid ads were noted, giving in greater or lesser detail the story of the Nazi persecution and extermination of the Jews. As in other years, the ads mainly were purchased by Christian missionary organizations evangelizing among Jews. Consistently, these organizations had used this medium of advertising to convey the message of the Nazi terror for Europe's Jews.[80]

A Full Assessment of What Was Reported, 1943–1944

By the end of 1944, the American Protestant press had fully reported what was happening to the Jews in the Nazi-occupied countries. The record for 1943–1944 was complete. No part of the Nazi-instigated plan was left out. Deportation, massacres, ghettos, gas chambers, crematoria, starvation, disease, "firing squads," gas vans, medical experiments, transport trains, brutality, mass graves and trenches, and death camps were reported. *The Churchman* reported incidents described in a book published by the Polish underground, *From the First Lines of the Battlefield,* which told of conditions at Sachsenhausen and Ravensbruck.[81] Auschwitz was named in reports on the deportation of Hungarian Jews, and Majdanek near Lublin, Poland, had been opened to the world by the Russians, with full reports given by Western news correspondents of proven reputation reporting for newspapers and news magazines of standing. And yet there remained skepticism, nagging doubts, concern over the possibility of "more atrocity stories," as expressed by Morrison in the editorial on Majdanek and by other editors. In fact, what was reported in the American Protestant press in 1943 and 1944 (from sources in Sweden, London, Lisbon, Geneva, and the Balkans and from the underground and resistance movements, the governments in exile, and the news wires and news services) was true. It was verified later.

Who in America knew? Among those who did know were the editors and writers of the American Protestant press, and, to the extent that the press informed its readers, so did the Protestant Christians of America. In spite of their openly expressed doubts about the authenticity of some reports and in spite of their openly acknowledged skepticism even when their information came from responsible, credible sources, the editors and writers told the story, complete in detail, of the planned wholesale extermination of Jews and others in Nazi-occupied Europe. It must be said again. Protestant Christians in America, based on reports published in the American Protestant press, could not have said then and cannot say now that they did not know.

CHAPTER

1945—"So It Was True":
Face to Face with the Death
Camps

*During and immediately after World War II, the shock of
the experience was too great. As the camps were liberated,
brutal media images of survivors who seemed hardly more
than walking skeletons were mixed with images of mounds
of unburied corpses.*

RICHARD L. RUBENSTEIN
The Cunning of History

KEY EVENTS

1945, General: January 11, Russians capture Warsaw; March 7,
United States Army crosses the Rhine; April 12, death of Franklin D.
Roosevelt; April 13, Vienna entered by Russians; April 25, United
Nations meeting in San Francisco; April 25, American and Russian
troops meet at the Elbe River in Germany; April 28, death of Mussolini; April 30, death of Adolf Hitler; May 2, Berlin falls to Russians;
May 7, Germany unconditionally surrenders; May 8, V-E Day; August 6, atomic bomb dropped on Hiroshima, Japan; August 9, atomic
bombing of Nagasaki, Japan; August 14, surrender of Japan.

1945, Relating to the Jews: January 26, Russians liberate Auschwitz;
January, liberation of remaining Jews in Polish ghettos; February 14,
90,000 Budapest Jews found by Russian troops; April 6–10, Buchenwald liberated; April 15, Bergen-Belsen liberated; April 23, Mauthausen opened; April 23–May 4, Sachsenhausen and Ravensbruck evacuated, with continued massacre of prisoners; May 2–10, Theresienstadt
opened and liberated.

203

Anticipating the End of the War

The last awful reality in the continued reporting of the Nazi persecution of the Jews by the American Protestant press came as the war in Europe drew to the end during the winter and spring of 1945. Hope for the war's end in Europe was being expressed in the press as early as January 1945, largely in the context of anticipating the immense, admittedly catastrophic problems facing the Allied nations and the Protestant Christians confronted with rebuilding Europe, feeding and housing millions of homeless, stateless refugees, and, of particular concern, rebuilding the church in Europe and Germany.

In the American Protestant press, three concerns emerged as paramount. The first was the commitment (or the attempt to generate a commitment) to help meet the needs of the catastrophic war's refugees and victims. When church leaders visited Europe during the winter and spring of 1945 and saw both physical devastation and human tragedy in the liberated countries, they wrote about what they saw in blunt, no-nonsense terms, urging American Christians to give money, clothing, food, livestock, and time to refugees.

To this end, the use of denominational resources and interdenominational agencies already at work was not only recommended, but urged. Where there were no denominational committees or structures available for this work, the establishment of such a centralized effort was also recommended, if necessary on an emergency basis so it could be done quickly. Interdenominational groups already at work were described in articles, as in *The Churchman*, where Henry Smith Leiper told of the work of the American Committee for Christian Refugees in relation to the larger efforts carried on throughout the war years and geared to expansion as the war ended, as a part of the World Council of Churches in Geneva. It was in this article that Leiper optimistically wrote, "the defeat of Nazism is near at hand." He also spoke of the enormity of the task to be undertaken. Having written of the displaced people in Europe in such terms as "a hundred million [who] moved to save their freedom if not their very lives" and of the high proportion of Christians among the 30 million so displaced. He then wrote, "Such staggering facts, which the average comfortable American has not even yet begun to grasp in all their stark tragedy, makes it clear that the World Council of Churches could not remain indifferent to caring for the refugees."[1]

During the remaining months of 1945 and afterward, Americans, especially American Christians, were made aware of the true dimensions of this need, as article after article appeared describing the devastation, the situation for the homeless and destitute, the mass migration of people in Europe as the zones of control were divided among the Russians, British, French, and Americans, and especially the need for food for Europe's children. As American Christians responded with food, clothing, money, and livestock, the reports about their contributions filled the pages of the American Protestant press.[2]

The second major concern reported in the American Protestant press was that of restoring America's broken contacts with European Christians in the liberated countries. American denominational leaders were sent to Europe as soon as such trips were possible to reestablish contacts, survey the needs, and bring back proposals and plans for assistance. Alice Shaffer sent home a letter written on July 25, 1945, telling of her efforts to locate what was left of the Quaker fellowship in Germany. Having had only names and old addresses in Frankfurt and Mannheim, she told of her difficulties, of the contacts she was able to make, and of the Quakers who had been imprisoned for a variety of reasons, including aiding Jews, and she reported who of the Quakers had survived. She also told of the devastation and extreme hardship she saw; houses damaged, nearly impossible living conditions, and destruction everywhere. She also suggested ways Americans could help. The letter was published in full in *The Friend* under the caption, "These Are They which Come Out of Great Tribulation."[3]

The Mennonites, as early as April 1945, were reporting on restored contacts, relief work, and workers sent to France to take up the interrupted relief efforts begun before the war, carried on during the occupation, and then reopened for assignment to American Mennonites. Three workers had been sent to France and were already at work.[4] The sending of food, clothing, additional workers, and funds through the combined efforts of Mennonite and Brethren in Christ congregations was reported in the "Relief and Service News" later in 1945.[5] The Church of the Brethren periodical reported the sermon delivered over the radio by their local pastor in Uniontown, Pennsylvania, at the victory service held in that city when the war ended. The sermon stressed the need for active participation in the massive relief effort to save Europe's people from starvation, using United Nations Relief and Rehabilitation Administration (UNRRA) statements, among others, to make the point.[6]

The Lutherans, acting jointly, sent three of their leaders to Europe for a six-and-one-half-week visit to make contact with Lutheran churches in Europe and to meet with Lutheran church leaders to plan postwar assistance, World Council of Churches officials, and chaplains in the military and to see prisoner-of-war camps and ministries when possible. The trip took place during the late winter and early spring of 1945, before the war in Europe was over. The Lutheran periodicals were filled with articles by Lorenz B. Meyer of the Missouri Synod, P. O. Bersell, president of the Augustana Synod, and Ralph H. Long of the National Lutheran Council. They wrote articles for Lutheranism at large and also for the periodicals of their own Lutheran denominations, which outlined in detail what they had experienced and also what action they recommended.[7] A number of Protestant periodicals also published articles by A. L. Warnshuis, who had visited Europe in December and January, 1944–1945, representing various Protestant agencies, including the Federal Council of Churches. His articles covered the news from Europe's churches (as much as he could obtain) but centered mainly on the need for the United States to assume world leadership in rehabilitating Europe and the role of the American Churches in urging that the United States accept this responsibility.[8] The Missouri Synod periodical raised the question of responsibility for Europe's rehabilitation directly in an article by Lawrence Meyer in The Lutheran Witness for May 8, 1945.[9] Samuel McCrea Cavert of the Federal Council of Churches published an article in The Messenger, "Hunger of Body and Soul: Christians of America Must Demonstrate Their Christianity in Healing Fellowship with Christians of Europe." He stressed the need for food and also the need for America's churches of all denominations to cooperate fully and sacrificially with every agency—religious, government sponsored, or independent—engaged in relief work in Europe, including reestablishing all contacts possible with the churches of Europe.[10] The denominational and interdenominational church leaders in America did not wait for the war in Europe to end. Leiper, Warnshuis, Cavert, the three Lutheran leaders mentioned earlier, and others were pressing American Protestant Christians to assume a major role in relief and rehabilitation, to support all efforts to resume Christian fellowship with Europe's Christians, and to sacrifice by giving food, clothing, and money to this effort, which began in late 1944 but went on mostly during the winter and spring of 1945.

The third major concern emerged in this context. P. O. Bersell, one of the three Lutheran leaders sent to Europe in early 1945, expressed an almost universal concern of American Protestant leaders in his article, "What Shall We Do with Germany?"[11] Cecil Northcott had raised the same question early in 1945 in *The Christian Century*, "The Treatment of Germany," and an editorial in *The Christian Century* was titled, "Germany's Rehabilitation."[12] The question was raised in another context when W. A. Visser't Hooft of the World Council of Churches and the Rev. Marc Boegner, president of the French Protestant Federation, visited the United States to report on the situation in Europe. Visser't Hooft's reports, made in a series of meetings throughout the United States, emphasized the situation in Germany and the Church in Germany and dealt with the questions of what should be done with former Nazis, collaborators, and German youths whose indoctrination as Hitler's youth had been complete.[13]

P. O. Bersell raised most of the fundamental questions that needed to be raised as American Protestant Christians confronted the monumental task of aiding in the rehabilitation of Germany and the reeducation of Germans, particularly in relation to the Protestant church in Germany. Bersell specifically stated that he was not going to discuss the political or military aspects of the way Germany would be governed. He spoke of the "baffling postwar problems, political, economical, social, educational and spiritual" as being more complex than winning the war. He wrote, "I am mindful of the dislocation of entire racial and national populations, of the entire disruption of social structures and the distortion of Christian morality."

He then went on to state that decisions about Germany to be made by the Allies were "pivotal and it will set the pattern for future actions." He continued, "As Christians and as Lutherans we are tremendously interested. What shall be our attitude toward the German people? Shall the spirit of hatred and vengeance prevail over against the concepts of the Kingdom of God and the genius of the Gospel of Christ?" He then told of what he had seen and heard when in Europe representing Lutherans. He spoke of talking "by the hour" to refugees, many of them "men of God. I do not believe they lied to me. I spoke to diplomats who had documentary evidence of terrible atrocities." He told of the terrible story told to him of the "almost unbelievable, wholesale liquidation of Jews and other 'undesirables,' political and religious." He described his own "frustration and futility as I pondered the thought that this was the homeland of the Reformation and the historic stronghold of the Lutheran Church." He then stated that the destruction and devastation in Germany, though accomplished by Allied military forces, were in fact the legacy of Hitler. "Hitler's crime was primarily a crime against the German people.

How and why they stood for it will continue to be one of the enigmas of history. Whatever the answer, the German people, as such, must share the blame for what happened."

At this point, Bersell became more optimistic. He spoke of the resistance to Hitler and the Nazis centered in the Confessing Church. He mentioned leaders such as Bishop Wurm and Bishop Meiser and Martin Neimoeller, Eugen Gerstenmeir, and Helmut Thielicke.

> They and thousands with them have stood heroically for the freedom fo the Church and for Christian principles. Under Bishop Wurm of Stuttgart, eighty-five percent of the Protestant churches (mostly Lutheran) have banded together in the "Einigungswerk" a united front of the churches for evangelical freedom and Christian liberty and for the liberation of the Church from the tyranny of the State.

He mentioned also that Presbyterians, Methodists, Lutherans, and other Protestant denominations were in the process of raising millions of dollars to aid in the material and spiritual rehabilitation of the Church in Germany. He concluded his article:

> Therefore, . . . let us Christians unitedly join in this battle for Germany's soul. The Church in Germany must be given aid to build tabernacles for religious worship to take the place of the thousands of churches destroyed, to integrate the congregational life, to furnish Bibles and Christian literature by the millions, to prepare and sustain pastors and other Christian leaders, to rehabilitate Christian institutions of mercy; in brief, to build up a vibrant, strong church life.
>
> The big task is to evangelize the millions of paganized German youth. . . . The leadership of the Church must be purged of all "that bowed the knee to Baal," and of all sympathizers with Jewish or other racial persecutions.
>
> . . . It is the battle for Europe's soul. The battle must be won, or else hell will break loose again with renewed fury.
>
> This is the day of the Church's opportunity. Let us not come with too little and too late.[14]

The scenario had been laid out. Reestablish contact with the Protestant church in Germany as quickly as possible; use the known leadership in the Confessing Church that had resisted Hitler and the Nazis; send literature; rebuild churches; train new pastoral and lay leadership; reeducate youths who were trained and indoctrinated into nazism; send funds in the millions of dollars; purge German

Christians, those who went over to the Nazi form of Christianity; purge anti-Semites and known racial persecutors; restore orphanages, homes for the aged, church-related hospitals, and relief agencies.

Through 1945, the American Protestant press was filled with articles detailing the activities and responses by agencies of American Protestantism to the various parts of the program that Bersell had described. Bersell's phrase "the battle for Europe's soul" was taken from a book by Stewart W. Herman, a Lutheran and the former pastor of the American Church in Berlin, who had been interned and then expatriated with the American diplomatic corps. In 1943, he wrote *It's Your Souls We Want*.[15]

Americans "On Site" in Germany and Europe

Stewart W. Herman was one of those sent back into Germany by the World Council of Churches at the earliest possible moment. As he stated in his second book, *The Rebirth of the German Church*, in hundreds of instances, he was the first foreign civilian seen by German churchmen. He was free to travel all over Germany, which he did, often bringing to German churchmen the first news about Western churches and activities that they had received for years. He also kept careful records of his travels so that, in retrospect, it is possible to confirm a great deal of what was reported about Germany immediately after the end of the war in Europe article by article and news item by news item in the American Protestant press. *The Rebirth of the German Church*, commemorating V-E Day plus 365, as he noted in his subscription at the end of the preface, was his own report of the events in Germany related to the German Protestant church during that first year.[16]

Herman was himself both reported about and reporting back to the American Protestant Press. As the official, on-site representative of the World Council of Churches, his reports were often the first news sent back from Germany about the German churches and clergy. He wrote of conditions as he saw them and also of the meetings he attended with other representatives of the World Council. In addition, he served as an escort for American church leaders when they visited Germany.[17]

Delegations soon were sent to Europe and Germany from America. The Federal Council of Churches sent Bishop Oxnam (its president and a Methodist bishop) and Bishop Sherrill of the Protestant Episcopal church as an official delegation also supported officially by the United States government.[18] The Lutherans sent a second delegation of five leaders traveling in two groups. J. A. Aasgard, Franklin Clark Fry, and Ralph C. Long were in the first group; J. W. Behnken and Lawrence Meyer, the second, Meyer from the Missouri Synod.[19] Samuel McCrea Cavert was "loaned" for six months from his position as executive secretary of the Federal Council of Churches to the World Council of Churches. He also sent back reports and articles, as did S. C. Michelfelder, who was sent by the Lutherans to Geneva as commissioner of the American section of the Lutheran World Convention.[20] Ewart E. Turner, also a former pastor of the American Church in Berlin, returned to Europe as the official special correspondent for the Religious News Service.[21]

Chaplains in the victorious army and in the occupation forces made contacts, often on behalf of their own denominations, sending back reports or articles and letters describing their work and contacts and reactions to the conditions that they observed. They reported assistance in the way of funds collected voluntarily from among their own troops, usually given to provide food for needy children, the opening of centers for literature distribution, rehabilitation, and evangelism, and occasional contacts with local pastors. Often the chaplains served as escorts for church leaders visiting from America since most such travel required permission from the military authorities. Part of the purpose of the Oxnam-Sherrill visit to Europe was to contact military chaplains and discuss their work.[22] The reports of visitors also included the visit from Europe to the United States of Marc Boegner (president of the Reformed Church in France and of the French Protestant Federation), W. A. Visser't Hooft (executive secretary of the World Council of Churches), and George K. A. Bell (bishop of Chichester).[23]

The interest in Martin Niemoeller continued to be great in the American Protestant press. The reports came in several phases. The first was the report of his liberation.[24] The second phase concerned the interviews he gave to Dorothy Thompson, Bishop Oxnam, and a number of chaplains while he was in Italy.[25] The third phase concerned his return to Germany and his church in Dahlem and to active work in the rebuilding of the Protestant church in Germany.[26] The last concerned his role in Germany during the Nazi years, what place he should be given as a hero or a collaborator, and the possibility of his visiting America. In other words, a controversy was reported, with Niemoeller's defenders and detractors representing their views quite openly.[27]

The Last Chapter in the Church Struggle

Events within the Evangelical church in Germany were also reported quite fully. Leaders of the Confessing (or Evangelical) Church came forward to assume leadership roles in reorganizing the Church in Germany and in reestablishing contacts with Christians in Europe and America. Bishop Theophilus Wurm, Bishop Otto Dibelius, Hanns Lilje, Bishop Meiser, Pastor Herman Asmussen, and Pastor Martin Niemoeller emerged as the central group selected to guide the newly formed Evangelical church in Germany. Conferences and meetings, particularly those in Treysa (August 1945) and Stuttgart (October 1945), were reported extensively. It was at the Stuttgart conference that the Evangelical church in Germany voted to join the World Council of Churches. It was also at this point that a mistake (referred to by Henry Smith Leiper and others) that was made after World War I was not repeated. After World War I, little or no attempt was made by Christian groups in Europe or America to reestablish ties with the churches in Germany for two or more years. Samuel McCrea Cavert, as well as Leiper and others, noted that this was not the case in 1945, largely because of the contacts maintained by the World Council of Churches through Holland, Switzerland, and Sweden.[28] In reports of the death of Dietrich Bonhoeffer, among the things Bonhoeffer was commended for was his constant contact with the World Council through Sweden before his imprisonment.[29] As for the reorganization of the German church, the American Protestant press reports were published regularly in the latter half of 1945.[30]

There can be no question, then, that the last chapter in the Church Struggle and the restoration of the Church in Germany and Europe dominated the American Protestant press in 1945. Throughout 1945, these two topics were coupled with the articles on the need for relief aid for Europe and Germany and reports of relief assistance given by American Protestant churches and denominations. In the thirty-nine American Protestant periodicals examined for 1945, well over 200 articles, editorials, news notes, and letters to the editor were recorded on these subjects which included those pieces devoted primarily to Martin Niemoeller.[31]

The Persecution of the Jews, Early 1945
and Afterward

There can also be no question that, as the war in Europe began to draw to a close and the concerns for the church situation in Germany and throughout Europe became the focus for major segments of the American Protestant press, that the amount of reporting on the Nazi persecution of the Jews declined somewhat. As the Allied Troops advanced deeper into Europe and countries that had been under Nazi occupation were freed, knowledge about the true dimensions of the Nazi persecution of the Jews began to grow so that, though the number of such reports was not large, the information in them was more explicit. The articles, editorials, news items and letters to the editor fell into three categories. The first category included the more general discussions of the Nazi persecution of the Jews. In this grouping, articles reporting the arrest or death of those killed or imprisoned for assisting Jews or hiding Jews appeared. The second category contained references to the concentration camps and the death camps, including descriptions of the transportion, deportation, or concentration of Jews (that is, evidence of the plan now known as the Final Solution of the "Jewish question"). The third category included pieces that very specifically used the word *atrocity* in relation to the death camps or in articles or editorials discussing the moral and ethical implications of the mass killing of Jews and others that came to light, fully, when the extent of the Nazi killing operation was revealed to the world.

In a manner of speaking, the wide publication of photographs, newsreels, and written accounts of the death camps and the reports in the religious press of eyewitnesses and news correspondents of credibility, plus the military's own record of these camps, might well be considered the closing chapter of the story of the Nazi persecution of the Jews. This is true only if the aftereffects of the mass killing of Jews are ignored—that is, what happened to those Jews who survived. Though the topic was reported in some degree, an examination of the thirty-nine periodicals used for 1945 and an examination of a selected number of periodicals for 1946 and into 1947 (eighteen in all), seemed to indicate that these periodicals, for the most part, ceased reporting about the Jews in Europe in relation to the Nazi persecution. Rather, they reported on the continuing problems of displaced persons (DPs) and, insofar as they were within this larger descriptive category, Jews were not singled out as a special group.

For much of the American Protestant press in late 1945, then, the Jews in Western Europe more or less lost their identity as Jews and became DPs.

The other category in which the Jews were discussed, but in much more detail, was in relation to Palestine. Already in 1945, as it had from time to time throughout the 1930s and early 1940s, the question of the opening of Palestine to Jewish immigration emerged as central to a discussion of the "Jewish Problem" or the "Jewish question." In 1945, as the war finally ended, articles and editorials appeared, as well as letters to the editor, on Palestine, Zionism, the question of a national homeland for Jews and, during the immediate postwar months, on how many of Europe's surviving Jews actually wanted to immigrate to Israel. This last problem was discussed at length, using liberal Protestant periodicals, in Hertzel Fishman's book *American Protestantism and a Jewish State*.[32] The problems of Jews who were kept in displaced-person camps for as long as five years and how the American Protestant press dealt with these camps and DPs, particularly the Jews, still have not been studied. The question would be whether the Jews "disappeared" into the larger category of displaced persons in the reporting in the Protestant press? If so, did this indicate the continuing difficulty evident in much of the press of dealing with Jews as Jews, apart from relief aid, emigration and the Palestine issue, and missionary efforts to convert Jews through Christian evangelism? In one sense, then, the last chapter in the Nazi persecution of the Jews was written in the displaced-person camps and in the emigration of survivors during the years after the war in Europe.[33]

The Persecution of the Jews and the Progress of the War in the East

The actual reporting of the Nazi persecution of the Jews in late 1944 and in the early part of 1945 seemed to reflect the course of the war itself. The invasion of "fortress Europe" from the west in June 1944, the progress of the Allied forces up the Italian peninsula, and the news of the rapid advance of the Russians in the east from the Gulf of Finland in the north to the Black Sea in the south raised the hope that the war would soon end. In fact, purely military necessities, decisions being made by general staffs, the time of year, and the contingencies of success mitigated against the war ending in late 1944. Quite apart from the stiffening resistance of the German armies on all fronts and the fanaticism of Hitler and his "scorched earth" policy (if Germany could not win the war, it should perish as a nation and as a people), the Allies in the west and Russia in the east had been so successful by December 1945 that they had outdistanced their ability to supply their armies for the last big drive into Germany. Russian troops had moved from within Russia itself to a line running from just east of Memel on the Baltic Sea to the Yugoslavian-Bulgarian border in the south, between July 1943 and November 1944. As it was described by Henri Michel in *The Second World War*, the tactic was to advance along the entire Eastern European front in coordinated actions that penetrated westward from 120 to 300 miles and then stabilize the front and await supplies of matériel and manpower until full battle strength was regained and then launch a new offensive.[34]

It was such an offensive in July–November 1944 that had overrun Lublin and in which the death camps in and around Lublin, including Majdanek, had been discovered. But the offensive halted in October–December 1944 in order to resupply for the next offensive. The Russians, at this point, stopped. Two results must be noted. The failure to occupy Warsaw in October–December 1944 doomed the Polish uprising in Warsaw. This Russian decision was then and remains now one of great controversy. The Poles accused the Russians of allowing the Germans to massacre thousands of Poles in and around Warsaw in order to eliminate Poles who would have been hostile to the Soviets and communism.[35]

The second result was that most of the concentration camps, the forced labor camps and factories, and the large camps where systematic extermination of Jews and others was carried out were not liberated. They were by and large within the areas still in control of the German armies and government. As the Russians advanced in the east, many of the forced labor battalions and the living inmates of the concentration camps had been transported back into Germany proper, making the populations at Buchenwald, Bergen-Belsen, Ravensbruck, Oranienburg, Sachsenhausen, Ohrdruf, Neuengamme, and Doranordhausen swell to hopelessly unmanageable sizes. This evacuation continued when the major offensives of the winter and spring were begun in late December 1944 and January 1945. Under the pretense of a need for labor, Jews and others were transported into the constricted areas that remained under German control. Many survivor's accounts tell of this period of transportation and relocation and the toll it took in lives among the emaciated inhabitants both of the work camps and the death camps. Details of this mass movement of forced laborers and Jews can be found in Eugen Kogon's *The Theory and Practice of Hell*, Martin Broszat's "The Concentration Camps, 1933–1945" (in Krausnick et al., *Anatomy of the SS State*), and *The Murderers among Us: The Simon Wiesenthal Memoirs*, edited by Joseph Wechsberg.[36] Kogon wrote:

> Soon after the liberation of Lublin, a huge stream of evacuees from the eastern camps to the interior of Germany began to take place. . . . The surviving inmates were driven westward on foot whenever transport facilities in the general exodus had become inadequate. As much of the physical evidence of the atrocities as possible was blown up. . . .
> In endless columns the wretched host rolled over the countryside, day after day, often for weeks, without food or adequate clothing. Those who could go no further were shot down by the SS or their armed prisoner minions, or simply left by the wayside. . . . More centrally located camps had to make room for thousands upon thousands of evacuees who reported stories of unrelieved terror. . . . One had only to look at the wretched figures pouring into the narrowing interior from every side to believe them.[37]

Broszat gave the figures for January 1945 as 714,211 concentration camp inmates held by 40,000 guards. At least one-third of the inmates lost their lives "on the exhausting marches, in the transport trains which took weeks to reach their destination, and (particularly) in the hopelessly overcrowded reception camps in the months and weeks immediately before the end of the war."[38]

Wiesenthal's personal narrative described his forced travel from Lvov to Janowska camp, to Plaszow near Cracow to Gross-Rosen within Germany, then to Chemnitz and Buchenwald, and then to Mauthausen in upper Austria. It was in Mauthausen that he was finally liberated by the Americans on May 5, 1945.[39] Dora Zaidenweber, a survivor of Auschwitz and Bergen-Belsen, told of a three-day forced march in January 1945 and then of being transported by train to Buchenwald and then on to Bergen-Belsen, where she was liberated on April 15, 1945. Her husband Jules Zaidenweber was in transport from Dachau to an unknown destination when the guards fled and the prisoners found themselves free in Garmisch-Partenkirchen, Germany.[40]

The Persecution of the Jews and the Progress
of the War in the West

In the west, the Allied advance toward Germany stopped, facing the Siegfried line. The map of positions held by the American, British, and French armies on December 25, 1944, shows them occupying territory from the southern sector of Holland down the French-German border south to the Swiss border and on into the south of France to the area of Nice, on the Mediterranean coast. Germany proper had yet to be entered. The Allied entrance into Germany was further complicated by the German counteroffensive known as the Battle of the Bulge, begun on December 15, 1944. At the most, this German attack delayed the attack on Germany by about a month. Since the Allied troops had not entered Germany proper before January–March 1945, the existence of the huge German concentration camps in the north and west of Germany was still not fully known. In particular, the fact that they were still functioning and that they were filled to overflowing with prisoners was not general knowledge. The final assaults on Germany were begun in the east on January 12, 1945, and in the west on February 8, 1945.[41]

For the American Protestant press, then, the war itself was determinative in terms of reporting on the Nazi persecution of the Jews. When the forward movement of the Russians in the east and the Allied forces in the west was halted in the fall of 1944, further news of the existence of the extermination camps, the forced labor camps, and the extensive movement of the inhabitants of these camps into Germany could be only partially known, if known at all. This was reflected in the reports and news items that were published through late March 1945. Since there was little direct, explicit news to report about the Nazi persecution of the Jews, what was reported was often in a generalized or indirect reference, rather than to a specific instance. In January 1945, *The Christian Century* published an editorial about the effort to have Jews seated on the board of the UNRRA, the umbrella organization under which relief effort was being coordinated by the Allies as the United Nations. The reason for this request by Jews was noted. "We are all aware of the anxiety which gave birth to these resolutions. The Jews have been so victimized, persecuted, knocked about that it is to be expected that they would wish in every possible way to protect their position in the postwar world."[42]

In an even more indirect manner, Cecil Northcott in an article on how to treat Germany in a postwar situation referred to an exhibition

a rescue report from Germany was tempered by the statement, "Most of the 15,000 Jewish children the Germans seized in France and packed off to Germany were not so fortunate. Nothing has been heard of them, and there is evidence that many were put to death in the gas chambers in Poland." The writer then said, "My story concerns the children the Germans didn't get."[51] One brief sentence about the protest of the Danish Martyr-hero Kaj Munk and his protest against the persecution of the Jews was contained in an article on Munk by Stewart Herman.[52] Since *The Christian Herald* was published monthly, it was even more difficult for it to keep up with current events; therefore, the selection of news items, editorial comments, and articles reflected this publishing schedule.

The Churchman, published twice each month, also reflected the difficulty of being close to current with its reporting and editorial comment. The problem seemed to have been handled by a type of selected topical reporting. Such a report appeared on January 15, 1945. It told of an orphanage near Le Mans, France, where a group of children were being cared for largely through the support of a chaplain and the troops of the American Air Transport Command stationed in the Loire section of France.

> Stolen from the gas chambers of Berlin and Lublin, hidden in the region when their parents were seized by the Germans recently quartered in the Chateau itself, these Jewish children, once marked for death, now play happily through a park and by the pond and sculptures in the Chateau grounds.

The brief news article described how the children were located in the area, that over $4,000 had been donated by American troops, and that the troops voluntarily gave up their own chocolate and gum ration and their cigarettes to be "swapped" for food for the children.[53]

A March 1, 1945, article reported on a French pastor who had aided refugees in southern France identified as "Jews, French Army officers and anti-Nazis." The pastor, Jules Jesequel, was well known as the French secretary of the World Alliance for International Friendship through the Churches. In reference to aiding Jews, the article reported:

> Then, Pastor Jesequel writes, "when the shameful persecution of the Jews began in my region . . . another task presented itself . . . to help the Jews avoid arrest and the deportation which threatened them. So I organized a kind of placement service for men and women who then disappeared into safe

homes, most often in the country on isolated farms. This activity involved many journeys which had to be made secretly.

The article reported further that only two Jews of all those whom he had aided had been killed. One was a Hungarian Jewish doctor who was shot by a German patrol while he was giving aid to a resistance fighter, and the other was a young German Jewish woman who was tortured to death by the Gestapo while being questioned.[54]

In the April 15, 1945, issue of *The Churchman*, a news item reported that Dutch-Jewish Protestants paid a special tribute to the churches of Holland for their aid and stand against the Nazi persecution of the Jews in Holland. The group of Dutch Jews had just been released from Theresienstadt, identified in an editorial note as a ghetto. The Jews had been released and taken to Switzerland, from where they had made their statement.[55]

The Evangelical Visitor, generally concerned with reporting the extensive relief efforts of the Mennonites and members of the Brethren in Christ Church, included one small item on the persecution of the Jews in its April 9, 1945, issue, and even this item centered on relief work.

A Jew from Austria, dejected by the callousness of the average N. American, asked, "Are there any Christians? If there are Christians in Kitchener, what are they doing for my people who are suffering so intensely, being persecuted, imprisoned, interned, starving, freezing, and often being murdered?" The answer was given in the form of a visit to the Kitchener M.C.C. [Mennonite Central Committee] office where he received detailed information about the relief work done by the Church, and by a visit to the MCC clothing center nearby. The Jew marvelled, he was speechless, it was unbelievable what his eyes saw. He left saying, "I have learned much today."[56]

The Gospel Messenger for April 14, 1945, reported that 5,200 Jews had been sheltered in 180 houses and institutions in Rome for a period of nine months during the Nazi occupation and thus saved.[57]

Even the two periodicals published by organizations engaged in Christian missionary work among Jews reported the situation of the Jews in less detail, or in a more generalized and nonspecific manner in early 1945. *The Friend of Zion* contained only two reports, both published in February 1945. One was general; the other more specific in that it cited a city, Minsk, and a direct report from a survivor of the persecution. The generalized reports simply stated that the 4 million

Jews presumed to be still alive in Europe were homeless, meaning stateless or without a country to return to if the war should end. The second small news item reported that only twelve Jews survived in Minsk from some 80,000 Jews who had lived in the city before the war. An additional 39,000 Jews had been brought to Minsk by the Nazis, making the total Jewish population 119,000, all of whom had been exterminated. The twelve who survived were skilled technicians employed as forced labor in repairing German military vehicles. The survivor giving the report, Ignatz Burstein, gave the information while standing outside the charred building where had had once worked.[58]

The Hebrew Christian Alliance Quarterly also reported in the winter and spring issues of 1945 in generalized terms. In a year-end report for 1944, published in the winter of 1945, reference was made to the War Refugee Board and its investigation of atrocities.

> Human life is cheap, almost worthless if we count the multitudes that have been destroyed . . . and among those who have suffered most stands the Jewish Nation, bruised and bleeding as a helpless minority in the world's great tragedy. The score against the Jew in this war is five million helpless human beings done to death by means so hellish and brutal that a recital of the facts beggars human language.

Thus, referring to the War Refugee Board's investigation that had been carefully verified by checking and rechecking, and citing the extermination of Greeks, Poles, Russians, Czechs, Hollanders, Belgians, Norwegians, and Danes by the Nazis, the report stated that Nazis, with particular bitterness and venom, had directed their extermination program against the Jews. "Millions have been put to death in concentration camps, by poisonous gas, bayonets, bullets and many other pitiless methods too horrible for public recital."[59]

In the same issue, John Stuart Conning wrote of the Nazi intention to liquidate the Jews of Europe and of the difficulty of getting accurate details "behind the censorship screen that has been cast about Nazi doings in Europe. . . ."

> But occasionally bits of information received through underground channels lift a corner of the veil. . . . The mass murders of the Jewish population in Poland, in fulfillment of the Nazi purpose to exterminate the Jews, transcend in satanic, cold-blooded cruelty anything that savagery has hitherto devised.

He then described the ghettoization of Germany's and Europe's Jews. He wrote:

> They are transported in limed freight cars as cattle. . . . Those who survive await the doom that has been prepared for them. Caravans of death are driven daily from these concentration centers to deathhouses in outlying districts where the victims are done to death by gas and blood-poisoning. Steam shovels dig trenches in the fields about into which the bodies are cast. No account is taken of age or sex. The only crime is that they are Jews. Already many towns and villages, hallowed in Jewish memory, . . . are declared by the Nazi press to be "Judenrein."

Conning then went on to describe the events that had taken place in the Warsaw ghetto and made particular reference to Sholem Asch, whom he described as having personal knowledge of the destruction of an entire institution of children, citing this as evidence of "the depth of degradation to which humanity can be brought by unmitigated hate."[60]

In the spring 1945 issue in a news page, "Happenings in Israel," reports of the Jewish survivors in Lodz (mostly German Jews who had been sent to the Lodz ghetto) and of Jews in Italy who were saved by Catholic Christians also noted the conversion of many Italian Jews to the Roman Catholic faith. The discovery of Auschwitz, here given its Polish name, was also reported.

> The Russian armies have occupied the Polish town of Osvientim with its infamous extermination camp where many hundreds of thousands of Jews have been executed in a most barbarous way. In September, 1944 alone the Nazis burned 20,-000 Jews alive in that camp. Before their evacuation the Germans removed the ovens so as to obliterate incriminating evidence. However, 5,000 Jews survived the mass murder.

This is one of the very few references to Auschwitz found in any of the American Protestant periodicals examined.

Victor Buksbazen, who compiled the news reported in "Happenings in Israel," included a lengthy quotation from *Opinion*, a monthly Jewish magazine. The citation was in the form of an indictment.

> "The most shocking of the war, indeed of all history, is the extermination of close to five million European Jews! Almost equally shocking is the indifference of the civilized world. If the Nazis had murdered five millions dogs or cats under simi-

lar circumstances, the denunciations would have risen to the
high heaven, and numerous groups would have vied with one
another to save the animals. Jews, however, has created hardly
a stir! Hitler certainly has scored a superlative success in at
least one field in the war on the Jews.

"More painful than the world silence is the failure of American Jewry and of American Jewish leadership to do anything
themselves or to compel government action in behalf of the
victims. True, international conferences have been held at Evian and Bermuda, but the results were precisely nil! Even national Jewish organizations charged with the task of overseas
relief did not do all that could have been done nor all that
should have been done!

"Ultimately and in the final analysis the guilt for the death of
five million Jews rests upon all of American Israel. If American
Jews had really been deeply aroused, our public officials
would have been compelled to initiate real rescue work. Our
failure represents another phase of the contemporary Jewish
tragedy without a parallel in Jewish history."

The *Opinion* article quoted closed with a citation of a speech by Senator Robert F. Wagner concerning the failure to make Palestine available for Jewish emigration to save Europe's Jews.[61] It is particularly
interesting to note that Victor Buksbazen, in including the *Opinion*
article, added no comment or additional information. In a later paragraph, he did note that some Germans were apparently befriending
the few remaining Jews in Germany as "good policy and a helpful
alibi in view of the unmistakable signs that an allied victory is at
hand. Hitler's Latest Outrage on Jewry."[62]

The Presbyterian Register, again indicating the relative difficulty of
obtaining accurate or comprehensive news from within the Nazi-held
areas in early 1945, reported in a very brief statement that the Jews
in Budapest and Vienna were being used as forced labor to build
fortifications. In the same brief report, it was noted that the holy
books and priestly garments of a Jewish community had been se-
creted in the cellars of the faculty of theology at Sarospatek (not otherwise identified) and thus had been preserved from destruction.[63]

But difficult as it was to obtain accurate, detailed accounts of the
Nazi persecution of the Jews in 1945, January to April, the organizations engaged in Christian missionary work among Jews in America
seemed able both to obtain and publish the more detailed reports.
Where Jews had survived (as in Lodz, Poland, and Hungary), this
fact was known and reported. Where extermination camps were

found as the Russians advanced into western Poland and into parts of eastern Germany, these discoveries were reported, as was the liberation of Auschwitz.

Paid Advertisements in 1945

The ability to obtain and then publish such information by these organizations and agencies was further confirmed by the paid advertising placed by such Christian missionary agencies that did not themselves publish a magazine or a periodical but who paid for advertisements in regularly published American Protestant periodicals.

The International Hebrew Christian Alliance's advertisement for February 1945 in *The King's Business* referred to 400,000 Jews starved to death or massacred in extermination camps. The source for the report was given as "missionaries in Europe." "'Many Hebrew Christians,' the report states, 'were shot or simply disappeared. From a whole congregation of Hebrew Christians in Chisinau, only one is now alive.'" A similar extermination of a small Hebrew Christian congregation at Jassy was also reported in the advertisement, but the major purpose of the ad was to announce that aid to the remaining Rumanian Jews was an imperative need, since Rumania was then free of Nazi occupation.[64] The same advertisement under the same title had appeared in *The Sunday School Times* in January 1945.[65] The February 17, 1945, advertisement placed by the International Hebrew Christian Alliance took another direction. It focused on the number of Jews exterminated, stating that of the 3 million Jews who had perished during the war, only 8 percent had fallen in actual warfare. "The remaining 2,770,000 deaths resulted from deliberate Nazi methods of planned starvation, forced labor, mass deportation and methodical massacres."[66] The Friends of Israel Missionary and Relief Society's advertisement in the same periodical on March 17, 1945, noted that "the tragedy of Israel in our day is so great and monstrous, that nothing in the annals of world history can be compared with it."[67]

Two weeks later, the International Hebrew Christian Alliance again placed an advertisement, but that ad referred to the Nazi persecution of the Jews in generalized, nonspecific terms. The ad stressed, instead, the relief work of the organization throughout the Nazi era.[68] The same advertisement was run in *The Sunday School Times* two weeks later, on April 14, 1945.[69] This organization continued to place advertisements in *The Sunday School Times* throughout 1945, but the character of the ads shifted somewhat to an emphasis on the extreme need of the surviving Jews in Europe. The one exception was the advertisement placed in the September 1, 1945, issue. It contained the following paragraph:

> It is estimated that the Nazis killed nearly five million Jews in Europe during the past ten years and that the remnant of European Jewry number no more than two million, aside from the 3,500,000 Jews to be found in Russia. In Poland, before the war, there were 3,500,000 Jews; today, the latest survey shows a mere 30,000. In Hungary there were nearly a million Jews before the war; today, perhaps 250,000. In Jugoslavia, there were 75,000 Jews; today, about 10,000. And so the painful story goes.[70]

The dire situation facing the Jews who had "survived the Nazi plan of extermination" was stressed by the organizations and agencies engaged in Christian missionary work among Jews. The ads reflected this.[71]

But what of those American Protestant periodicals that were not published by organizations engaged in Christian missionary work among American Jews? The majority of periodicals in 1945 reported nothing about the Nazi persecution of the Jews during the first four months of 1945. Even those that accepted paid advertising reported nothing in their news pages, editorials, or articles. Only eight of the thirty-nine periodicals examined for 1945 included any references at all to the Nazi persecution of the Jews, and, as has been noted, many of these references were generalized, indirect, and nonspecific. The course of the war and the prevailing censorship apparently precluded detailed, accurate reports. Most of the paid advertisements appeared in only two periodicals during these same months, January–April 1945, and those periodicals were most closely tied to Christian missionary work among the Jews. The Friend of Zion and The Hebrew Christian Alliance Quarterly published items from the general to the more specific but only as such information came out of what had been Nazi-occupied Europe.[72] Thirty-one of the periodicals reported nothing during this time period.

The Liberation of the Death Camps

The Allied and Russian advances into the heart of Germany itself changed all that. By April 15, 1945, the Allies had advanced into central and southern Germany and the Russians had advanced to a line west of Berlin. On April 25, 1945, Allied and Russian troops met at Torgau in central Germany. As the Allied forces advanced, the remaining concentration camps and their inmates were discovered and liberated. The liberation of prisoners in these camps had begun in the summer of 1944 with the advance of the Russian armies into Poland. Though most of the world's attention was focused on Majdanek and the revelations of the extermination process in that camp, a number of other forced labor camps and extermination camps also had either been liberated or evacuated ahead of the Russian advance. A chronology of the evacuations and liberations of the camps follows.

Fall 1943	Treblinka Sobibor Belzec	Camps in eastern Poland, evacuated by Germans
July 1944	Lublin Majdanek	Camps in eastern Poland, liberated by Russians
	Radom Cracow Blzyn Prestkowa	Forced labor camps in eastern Poland, evacuated by Germans
	Riga Vilna Kovno	Camps in Estonia, liberated by Russians
January 26, 1945	Auschwitz Birkenau	Camps in Upper Silesia, liberated by Russians
February 1945	Stutthof	Camp in eastern Prussia, liberated by Russians
April 1945	Nuengamme	Camp in northern Germany, evacuated by Germans
	Oranienburg Ravensbruck Sachsenhausen	Camps in northern and eastern Germany, probably liberated by Americans or evacuated by Germans

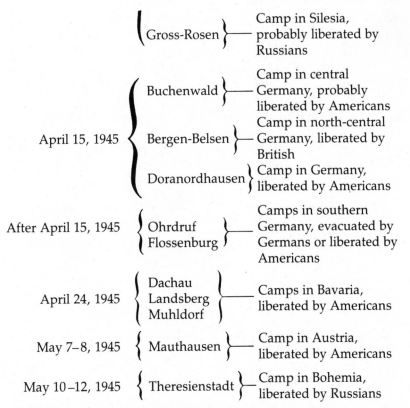

April 15, 1945
- Gross-Rosen — Camp in Silesia, probably liberated by Russians
- Buchenwald — Camp in central Germany, probably liberated by Americans
- Bergen-Belsen — Camp in north-central Germany, liberated by British
- Doranordhausen — Camp in Germany, liberated by Americans

After April 15, 1945
- Ohrdruf / Flossenburg — Camps in southern Germany, evacuated by Germans or liberated by Americans

April 24, 1945
- Dachau / Landsberg / Muhldorf — Camps in Bavaria, liberated by Americans

May 7–8, 1945
- Mauthausen — Camp in Austria, liberated by Americans

May 10–12, 1945
- Theresienstadt — Camp in Bohemia, liberated by Russians

At best, such a chronology can only be approximate. For instance, specific references to the evacuation or liberation of the camps at Ohrdruf, Gross-Rosen, Landsberg, Doranordhausen, and Muhldorf can only be inferred from the time when the area was occupied by American troops. No direct reference to the time of this liberation or evacuation could be found.[73] According to Henri Michel's *The Second World War*, many of these camps combined forced labor, concentration, and extermination, and they also functioned as a part of a local network (*Kommando*) of camps in various areas in Germany, Bohemia, and Bavaria.[74]

The extent of the whole network of camps seems to have been largely unknown to the American Protestant press at the time the war was ending in Europe. It is not surprising, then, that the names of many of the camps did not appear at all in the general news reports and editorials. Some of them did appear by name and with descriptions in the letters from military personnel who were in the area during and after the capture and liberation of some of the camps.

Face to Face with the Death Camps

Shock, horror, and a reluctant acknowledgment that rumor was reality was the immediate editorial response. But, even then, the full force of the extent of the extermination process in the death camps did not come home immediately. In the first direct reference to the death camps after they had been found, Charles Clayton Morrison described the policy of requiring German civilians to visit the camps to see for themselves what had been happening in them.

> As the concentration camps are captured, German civilians by the thousand . . . are being forced to look on the evidence of the fiendish atrocities committed in them and to bury the thousands of still unburied dead. This has already happened at Buchenwald, Gardelegen and Nordhausen, and it is said to be a policy which will be continued as all the other concentration camps are reached.
>
> It is, admittedly, a revolting business thus to make civilians, women as well as men, look at the stomach-turning sights. . . . But there is sound reason behind it. Unless great numbers of the German survivors of the war see the horrors for themselves no written descriptions, no photographs would convince them that they had ever taken place.

The editorial then went on to discuss the hoped-for effect of such a policy, the problem of these revelations becoming part of a denial that these things ever happened at some future time, and the expressed hope that "decent Germans" would never again turn to "such a vile thing as nazism."[75]

One week later, Charles Clayton Morrison wrote of his own direct confrontation with the death camps. His editorial was titled "Gazing into the Pit."

> The horrors disclosed by the capture of the nazi concentration camps at Buchenwald, Belsen and Limburg and a dozen other places constitute one of those awful facts upon which a paper such as this feels under obligation to comment, but concerning which it is almost physically impossible to write. What can be said that will not seem like tossing little words up against a giant mountain of ineradicable evil? What human emotion can measure up to such bestiality except a searing anger which calls heaven to witness that retribution shall be swift and terri-

ble and pitiless? How can men (and, it is alleged, women) who
have been capable of such deeds be thought of or dealt with
save as vicious brutes who must be exterminated both to do
justice and in mercy to the future of the race?

We have found it hard to believe that the reports from the
nazi concentration camps could be true. Almost desperately
we have tried to think that they must be wildly exaggerated.
Perhaps they were the products of the fevered brains of prisoners who were out for revenge. Or perhaps they were just
more atrocity-mongering like the cadaver factory stories of the
last war. But such puny barricades cannot stand up against the
terrible facts. The evidence is too conclusive. It will be a long,
long time before our eyes will cease to see those pictures of naked corpses piled like firewood or those mounds of carrion
flesh and bones. It will be a long, long time before we can forget what scores of honorable, competent observers tell us they
have seen with their own eyes. The thing is well-nigh incredible. But it happened.

The editorial went on to raise the general question, what does this all
mean? He reported similar atrocities from missionaries coming out of
China, he mentioned Poland and the Baltic states, and he said that a
similar story could be told about Russia were the details available.
Even the lynch mobs in America were cited. Then the editorial stated:

No, the horror of the Nazi concentration camps is the horror of
humanity itself when it has surrendered to its capacity for evil.
When we look at the pictures from Buchenwald we are looking, to be sure, at the frightful malignity of nazism. This perv-
ersion of all values which in its final extremity is actually intent, as Hitler himself has said, on reducing Europe to "ruin,
rats and epidemics." But in the nazis and beyond them we are
looking into the very pit of hell which men disclose yawning
within themselves when they reject the authority of the moral
law, when they deny the sacredness of the human personality,
when they turn from worship of the one true God to the worship of their own wills, their own states, their own lust for
power.

Buchenwald and the other memorials of nazi infamy reveal
the depths to which humanity can sink, and has sunk, in these
frightful years.

Then, in effect, Morrison called for a spiritual awakening, both of
the Christian conscience and of the proclamation of the Gospel, not
"dispassionately, tentatively or listlessly . . . the time has come when

the Christian must proclaim his gospel 'like a dying man to dying men.'" Morrison then called upon the World Council of Churches to lead this renewed proclamation of the Christian Gospel, naming Niemoeller and Bishop Berggrav of Norway, survivors of Nazi prisons, as men who should lead the way, with every Christian "who sees the peril and knows the means of escape" following.[76]

Guy Emery Shipler, the editor of *The Churchman*, published three editorials on May 15, 1945. The first dealt with Hitler the man and contrasted *Mein Kampf* with the Bible, particularly quoting the prophet Isaiah. "Because of this one being cast in the mold of a man—one who called evil good, and good evil—'hell hath enlarged herself, and opened her mouth without measure' throughout the world."[77] The second editorial, "Think on This," mentioned that American prisoners of war were among the victims of Nazi bestiality.

> It is their beaten, starved, and burned bodies which are found in these charnel houses, along with the bodies of Russians, Poles, Frenchmen, Czechoslovaks, and Jews. There is meaning to this. The meaning is that the atrocities which Nazis began years ago to practice on the Jews of Germany—without too much protest from the Christian world—at last reached our own flesh and blood, precisely as every opponent of anti-Semitism predicted that they would eventually. For anti-Semitism— in Germany, in America, or anywhere else—never has, as its real objective, the persecution of the Jews alone. It is always a diabolical way of destroying the dignity and humanity of the whole human race—beginning with the Jews. . . . When the Nazis began to persecute the Jews they were testing the conscience of mankind. . . .
>
> The whole Christian world, inside Germany and out, should have thrown all its strength against the Nazis from the moment that its anti-Semitic program was announced and the first Jew was subjected to persecution as a consequence of it. Had we done that we should not today be looking upon the mutilated corpses of American prisoners in Nazi concentration camps.
>
> Americans—and Christians—who permit anti-Semitism in America to go unrebuked—please note and ponder!

Shipler was consistent in that he shaped his response to the death camps to the long-established campaign of *The Churchman* against anti-Semitism. At the same time, he indicted the Christian community for its failure.[78]

The third editorial was a guest editorial written by Wilbur L. Caswell. It was based, in turn, upon an editorial published in the *New York Herald-Tribune*, from which Caswell even borrowed the title, "The Shape of Buchenwald." Caswell also shaped his remarks around a condemnation of mankind and around the role of religion in devising means for destroying people in the name of a cause. Caswell wrote:

> The editorial writer believes that the public should see the moving-pictures of the butchery and atrocities in the German concentration camps, but insists that they "must be more to the public than a mere shrilling pitch-pipe to set the key for a hymn of hate and reprisal against the Nazi enemy."
>
> In condemning the Germans, we . . . are condemning the human race which is capable of such atrocities, for "Germany has no monopoly on atrocity. No nation's history is above reproach, and Buchenwald is only a new entry on a long list of crimes for which all mankind must inevitably take the blame."

Turning again to the *Herald-Tribune*, he continued:

> "It is the entire breed of the proud, two-legged animal that has been guilty of atrocity . . . and Buchenwald is the latest link in a chain of proof that the jungle mud has not yet been washed from him by all the mighty currents of his civilizations. The furnaces designed for cheap killing are cold now. . . ." It is not enough "to take grim resolve, in the manner of one who is free from blame, that they who have committed this crime shall be punished. The horror must be impressed upon every conscience."

Referring to intentions too often "marred by humanity," Caswell concluded:

> Most of the prophets of Nazism probably really believed that they were fighting for a worthy cause—the purging of the Elect Race. The most relentless cruelty has often been exhibited by those who believed themselves fighting the battle of the Lord.[79]

The Living Church chose to publish excerpts from the *Christian News-Letter* of Dr. J. H. Oldham, who also spoke of a collective blame "for the infamy of the German concentration camps," referring to the fact that the inhumanity and torture being carried out in the camps had been known for years before the war and that "the public as a whole was apathetic and the disposition in influential quarters was to hush things up." Citing Oldham further, the article stated, "When its most hideous manifestations strike us in the face we recoil in horror, but corruption from which they spring has lodgment in ourselves. All pride, selfishness and callous indifference to needs of others are a siding with the enemies of Christ." For Oldham, the German concentration camps were evidence of the "web of sin."[80]

The first editorial in *The Messenger* was very brief and titled "Hope in Horror." "It would have been still more horrible if no wave of horror had swept across the country when the German prison camp atrocities were revealed. That men and women recoil . . . from such fiendish brutality is evidence that at least some standards for human conduct have survived these years of barbaric warfare."[81] The second editorial, published two weeks later, was introduced by a quotation from J. H. Oldham's *Christian News-Letter*, as had *The Living Church*, and then introduced the editorial, "Gazing into the Pit" from *The Christian Century*, with an acknowledgment for permission to publish it. The editorial from the *Century* was then printed in full.[82]

The Presbyterian Register, first reminding its readers that some of the churches in the Reformed tradition had been on the opposite side during the war nevertheless went on to write:

> The sinister revelations made of the maltreatment and butchery of human fellow-creatures under the devildoms of Buchenwald or Dachau, or in such extirpations as occurred at Lidice and many another place, must surely have afflicted *all* Christian souls alike and equally. . . . It passes our weak powers to believe that the causing of so great pain with so much cruelty and wicked design can be justly ignored. . . . But it is with heart-ache and heart-quake and heart-break that the very thought of retribution bows us down. May God have mercy indeed upon our souls.

The editorial was entitled, "Judgment."[83]

The Sabbath Recorder, a weekly serving the Seventh-Day Baptists, wrote in an editorial entitled, "Let Us Maintain Our Honor," that the atrocities and "the horrors of the concentration camps where prisoners have been starved to death and have suffered other horrors too dreadful to mention, stir the hearts of Americans as nothing else has. Papers are full of these atrocities, and the radios tell of these horrors." The editorial went on to discuss the reaction of some Americans who were apparently calling for retaliatory measures to be taken against German prisoners of war being held in the United States. Referring to the Geneva Convention calling for "honorable treatment of war prisoners," the editorial urged that the pledge to treat German war prisoners as human beings be kept. "We are giving our war prisoners honorable treatment, and we cannot afford to come down to the Nazi level."[84]

But no editorial or article in May or June of 1945 so captured the essence of the response to the death camps in the American Protestant press, while at the same time pointing up the dilemmas and cautions inherent in such a news revelation, as did the editorial published in *The Signs of the Times* on May 22, 1945. Its title was "So It Was True!"

> It was hard to believe that human beings could sink so low as to starve and torture and burn alive their fellow creatures. When the stories first came out of Nazi Germany, . . . many scoffed and said, "Propaganda!" They remembered the last war and how many of the supposed atrocities were ultimately proved to be without foundation in fact. They assumed that these new horrors had been similarly invented to stir up the war spirit and build up home "morale."
>
> But this time, alas, the stories were true. Only they did not begin to depict the satanic nature of the abominations inflicted on a helpless people.
>
> As the allied armies swept with giant strides across the broken defenses of Germany, they came across evidence of a reign of terror the like of which the world has never seen. So rapid was the advance that concentration camps . . . were captured before the depraved guards and overlords could escape. In one village they found the still smoldering bodies of 1,100 prisoners deliberately crowded into a barn and burned to death. At Belsen they seized a camp where the naked, emaciated dead were still in heaps, awaiting burial. Thousands more, still alive, were but walking skeletons. In Poland and Alsace they uncovered the dread gas chambers where hundreds have been put to death. Almost every day brought new revelations of savagery no words can describe.
>
> Yes, it is all too true. General Eisenhower himself reported to Washington that the facts are almost incredible. At his suggestion many Congressmen and editors are in Europe to see the awful sight for themselves.
>
> Photographs have been taken, too, and moving pictures, so that the reports are authentic, . . . the information . . . a fearsome record of the depths of sin to which humanity was descended.

The writer concluded the editorial, "Surely the horrors of human degradation now uncovered for all mankind to see affords [sic] overwhelming testimony that 'the last days' are upon us, and that the day of judgment must be near at hand."[85]

This editorial and that of Charles Clayton Morrison ("Gazing into the Pit") raised all of the questions inherent in such reporting. Were these "more atrocity stories," like those from World War I? Were they "propaganda?" How was the reporting authenticated? Was it credible? From what sources did these stories come? Who would stand as witness to the accuracy of what was being said as well as seen?

Credibility and Authenticity

Morrison tried to answer these questions by referring to the fact that German civilians were being taken through some of the camps in order to authenticate what has been done in them. In letters sent to some of the periodicals, chaplains told of being present when Germans were brought into one of the camps and the reactions of some of them. Morrison also referred to photographs and to "competent observers."

In the same way, as though particularly concerned to offset criticism and to provide strong, credible witnesses to what was being written about, the editorial in *The Signs of the Times* had referred to General Eisenhower, to members of Congress, to editors, to photographs, and to motion pictures "so that there could be no doubt that the reports were authentic."

Indeed, the "more atrocity stories" theme did appear in a variety of forms in some American Protestant publications. The editor of *Advance*, while admitting that atrocities were a part of the process of making war, in effect said that such stories were of no interest to him and in a later editorial suggested caution in all such reporting. John L. Scotford wrote in March 1945:

> Although they have not been scattered abroad in the whole-sale fashion of 1918, atrocity stories still get around and afford some people a chance for emotional debauch. We believe that the less said about such matters the better. Against the total picture of the war's destruction, all horror tales are a minor matter. . . . The military system gives some men power over their fellows. . . . War puts tremendous pressure on all its participants. In the heat of the conflict men become mad; they are not accountable for their actions. They tell what the enemy has done to our men but they do not tell what we may have done to them. They distort the truth by not also telling of the many

instances when the enemy has been compassionate. Even at its best, war is bad enough; let us not further blacken the countenance of the villian.

The editorial was entitled, "Atrocities."[86] In October 1945, Scotford was still cautious in an editorial, "Atrocities That Weren't." Based on what he referred to as personal conversations with former Canadian and American prisoners of war in Germany and Japan, he wrote:

> All sorts of things happen during the war. . . . However we feel that the black spots have been over-publicized on the radio and in the press and the bright spots almost completely neglected. Our suggestion is that so far as possible these highlighted horrors be checked against the experience of the mass of returning prisoners.

Scotford did not differentiate between prisoner-of-war camps and the death camps. In fact, they were not the same at all, particularly in Germany.[87]

Gerhard E. Lenski, writing for *The Lutheran Standard* in his regularly published "Washington Comments," took a completely different approach. He first mentioned the subject of atrocities in "A Word about Atrocities" on June 2, 1945.

> The widespread showing of pictures depicting certain German prison camps, notably those at Buchenwald and Dachau, has deeply stirred our city and country. It would be hard to say that these pictures are not authentic. . . . Beyond doubt, these pictures are real, and as such they are shocking in the revelation they bring. . . . *They tell us vividly just what war is.* . . . Look at the horrors of Buchenwald and Dachau and Lublin— these are true pictures of what war is and what war does [emphasis his].[88]

In August, Lenski again took up the same theme. In "Atrocity Pictures," he wrote:

> We ourselves have seen the enlarged photographs shown as murals at the Congressional Library. We also saw the army movies depicting German prison camps. Then we heard two reports, given by eye witnesses, who had inspected these camps. . . . Will the showing of these pictures prevent war and further atrocities? No doubt that is the purpose intended. But we are not sure the desired result will be attained. For one thing it is hard to think that the general public is deeply inter-

ested in these pictures. Somehow the average American, having read *Life* magazine, . . . has grown blasé and case-hardened. Then all these horrors took place in Germany and, of course they can't ever happen here. That seems the common reaction.

Lenski then repeated his earlier statement regarding what war is and what war does, adding that war makers—munitions manufacturers, international schemers, and students at war colleges—ought to be the ones to see the pictures.[89]

The Cautious and the Skeptical

A third approach, different from Scotford's in *Advance* and Lenski's in *The Lutheran Standard*, appeared in *The Concordia Theological Monthly* and in *The Mennonite*. In the former, the editor wrote:

Is it possible to love the perpetrators of the atrocities of Buchenwald and Dachau and of the horror camps in the Far East? To one endeavoring to escape in this instance the application of the command of love proclaimed with unsurpassed clarity and force by Jesus and His Apostles, the thought might suggest itself that the people responsible for these shocking crimes against humanity have ceased to be human beings, that they have become obnoxious reptiles and simply must be exterminated with as little feeling of regret as when one kills a man-eating tiger or a cobra. First of all, a word of caution is not out of place. How easy it is for people to be misled we remember from the first World War when the blackest of stories were spread about inhumanities committed in Belgium and elsewhere which afterwards proved to be fabrications. . . . Still, all who recall the air of truth with which the stories of 1917 were told and the pictures which were presented in proof will be somewhat wary when they come upon the descriptions of brutalities said to have been committed by the Nazis and the Japanese.

He concluded by saying that, even if the stories were true, Christian love should prevail over a spirit of retribution.[90]

The editor of *The Mennonite* wrote an editorial on the topic on June 3, 1945. "Atrocity stories may be considered in the light of the following points," which can be summarized as follows: (1) God "hath made of one blood all nations" and the Germans are no different than we are. If we argue that Germans are inferior, then we use the same argument that the Germans used against the Jews. (2) The Allies are not blameless in regard to what are "unwholesome characteristics" in the German culture. (3) The Allies have been more deadly than the Germans in order to win victory. (4) Atrocity stories from the last war were largely false, and there were atrocity stories about us. (5) The current atrocity stories have come out after the cessation of fighting in Europe but look what we are doing in the Pacific area. (6) Vengeance belongs to God and not to us. (7) "'I saw with my own eyes' stories written by local boys who are across may be accepted with the knowledge that human observation is very fallible and especially so when handicapped by limited time and unfamiliar conditions. Who produced what in Europe is not always very clear—even in the atrocity pictures of the famous magazines. One such showed Allied soldiers laying out nearly three thousand dead bodies along a bombed street for burial. Were the Germans responsible for these many dead or was it the Allied bombing that killed them? To believe everything that is printed hardly seems justifiable." (8) "That atrocities have been committed in this war need not be questioned." The remainder of the eighth point then discussed the "atrocity of all time," the crucifixion of Jesus of Nazareth by the Roman military troops, and the need for forgiveness as Jesus cried, "Father forgive them for they know not what they do."[91] Both the "more atrocity stories" problem and the problem of skepticism about what was being reported about the death camps in Germany hung on tenaciously in spite of efforts to authenticate fully what was being said and shown.

At no point was this skepticism revealed more clearly than in an article by James Morgan Read, published in *The Christian Century* with the title "Trials for War Criminals." Read, who had held several college teaching posts during the 1930s, had received two earned doctoral degrees, one from Marburg University in Germany in 1932, one from the University of Chicago in 1941.[92] Also in 1941 he had published a book on atrocity propaganda in World War I. It is to this work that he makes a slight reference in his article.[93]

Finally, trials for war criminals would establish the truth concerning atrocities. I have had a little experience in trying to weigh the evidence in atrocity stories. It is not easy when you have to rely on the testimony of reporters, *ex parte* official commissions, and even eye-witnesses unchecked by cross-examination. . . . Are these atrocities on a scale large enough to indict 5,000,000 Germans, as the Russians have suggested when they speak of the many war criminals? Or do they represent the work of a small number of sadists?

One illustration of what is needed in the way of impartial investigation into atrocity charges is provided by the account of death chambers in German camps. Many of these camps were obviously fighting typhus epidemics and using fumigation chambers to delouse the prisoners as a preventive measure. The question is, "How many of these chambers represented genuine efforts to kill *lice,* and how many of them were flimsy excuses or even undisguised efforts to kill *people*? Court trials could establish such facts beyond reasonable doubt. [emphasis his].[94]

In retrospect, Read's statement, formed as a question, was startling, if not incredible. It must be noted, however, that he had credentials for commenting on the problem, it had been a problem in World War I, and it had been a constant problem for editors and writers in the American Protestant press throughout the Nazi era. Were the things reported to be happening in the German concentration camps going to prove to have been largely propaganda, or had they actually happened?

Also, assuming that Read had submitted his article to the *Century* at least two weeks before the time of its publication (May 30, 1945), he must have written it early in May before the revelations about the death camps were fully comprehended. Read probably rushed into print prematurely, both in light of the subsequent evidence and from the perspective of distance. In any event, his "genuine efforts to kill *lice* . . . undisguised efforts to kill *people*" statement was an unfortunate juxtaposition. Two interesting but unanswerable questions arise. Why did *The Christian Century* publish the article? And, more important, why did Read go unchallenged in the published letters to the editor in the *Century* during subsequent weeks? No letters to the editor, even on the central theme of the article, the trying of war criminals, were published. But the fact that the atrocity stories and the showing of atrocity films resulted in controversy was evident in an editorial in *The Messenger,* which noted that the faculty and students of Eden Seminary in St. Louis had sent a letter to the local newspaper opposing the showing of such films as hinderances to reconciliation. The editor of *The Messenger* agreed with the seminarians.[95]

Eyewitness and Firsthand Reports about the Death Camps

Both the editor of *The Mennonite* and James Morgan Read questioned the reliability of eyewitness accounts and firsthand accounts of the reports coming out of the death camps. Several means of dealing with this credibility problem were used by editors and writers in the American Protestant press. References to prominent persons and to well-authenticated motion pictures and photographs have already been noted. At least three other ways of establishing the credibility of the revelations about the extermination processes used in the death camps were employed by the press. One was to publish directly statements by credible, respected, professional journalists whose reputations as newspeople could not be questioned. The second was to publish letters, and later articles, written by military personnel—enlisted men, officers, and chaplains—who actually had seen the death camps and who had written home to their denominational periodicals to describe what they had seen. The third was what Martin Niemoeller had to say about the death camps.

The Churchman, using the first criteria, gave a lengthy report of the statements made before the Economic Club of Detroit by Malcolm W. Bingay, identified as "editorial director of the *Detroit Free Press*, . . . one of 18 American editors who went to Europe on General Eisenhower's request to visit the Nazi horror camps. . . . 'Are the stories "propaganda"?' Mr. Bingay: 'We found that these reports were not propaganda. Rather they were inadequate in telling the full horror. Statistics are utterly impossible.'" A series of questions followed the first one, most of which related to the possibility that such things could happen in America. Two questions related to the atrocities and to the German people. "'How could these atrocities have happened?'" Bingay's answer was "'No moral law.'" "'Why did the German people yield to the Nazis?' . . . We talked to scholars, we talked to industrial leaders, we talked to scientists, we talked to the little people of Germany, and always it was the same story. "No, we didn't believe in the Nazi principles, but we had to join up—or else." They were afraid.'" Bingay's concluding reference was to the Sermon on the Mount and to Calvary, by which he meant the moral law. "'That is what the Nazis threw away to launch their crime of the ages.'"[96]

The eyewitness accounts of military personnel were printed in some publications, sometimes in an edited form, sometimes in the form of the original letter. Generally, these accounts tended to appear somewhat later in 1945 because of the time involved in sending the letter from overseas or in some instances because the account was prepared for publication after the person giving the details had returned to the United States.

One such account was published in *The Gospel Messenger* on August 18, 1945. A prefatory statement read, "The following letter was written amidst the smells of one of the widely publicized prison camps of Europe on the day of its liberation, by one of the corporals, Orlando J. Woodward, who helped liberate it." The content of the letter follows.

> Today is V-E day in the European theater of operations. The Allies have won a great military victory. But actually, what real worth-while victory has been gained?
>
> Today I visited a Jewish camp. Most of the inmates were former residents of Poland, but were made prisoners by the Germans upon their occupation of that country. These people are dying of starvation and disease.
>
> Upon arrival at the camp, which was made of mere logs and sticks, the first thing I saw was a man who had been starved so much that he would not weigh more than eighty pounds. The further I progressed into camp the stronger the stench got. People were dying in piles. The Americans were having them brought out of the muddy huts, or pens, to drier ground. In one to two minutes many were dead. Of the thousands there, they were literally dying by the hundreds. They were reached too late by Allied armies. Unless one could see things he can hardly believe it; but it is true!

Mentioning that all the aid possible was being given to the freed prisoners, Woodward then wrote:

> This is the crop that was planted by militarism, cultivated by hatred, and the harvest is destruction for millions of people. . . . Christ was forgotten. The idea of the brotherhood of man was denied, for no human could treat his brother with so much cruelty.[97]

Neither the camp nor the man's army unit was identified. The description could serve for any number of the death camps liberated by American troops.

A similar letter was sent directly to the editor of *The Calvin Forum* by F. W. Van Houten, identified only as being stationed in Kassel,

Germany. He told of visiting Buchenwald and Nordhausen and of a planned trip to Dachau. The letter was written on June 11, 1945. The letter is long, for a reason.

> For the last six years you have heard many reports of the S.S. atrocities and you have questioned their veracity. I offer my observations and relate them factually. The walls still echo the terrible agonies of victims and the horrible atrocities of the S.S.

Van Houten then gave a detailed, eight-paragraph description of Buchenwald. He described the population of the camp, some 55,000; how the prisoners were housed under impossibly crowded conditions; how they were dying of malnutrition; how prisoners had been used for medical experimentation (he included a description of "an array of hearts and lungs preserved in jars of alcohol" that he had seen); how they had been put to death by injection. He described the blood-stained walls and floor in a dispensary room, the crematoria, the gallows, the torture racks, and all of the other evidence of the extermination process. He noted that American soldiers had found bodies awaiting the crematoria, most of whom had starved to death.

He also described a room that prisoners had been forced to enter. They fell into a concrete trap or pit, described as being three feet square and about nine feet deep. Metal spikes were a part of the torture process. Prisoners were then hung and apparently left to die. "Even though the place was cleaned and whitewashed, I could see the marks on the wall where the unhappy victims had scratched and kicked in the agony of death."

He then described how the bodies were placed on a hand elevator and elevated to six gas ovens, three bodies to an iron stretcher, to be burned. "When the American soldiers came they found the furnace burning with partially burned bodies in the ovens. The guides claim that thousands of bodies were cremated there." Van Houten's guide was a Yugoslavian who had lived in the United States, who had returned to Yugoslavia after World War I, and who had become a prisoner because three of his sons were in Tito's Yugoslavian partisan army. "In a vivid way he described these horrors which he had witnessed during his eleven months imprisonment. Night after night he watched vigorous flames belch from the colossal chimney of the mammoth furnace with its six ovens."

Van Houten then spoke of his planned trip to Dachau. "Of all the concentration camps in Germany—and there were many—this is the most notorious." He also told of his visit to Doranordhausen, the huge underground V-1 and V-2 rocket factory run by forced labor. His guide was a young Dutch former medical student who had been imprisoned at Nordhausen. Van Houten told of seeing in the hospital the emaciated bodies of those whom the Allies were trying to save and of the crematorium. "Outside the crematorium were two pits of human ashes. The pits were 5 × 5 × 5; one was filled with ashes and covered with dirt; the other was half full of ashes." Van Houten continued, "Thus, you are able to perceive something of the diabolical system of the Nazi State as executed by the Satanic S.S. These concentration camps are an actuality of slave labor, punishment, and execution accompanied by that dreadful and slow murderer of men— malnutrition." He also told of the shooting of seventy-eight Italian prisoners near Kassel and the forced exhumation of the bodies by German civilians to "give them a decent burial. I saw these bodies exhumed." He closed his letter by comparing Germany to the biblical Tyre and Sidon after their destruction and with a quotation from Psalm 46.[98]

Similar accounts were sent home from Europe by army chaplains. Chaplain (Captain) Thomas P. Bailey sent a letter to *The Alliance Weekly*. Bailey told of entering one of the liberated camps with the Third Army. "Those who were still alive were skeletons of forty or fifty pounds. As we entered the camp some civilians lifted their caps to us. I didn't understand why they did that until I had seen the horrors of the place they had been, and understood what their deliverance had meant to them." He then described the sight of the dead bodies in the camp.[99]

Division Chaplain (Major) George B. Wood, a Protestant Episcopalian clergyman, wrote to *The Living Church*. He, too, described details similar to the other accounts but with other emphases. He spoke of going to a camp where he saw "stark and naked cruelty and it is a horrible sight. . . . In one building I saw the bodies piled high like disordered cord wood; in others I saw the sick and dying lying with the dead in their own feces and vomit—no stables were filthier than these." He also described a nearby camp for Polish women, where conditions were somewhat better because it was a forced labor camp.

Chaplain Wood then described a burial service held on V-E Day for 200 "atrocity victims." He told of 5,000 German civilians who

filed by to view the remains laid out in state by the graves which they had dug. German officers, including generals were made to see the horror of their own brutality. . . . The local

Pre-Nazi Burgomaster addressed his people to the effect that they were now being given the opportunity to right a wrong committed by the German nation.

Every fourth cross was marked by a Star of David since camp records indicated that 25 percent of the camp's inmates had been Jewish. "It is hoped that a deep impression is made upon these German people, many of whom were seen to be weeping during the ceremony. One woman was overheard to say, 'It is a disgrace to be a German.'" The letter concluded with a note that local churches (Lutheran) were available to him for the services he conducted, presumably for the American troops.[100] A full report of the actual service described by Chaplain Wood, including a complete copy of the statement read by Chaplain Wood, was published one week later in *The Living Church*.[101] Here, the military unit was identified as the 82nd Airborne Division.

But perhaps no such account quite equaled that of Chaplain (Captain) Donald G. Davis, identified as "pastor-on-leave of the First Baptist Church of Wasco, California." Davis was a clergyman in the German Baptist denomination in America, and his article was requested by the editor of *The Baptist Herald*, the publication of the German Baptist Publication Society, because of a speech Chaplain Davis had given at a youth service in July 1945. "What I Saw at Buchenwald" was published in the November 11, 1945, issue of *The Baptist Herald*.

> My mother was born in Germany. I spent a summer at the University of Berlin in the middle 20's. When atrocity stories from German concentration camps began to be made public before and during the early years of the war, I felt that they must be a part of the propaganda against Germany which might be expected in such times.
>
> This spring I had the opportunity to see for myself.

He then told of being assigned to Buchenwald with the 120th Evacuation Hospital, on April 15–16, 1945. He was the chaplain for this unit. The war was still going on in the area, snipers were active, the enemy dead were strewn about the streets, and enemy planes still strafed the area. He described in detail the scene at Buchenwald— the wooden barracks, the tiered wooden bunks, the filth and misery, and the condition of the remaining prisoners. His unit removed the living to a hospital, "which we had set up in the beautiful and modern barracks in which 3,000 S.S. (Schutzstaffel) guards had lived."

He further stated that what he saw had been going on for more than ten years and that he had attended a memorial service for 50,000 "who by actual headquarter records had died or been killed in Buchenwald." He saw the crematoria, still holding the charred remains of bodies, young and old, and the piled up skeletons and bodies of the unburied dead, "stacked up like cordwood on the ground and in wagons and trucks." He mentioned Frau Koch, wife of the commandant, and her penchant for tattoed skin in lampshades, sails for model ships, and ornamental articles. He told of speaking personally with inmates of the camp and of the marching of adult citizens of Weimar to Buchenwald so they could see for themselves and talk with the inmates. "Fainting men and women who could not retain their food were to be seen in each group." Each group was also addressed by an American lieutenant and told why they had been brought to the camp.

Chaplain Davis then said:

> I write only of the things I saw for myself. I could write of things told us by prisoners—of water tortures and other forms of inquisatorial torture and death meted out to prisoners—of the 400 children remaining from an original group of 2,000, who upon their own testimony were at the disposal of the S.S. guards.

The remainder of the article addressed the question of how this could have happened and what the German Baptists could do for Germany in the postwar situation.[102]

Chaplain Davis's article was doubly significant not only as an eyewitness account but also because of his own German heritage and because of his ministerial relationship to the German Baptist denomination in America. Further, The Baptist Herald, during the 1930s, had published articles from time to time that were between favorable and neutral regarding Hitler and the future of Germany. In 1934, several representatives of the denomination had attended the Baptist World Alliance meetings in Berlin, and some of them had written articles following their return.[103]

Chaplain Davis did observe that the situation at Buchenwald could be multiplied "many dozens of times for all the concentration camps in Germany and the occupied countries" and that a Polish Jew who had been in ten different camps in Poland and Germany told him "that Buchenwald was the best he had seen: it was spoken of as a rest camp."[104] Curiously, no other account or reference to the death camps as such appeared in The Baptist Herald. One letter from Chaplain Frank Woyke, dated September 10, 1945, Berlin, Germany, referred indirectly to deaths by starvation and torture but spoke mostly about the plight of refugees. Woyke was one of those who had gone to Berlin in 1934.[105]

Martin Niemoeller and the Death Camps

Pastor Martin Niemoeller was witness to the death camps and to Nazi practices in the concentration camps. Many people interviewed him, and some asked him about these camps. G. Bromley Oxnam, with several others, met with Niemoeller on May 15, 1945, in Naples, Italy. One part of the conversation turned to the camps.

> I took another line for a moment and asked, "How could Germans do the brutal things done in the camps?"
> "What has been reported is true. Indescribable and incredible things were done. A preacher knows the reason, because he knows sin. A man commits adultery. He is under the conviction of conscience, suffers remorse. But he commits the second act, and conscience does not speak so sharp. And finally he commits adultery without remorse. At first, those ordered to torture and kill did so because they were afraid they would be killed if they did not. Then they became accustomed to brutality, they killed with little feeling, and finally they did their terrible work as a matter of routine. The camps were worse than reported. It is like a terrible dream within a dream. All is still a nightmare, and you awaken to disbelieve what you know was true just the day before.[106]

Niemoeller also spoke for himself in an article published in *The Living Church*, "The Spiritual Outlook in Germany." In the article, he reminded his readers, "We cannot forget—and the world should not, either—that concentration camps and extermination camps were not an invention of the war that began in 1939, but of 1933, and that 'war crimes' had their beginning many years before the war began." He then spoke of the loss of "spirit" of the German people over the years. "What was left was sheer emptiness of mind and soul. . . . And that is what the G.I.'s saw when they entered Germany and found our people dumb, dull and apathetic. The news and pictures of crimes and atrocities has infinitely deepened the abyss."[107]

The Lutheran Standard editorialized from Bishop Oxnam's visit with Niemoeller, stressing particularly his response about "alleged Nazi atrocities" and noting that Niemoeller had said that they were true.[108] One week later, an article by P. O. Bersell was published. The article was based on the writer's travels in Europe in the spring of 1945 and appeared under the heading "Almost Unbelievable Atrocities."

> I saw with my own eyes what the Germans had done so ruthlessly and barbarously to conquered people. I listened by the hour to stories of refugees. Many of them were men of God. I do not believe that they lied to me. I spoke to diplomats who had documentary evidence of terrible atrocities. I heard the story, as told by men who had come right out of Germany, of almost unbelievable wholesale liquidation of Jews and other "undesirables."

Photographs of Niemoeller and Bishop Hans Meiser of Bavaria accompanied the article.[109]

On July 7, 1945, *The Lutheran Standard* published the Religious News Service's article by Niemoeller.[110] On September 15, 1945, another interview with Niemoeller was published. The interviewer was Chaplain David L. Ostergren, a Lutheran clergyman serving in Italy. Ostergren was Niemoeller's "neighbor" in Italy and saw him almost daily. Among the questions asked by the chaplain was "if the cruelties described at Buchenwald and Dachau were exaggerated."

> He replied that he had no reason to believe that they were anything but true. He had seen many acts performed in the prison that were horrible and terrible and that made it possible for him to believe that these inhuman atrocities were as described. He furthermore stated that the element of fear impressed upon each individual in the concentration camp was almost unbearable.[111]

Chaplain Ostergren published a second article in *The Lutheran Companion*, also in September of 1945. Here, the chaplain was more specific in his explanation of some of the questions he had asked of Niemoeller. One was related to Niemoeller's opposition to, or at least objection to, national socialism. Among the reasons Niemoeller gave for his opposition to national socialism was that "National Socialists murdered cruelly without cause the Jews and many others. This was a violation of the commandment 'Thou shalt not kill.'" He then was quoted as saying that national socialism

> disregarded the rights of the individual, making him only a machine in the eyes of the State. . . . It got so that every time I spoke I thought, "This will be my last." . . . Later they said I was a Jew lover and dangerous to the State. My underground

activities were discovered. I was arrested and sent to the concentration camp.

The Ostergren article repeated essentially the same information as
had appeared in *The Lutheran Standard* article about atrocities at Buchenwald and Dachau and a slightly longer version of the analogy of
sin and committing adultery, mentioned in the article in *The Christian
Century*, by Bishop Oxnam. The remainder of the article covered subjects other than the death camps and atrocities.[112]

The Death Camps and Response through Letters to the Editor

Credible, authoritative, responsible witnesses there were upon
which editorials, articles, and accounts were based. These, in turn,
elicited response from readers. Not all American Protestant periodicals published letters to the editor. Those that did were not wanting
in comments on the death camps, particularly on the subject of atrocities. Three letters were published in *The Christian Century* for May
16, 1945. The first began, "In view of the factual revelation of the
astounding nazi atrocities in prison camps" and then took exception
to an article published earlier, "The Perils of Victory." In the second
paragraph, the writer, Willis W. Willard, Jr., continued:

> In the light of the horrible nazi practices, which were going on
> years before Hitler actually started the war, let us be done with
> this superficial pacifistic sentimentalism. . . . Germany stands
> condemned at history's bar of judgment, and nothing can ab-
> solve that whole nation from the guilt which has brought this
> tragic doom upon her.[113]

Woodrow K. Kern, in the second letter, argued for the "saving remnant" of the few good Germans, "however small the group may be,"
who would "help in making the German people see the error of their
ways."[114]

Homer L. Rickel wrote:

> Yesterday, I opened my evening paper to find on the editorial
> page the follow-up of all the flood of German atrocities which
> have been part of the news the last few days. It was an edito-
> rial entitled "Now Americans Can Believe," accompanied by al-
> most a whole page of pictures. . . . They lament the fact that
> after we were so badly fooled by our own government in the

last war nobody believes the stories this time. . . . I think that most Americans accept these stories as true.

The thing that we ought to learn from these pictures is not so much that the Germans are beasts but that war is a beast.

The letter went on to suggest that death by burning in a concentration camp and death "in my own home by the liquid fire bombs" are little different and that the editorials ought to have condemned war, the real cause of atrocities.[115]

Letters were sent responding to the two editorials in *The Christian Century*, "Bringing Infamy Home to the Germans" and "Gazing into the Pit." The first suggested that American bombing (obliteration bombs and incendiary bombs) should be brought home forcibly to Americans to "expand the technique" of observing horrors. The second compared the German concentration camps and the CPS camps as being different only in the degree of horror.[116] The letters to the editor at this point apparently reflected a failure to comprehend the full force of the revelations on the extent of the planned extermination carried out by the Nazis.

A lawyer, who also identified himself as a war veteran and a Christian, wrote to *The Churchman* about what the Christian position should be "toward those responsible for Buchenwald, etc." Essentially, his argument was that Americans should from both a practical and a Christian standpoint "fix responsibility with impartial justice," with the facts determined through the judicial process, involving neither malice nor revenge.[117]

Joseph A. Leighton, who had been in Germany in 1939 and who stated at the conclusion of his letter that he had been a student "and expositor of the German idealist philosophers—Kant, Fichte, Hegel and Goethe," wrote in quite direct terms:

As the ghastly and foul horrors, the diabolical and thoroughly sadistic cruelties of the German concentration camps, pile up before our eyes, revealing the frightful and gigantic moral degradation and inhumanity practiced with cold-blood deliberation by the leaders of a people which boasted of its KULTUR, its science, its technology and social organization, the question is debated—how far are the German people as a whole to be held responsible for this holocaust of deviltry. The reports are that, in general, they disclaim responsibility and proclaim ignorance. If we accept their disclaimers we are indeed suckers. They must have known, if not in every detail certainly in the main, what went on in these camps. For the camps were not concealed by high stone walls and free Germans who worked in them came and went. Moreover Germans suffered in them.

Leighton went on the describe the overwhelming support for Hitler that was reflected in German plebiscites and that he had observed during his visits to Germany in 1936 and 1939, and he cited conversations he had had with German tourists in Italy. He then went on:

> There was only one conclusion to be drawn: *so long as Hitler and his gang were succeeding and Germany was on top of the wave the great majority of Germans supported him, because they thought it paid.* Germany had become a country without any more principles or humane standards of conduct. . . . These conclusions were very painful for me [emphasis his].[118]

Leighton was the most condemnatory of the German people as a whole of those who wrote letters to the editor, but the surprising thing was that more letters to the editor were not published. The death camps and the extermination program, particularly in relation to Jews but not only to Jews, received significant coverage in the American Protestant press. It seems to follow that more readers would have commented by sending in letters. They may have; perhaps editors chose not to publish such letters.

Survivors of Death Camps as Credible Witnesses

Some people did survive the death camps, forced labor camps, and concentration camps. Niemoeller was the most prominent and easily the most publicized survivor but he was not the only source for survivors' accounts. A two-article series was published in *The Messenger* about the 1,000 mostly Jewish refugees who had been brought from Italy in 1944 and who were housed in Fort Ontario, Oswego, New York. The first article was mainly historical, explaining the process by which these refugees had been brought to the United States.[119]

The second article focused on the concentration camps, particularly as they operated from 1938 to 1944, through an interview-article written by a twenty-nine-year-old Yugoslavian refugee staying at Fort Ontario. The article recounted what he had first heard from those fleeing through Yugoslavia and then what he and his family experienced, beginning in 1942. His father was taken to a camp in 1942, with 400 other men. He returned, frozen and fifty pounds lighter, in three weeks. The article then told what his father had witnessed and heard about exterminations in the camp. The man then recounted how he had told the story in Italy and again in America, but no one would believe him. "Only when the American and Russian armies in their advance toward Berlin discovered the extermination camps, and the first newsreel and eyewitness accounts came over here— only then did people begin to believe it."[120]

Edward L. R. Elson, a Presbyterian clergyman, toured Dachau on May 9, 1945. He told about his visit, particularly to block 26, where imprisoned clergy were housed. He described going by the crematorium, where 3,000 bodies were awaiting burial outside the camp. He noted that there were about 31,000 prisoners still in the camp and that many were dying of typhus. Then he found block 26, where 2,400 clergymen had been imprisoned. The prisoners had represented twenty-four nationalities; this fact was known from a very careful census that had been kept by one of the prisoners, a Jesuit priest, Fr. Peter Van Gestel, and others. There were 1,143 survivors still alive in block 26, and only 108 clergymen had ever been released from Dachau.

Elson then described the living conditions and the torture and humiliation suffered by these clergymen, for example, the use of many of the clergymen for medical experiments by Prof. Kurt Karl Schilling, a biochemist, and the consequent deaths of thirteen of the forty "guinea pigs." The Holy Week was particularly dreaded by the imprisoned clergymen because of the special humiliations they were forced to endure at that time. These were also described by Elson. The article closed with interviews with two of the surviving pastors, Fr. Peter Van Gestel (rector of the Jesuit College at Maastricht in Holland, who had been imprisoned in 1942) and Pastor Nicholas Padt (of the Reformed Church in Zutphen, Holland, who had also been imprisoned in 1942). Elson clearly ascribed to Van Gestel the place "as principal informant as to the facts here recorded." Each man was permitted to tell of his arrest and of his subsequent survival in spite of torture and beatings and also of the maintenance of a successful underground resistance network and even a clandestine radio. Van Gestel was forty-seven years of age; Padt, fifty-eight.[121]

The Churchman published selected portions of the Jewish Black Book of the World Jewish Congress just before its publication. The article focused on the destruction of Jews in the notorious extermination camp at Treblinka, in Poland. Survivors of this camp were interviewed. A full description of the camp—its special rail siding, extra security precautions, and physical layout—was given. The transport system was described, including the playing of an orchestra for the arriving prisoners. Then described was the separation for the "baths" as people were unloaded from the trains at the siding, disguised as a passenger station. The "death haircuts" of the women were described, as were the removal of all clothes and the six- or seven-minute walk to the beautiful stone structure, the bath house, wooden trimmed and with potted plants, "but [where] chaos reigned all around. The roar of the colossal machine digging huge pits . . . graves."

The killing process was then described in detail, even the noise of the victims' screams, at times so loud as to cause the inhabitants of a nearby village to flee into the woods to escape the sound. "One must remember that the Treblinka execution block was not a plain execution block. It was a conveyor block organized on the lines of a modern, large industrial enterprise." Some 4,500 were exterminated at a time in the ten chambers. The use of faulty equipment, experiments with various kinds of exhaust gases, and suffocation and other extermination methods were then described; these often caused prolonged and agonized suffering for the victims before they died. It was estimated that 3 million people were exterminated in the thirteen months the camp was operative, according to the Jewish Black Book.

The article itself was introduced by an editorial statement. In retrospect, the editorial statement was as significant as the content of the article was. Referring to the article as being excerpts from the Jewish Black Book, Albert Einstein was then quoted by the editor, who then described the destruction of the Jewish people as the reason why the information was gathered and published in the Black Book.[122] Then:

> It was written from eye witness accounts gathered on the spot (in Eastern Poland). Says the author: "It is terribly hard to read about it. Please reader, believe me that it is no less difficult to write about it. Perhaps someone will ask: 'Then why write, why recall all this?' It is the duty of the writer to tell the whole truth, it is the civil obligation of the reader to know it. He who turns away, who shuts his eyes and passes by, offends the memory of those who perished."[123]

Thirty-three years later, it is still hard to read (and write) about it. Treblinka, Himmler's plan, and Himmler's secret were the epitome of the efficient, well-run killing operation used for the extermination of Jews, "subhumans," and enemies of the Reich. The chill of its march to death reaches through the years. Through Treblinka (and Dachau,

Auschwitz, Buchenwald, Majdanek, Belzec, Sobibor: the death camps), the dead as well as those who survived speak of the terror of the Nazi death factories.

Not Facing the Death Camps, The Oblique Approach

But some editors of American Protestant press took a different approach when they stood face to face with the death camps. John L. Scotford, editor of *Advance*, had written, "We believe that the less said about such matters the better" about the atrocity stories and by inference about the death camps.[124] Other editors chose the less blunt approach of making generalized, indirect references to the discussion of the death camps. The editorials indicated that something would be said about these camps; in reality, the death camps and the details of their functions or a description of what was found in them were not included in the editorials at all. The subject discussed was something else related to them, but only indirectly. The editor of *The Presbyterian* wrote an editorial in this style about Buchenwald. "There is a sombre symbolism in the name. 'Keep the heart with all diligence, for out of it are the issues of life.' Buchenwald is part of the fruitage of 'Mein Kampf,' a book. Behind that volume stands the disintegration of Germany in 1919." The remainder of the editorial spoke about the differences between Great Britain and Germany and why one was strong, the other not strong. No direct confrontation with the meaning and significance of the death camps appeared, not even as straight news in the discussion of Buchenwald. There was no other editorial published on the death camps in this periodical.[125]

The editor of *The Watchman-Examiner*, quite late in 1945, published an editorial called, "Disregard for Human Life." "We gasp with horror over revelations concerning the needless slaughter of thousands of human beings in Europe's concentration camps." But the editorial was really a condemnation of the liquor industry in America as being the chief cause of accidental deaths caused by drunken drivers and by people who were drinking when accidents happened on the job.[126] Again, there was no other editorial on the death camps published in *The Watchman-Examiner. The King's Business* carried one brief paragraph referring to Buchenwald in its "The Bible in the News" section in the July 1945 issue. It stated that 42,000 prisoners from thirty-nine nations had been found in the camp and then referred to "the indescribable torture which was responsible for the death of thousands." That was all that was reported on the topic in this publication.[127]

The Death Camps, Palestine, and Prophecy

A number of subjects were discussed in this generalized, indirect fashion, using the death camps and concentration camps as a reference point only. The subjects were retaliation in kind against German war prisoners held in the United States, man's inhumanity to man, anti-Semitism, the war as the real cause of such actions as were revealed in the discovery of the camps, the horrors of war, the need to reassert the full force of the Christian Gospel in the world, evangelization as the primary need of the hour, and for some, the signs of the "last days," in a continuation of the theme of the dispensational-prophetic analysis of these events. The latter was often in the context of a discussion of Palestine as a haven for the Jews in Europe who had survived the extermination process and who were in the camps as refugees (soon designated as displaced person, or DPs).

An example of the latter emphasis appeared in an editorial article in *The Watchman-Examiner* on "The Jewish Problem." After discussing the condition of Jews in Europe following the end of the war in Europe, the editorial writer strongly supported the opening of Palestine as a place of refuge for European Jews because many could not return to their former homes and many did not want to return to their former homes. This position of support was taken in spite of the known resistance to such a plan by the Arab-Moslem world. Also, the article stated, American Jews would strongly support such a solution to the "Jewish problem" in Europe. The writer then discussed the significance of such a possibility from a Christian perspective. The theme became the fulfillment of the prophecies of the Scriptures. Such statements as "they remain God's elect people in spite of themselves" and "they are enemies of the gospel for the Christian's sake" appeared. Then, he wrote:

> Jewish sufferings of the past few years will in the end prove divine compulsions driving an apostate people out of their ghettos in order that they might ultimately arrive in the land which God originally gave to their fathers. While he is out of his own land and unconverted, the Jew is a stumbling block to the Gentiles. It is the purpose of God, and not any international act of the Jews themselves, which has made Israel—as the nation which has most definitely rejected Christ—a token to other nations.

The horror of the persecution of the Jews and of the death camps had changed nothing for at least one segment of the Protestant press.

This statement was similar to ones found in *The Brethren Evangelist* (the Brethren Church, Ashland, Ohio), *The Brethren Missionary Herald* (Grace Brethren, Winona Lake, Indiana), *The King's Business, Moody Monthly, The Sunday School Times, The Gospel Herald* (conservative, interdenominational), *The Hebrew Christian Alliance Quarterly* (conservative, Christian mission to Jews), *The Signs of the Times* (Seventh-Day Adventist), *The Alliance Weekly* (Christian and Missionary Alliance), and numerous Baptist papers from as early as 1933, 1934, and 1935. For these periodicals, prophetic fulfillment and Christian "triumphalism" dominated all other discussions and analyses.[128]

But whatever the theme or subject, the failure to confront the existence of the death camps directly by many periodicals of the American Protestant press remains a mystery. Without directly interviewing the editors who were responsible for these publications in 1945, no certain conclusions or even suggestions can be made as to why there was such an aversion to speaking directly or descriptively or from the perspective of Christian ethical and moral concerns about the revelations of extremes to which the Nazi extermination programs had gone. Speculation might be possible, but it certainly would not be wise.

Paid Advertising and the Death Camps

Some of the periodicals said nothing at all. No editorial, article, news item, letter to the editor, or other reference to the Nazi extermination program and the death camps or even a generalized, indirect statement on the subject was found in *The Baptist Bulletin, The Baptist and Reflector, The Brethren Evanglist, The Brethren Missionary Herald*, the *Federal Council Bulletin, The Gospel Herald, Moody Monthly, The Sunday School Times,* or *The Pulpit.* But *Moody Monthly* and *The Sunday School Times,* as well as a few other periodicals, did continue to accept and publish paid advertising on behalf of the Jews. Most of these ads, as had been true since 1934 when they first appeared, were purchased by Christian groups and organizations actively involved in Christian evangelization and missionary work among Jews. Again, as they had been from their inception in 1934, these ads were very explicit, changing their emphasis only late in 1945, when the ads concentrated on raising funds for refugee aid. The major references during the winter through the early fall of 1945 were to the extermination of the Jews. One such advertisement placed by the Friends of Israel Missionary and Relief Society, Philadelphia, in *Moody Monthly* read in part:

> And now the Gospel of Salvation instead of Mein Kampf.
> We rejoice that the Lord has, through victory in Europe, made it possible for us to proclaim Christ once again in those countries where the evil spirit of hatred and murder has destroyed the lives of seven million Jews. We are burdened for the remnant of Israel that has survived this unprecendented ordeal of suffering and sorrow.[129]

But the most direct story of the extermination of the Jews was given in advertising paid for by the International Hebrew Christian Alliance of Chicago. The advertisement for February 1945 reported that 400,000 Jews in Rumania had either starved to death or had been massacred in camps. The ad continued. "Many Hebrew Christians, the report states, 'were either shot or simply disappeared. From a whole congregation of Hebrew Christians in Chisenau, only one is now alive.'"[130] The ad for October read, "It is estimated that the Nazis killed nearly five million Jews in Europe during the past ten years and that the remnant of European Jewry number no more than two million, aside from the 3,500,000 Jews to be found in Russia." The ad then went on to list, country by country, the number of Jews left: Poland, of 3,500,000, 30,000 were left; Hungary, of 1,000,000, perhaps 250,000 were still alive; Yugoslavia, of 75,000 before the war, perhaps about 10,000 remain. "And so the painful story goes."[131]

The paid advertisement produced by this same group and published in the same periodical for December 1945 told of a young German Jew who had escaped to England in 1938 and of his search for his family and his learning that they had been victims of the gas chambers and then of the young man's efforts to help Jewish families in Czechoslovakia.[132] Many of these advertisements were published in more than one periodical, the greatest number appearing in *The Sunday School Times*.[133]

The Protestant Press and the Death Camps, An Assessment

Face to face with the death camps; after twelve years and four months, the Nazi rule of Germany was ended. After just under six years, the European war was over; after four and one-half years,

America's direct, military involvement in the war in Europe was also ended. The Allied armed forces were the victors; Germany was defeated and Adolf Hitler was dead. But the war in Asia continued, and the sobering revelations of the forced labor camps, concentration camps, and death camps gave pause to many. As the news was spread in the newspapers, weekly news magazines, photographs and newsreels, as well as by radio, the growing awareness of the full extent of the Nazi persecutions and the extermination process became known. And with this knowledge came the added awareness that the Jews of Germany and occupied Europe had been the major victims of the Nazi mass exterminations.

The information was available. The periodicals published by Christian groups and organizations engaged in missionary work among Jews in America and the paid advertising placed by these groups in other Protestant periodicals attest to this. The evidence of the .planned, systematic effort to exterminate the Jews and others was overwhelming. No one who could read the reports, see the photographs, or listen to the radio could plead lack of knowledge. The story of the Nazi death camps was everywhere where news was published or broadcast.

The American Protestant press's response to these revelations ranged from expressions of shock and near disbelief, through a reluctant acceptance of the fact that all the rumors and stories that they had heard about and even published (some as early as 1933) were indeed a horrible reality, to the establishment as credible and verified beyond a doubt that what they were then confronting was an awful truth, far worse than even the rumors had indicated. Many of these periodicals—through a variety of editorials, articles, news items, and letters to the editor—gave to their readers a full range of information, description, and response—commentary on the death camps and what was found when they were liberated. Some periodicals were less direct and more inclined to be general or indirect. Some could face the death camps only within an already-established context of meaning (that is, moral and ethical stance; theological and doctrinal stance; denominational commitment or concern; Christian missionary and evangelistic opportunity; refugee aid and service; the continuing Church Struggle in Europe and particularly in Germany; the dispensational-premillenial-prophetic stance and the search for evidence of fulfilled prophecy, the "last days," preceding the Second Coming of Christ; and Christian "triumphalism," that the Christian message and the Christian faith would ultimately triumph over wars, nations, unbelief, and particularly over unbelieving Jewry.) All of these themes were present in one form or another in that part of the American Protestant press that did not directly write about the death camps.

Some of this press remained silent. They wrote nothing at all. A strange time to be silent, but silent they were, committing the ultimate avoidance. It was also itself surprising to note the surprise with which some of the editors responded when the full news of the death camps became known and the facts were verified beyond any question. However, some of the editors (Charles Clayton Morrison of *The Christian Century*, for instance) had been publishing information about the persecution and extermination of masses of people by the Nazis all along.

Hitler's statements about his intention to destroy Europe's Jews had been published and commented on; *Mein Kampf* had been reviewed and discussed; reports from the observation centers in Europe and from the World Council of Churches and its affiliated groups had been published. After 1939, governments in exile, refugees, and escapees from the Nazis told their stories. Martin Niemoeller's eight-year imprisonment was followed intently.

And yet, upon reading "Gazing into the Pit," an editorial that can represent the opinions of several other editors in addition to Morrison, it seems as though Morrison was completely surprised to discover that what his own periodical and other Protestant periodicals had been writing about for years was indeed exactly what had happened under the Nazis and Hitler.[134]

Morrison's words, "We have found it hard to believe that the reports from the Nazi concentration camps could be true," when read in the context of twelve and one-half years of reporting about the Nazi persecution of the Jews, the existence of the concentration camps, and everything else, are not a false sentiment; but they ring hollow. Perhaps the editors did not read their own periodicals.

But, in the final analysis, Arthur S. Maxwell, editor of *The Signs of the Times*, really caught the sentiment of the moment for those facing the death camps as editors and writers in the American Protestant press. He did not express surprise so much as resignation. "But this time, alas, the stories were true. . . . Yes, it is all too true."[135]

Epilogue

Two questions should now be asked and, insofar as possible, answered. Did American Protestant Christians know what was happening to the Jews in Germany and Europe under the Nazis, based on information published in the American Protestant press? This is the first question. A review of the materials published during the period of Nazi domination in Germany and Europe (1933–1945) centering on specific events and information states clearly that American Protestant Christians did know what was happening to the Jews under Hitler and the Nazis, from early 1933 through to the liberation of the death camps, concentration camps, and slave-labor camps in April and May of 1945. The information was published extensively, continuously, and often comprehensively in the American Protestant press. The major events were reported: the boycott-pogrom of April 1, 1933, the "Aryan paragraph," the Nuremberg laws of 1935, Kristallnacht (the Night of Broken Glass), the ill-fated Evian Conference, the mass deportation of Jews, the whole story of the killing operations from euthanasia to medical experiments, from mass killing by starvation, disease, and massacre (committed by the *Einsatzgruppen*) to the death camps.

The second question requires going back through the same reports, the same information, and the same events and asking, what, if any, meaning can be given to all of this, particularly in relation to what Jews call the Silence of Christians (including American Protestant Christians) while all this was happening to the Jews under the

Nazis? Since the reporting was extensive, continuous, and sometimes comprehensive, why was there not more intervention on behalf of the Jews? Why did not the Christians of America speak out? Demand assistance for the Jews? Pressure the American government to act? Why did not the American Protestants themselves act in concerted, massive, total Christian coalitions of protest and assistance? These questions flow from the primary question, what did having the information reported in the press mean to American Protestant Christians? Certainly there was not as much of a "silence" as had been assumed when what was reported is taken as the measure. As has been shown, the Protestant press reported far more than it was generally thought that they had. But there occurred another kind of "silence" that was more disturbing in its consequences, the "silence" that followed the lack of intervention on behalf of the persecuted Jews and the almost total failure of such interventions as were attempted. Such conclusions may seem stark and uncompromising, but they are based squarely on the evidence reported in the American Protestant press from 1933 through 1945.

PART II

Christianity and the Holocaust

Complicity or Complacency: "A Standing Reproach"

It would be a standing reproach against Christendom if the true Christians of the world were callously indifferent when Jews have been made victims of unchristian policies perpetrated by nominal Christians.

"A Challenge to Christendom"
Federal Council Bulletin

The Protestant Christians who read the periodicals published by their denominations and independent sources did know what was happening to the Jews in Germany under the Nazis from 1933 on. As the conquest of Europe by Hitler and the Nazis took place between 1937 and 1940, the Nazi persecution of the Jews extended with the conquest. Austria, Czechoslovakia, Poland, Eastern Europe, Western Europe, Denmark, Norway, each in its turn became victim, not only of German and Nazi occupation, but of the accompanying persecution of "enemies of the Reich," including the persecution, transportation, and extermination of Jews from these countries. No conquered nation escaped.

The Range of Reporting in the
Protestant Religious Press, 1933–1945

American Protestant periodicals, representing the full theological spectrum common during the 1930s and 1940s, reported the events in Europe in full from the time that Adolf Hitler became chancellor of Germany until the defeat of Germany and the end of the war in Europe. The revelations about the death camps and the growing sense of the full implications of the destruction of the European Jews were only the final chapter in the series of events promised in the platforms of the National Socialist German Workers' party in the 1920s, confirmed in Hitler's Mein Kampf published in 1925 (volume 1) and 1926 (volume 2), and carried out with ruthless and increasing efficiency from 1933 through the Final Solution of the "Jewish question," between 1942 and 1945.[1] Though the full importance of the Nazi anti-Semitism was neither understood nor believed by American Protestants in 1924, in 1925–1926, or in 1933, once Hitler gained power in Germany and the Nazi party became the government in Germany, the American Protestant press did report the plight of the Jews in Germany. Reports on incidents of direct persecution appeared in the press as early as February 1933. By late April 1933, editorials condemning the pogrom of April 1, 1933, and editorials and articles condemning the Nazi persecution of the Jews in Germany also began to appear.

From this point on, as the events within Germany and later in conquered Europe occurred and as the persecution of the Jews escalated, the American Protestant press took note of what was happening, if only in brief references and short news items. Report they did. The story was being told, and Protestant Christians, those who were readers of their own press, could not say that they did not know.

Within the American Protestant press, the reporting of the Nazi persecution of the Jews was presented in every conceivable form usually used within these publications. Editorials and articles were published, as were news items, letters to the editor, devotional pages, and youth pages, lessons for teachers in Sunday schools and Christian Endeavors, and letters from military personnel overseas during and immediately after the war. These letters, as a special category, were published apart from the letter-to-the-editor pages common in some of the periodicals.[2] They often appeared in article form and in special sections devoted to military personnel from particular denominations.[3]

Some periodicals also regularly accepted paid advertisements. With few exceptions, these paid advertisements, first in 1934 and through 1945 (and presumably beyond), were placed by organizations, agencies, and groups involved in Christian missionary and evangelistic efforts among Jews in the United States. In addition, they were a part of a larger network of such Christian missionary efforts among Jews in Europe and other parts of the world. These advertisements served two purposes. The first in importance was that of solicitation of funds in order to continue to do the work of the sponsoring organization, agency, or group. The second was to convey in the text and illustrations what was happening to Jews under

Nazi rule. An attempt was made to make the information comprehensive and persuasive for itself and also to demonstrate what the
organization, agency, or group was doing for Jews in Germany and
Eastern and Western Europe that justified the request for funds to
support their work. In many instances, the copy in these advertisements was more explicit, more accurate, more comprehensive, and
more forthright than what was published elsewhere in the periodicals in which the advertisements appeared. Sometimes such an advertisement was the only published item referring to the Nazi persecution of the Jews at all.

News items culled from wherever possible, including other periodicals, were also published in a special section devoted to a brief
summary of world events. The regular wire services were used, as
were the so-called secular newspapers and news magazines. As the
services and personnel of the Religious News Service grew, the news
pages were often taken from its releases. The Religious News Service
operated as a division of the National Conference of Christians and
Jews, as it still does.[4]

Reporting about the Nazi persecution of the Jews from 1933
through 1945 reflected generally the course of events within Germany, as the Nazis first gained power and then consolidated their
hold on Germany and on German politics. When notable instances
of persecution of Jews took place (as in March–April of 1933 or as in
the passing of the Nuremberg laws in September 1935), reporting of
the effect on Jews in Germany seemed to increase. During periods of
quiet (that is, when persecution of the Jews by the Naxis was less
obvious), the American Protestant press said less. Major events in
the spring of 1933, the final effect of the "Aryan clause" as embodied
in the Nuremberg laws of September 1935, Kristallnacht in November of 1938, and the first deportations of Jews to Poland in 1938 after
Austria was occupied were events that received considerable attention in the press until the outbreak of the war itself, when Poland
was invaded and Western Europe was overrun by the Nazis.

Reporting about the Persecution of the Jews
under Wartime Conditions

At this point, new problems arose in reporting about the Nazi persecution of the Jews. Wartime conditions prevailed. News censorship
and propaganda impinged more than ever on news of current
events. In particular, the program known as the Final Solution of the

"Jewish question" was carried out by the Nazi leadership with a continual emphasis on the necessity for secrecy. Secrecy took two forms. First was secrecy maintained about the plan for the program of extermination through the expansion of the SS police apparatus, the creation of the concentration camps, and the development of the extermination system identified with the camps.[5] Second, by the use of euphemisms, the language used to describe the extermination process was never direct but rather was deliberately indirect, almost as though it were a code understood only by those involved in the killing operations. "Special treatment," "protective custody," "final solution," "selection," "hygiene measures," "disposition," "liquidation," "transport," "deportation," "elimination," and "resettlement" were what Bracher called the "camouflaged instructions" and the "Aesopian language" used to disguise the execution process.[6]

In one sense, this two-pronged secrecy was the central subject of Raul Hilberg's monumental study *The Destruction of the European Jews*, in which he traced the steps of the process from definition to expropriation to concentration to annihilation, adding only that most characteristic word *efficiency*; characteristic, that is, of the German civil service's bureaucratic approach to accomplishing any assigned task. "If it is to be done, do it efficiently." Hilberg also showed how the SS functioned both apart from and through the entire German governmental and bureaucratic structure, with Himmler and the SS first claiming and then gaining all of the authority over the concentration and liquidation processes.[7] As for the use of a disguised language in relation to the whole process of extermination, Hilberg, in describing some of the terms, spoke of them as "not the product of naiveté; they were convenient tools of psychological repression."[8]

No statements captured the essence of the Nazi effort to keep as much of this killing process secret as did those of Himmler in a speech at Posen on October 6, 1943, which urged his audience to secrecy. "I am talking to you within these four walls and you must listen to what I say and let it go no further." In the same vein, Hans Frank, governor-general of Poland, in speaking of the SS and the carrying out of the policy of extermination, said, "As National Socialists we are facing so immeasurably difficult and responsible a task *that even in our inmost circle we cannot really speak of these things*" [emphasis in the original].[9]

Himmler seemed to have concluded his speech at Posen, or at least that part of it dealing with the "Jewish question," with:

That is all I have to say on the Jewish question. You now know the full story, and you will keep it to yourselves. In the distant future it will perhaps be worth considering *whether the German people should be told more on this subject.* I believe it to be better that we—all of us—should carry this burden for our people, and that we should take the responsibility upon ourselves (responsibility for the action not the concept) *and carry the secret with us to the grave.* [emphasis in the original].[10]

But the Nazis could not keep the secret.[11] In fact, virtually all phases of the Nazi program from the early application of the Aryan laws and the first active persecutions were reported in the American Protestant press. From 1933 the process of placing Jews under restrictive laws and regulations (what Hilberg calls *definition*) through the nationwide pogrom of Kristallnacht in 1938, from the formal beginnings of mass concentration in 1938 and 1939 to the existence of the mass concentration camps in eastern Poland and the mass shootings by the *Einsatzgruppen* and the first rumors of the existence of "death factories"—all of this was reported in the American Protestant press. Based on the information published in the fifty-two such periodicals examined for the period 1933–1945, with some examined into 1947 on the one subject of the death camps, I can say conclusively that American Protestant Christians did know what was happening to the Jews in Germany and later in occupied Europe under the Nazis. This conclusion assumes that those who subscribed to the periodicals read them, even at the "scan" level, as well as having other sources of information available to them through newspapers, magazines (secular), and radio broadcasts.

If Protestant Christians Read Their Press, They Knew, 1933–1945

The cumulative total of references to the Nazi persecution of the Jews published in these periodicals over the span of approximately twelve and one-half years argues against the plea of ignorance by American Protestant Christians. Too many articles, editorials, devotional pages, youth pages, Sunday school lessons, letters to the editor, and paid advertisements about the Nazis' treatment of the Jews were published during those twelve and a half years for the subscriber-readers to say truthfully, "we did not know." Before the evidence, the most that American Protestant Christians can say is that they were not persuaded as to the significance or meaning of what they were reading.

Why? Because other matters dominated their concern. Insofar as they were concerned at all about events in Germany, other matters more immediate seemed to many more critical. The Church Struggle and the growing effort of German churchmen, Protestant and Roman Catholic, to resist the Nazi German Christian movement whereby the Church would become an arm of the Nazi state, received full attention in the American Protestant press. The "Aryan paragraph" restricting professing Christians defined as Jews under the Aryan laws was only one phase of the increasingly intensified conflict involving the Church in Germany and the Nazis. As the resistance of the Church hardened and as outspoken clergy and lay leadership emerged, the leaders of the resistance became subject to confinement under house arrest, to restrictions on the church duties they were permitted to carry out, and to imprisonment. For many, it meant death.

In a very real sense, though both struggles were going on simultaneously in Germany (the Church Struggle and the struggle of the Jews to survive), the natural concern of American Protestant Christians was for their brethren in the faith. Insofar as Roman Catholic Christians were also being persecuted or were resisting the Nazis, the natural affinity was for Roman Catholic Christian heroes and heroines. Thus, editors and writers tended to pay a great deal of attention to all aspects of the Church Struggle at the expense of the struggle of the Jews. This was not deliberate. Almost every editor and writer had direct historical-theological ties with Germany since their denominations were products of the Reformation. Many had traveled in Germany on study tours between the wars. This was particularly true for the Lutheran, Reformed, Mennonite, Brethren, and Brethren-in-Christ churches and for those churches having membership in Germany such as the Methodists, the Baptists, and the Friends (Quakers). For members of these groups and those denominations whose leaders were becoming increasingly involved in the emerging World Council of Churches, what was happening to the Christian church in Germany, as well as what was happening to individual Christians, was of paramount significance and interest.

Reporting about the Resisters, 1933–1945

It was in this context that heroes in the resistance to the Nazis began to appear. First was Bodelschwingh and then a succession of clergymen who were silenced or imprisoned, such as Hans Lilje and Otto Dibelius, or who openly resisted, such as Theophilus Wurm, and those less-prominent clergymen who opposed the Nazis, aided Jews, or prayed or preached from their pulpits in defiance of Nazi decrees and practices. Dietrich Bonhoeffer was among this latter group. Best known and most admired of all the resisters from the clergy was Martin Niemoeller. His eight-year imprisonment under Hitler's direct order and his release from his eight-year ordeal were reported almost universally in the American Protestant press. The longer he succeeded in staying alive, the more of a hero he became, and the passing of each succeeding year was noted by all segments of this press from liberal to fundamentalist. Even the controversy that developed in the summer and fall of 1945 over his role in Germany and whether he should be invited to the United States or not could not detract from the ultimate fact that Martin Niemoeller had defied Hitler and the Nazis, had been imprisoned, had survived eight years in concentration camps, and had emerged alive. Hero, indeed!

Reporting about Anti-Semitism and Race, 1933–1945

Also a dominant issue was the question of anti-Semitism and racism within the United States. Perhaps no American Protestant periodical devoted as much of its publishing effort to exposing anti-Semitism in the United States as did *The Churchman* under the editorship of Guy Emery Shipler and his son Guy Emery Shipler, Jr. From 1935 until the editorials on the death camps in 1945, *The Churchman* pursued this theme relentlessly. In the Shipler-written editorial on the death camps, the final sentence reiterated this central theme. "Americans— and Christians—who permit anti-Semitism in America to go unrebuked—please note and ponder."[12]

The "Negro question" was also discussed in relation to the Nazi persecution of the Jews. The concern of the American Protestant press and of some church members and denominations about facing the race question, particularly in the South and particularly for black Americans, was reflected in what was written and what was done. Incidents of lynchings were widely publicized and condemned. The *Federal Council Bulletin* throughout the 1930s and until the middle of 1945 contained frequent articles discussing study groups, commissions, programs, and literature about the race question. In part, some of the articles did make comparisons between the plight of the Jews in Nazi Germany and the plight of Negroes in the South. Also, occasional references were made to the Nazi propaganda effort to blunt the criticism of the Nazi treatment of the Jews by pointing out that the United States had its own problem, the Negro, and that its record in race relations was not all that good.

Generally, however, direct references to the situation of the European Jews and the American blacks as in any way similar did not occur. The tendency in the American Protestant press during the 1930s and 1940s was to treat anti-Semitism and racism as two separate questions. In light of the more recent use of the term *race* to mean minorities in a broad sense, the term was in fact consistently restricted to Negroes in the press during the 1930s and 1940s. Even the internment of Japanese Americans at the beginning of World War II was not seen by most Protestant periodicals as a matter defined by "race" or as a "racial question." The problems related to Jews in America were not discussed under the rubric of "race" at all but rather as the "Jewish question" or as anti-Semitism. In the commonly used terminology of the 1930s and through 1945–1946, the term *race* and the phrase *racial problem* were used almost exclusively with reference to Negroes, including discussions of the "race riot" in Detroit during the war years. The German propaganda effort was aimed at taking advantage of America's racial problems as much as possible, however, especially during the years immediately preceding World War II. Clearly, this was a diversionary tactic used to draw attention away from the Nazi persecution of the Jews. Some effort to measure the attitudes of Americans toward Jews and Negroes during and immediately after World War II was made by several different organizations but not with specific reference to American Christians. These surveys were reported on and discussed in Bettelheim and Janowitz, *Social Change and Prejudice.*[13] A study of the attitudes toward Jews and Negroes in the American Protestant press for the period 1933–1945 needs to be made. The published material in the Protestant press on this subject fully warrants such an undertaking.

Reporting American Protestant Christian Response and Action, 1933–1945

As the news of the persecution of Jews by the Nazis began to be reported in 1933, the response of American Protestant Christians also began to assume definition. For those denominations and those active churchmen, the early concern was to bring pressure to bear on the government of Germany, generally perceived of as going directly to Adolf Hitler, with expressions of concern and protest. The American Protestant press reported such efforts, particularly noting the number of vocal protests, rallies, and statements issued from such rallies. When rallies were held, as in New York, Chicago, and elsewhere, Jews and Christians commonly met together in large numbers to hear speakers condemn the Nazi practice of persecuting the Jews and to make some sort of official statement of protest in the name of the gathering.[14] During the ensuing years and until the coming of the war changed everything, statements from protest rallies were regularly made from time to time. The American Jewish Congress, the American Jewish Committee, the World Jewish Congress, the Federal Council of Churches, the National Conference of Christians and Jews, and local city or area councils of churches commonly sponsored, cosponsored, or cooperated in such protest rallies and meetings. Prominent Jewish, Protestant, and Roman Catholic clergymen and Jewish and Christian laypersons of note were the speakers at the rallies. From 1933 to 1938–1939, such meetings were common, and they were reported, often with the rally's official statement being either published or excerpted in the report.

As the years passed and the Nazi oppression of the Jews increased, such statements from rallies and protest meetings were often addressed to President Roosevelt, the State Department, or the Congress of the United States, calling for intervention or some other action, including opening the quotas for refugees from Germany, as evidence of the disapproval of Americans toward the Nazis' policies. Such statements of protest seem to have had little or no effect.[15]

Answering the Central Question, Did American Protestant Christians Know?

But the central question remains. How much information about what was happening to the Jews in Germany needed to be reported in the American Protestant press in order to be able to state categorically that American Protestant Christians could not say that they did not know? Several hundred items were published in the Protestant press from early 1933 through 1945. The question is not about quantity (how much) but about accuracy. The reports, from the beginning, were accurate.

First would be the report of the pogroms of April 1933. These pogroms in conjunction with the first application of Nazi-Hitler racial theory in the use of the "Aryan clause" were reported more fully that has generally been appreciated by scholars in the field. The story of this first pogrom and the concern over the meaning and application of the "Aryan clause" were reported in the press thoroughly and accurately.[16] The second item offered in evidence would be the documents submitted by James G. McDonald, the letter of resignation and the accompanying "Annex" published in *The Christian Century* on January 15, 1936.[17] McDonald's letter of resignation and "Annex" are a total indictment, as well as a complete explanation, of the Nazi program for the persecution of the Jews and of the system of laws that legalized this program, which were passed on September 15, 1935, at the annual meeting of the National Socialist party sitting as the German Reichstag. Though the American Protestant press virtually ignored McDonald's letter of resignation and "Annex," nonetheless, in publishing it, *The Christian Century* put into the record and before the public in America a complete, thoroughly documented description of what was happening to the Jews in Germany at a relatively early date in the history of the Nazi persecution. McDonald's resignation came before the larger truth of the Nazis' intentions began to be comprehended except by the prescient few. McDonald's failure to bring the League of Nations into intervention on behalf of German Jews in no way detracts from the forceful documentation that he presented to American Protestant Christians and the American public. That almost no one, including the American Protestant press, seemed to fully understand or act upon McDonald's indictment of the Nazis and the suggestions that he put forward for intervention on behalf of Germany's Jews compounds the tragedy. The opportunity, albeit an early one, to confront Hitler and the Nazis directly with the incontrovertible evidence as presented by James G. McDonald was missed. Other such opportunities were also missed.[18]

Such an opportunity existed when the Baptist World Alliance decided to hold its meeting in Berlin, which had been postponed from 1933 to 1934. This world body represented a major Protestant group with a reputation for defying governments, speaking on controversial issues freely, advocating on behalf of the downtrodden, and challenging systems and laws considered abhorrent, un-Baptist, and unchristian. The Baptist World Alliance in its statements on anti-Semitism and racial theories appeared quite forthright at the congress in Berlin in 1934. In fact, there was no direct confrontation of the Nazis on the question of the persecution of the Jews, ostensibly out of a fear that Baptists in Germany would be jeopardized unduly through such a direct challenge. This failure was glossed over in the resolutions and the subsequent reports of the congress's sessions published by the American Protestant press. Only Robert Ashworth, a member of the Executive Committee of the Baptist World Alliance, spoke out on this failure in his open letter to M. E. Dodd, president of the Southern Baptist Convention, which responded to Dodd's glowing report on the Berlin meeting. At that point, the entire matter was dropped.[19]

So also in 1936 was there another opportunity to protest the Nazi persecution of Jews—the Olympic Games. American Protestants, their press, and others called for moving the Olympic Games to another site. Such pleas went unheeded by the American Olympic Committee. Both the winter games and the summer games were reported in the American Protestant press. Only the more obvious evidences of persecution were removed in Germany for the games, such as signs forbidding Jews to enter German towns, et cetera. As a result of this sort of sanitizing process removing the overt evidence of persecution, not much more was said about the persecution of the Jews in Germany in relation to the Olympic Games in Berlin. Again, an effort to muster public opinion in order to force a relocation of the Olympic Games to a site other than Germany was not successful. Insofar as the American Protestant press took an active part in this effort, and some publications did, they were also unsuccessful in mustering opinion to the point where the American Olympic Games Committee would have supported such a move. The opportunity to use the Olympic Games as a public, worldwide event by which to support the persecuted Jews in Germany by American Protestant Christians proved to be a missed opportunity.[20]

The Central Question and the Role of Paid Advertising

Added to the reporting of the pogroms, the McDonald documents, the Baptist World Alliance meeting, and the 1936 Olympic Games was the appearance of paid advertisements, the first of which were published in February 1934.[21] The message carried in these paid advertisements was unrelenting. They often contained the most bold, direct information about what was happening to Jews in Germany and later in occupied Europe.

Though the organizations placing the advertisements were based in the United States, they often carried on active missionary work among Jews in Europe, Latin America, and Asia, as well as among Jews living in the United States. In this way, these organizations had links to missionary work in Europe and in Germany. News of what was happening to the Jews in Germany was often obtained through personal correspondence and through people who were making active efforts to assist refugees who were fleeing from Germany and who told their own personal stories of the Nazi persecution of the Jews. The paid advertisements were often based on such personal information rather than on reports from the news services and secular press.

The story of the Nazi persecution of the Jews thus was made explicit and was based on eyewitness accounts from missionary observers who were on the scene actively assisting the Jews who were being persecuted or who were themselves fleeing as refugees. Such detailed, personal accounts of persecution could seldom be found elsewhere in the American Protestant press, particularly between 1933 and 1938.

In many instances, the publications accepting and publishing these paid advertisements published nothing else about the persecution of Germany's Jews in the issues containing the advertisements. This, in itself, says a great deal about the publishing of news about the Nazi persecution of the Jews. Periodicals would accept paid advertisements, but they would not themselves publish editorials, articles, or reports on the subject. Explanations were sometimes given by editors for this lack of reporting, but usually they were not. For whatever reasons there were—the fear of "more atrocity stories"; anti-Semitism as a force to be reckoned with by much of the press; plain neglect or, worse, disinterest; the success of the Nazi propaganda effort in the United States until the country entered World War II in 1941–1942; or the "business as usual and serve the constituency" character of many individual periodicals—the fact remains that there were many periodicals that regularly accepted paid advertisements about such persecution contained in the copy printed in the advertisements. In some instances, this was true after 1938, when conditions for the Jews in Germany and other parts of Europe worsened, on through the war years, when the Nazis occupied much of Europe, up to 1945 and the discovery of the death camps. Many of these publications confronted the Nazi persecution of the Jews, the concentration of Jews in eastern Poland, the known massacres of Jews from 1942 on, and the revelations about the death camps *not at all*; yet, they continued to accept the paid advertisements in which these issues were confronted. It is a strange sort of silence, but a silence nonetheless.

The Central Question, Kristallnacht, and the Reporting,
1938–1942

The year 1938 was a bad one for the Jews of Germany and in the parts of Europe controlled by the Nazis; 1939, 1940, and 1941 were not any better. For Jews, the culmination of persecution in 1938 was Kristallnacht, the Night of Broken Glass. In fact, the entire year of 1938 saw the situation for Jews in Germany and Austria deteriorate drastically. To use Lucy S. Dawidowicz's phrase, the war against the Jews accelerated dramatically after 1938. As it was noted in chapter 3, the number of references to the persecution of the Jews, apart from those referring to Kristallnacht, in the American Protestant press exceeded the references to the Church Struggle, 165 to 113, in 1938. Including Kristallnacht, the number was almost double, 201 to 113.

The reporting of the events of Kristallnacht, including what happened to Jews in Germany and Austria from 1938 on, can be added, then, to the earlier evidence that the reports in the American Protestant press were of sufficient breadth and accuracy that American Protestant Christians who read these reports had no excuse to say that they did not know what was going on.

The evidence that such reporting not only continued but increased after 1938 can be shown by the single recorded fact that the number of references to the Nazi persecution of the Jews found in the American Protestant periodicals examined for 1939 through 1942 continued to be greater in the aggregate than references to the Church Struggle or to the other themes in this press about the Nazis and Germany. As it was noted in chapter 4, over 600 direct references to the persecution of the Jews were recorded in thirty-eight periodicals for 1939, thirty-three for 1940, thirty-five for 1941, and thirty for 1942, excluding specific references to the early indications of the Final Solution.

The Central Question and the Reporting
on the Final Solution

As for the direct reporting of the Final Solution in the American Protestant press, it is possible to identify a specific periodical, issue, and title for a piece in which such a reference is unmistakable. The date was December 28, 1939; the periodical, *The Watchman-Examiner*; and the piece, an editorial, "The Suffering of the Jews." In this editorial, a direct reference was made to a speech by Adolf Hitler on October

6, 1939, in which he spoke of the "regulation of the Jewish problem," which was identified further in the editorial as a proposal made to the Reichstag. The editorial quoted Hitler's plans for "a special region for Jews . . . around Lublin in the southeastern part of Poland."[22] The specific names of the "settlements" in the "region" were not known by American editors and writers at that point—but they were Treblinka, Majdanek, Belzec, and Sobibor, the dread Polish extermination centers. That Jews were being transported for mass concentration in the area of Lublin as a part of the planned "regulation of the Jewish problem" was known and was reported.

Further, in 1940, 1941, and 1942, the fate of the Jews in the occupied countries was linked to the concentration, deportation, and ghettoization of Jews and to the increasing number of reports of Jews dying from starvation, disease, and shooting, often described as massacre. The mass transportation of Jews had begun, and with it began the attempts of Jews to escape the consequences of such transportation, or to use the term from the Nazi vocabulary, "resettlement to the east." Thus, in late 1939 and in 1940, Jews were described in the American Protestant press as being homeless, destitute, and wandering in the fields and forests, sick, starving, and seeking escape routes through the Balkans in an effort to reach Palestine.

The beginning of the ghettoization of masses of Jews in the cities of Poland was also being reported by 1940. Warsaw, Lodz, Vilna, Radom, and other Polish cities were soon to see Jews ghettoized in their midst, a further step toward the destruction of Europe's Jews. In March 1940, Elias Newman, who had witnessed this ghettoization, wrote to *The Friend of Zion*. He said, "After the last World War 3,000,000 Jews became beggars. Before this war ends, 7,000,000 will be corpses."[23] Newman, a Christian missionary who worked among Jews in Eastern Europe, was an early prophet whose accurate estimate of the number of Jews who were to become victims of the Nazis had little or no effect on those who read what he wrote, apart from the small number of dedicated supporters of *The Friend of Zion*, if some sort of reported action or assistance plan is looked for as the criterion for such a statement. That 6 million Jews did become corpses is not only historical verification of Elias Newman's foresight, it is also the witness to the world of the efficiency of the Nazi killing operation.

The course of the war and the Nazi successes of 1940 and 1941 determined also the course of the execution of the extermination of Jews and "enemies of the Reich." The mass transportation of Jews

into concentration camps and the "resettlement to the east" were reported through the remainder of 1940 and into 1941. But, with the
Nazi attack on Russia in June of 1941, a new element in the mass-
killing process began to appear in the pages of the American Protestant press. In the context of the Russian invasion and as a planned
strategy devised as a part of the Final Solution of the "Jewish problem," word began to come out of Eastern Europe about the use of
firing squads to massacre large numbers of Jews. It has been estimated that 2 million Jews were killed by the firing squads, the *Einsatzgruppen*, whose special training was designed to accomplish this
one task in the wake of the Nazi invasion armies as they moved into
Russia. Of all the sites where mass shootings took place, Babi Yar,
near Kiev, stands as mute witness to this method of extermination.
Nora Levin stated that 35,000 Jews were killed at Babi Yar in two
days. She also cited the poem "Babi Yar," by the Russian poet Yevgeny Yevtushenko, a part of which reads:

> On Babi Yar weeds rustle; the tall trees
> Like judges loom and threaten. . . .
> All screams in silence; I take off my cap
> And feel that I am slowly turning gray.
> And I too have become a soundless cry
> Over the thousands that lie buried here.
> I am each old man slaughtered, each child shot.
> None of me will forget.[24]

My thanks to Nora Levin for permission to use a part of the Yevtushenko poem, translated by Maria Syrkin and published in Nora Levin, *The Holocaust: The Destruction of
European Jewry, 1933–1945*, New York, Thomas Y. Crowell Company, 1968, pp. 255–56.

The use of firing squads was a part of the "radical solution of the
Jewish question in all conquered countries" reported *The Hebrew
Christian Alliance Quarterly* in the fall of 1941.[25]

During the latter months of 1942, there was no longer any question
about the fate of the Jews in Germany and in Nazi-occupied Europe.
The Christian Century, The Churchman, the *Federal Council Bulletin, The
Messenger, The Gospel Messenger, The Presbyterian, The Signs of the Times*
and *The Watchman-Examiner* reported all or part of the full story. As
described in *The Churchman*, it was the story of "persecution, murders, mass slaughters, tortures of prisoners, brutal treatment of
women."[26]

In December 1942, Charles Clayton Morrison, editor of *The Chris-*

tian Century, wrote, "Extermination of a race has seldom, if ever, been so systematically practiced on a grand scale as in the present mass murder of Polish Jews by the Nazi power." Morrison was right in the main point, the extermination of Jews had one cause only, racism. He was wrong in limiting the killing to only Polish Jews; he should have included all Jews in occupied Europe as victims or potential victims of the exterminations.[27]

When Dr. J. H. Hertz, chief rabbi of England, responded to the request of Dr. J. H. Rushbrooke, president of the Baptist World Alliance in late 1942, the letter of Hertz to Rushbrooke confirmed the rumors. "A sentence of death has been pronounced upon the entire Jewish population on the Continent, and—by machine gun and poison chamber, by torture and famine—millions of my brethren have already fallen victim to the Nazi fury."[28] The Final Solution of the "Jewish problem," more properly the mass, planned, efficient killing of Jews had become an established fact. All that the American Protestant press lacked was the formal name used by the Nazis (the ultimate form of what Lucy S. Dawidowicz called Nazi-Deutsch doublespeak) now commonly shortened to the three terrible words—the Final Solution.[29]

The Central Question and the Existence of the Death Camps, 1943–1944

In 1943 and 1944, through Sweden, Portugal, Switzerland, and Turkey and through the resistance and underground reports received in London by the various "free" governments headquartered in that city, news of the Jews came out. The censorship, the propaganda, the silence of the military and the governments, the question of the reliability of the reports, and the ever-present fear of "more atrocity stories" were screens that in one way or another blocked access to the news about the destruction of Europe's Jews. But bits and pieces did filter out. Refugees and escapees from the Nazi terror told their stories; word was sent out through underground sources; the Red Cross and the World Council of Churches through their own networks and contacts received news of what was happening to Jews in Germany and elsewhere in occupied Europe and they reported what they heard.

Editors of the American Protestant press understandably were cautious. The sources of such reports were inaccessible, the news at times hardly above the level of rumor; nonetheless, they did report in editorials and articles and in their news sections what they had heard. Wherever possible, credible attribution was given to the source for what was being reported in an effort to make it believable in the face of the sheer unbelievableness of what they were reporting. Henry Smith Leiper in *Advance* wrote bluntly, "The tales that come out of unhappy Poland are not mere rumors of atrocity stories." The headline of this news item read, "Six Thousand Jews Executed Daily in Poland."[30]

Also, a measure of credibility for the reports of the Nazi extermination of Jews came about through the linking together of the well-established concern in the American Protestant press for the Church Struggle and what was happening to Jews. In the reports coming out of occupied Europe in 1943 and 1944, the persecution and killing of Jews and the heroic actions of Protestant and Roman Catholic clergymen, religious people, and laypersons who intervened to try to save Jews would often appear in the same news item or release. In fact, all of the themes carried in the press since 1933 came together in 1943 and 1944. The refugee problem, the "Jewish question," and "national home" in Palestine for the suffering Jews of Europe, the need to save children, the failure of England and the United States to do more, and especially the failure of the United States to lift the quota restrictions and admit more refugees, the failure of England to make Palestine more accessible to those Jews who did escape the Nazi terror, and the Church Struggle were inextricably woven together during these critical war years.

But the central fact reported during these two years was the clear identification of the death camps, that is, those concentration camps specifically provided with the apparatus for the mass killing of Jews and others in gas chambers, which first used carbon monoxide gas and later Zyklon B. (hydrogen cyanide) because it was "more efficient," or quicker.[31] Rabbi Hertz had mentioned poison gas in his reply to Rushbrooke. In an editorial in *The Brethren Missionary Herald* in July 1943, Louis S. Bauman made three direct references to poison gas or gas-filled rooms and to camps in Poland as places where only death awaited the Jews transported there from Greece, Latvia, Lithuania, Holland, and Belgium.[32] Later, the same periodical referred to "steam chambers" erected in several concentration camps for the mass killing of Jews and named one of the camps—Treblinka. The original information came from the Jewish Telegraph Agency of London.[33]

The Churchman, The Baptist and Reflector, The Calvin Forum, The Chris-

tian Century, Current Religious Thought, The Pulpit, The Friend of Zion, The Hebrew Christian Alliance Quarterly, The Gospel Herald, The Presbyterian, Advance, The Friend, and *The Watchman-Examiner* all contained reports in varying detail on the extermination of the Jews by the Nazis in 1943 and 1944. So did the agencies and organizations who purchased paid advertisements, as they had in every year since 1934. Their witness to the extermination of the Jews by the Nazis was unrelenting. The information in these paid advertisements, especially those purchased by the International Hebrew Christian Alliance, were accurate and explicit descriptions of the extermination process. But of all the periodicals reporting, especially in 1943, the most explicit, detailed news articles concerning the extermination of Europe's Jews came in two small, fundamentalist, or at least strongly evangelical, periodicals with a relatively small readership, *The Brethren Missionary Herald* and *The Hebrew Christian Alliance Quarterly.* Why did not the larger, more influential American Protestant periodicals also report as these two did? The same news was available to them, particularly the news reports originating with the Jewish Telegraph Agency of London and those originally published in the secular press both in England and in the United States. Louis S. Bauman, in writing in *The Brethren Missionary Herald,* cited these sources in his editorials and articles; so did the writers in *The Hebrew Christian Alliance Quarterly,* to some extent. Bauman, for clearly stated reasons, paid a great deal of attention to the daily news, and quite evidently he read the many sources available to him, including the secular press and the news services. He was also particularly interested in what was happening to Jews, and he did react with horror and dismay at what he read and reported. But, in the final analysis, his purpose for such close attention was defined by his opinion that the Jew was the key to fulfilled prophecy from the Bible. What was happening to the Jews in Europe was ultimately a part of the prophetic schematic described in the Scofield Reference Bible, premillenial and dispensational, that was taking place in the "last days" just before the Second Coming of Jesus Christ as promised for the believing Christians and the coming of the promised Messiah for the Jews.[34]

But regardless of his primary objective—prophetic analysis and interpretation—Louis S. Bauman over an eleven-year span provided American Protestant Christians with continuous, substantive information about what was happening to Jews under Hitler and the Nazis in the several periodicals in which his articles and editorials appeared, including reports about the existence of the death camps. For this he is to be commended.

Reports about Auschwitz and Majdanek and letters from chaplains constituted the only new basis for reporting about the Nazi persecution of the Jews in 1944. Auschwitz appeared in the American Protestant press reporting for the first time in relation to the transportation of Hungarian Jews for concentration and untimely death. The discovery and liberation of the death camp at Majdanek, near Lublin in southeastern Poland, constituted the first conclusive evidence that such death camps did exist. Found by advancing Russian troops in July 1944, the camp was opened to thirty journalists, including representatives of the American press. The reaction in the American Protestant press was a combination of horror, caution, and even some disbelief.[35]

The letters from chaplains later in 1944 told of finding Jews still alive who had never been sent to concentration camps and of instituting Jewish religious services, restoring synagogues, and giving assistance to Jews, especially children, when such assistance was possible. By the end of 1944, American Protestant Christians were given one bit of additional information not previously published, the names of some of the concentration camps and death camps. Treblinka, Auschwitz, Majdanek, Sachsenhausen, and Ravensbruck were clearly named as places where the killing of Jews in great numbers had been taking place.

The Central Question and the Discovery of the Death Camps, 1945

In the spring of 1945, as the Russian armies advanced into Germany from the east and the Allied armies advanced from the west, the worst fears about the fate of Europe's Jews were confirmed. The death camps, many of them with the gas chambers intact and the crematoria containing partly burned bodies, were found. As camp after camp was discovered between April 15, 1945, and May 12, 1945, the pictorial and written record of what had been discovered was reported to the world. The series of editorials, articles, and letters from military personnel (chaplains, officers, and enlisted men) published in the American Protestant press told the story of the death camps to American Protestant Christians. Words proved inadequate as the editors and writers of articles attempted to come to grips with the reality of the death camps, even though many of them had been reporting about the mass killings of Jews for several years. Charles Clayton Morrison's phrase, "what can be said that will not seem like tossing little words up against a giant mountain of ineradicable evil?" could stand for almost every editorial response, except for those who, even in the face of the evidence, continued to voice caution, skepticism, or disbelief.[36] The despairing note of William S. Maxwell, editor of *The Signs of the Times*, breathes like a shuddering sigh across the years; he wrote, "So It Was True!" and then reiterated, not once but twice, "but this time, alas, the stories were true" and "yes, it is all too true." He then did what almost all the editors and writers did as a reflex action to the possible charge of "more atrocity stories" by referring to the bringing in of prominent persons by General Eisenhower to see what the death camps revealed and by citing both photographs and motion pictures taken on the sites of the camps to perpetuate the authenticity of what was seen.[37]

The letters from service personnel published in a number of American Protestant periodicals only served to add specific credibility, the credibility of those within denominations whose integrity was unquestioned, to the already well-authenticated story of the death camps. Members of one's own denominational "family" would speak the truth was the unstated message of editors who published such eyewitness accounts written by servicemen who had participated in the events they were describing. One of the most detailed accounts was published in *The Calvin Forum* in a letter sent by F. W. Van Houten, who was not a chaplain.[38] Of the chaplains who told their stories, none spoke more authentically than did Chaplain Donald G. Davis. He was of German descent; he was a minister of the denomination calling itself the German Baptists of North America. He had to tell the story of the German-Nazi-Hitler supreme effort to exterminate Jews and others as he had seen it for himself at Buchenwald to the people of his own denomination, themselves mainly of German descent. His story was presented in a straightforward and unapologetic manner. The periodical, *The Baptist Herald*, had no other word to offer in all of 1945 on the death camps.[39]

The paid advertisements continued to tell the story of the mass extermination of the Jews and of the death camps and the decimation of the Jews of Europe. These advertisements named sites; they cited the numbers of Jews estimated to have been killed and compared the figures to the relatively small numbers of Jews who remained alive. For the organizations and agencies who had placed these advertisements, the finding of the death camps was only the last, awful detail in the story they had been telling since the first advertisement had been published in *The Moody Bible Institute Monthly* in February of 1934.[40] The message of the first advertisement largely had gone unheeded. The headline had read, "Shout It from the Housetops: It's Time to Help the Jews." Such help had not been forthcoming, and the 6 million Jews who were among the victims of the Nazi extermination process bore testimony to that failure.

The advertisements were consistent in their message, however ineffective they may have been in persuading readers of the central fact that they repeated over and over, the terrible persecution and the mass killing of Jews by the Nazis. So consistent were these advertisements, regardless of which organization or agency placed them, that it can be strongly suggested that, were no other evidence available than what these paid advertisements reported from 1934 through 1945, enough evidence of what was happening to Jews under the Nazis was given so that American Protestant Christians could not, and cannot, say that no one told them that they did not know.[41] In fact, as has been discussed, there was much more evidence in the American Protestant press and the paid advertisements did not have to stand alone. They became a significant part of the larger record in the press of reporting about the Nazi persecution and extermination of the Jews.

The Central Question, A Summary

In summary, what was reported in the American Protestant press from 1933 through 1945 supports the statement that American Protestant Christians who read the periodicals even minimally could not plead ignorance or say that they had little or no knowledge about what was happening to Jews under the Nazis. In 1933, the reporting of the April pogrom and the first application of Nazi racial theories, the "Aryan clause" or "paragraph"; in 1935, reports of the adoption of these racial theories as formal laws, the Nuremberg laws; in 1936, the "annex" and resignation letter of James G. McDonald as the high commissioner for refugees of the League of Nations; in 1938, the reports of increasing persecution throughout the year, culminating in Kristallnacht, the Night of Broken Glass; in the years 1939 through 1942, the reports of increasing evidence of the transportation of Jews to concentration camps, the ghettoization of Jews, and the increasing evidence of mass death from starvation and disease or by mass killing confirmed finally and fully in the letter of the chief rabbi of England to the president of the Baptist World Alliance in December 1942; in the years 1943 and 1944, the increasing, persistent rumors of the existence of the death camps, or "killing factories," with the names of some of these camps beginning to appear in the reports, and the discovery of Majdanek, reported in August and September of 1944, with accurate details even though reported with caution and skepticism; the consistent record carried in the paid advertising from 1934 through 1945; and finally the face-to-face encounter with the death camps reported first in May 1945.

Each one of these reported events stands as witness that American Protestant Christians were informed by their own press about the Nazi persecution of the Jews. The cumulative record is impressive, if not overwhelming. American Protestant Christians, by the evidence reported in their own press, knew. Unquestionably, they knew!

In February 1934, an editorial was published in the *Federal Council Bulletin* with the title, "A Challenge to Christendom." The editorial began "The plight of 60,000 refugees from Germany presents a peculiar challenge to the conscience of Christendom—a challenge which thoughtful Christians cannot escape." The editorial then pointed out that the all refugees were not Jews and then stated:

> the greater majority of them are Jews—Jews who are suffering bitter injustice at the hands of those who call themselves Christians. It would be a standing reproach against Christendom if the true Christians of the world were callously indifferent when Jews have been made the victims of unchristian policies perpetrated by nominal Christians.[42]

Neither written as a prophecy nor as a prelude to the events of the next eleven and one-half years to the shock and revulsion voiced in the American Protestant press when editors and writers faced the death camps, nonetheless, the statement written so soon after the beginning of the Nazi persecution of the Jews reaches through those years and beyond, to the present. The cumulative evidence that the American Protestant press reported from 1933 through 1945 only reinforces that early editorial in the *Federal Council Bulletin*. The Jews were the victims; Christians, those who proved to be "callously indifferent," including American Protestant Christians, must bear the weight of "a standing reproach."

CHAPTER 8

"Too Long Have We Christians Been Silent"

> Men are always accomplices to whatever leaves them indifferent.
>
> GEORGE STEINER
> "Jewish Values in the Post-Holocaust Future

The editor of The Hebrew Christian Alliance Quarterly wrote an article for the winter 1943 issue. His title was "Hitler Plans to Destroy European Jewry." His article was based on information provided to President Roosevelt, the reports of the Jewish Telegraphic Agency, and a Polish underground newspaper.[1] After rehearsing the details, including a country-by-country assessment of the fate of Jews in occupied Europe, the author wrote, "What do these revelations of German atrocities do to you? Are you sick at heart? Are you indignant? You should be. Too long have we Christians been silent. Our voices of protest should have been heard long before this happened."[2] The phrase "we Christians" should be noted. The editor, David Bronstein, was an ordained minister; he was also a Jew and a convert to the Christian faith who was associated with an organization and a periodical whose purpose was to carry on a Christian witness and missionary effort among American Jews. His indictment of the silence of Christians has in it a very personal, even despairing note; he was writing as a convert to Christianity but his empathy was with the suffering Jews of Europe. His central message was the indictment of Christians for their silence, a silence before not only the growing knowledge of what was happening to Jews in Poland in 1942 and early 1943, which he reported in his article, but what seemed to him to be the longer silence that had been evident since 1933, when the Nazi persecution of the Jews under Adolf Hitler's dictatorship had begun.

Another comment also written in 1943 heightened the significance of Bronstein's indictment. In "The Observer," edited by R. Paul Miller, in *The Brethren Missionary Herald* for November 20, 1943, there appeared a news note, "The Greatest War Casualties." One paragraph read:

> But the staggering loss of this war is among Jews. With a world population of not more than sixteen million, they have already been tortured to death and murdered to the extent of close to four million. This is practically twenty-five percent of all—the most tremendous loss of all the peoples of the world. And Israel is not at war with anybody.[3]

Indeed, the Jews (the meaning of *Israel* in this context) were not at war with anybody. No Jews were fighting as Axis soldiers. Rather, the Jews were the victims, suffering the most "staggering loss of this war." When the war in Europe ended, the final assessment of the total of number of Jews who were victims of the Nazi terror and extermination policy was fixed at 6 million, just under 27 percent of the Jewish population of the world.[4] A statistic? As Malcolm W. Bingay, then the editorial director of the *Detroit Free Press*, said to the Economic Club of Detroit, as reported in *The Churchman*, "Statistics are utterly impossible." He was answering a question as to whether the stories of the death camps were true or not.[5] Bronstein's indictment of "we Christians" and "the silence" was not an indictment of a silence before a figure, the statistic that 6 million, or 27 percent, of the Jews of the world had been victims of the Nazis. Rather, it was the indictment of a silence of Christians when 6 million human beings were being murdered by methods of torture, terror, massacre, disease, starvation, experimentation, and gas chambers. The persecution that culminated in the Final Solution was reported in the American Protestant press from the very beginning. About this there can be no question.

The Silence, The Failure of Information to Persuade

What then is the nature of the silence that Bronstein wrote about and that has now been raised in the postwar period to a central place in all discussions of the meaning of the Holocaust? The Silence was not a silence of ignorance or of lack of information. Based on what was published about the Nazi persecution of the Jews in the American Protestant press alone, an argument for a silence based on lack of information would not hold up. This is even more true when the information that was given in the daily press, by the radio, in the news and picture magazines is taken into account. Indeed, these sources were sometimes cited as the basis for the information being published in the American Protestant press.

What is called the Silence in a post-Holocaust context must be something other than lack of information. Elie Wiesel, in an address at the annual Bernhard E. Olson Scholars' Conference on the Church Struggle and the Holocaust, referred to the abundance of reported information specifically citing the daily press. He stated that the problem was not information but persuasion.[6] One meaning of the Silence, then, can be defined, in Wiesel's terms, as having the information but the information by itself was not persuasive in the sense that no significant action or intervention took place by governments or by large groups of influential people that slowed or halted the extermination of 6 million European Jews.

The Silence, The Failure of Concerted Effort

In the sense of not being persuaded, American Protestant Christians can also be said to have been silent since what they read from their own religious periodicals over a period of twelve years about the Nazi persecution of the Jews did not result in massive actions or interventions that might have halted the destruction of Europe's Jews or saved large numbers of them from extermination. That prominent churchmen—leaders of denominations, editors and writers, officers in the Federal Council of Churches of Christ in America, and clergymen—here and there did attempt to arouse American Protestant Christians about what was happening to Jews under the Nazis is clear. That they were basically unsuccessful in arousing Christian support on behalf of the Jews is also clear. The programs and plans that were put forward were often modest, focusing on non-Aryan Christians to the exclusion of all other Jews or emphasizing assistance to those fleeing the persecution to the exclusion of those who remained under the Nazis and who did not or could not flee. It is in this context of a failure to intervene using the full weight of American Protestant Christian opinion and resources that a second definition of the Silence can be found, the failure of concerted effort.

The Silence, The Failure of Modest Actions

American Protestant Christians gave money; held rallies or participated in rallies; wrote, approved, and signed statements of protest; sent representatives to Germany, some of whom met with Hitler and other leading Nazis; petitioned President Roosevelt, the United States State Department, and the United States Congress; formed committees within denominations and interdenominationally; cooperated from time to time with concerned Jewish organizations and Jewish leaders; and offered petitions of prayer. As an individual effort and as a combined effort judged in the aggregate, never was this activity or any part of it sufficient enough to do anything beyond slightly delaying the Nazis' movement toward Hitler's often-stated goal—destroying the Jews of Europe. Hitler's calculations of the risks involved proved correct. Massive protest and massive outcry against what the Nazis planned and carried out did not happen, from the early pogroms, through manipulated laws, through the restructuring of the legal system and the political system and the creation of a Nazi totalitarian state, and through the systematic elimination of the "enemies of the state," including Jews. The Nazis carried out these actions for years, with no fear of interference from the nations of the West.

Only after the policy of *Lebensraum* had been instituted and Western Europe had fallen victim to Nazi occupation did intervention come in the form of war and even then the United States did not become a part of the "fighting war" until the nation itself was attacked on December 7, 1941. This gave Hitler from January 30, 1933, to December 7, 1941, seven years and ten months to mount successive challenges to world opinion and intervention, short of war itself, on behalf of the persecuted. None came, at least none of enough force to persuade Hitler to give up or seriously modify the planned extermination of Jews and others. Rather, in the negotiations following Kristallnacht in late 1938 and in early 1939, Germany's Jews became pawns, hostages in a plan of international blackmail, the plans for which were not a failure because they were never instituted but because they were dropped, scuttled, abandoned. Jews could not even be ransomed by their own money.

American Protestant Christians, a significant voice in the United States, did little or nothing to change any of this. Whether through refugee aid, hope for small successes put forward in relation to the Schacht plan, or larger successes expected from the conference held at Evian-les-Bains, nothing even modestly substantive resulted, but Rufus M. Jones writing in *The Christian Century* and in *The Friend* in early 1939 could and did write with a note of hope that, finally, some sort of intervention on behalf of Germany's Jews had been achieved. His hopes proved misplaced.[7] J. Hoffman Cohn, by March 25, 1939, could state flatly that Evian was a failure, if not an outright farce.[8] So yet a third definition of the Silence is suggested. There was not only the failure to be persuaded and the failure of concerted effort, there was the failure of modest attempts. What things that were tried did not work or worked so modestly as to make little or no impression. Nothing changed for the majority of Germany's and Europe's Jews, save that more of them became victims as the persecution and extermination of the Jews was extended to all Nazi-occupied countries.

The Silence, The Failure of World War II as an Intervention for Jews

Even the one great intervention, World War II, did nothing for the Jews and those classed as "subhumans" by the Nazis. The war effort was against Hitler and nazism, against Mussolini and fascism, against the Japanese and its Imperial Army and Navy; World War II was not *for* the saving of Jews who were being gassed or shot in massive numbers, which remain to this day incomprehensible. It was not *for* the bombing of the rail lines that led to Auschwitz and Chelmno and Treblinka and Buchenwald and Sobibor, the known "death factories"; it was not *for* the bombing of the great Buna factory system or the aircraft and missile factories of Doranordhausen or the slave-labor-run quarries near Mauthausen (that is, it was not against the slave-labor system of the Nazis.) The purpose of World War II, as stated by President Roosevelt and by the military leaders, was to win the war and in this way only help the Jews and others held prisoner in the slave-labor system and in the concentration camps.

The American Protestant Christian denominations went to war along with the nation, fully in support of the goal to defeat Hitler and all forms of fascism, German, Italian, and Japanese. Even the traditionally pacifist churches, consistent in their stance, provided a form of alternate service for their young men affected by the prosecution of the war and the need to interact with a war stance and a wartime economy. The concern for Jews as victims of German-Nazi persecution receded into the larger and inarguably correct need to win the war. The existence of a plan for the extermination of the Jews and the existence of "death factories" for this purpose remained a nagging, persistent news item reported from 1942 on in the American Protestant press, which was held under the cloud of suspicion about "more atrocity stories." But the rumors would not go away. Quite the contrary, as the prosecution of the war increased the possibility of an Allied victory, more substantive information appeared to indicate that such extermination camps did exist and that they were functioning successfully.

What intervention might have been undertaken on behalf of the concentrated, doomed Jews at this point? George M. Kren and Leon Rappaport raised an interesting point. Their subject was the survivors of the concentration and death camps and how some had managed to survive through all or part of the interminable ordeal. But, they also noted, those who survived the first few weeks in a camp often died after seven or eight months through a loss of will and a loss of hope. All their psychic energy was used up. Kren and Rappaport then wrote:

> Virtually every survivor memoir contains descriptions of persons who gave up the struggle for life when they finally lost all hope of rescue. A few propaganda broadcasts or leaflet raids directed at the camps might have made a great difference, for if there is anything more crushing than the burden of an atrocious captivity, it is the sense of being forgotten in that captivity.[9]

The question is a haunting one. Could such raids or bombardments with leaflet or broadcasts have been undertaken? More to the point, could exerted, persistent pressure have been brought to bear at the proper levels to institute such a program? The effects of propaganda by print media, both in a positive and in a negative sense, were both known and used. Dropping propaganda leaflets was a known practice, but it was not done for the inmates of the Nazi camps. World War II and the prosecution of the war was not an intervention on behalf of the Jews. Only the final victory by the Allied forces brought their deliverance, six years and 6 million Jewish victims after World War II had begun in Europe. The fourth definition of the Silence can then be stated as the failure *within* the prosecution of World War II, the final and massive intervention against nazism and Hitler, to do anything specifically aimed at informing Jews held in the concentration, slave-labor, and death-camp system that they had not been forgotten. Leaflets, broadcasts, and bombings of rail lines, the barracks of the SS, even the camps themselves would have been a welcome sign that the Allies knew what was going on and that they cared. The masses of Jews and others held in these camps never received such a sign.

The Silence, The Failure to Speak in "Moral Passion"

Majdanek was overrun by the Russians in July 1944, and the world received the first eyewitness stories of an actual "death factory" not told by an escapee-survivor. But the continuation of the fighting and the somewhat unexpected delay of the end of the war served to blunt the full force of the discovery of Majdanek. Only during the final weeks of the war were the extermination centers liberated and then somehow comprehended as being a part of a very large, long-existing system of camps in which thousands of human beings had been held as slave laborers and other multiplied hundreds of thousands had been systematically put to death. Yet, in spite of the eyewitness accounts of chaplains, service personnel, military officers of high rank and distinction, prominent visitors invited by General Eisenhower to see for themselves, in spite of the motion pictures and still photographs exhibited throughout the world, in spite of the accounts of survivors, these camps remained almost incomprehensible.

It is in the context of the discovery of the death camps and the response to them that a fifth definition of the Silence can be proposed. J. H. Oldham was the editor of a newsletter published in England. Selections from his newsletter were published in *The Living Church* on May 20, 1945, under the headline, "Sees Lack of Moral Passion Helping Growth of Barbarism." As printed, the article read:

> Asserting that "our own lack of moral passion contributed to the rank growth of barbarism" in the world, Dr. J. H. Oldham said in the Christian News-Letter of which he is editor that "even for the infamy of German concentration camps we cannot wholly divest ourselves of responsibility."
>
> "The inhumanity and torture being practiced in them were known in this country in the years before the war," he declared. "A few courageous individuals raised their protest and did what they could to succour the victims, but the public as a whole was apathetic and the disposition in influential quarters was to hush things up."
>
> "The web of sin is all of one piece," he wrote. All pride, selfishness and callous indifference to needs of others are a siding with the enemies of Christ.
>
> "We especially need to remind ourselves of this," he added, "when we encounter revolting wickedness. We are then more than ever in danger of externalizing and localizing evil by identifying it with those guilty of these particular abominations."[10]

Oldham raised the central question, which remains in any assessment of the response in the American Protestant press to the discovery of the death camps. The subjects are two, lack of "moral passion" and a sense of complicity for failure to act, but not only for failure to act but a more direct charge of complicity through apathy, "the disposition in influential quarters . . . to hush things up," pride, selfishness, and "callous indifference."

The reaction was shock, horror, disbelief, or finding a prophetic meaning in the events, and it was silence. But there was no indignation or moral passion, words of moral outrage at such evidence of human degradation and utter disregard for human life.[11] Further, there were very few words specifically addressed to Jews, either survivors or Jews in America, addressing this sense of moral outrage that the Jews of Germany and Europe had become the victims of the Hitler and the Nazi-planned extermination and that the world, particularly the Christian world, had "passed by on the other side" in the classic sense of the parable of the Good Samaritan.[12] The fifth proposed definition of the meaning of the Silence, then, is the silence in the absence of moral outrage and moral indignation. As resigned or as compassionate as Maxwell's "So It Was True!" editorial may have been or as overcome with horror as Charles Clayton Morrison professed to have been almost to the point of not writing and then saying, "What can be said that will not seem like tossing little words up against a giant mountain of ineradicable evil?" or Caswell's "in condemning the Germans, we must remember that we are condemning the human race . . . , 'Buchenwald is only a new entry in a long list of crimes for which all mankind must inevitably take the blame,'" they still do not seem to have said what needed to be said.[13]

Guy Emery Shipler in *The Churchman* did center his editorial on the Jews, but only in part. The central theme of the editorial was the American prisoners of war whose bodies had been found among those in the "charnel houses, along with the bodies of Russians, Poles, Frenchmen, Czechoslovaks, and Jews." Shipler went on to state that the Christian world failed to protest in any significant degree when the Nazi's first began their persecution of the Jews "years ago." He also said that the Nazi intention had been not to destroy Jews only but to destory "the dignity and humanity of the whole human race."[14]

Opinion, a Jewish monthly magazine, brutal as its condemnation may now seem, may have come closest to the realities of the spring of 1945 and the finding of the death camps as the final chapter in the program of the extermination of the Jews by the Nazis. Even this *Opinion* article would have escaped the attention of Christians if it had not been quoted at length in "Happenings in Israel" in *The Hebrew Christian Alliance Quarterly.*

> "The most shocking of the war, indeed of all history, is the extermination of close to five million European Jews! Almost equally shocking is the indifference of the civilized world. If the Nazis had murdered five million dogs or cats under similar circumstances, the denunciations would have risen to the high heaven, and numerous groups would have vied with one another to save the animals. Jews, however, has created hardly a stir! Hitler certainly has scored a superlative success in at least one field in the war on the Jews.[15]

That the original article in *Opinion* also went on to blame American Jews only compounds the fact that American Christians, with or without their Jewish "elder brothers," did not intercede or intervene effectively or respond in indignation and outrage when the full story of the extermination of the Jews became known. It is this silence, the silence of moral indignation, that may be the closest definition of the Silence in the meaning in which the Silence is now used in post-Holocaust times. In truth, the Silence may best be defined as having a multiple, comprehensive meaning, in the context of what was published over a period of almost twelve years in the American Protestant press. First, American Protestant Christians knew, but they were not persuaded to take significant action. Second, the Silence may also be defined as the failure of a concerted effort by a unified American Protestantism to do anything for Germany's or Europe's Jews during the Nazi years. Those attempts to assist or intervene that were undertaken, even on a modest scale, failed. Third, yet another definition of the Silence, then, may be the failure of modest attempts to intervene on behalf of Jews.

A fourth meaning of the Silence concerns the failure to encourage the concentrated, slave-labor and death-camp populations through bombings, broadcasts, dropping leaflets, or other assistance, thus leaving the camp's inmates with a sense of hopelessness born of the seeming indifference of the world, particularly the Western and Christian world. In this sense, then, World War II as an act of intervention on behalf of condemned Jews was a failure for those who died without hope. To those Jews who did survive and were rescued by Allied forces, those who had lived through the horrors of concentration camps, the deliverance was bittersweet. They knew the seeming miracle of their own survival amidst the terrible memory of those who had not survived, compounded by the added knowledge of how they had died. Finally, there was the awful silence when the death camps were found, the silence of a morally indignant and outraged world of Christians, including American Protestants, who failed to speak out about the death camps and who in subsequent years failed even to remember. These five meanings of silence—knowing but not being persuaded; the failure to act in concert; the failure of modest actions; the failure of World War II as "containing" specific intervention for Jews; and the failure to speak in words of moral indignation, confession, or moral outrage in the face of the death camps—these together are the Silence against which the voice of survivors and of Jews alike cries out "remember."

A Contrast, The Death Camps and Hiroshima/Nagasaki

In reading and rereading the articles in the American Protestant press (through the late spring, summer, and fall of 1945 and on into 1946 and 1947) used in this study, I looked in vain for a lucid, burning prophet's message. Where is the profound, soul-searching, seering condemnation-confession of a man of Christian faith, an American Protestant, a Poling, a Morrison, a Shipler, a Fosdick, or any of a host of other such Christian leaders who would step forward to say in our blindness, in our preoccupation with ourselves, that we have failed at the very heart of the most fundamental of all Christian commandments, to love our neighbors as ourselves. In this, by ignoring the most basic of Christian responsibilities, we have sinned against our "elder brother." No such statement was found.

Such moral outrage or moral indignation and a sense of culpability by American Protestant Christians was felt later, and it was widely reported in the American Protestant press. The subject, however, was not the Nazi persecution of the Jews or the death camps, but the dropping of the atom bomb on Hiroshima and Nagasaki, Japan. Two interesting questions must be asked. Would the treatment of the revelation of human suffering, torture, and death in the gas chambers and crematoria of the death camps have been different if the war had ended on all fronts in May 1945? Asked in a different way, did the two-front ending of World War II, first in Europe and then later in the Pacific, have an effect on the way the death camps were reported and discussed? The question is interesting and highly speculative; a definitive answer cannot be given, at least not in this study. The question is worthy of further examination.

The second question is, why was there such an outpouring of moral indignation when the atom bomb was dropped twice on Japanese cities but not when Buchenwald, Bergen-Belsen, Mauthausen, Sachsenhausen, Auschwitz, Dachau, and the other concentration camps were found?

The Atom Bomb

An article in *Advance* quoted Pope Pius XII as saying that the atom bomb ought to have been destroyed by its inventors, the *Christian Century* as saying that Japan should only have been threatened with the bomb, and Kagawa of Japan as saying that the Allies had been "morally" defeated because they had used the bomb.[16] The headline of an editorial in *The Brethren Missionary Herald* read "Atomic Bomb Shocks World."[17] *The Christian Century* described as a part of its first editorial on the atom bomb, "the ultimate in violence," the fear that it would lead to the extermination of humanity and concluded, "we should now be standing in penitence before the Creator of the power which the atom has hitherto kept inviolate, using what may be our last opportunity to learn the lost secret of peace on earth."[18]

One week later, the full force and editorial power of *The Christian Century* was turned loose in four editorials, the last two of which were directly about the atom bomb. The first of the last two, "Man and the Atom," noted that for the first time a great scientific breakthrough had not been hailed or acclaimed. "Has science gone too far? Is man worthy of such knowledge? Has he not violated the sanctities of nature's own secret and brought upon himself vast reprisals, perhaps the destruction of civilization and his own annihilation?" Reference to the world's horror, the doubt of the scientists who had worked on the atom bomb, the fears and questions of the "man on the street," and the problems confronting the Christian church also were discussed in the editorial. The last of the four editorials discussed "The Church's Responsibility" in light of "the apocalyptic end of the war," if "the abyss into which [man] has stared in horror is not to engulf him."[19]

On September 29, 1945, an editorial in *The Christian Century* was entitled "America's Atomic Atrocity." It began, "Something like a moral earthquake has followed the dropping of atomic bombs on two

Japanese cities." The editorial then described the "correspondence and much more like it" that had arrived in the offices of the *Century* unsolicited, part of which was published in the same issue. The editorial generally spoke of the validity of arguing military necessity for the use of the bomb and Japan's reaction, and then it spoke of the complicity of the Christian church, particularly of the American churches, and the difficulties of disassociating themselves from the dropping of the atom bomb in terms of returning to effective missionary work in Asia, particularly in Japan. The editorial concluded:

> The writers of the letters which appear in this paper have been profoundly shocked that their government was capable of such wantonness. Their protest will, we believe, be taken up by Christian people throughout the nation. And this protest will swell in volume until it reaches the shores and people of Japan.[20]

Seventeen letters to the editor were published in the same issue, all on the atom bomb.[21] Outrage, shame, scorn for the Church and its weakness, pleas for the Church to become strong and protest, confessions of complicity through personal inaction, apologies to Christian friends in Japan, calls for repentence and prayer, discussions of the moral issues raised by the action, calls to "outlaw" the atom bomb, discussions of the loss of spiritual and moral controls—all of these appeared in one form or another in the letters, all of which were from people within the United States. Only one of the letters even remotely related the atom bomb to the destruction of Europe's Jews. Fred Eastman from Chicago Theological Seminary put this comment in his letter, "We have beaten Hitler at his own game. But that game was a devil's race to see which could destroy human beings more effectively."[22]

Also in the same issue, the "News of the Christian World" section opened with an item entitled, "Leaders Protest Atomic Bombs: Oxnam and Dulles of Federal Council's Commission Issue Statement on Implication for Religion." Central to the Oxnam-Dulles statement was the concern that the world would become uninhabitable as a result of the invention and use of the atom bomb.[23] One or two other leaders (including Bernard Iddings Bell) were also cited, particularly regarding the effect of the use of the atom bomb on Japan on Christian missionary work being done in Asia because of a "worldwide moral revulsion against us."[24]

The editorials in *The Churchman* as well as the articles and news items paralleled those of *The Christian Century*.[25] *The Concordia Theological Monthly* wrote of the atom bomb as a "foretaste of Doomsday."[26] *Current Religious Thought* published a radio sermon given by George W. Phillips, pastor of the Tenth Avenue Baptist Church, Oakland, California. The title was "At the Portals of Tomorrow." In it he had a section, "The 'Blast' Felt around the World," which he called "the most tremendous moment in the history of man" with the exception of Calvary. He then wondered about how the atom bomb would be controlled and if "one world" was now inevitable. He then turned to the question of human righteousness in such a world. In this context, he made a brief reference to Hitler's extermination camps as an evidence of racial hatred. This was one of the very few articles linking any discussion of the atom bomb to the extermination of Jews under Hitler.[27]

The Friend introduced its discussion of the atom bomb in a brief editorial in order to mention an article by Richard M. Fagley, "The Atomic Bomb and the Crisis of Man," which called for international controls under the United Nations.[28] *The Friend* also published some letters to the editor on the subject of the bomb.

The Lutheran Companion's editorial was called "Our Tragic Victory." "The atomic bomb is a stain upon our national life. . . . We Americans . . . have set a new standard for hell's atrocities. . . . As a nation we have sinned atrociously, though perhaps not unforgivably."[29] *The Lutheran Standard* also published the article by Fagley that had been published in *The Friend*.[30] The editors of *The Messenger* felt "Remorse in Victory," fearing greater destruction in America through loss of respect in the world than in Japan by physical destruction. The editorial cited Robert Brodt, youth director of the staff of the Board of Christian Education and Publication, as having written, "Beside the awful horror of Hiroshima, Lidice and Dachau and robot bombs begin to fade into insignificance."[31] *Moody Monthly* published two editorials, one a solemn caution over undue flipancy and a call to act reasonably; the other pointing out that a Mrs. Lise Meitner was a mathematician whose calculations aided in the work on the atom bomb, that she was Jewish, and that she was a refugee from Germany. Her work had been done first in Germany in the early 1930s.[32] *The Pulpit* published an article, evidently first given as a sermon, by Marshall Wingfield, "The Atomic Bomb and Its Implications." No insights not already discussed in other publications were given in the article.[33]

The Death Camps and the Atom Bomb, A Summation

So the American Protestant press spoke out on the atom bomb and the dropping of the bomb as an act deserving shame. As for the moral and ethical consequences of this action, the evidence was clear. By the use of the atom bomb to end the war with Japan, America had lowered itself in the eyes of the world. A democracy proud of its moral strength by this single action had undone its reputation as a moral leader and a guide among nations. If nothing else, at least the continuance of an effective missionary outreach in the Orient would be much less possible because of the immoral action taken, the dropping of atom bombs on Hiroshima and Nagasaki.

Not so on the death camps. On March 9, 1944, just over a year before the end of the war in Europe, a meeting was held in Washington, D.C., attended by leading Protestant, Roman Catholic, and Jewish leaders, some of whom were members of Congress. Vice-President Henry A. Wallace was present, and at the dinner a telegram from President Franklin D. Roosevelt was read. The meeting had been called by the American Palestine Committee in conjunction with a number of other groups. The papers, resolutions, and the list of delegates to the conference were published as *The Voice of Christian America: Proceedings of the National Conference on Palestine*. One of the speakers was William B. Ziff. He spoke on "Palestine in the Present Crisis." He referred to what was happening to Jews under the Nazis, saying:

As a result of the current phase of the Nazi brutality almost three million Jews, men, women and children have been wantonly butchered under conditions of savagery and lust scarcely equalled anywhere in the long, sad history of man's faithlessness and inhumanity to his own kind.

One is compelled to stand aghast, not only at the brutishness which created these acts, but at the indifference and apathy of the Western world which lifted no hand to save these people. . . . They were hermetically sealed in with the full desperate knowledge that their death sentence had been written. These three million lie in nameless graves together, poets, dreamers, businessmen, scientists, grimy-handed workers, housewives and little children. Many were said to have been buried even before they died. Eye witnesses have stated that the very earth in these mass graves shook with the last convulsive breathing of these tragically broken people.

The stark measure of this crime and the irreparable loss it

has cost humanity can never be plumbed, but even more terrible has been the silence of the West. . . . If this silence is a
symbol of that inner demoralization for which Hitler has
prayed, it represents a subtle alteration of standards which
should well make the West tremble.[34]

Just two months before the meeting in Washington, D.C., Alfred
Kazin had written an article published in the *New Republic*. His article
was a commentary brought about by the death of Shmuel Ziegelboim, a Polish Jew, who committed suicide in his London apartment
on May 12, 1943, leaving a letter addressed to the president of Poland
and the premier of Poland. The entire letter was included in Kazin's
article. Among the things Kazin wrote were comments on the failure
of the world to comprehend what was happening to the Jews.
"Shmuel Ziegelboim came from a ghetto-driven, self-driven, but spiritually generous culture; and I honestly think he was thinking not
only of his own people at the end, but of the hollowness of a world
in which such a massacre could have so little meaning." A few sentence later, he wrote:

I do not speak here of the massacre of the Jews, for there is
nothing to say about it that has not already been said. . . . For
the tragedy is in our minds, in the basic quality of our personal
culture. . . . The tragedy lies in the quality of our belief—not
in the lack of it, but in the unconsciousness or dishonesty of it;
and above all in the merely political thinking, the desperate
and unreal optimism, with which we try to cover up the void
within ourselves.

Kazin's article closed with an indictment of those

—not liberals, not radicals, certainly not reactionaries—who
want only to live and let live, to have the good life back—who
think that you can dump three million helpless Jews into your
furnace, and sigh in the genuine impotence of your undeniable
regret, and then build Europe back again. . . .
For I know that the difference . . . is far more terrible than
physical terror and far more "tangible" than conscience. Something has been set forth in Europe. . . . That something is all
our silent complicity in the massacre of the Jews (and surely
not of them alone; it is merely that their deaths were so pecu-
liarly hopeless). For it means that men are not ashamed of what
they have been in this time, and are therefore not prepared
for the further outbreaks of fascism which are deep in all of us.[35]

Ziff and Kazin, in 1944 and separate of each other, spoke of silence, the "silence of the West," and "the silent complicity in the massacre of the Jews."

The Silence, A Closing Word

It is now time to go back to that first year of the Hitler era, to September 21, 1933. On that date, Robert A. Ashworth, who was associated with the National Conference of Jews and Christians and who was a former editor of *The Baptist*, had his letter to the editor to *The Reformed Church Messenger* published. He was responding to an article by Dr. E. G. Homrighausen, "Behind the German Jewish Problem," and disagreeing substantially with Homrighausen's analysis. "Germany's treatment of the Jews," Ashworth wrote, "is an offense against humanity, a violation of the most basic human instincts, a revival of sadism on a wide scale, and from a Christian point of view, a denial of all that we hold most sacred." He concluded his lengthy letter with the following statement:

As Hilaire Belloc says in the article from which we have quoted, "As it seems to be a particular and flagrant injustice of this kind affects not only the individual who suffers from it, nor only the unhappy men who perpetuate the outrage, but also those who are silent in the presence of it. They themselves will be poisoned if they do not protest, for it is their duty to protest."[36]

Ashworth, quoting Belloc, was right. What the Nazis, Hitler, and Germany did to the Jews was an offense against humanity, and American Protestant Christians stood witness in the presence of it, from 1933 to 1945. The American Protestant press did report what was happening to the Jews in Germany. As has been shown, the press reported far more extensively than has generally been thought to be the case. The accepted view has been that the press had said little or nothing. Clearly, this was not true. It must be said, then, that American Protestant Christians did know, for, if the people read, the people knew. But the editors and writers of the American Protestant press tried to deal with the mass extermination of the Jews of Germany and Europe as if it were a part of an ordered, stable, normal world. In fact, it happened in a world gone mad. In the end, editors and writers seemed unable to cope with something as unreal, even unimaginable, as the mass slaughter of millions of people, among them 6 million Jews, in an organized, bureaucratic, planned extermination. They could report this madness, this unreality, but, beyond the reporting and even beyond the expressed shock and horror over the discovery of the death camps, there remains the awful pall that hangs over this entire episode in modern history.

APPENDIXES

Appendix A

American Protestant
Religious Periodicals
Examined, 1933–1945

All of the periodicals were not available for all of the years between 1933 and 1945. Some published in 1933 became the victims of the Great Depression and either went out of business or
merged with other existing periodicals. Denominational mergers resulted in either a combined publication or a new one. Denominational divisions ("splits") resulted in there being two publications
where there had been one. And some publications begun at some
point after 1933 and before 1945 were entirely new ventures. Some
publications were owned by private corporations and were nondenominational; some privately held publications were denominational
even though they were not officially affiliated with a denomination.
The denominational names mentioned are those that were being
used during the years 1933 through 1945.

Number of Periodicals Examined, by Year

1933 . . . 30	1938 . . . 36	1943 . . . 31
1934 . . . 28	1939 . . . 37	1944 . . . 32
1935 . . . 33	1940 . . . 33	1945 . . . 39
1936 . . . 32	1941 . . . 35	(1946 . . . 19)
1937 . . . 31	1942 . . . 30	(1947 . . . 4)

Total number periodicals examined . . . 52

Analysis of Periodicals Examined

Name of Periodical	Denomination Affiliation	Place Published	Frequency of Publication
Adult Class and Adult Leader	Northern Baptist Convention	Philadelphia, Pennsylvania	Monthly
Advance	Congregational Christian Church	Chicago, Illinois	Biweekly
The Alliance Weekly	Christian and Missionary Alliance	Harrisburg, Pennsylvania	Weekly
The Arizona Baptist	Northern Baptist Convention	Phoenix, Arizona	Monthly
The Arkansas Baptist	Southern Baptist (state paper)	Little Rock, Arkansas	Weekly
The Banner Herald	Primitive Baptist	Columbus, Georgia	Monthly
The Baptist and Reflector	Southern Baptist (state paper)	Nashville, Tennessee	Weekly
The Baptist Bulletin	General Association of Regular Baptists	Butler, Indiana	Monthly
The Baptist Herald	German Baptist Publication Society	Cleveland, Ohio	Monthly
* *The Bond*	Lutheran Brotherhood Insurance Company	Mount Morris, Illinois	Monthly
The Brethren Evangelist	Brethren church	Ashland, Ohio	Weekly
* *The Brethren Missionary Herald*[a]	Brethren Missionary Herald Company (Grace Brethren Church)	Fort Wayne, Indiana	Weekly
The Calvin Forum	Christian Reformed	Grand Rapids, Michigan	Monthly
* *Christendom*[b]	Willet, Clark and Company and the Federal Council of Churches	Chicago, Illinois and New York, New York	Quarterly
†*The Christian Advocate*	Methodist Episcopal church (regional)	New York, New York, and Chicago, Illinois	Weekly
The Christian Century	Christian Century Foundation	Chicago, Illinois	Weekly
Christian Faith and Life[c]	Christian Faith and Life Publishers	Reading, Pennsylvania	Monthly
The Christian Herald	Christian Herald Associates	New York, New York	Monthly
Church Management	Church World Press, Inc.	Cleveland, Ohio	Monthly
The Churchman	Churchman Associates (Protestant Episcopal)	New York, New York	Weekly
The Concordia Theological Monthly	Missouri Synod Lutheran	St. Louis, Missouri	Monthly
Current Religious Thought[d]	Current Religious Thought	Oberlin, Ohio	Monthly
The Evangelical Visitor	Brethren in Christ	Nappanee, Indiana	Biweekly
Federal Council Bulletin	Federal Council of Churches of Christ	New York, New York	Monthly

Periodical	Sponsor/Publisher	Location	Frequency
*The Friend	Contributors to the Friend (Quaker)	Philadelphia, Pennsylvania	Biweekly
*The Friend of Zion	Zion Society for Israel (Lutheran)	Minneapolis, Minnesota	Monthly
*The Gospel Herald	Union Gospel Press	Cleveland, Ohio	Weekly
The Gospel Messenger	Church of the Brethren	Elgin, Illinois	Weekly
The Hebrew Christian Alliance Quarterly	Hebrew Christian Alliance of America	Chicago, Illinois	Quarterly
The Hebrew Lutheran	United Lutheran church, Jewish Missions Committee	Baltimore, Maryland	Quarterly
*The King's Business	Bible Institute of Los Angeles	Los Angeles, California	Monthly
The Living Church	Protestant Episcopal church	Milwaukee, Wisconsin	Weekly
The Lutheran	United Lutheran church	Philadelphia, Pennsylvania	Biweekly
The Lutheran Companion	Augustana Lutheran	Rock Island, Illinois	Weekly
The Lutheran Herald	Norwegian Lutheran	Minneapolis, Minnesota	Weekly
The Lutheran Standard	American Lutheran church	Columbus, Ohio	Weekly
The Lutheran Witness	Missouri Synod Lutheran	St. Louis, Missouri	Biweekly
*The Mennonite	Mennonite General Conference of America	Berne, Indiana	Weekly
The Mennonite Quarterly Review	Mennonite	Goshen College, Goshen, Indiana	Quarterly
†The Messenger^e	Evangelical and Reformed Church	St. Louis, Missouri	Weekly
The Moody Bible Institute Monthly	Moody Bible Institute	Chicago, Illinois	Monthly
The Northwestern Lutheran	Wisconsin Lutheran Synod	Milwaukee, Wisconsin	Monthly
The Presbyterian	Presbyterian Church in the U.S.A.	Philadelphia, Pennsylvania	Weekly
*The Presbyterian Banner^f	Presbyterian-Banner Publishing Company	Pittsburg, Pennsylvania	Weekly
The Presbyterian Guardian^g	Presbyterian Guardian Publishing Corporation	Philadelphia, Pennsylvania	Monthly
The Presbyterian Register	Alliance of Reformed Churches (holding the Presbyterian system)	Edinburgh, Scotland	Quarterly
*The Pulpit	Christian Century Foundation	Chicago, Illinois	Monthly
†The Reformed Church Messenger	Evangelical Reformed Church (See The Messenger)	Philadelphia, Pennsylvania	Weekly

Analysis of Periodicals Examined

Name of Periodical	Denomination Affiliation	Place Published	Frequency of Publication
*The Sabbath Recorder	American Sabbath Tract Society (Seventh-Day Baptist)	Plainfield, New Jersey	Monthly
The Signs of the Times	Seventh-Day Adventist	Mountain View, California	Weekly
*The Sunday School Times	Sunday School Times Publishing Company	Philadephia, Pennsylvania	Weekly
The Watchman-Examiner	Northern Baptist Convention	Philadelphia, Pennsylvania	Weekly

* Owned by a private corporation and/or a nondenominational publication.
† A merged publication or a publication resulting from a denominational merger.
ᵃ Began publication in 1940.
ᵇ Began publication in 1935.
ᶜ Published between 1933 and 1937.
ᵈ Began publication in 1941.
ᵉ Began publication in 1936. See *The Reformed Church Messenger*.
ᶠ Ceased publication in 1937.
ᵍ Began publication in 1936.

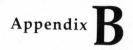

Glossary
of Terms and Names

Aryan: A term peculiar to Nazi-German usage. It was taken from Gobineau's *Essay on Inequality of the Human Races* (1853–1854), in which the phrase "Aryan German" appeared, initially as a description of Germans as superior members of the white race. The Nazi use of *Aryan* initially covered all Germans as "pure Nordic Germans," but in strict definition the term *Aryan* was used with many meanings, some contradictory, in the Nazi lexicon. In 1935, in the Nuremberg laws, an *Aryan* was defined as a person "of German or cognate blood." The so-called "Aryan paragraph," or "Aryan clause," was cited in the American Protestant religious press between April 7 and April 11, 1933, as in the Law for the Restoration of the Professional Civil Service, and the definition of a *non-Aryan* as anyone "descended from non-Aryan, especially Jewish parents or grandparents." See *Non-Aryan.*

"Aryan Clause" ("Aryan paragraph"): As used in the American Protestant press, the term refers to the exclusion from the professional clergy of the church of Germany of any person whose parents or grandparents had been Jewish. See **Aryan; Non-Aryan: Church Struggle.**

Auschwitz: (1) Auschwitz was a German concentration camp established in 1940 as a transit camp for Polish prisoners; it was expanded in 1941 to accommodate 100,000 prisoners, including nearby Birkenau. The camp was the source of slave labor for Buna, the IG-Farben AG synthetic rubber factory and one of thirty-nine "outside detachments" supplying slave labor in Upper Silesia, Austria, for German factories. The gas chambers and crematoria for Auschwitz were set up in Birkenau. (2) Auschwitz is-used symbolically (as in Richard L. Rubenstein's treatment of the Holocaust) as the basis for a radical Jewish theology (thus, *After Auschwitz: Radical Theology and Contemporary Judaism,* and Eva Fleischner, editor, *Auschwitz: Beginning of a New Era? Reflections on the Holocaust*). *Auschwitz,* and sometimes Buchenwald and Dachau, is also used symbolically to stand for all the Nazi death camps.

Baptist World Alliance: The alliance was founded by adoption of a constitution and organization plan July 11–18, 1905, in a meeting of Baptists from twenty-three countries. Membership was open to any "general Union, Convention or Association of Baptist Churches"; thus, membership was by organizational affiliation, not as individuals or churches. The alliance met at five-year intervals as a world conference of Baptists. Meetings were held in Berlin in 1934 and in Atlanta, Georgia, in 1938. The 1934 meeting was out of the five-year sequence, 1928, 1933, 1938, because of the internal political situation in 1933 and the decision to delay the meeting until 1934.

Church Struggle (German: *Kirchenkampf*): The term signified the collective resistance by Protestants and Roman Catholics to the National Socialist party and its attempt to make the Church a part of the German state and to control it as a part of the Nazi bureaucratic structure. The resistance was not universal; it divided the Church in Germany and created opposing factions within the Church.

Cold Pogrom: Generally, this included persecution; harassment; deprivation; humiliation; boycotts of Jewish businesses; loss of professional positions or jobs; restrictions on travel, housing, availability of health care, schooling, recreational facilities, and public services; but it was short of deportation, concentration, massacre or mass killing, and extermination. It was accompanied by extreme anti-Jewish propaganda and harassment.

Conservative-Evangelical: Within the divisions of Protestantism of the period 1930–1945, conservative-evangelicals were those Protestant denominations, churches, or individuals who held traditional views concerning the Bible, the person and work of Jesus Christ, the Atonement, the Resurrection, the Virgin Birth, and the Second Coming of Christ but who did not, commonly, align themselves with the movement known as fundamentalism. See **Fundamentalist; Modernist.**

Dispensationalism: Most commonly, a belief in the division of history into distinct eras called *dispensations* or different periods of God's work among humans and in the world in which God's work is considered unique to that period. This concept of periods is alluded to in the Scriptures, and the periods are correlated with events in the Scriptures. This system of periodization is then considered to be the correct interpretation of the Scriptures; thus, dispensationalism is raised to the level of a hermeneutical method or method of interpretation. Some dispensationalists were also millenarians, and some also held to premillenial views or what is called the "Secret Rapture" or any-moment coming of Jesus Christ.

Evian-les-Bains: An international conference on the refugee crisis was called for by President Roosevelt and held at the Hotel Royal, Evian-les-Bains, France. Representatives of thirty-two nations were present from July 6 through July 15, 1938. For a detailed account, see Henry Feingold, *The Politics of Rescue*, New Brunswick, New Jersey, Rutgers University Press, 1970, pp. 22–44.

The Final Solution: *Endlösung* (the Final Solution) was the plan adopted at the Wannsee Conference on January 20, 1942, in which the extermination of the Jews was made policy, thereby formalizing the various procedures that enabled Jews to be transported to the extermination centers and massacred by mass shootings. Parts of the extermination process were already being carried out prior to the Wannsee Conference. The responsibility for administrating the Final Solution belonged to Reinhold Heydrich as head of the RSHA (Reich Security Main Office). He was assisted by Adolph Eichmann, head of the office for Jewish Affairs and Evacuation Affairs (RSHA, IV-B-4).

Fundamentalist: (fundamentalism): As a movement, it stressed the Second Coming of Christ (millenarianism), dispensationalism, opposition to liberalism and modernism, the inerrancy of Scripture, the Virgin Birth of Christ, the Atonement of Christ, the resurrection of Christ and a pessimistic world view.

German Baptists: (1) These were members of the denomination in the United States and Canada known as the German Baptist church, who published *The Baptist Herald*, put out by the German Baptist Publication Society. The denomination is known today as the North American Baptist General Conference. (2) The term also applied to Baptists in Germany, who were members of a "free church," that is, one not considered a part of the Evangelical church in Germany. It had its own leaders, congregations, mission programs, and institutional structures and was the host body for the Baptist World Alliance Congress held in Berlin in 1934.

German Christians (*deutsche Christen*): These Christians, primarily Protestants, supported Hitler and the Nazis and participated in and supported the formal structures whereby the Church was made an arm of the state, that is, a part of the Nazi political apparatus. Opposition to the German Christians by a part of the Evangelical church (*Bekennende Kirche*), or Confessing Church, constituted a major part of what is known today as the Church Struggle.

Hebrew Christians (Jewish Christians): These were baptized or converted Jews who had become Christians. This designation was used commonly in the American Protestant press to refer to Christian Jews both in the United States and in Germany. *Hebrew Christian* also appeared in the titles of organizations (or their publications) engaged in Christian missionary and evangelistic work among Jews in the United States and in overseas missionary work. See **Non-Aryan Christian.**

Hermeneutics: In the context of the American Protestant press, this term refers to the methodological principles of interpretation of the Bible. In this sense, dispensationalism would be an example of hermeneutics, that is, an interpretation of the Bible in a structured, methodological manner, as in Daniel P. Fuller, "The Hermeneutics of Dispensationalism" (unpublished Th.D. dissertation, Northern Baptist Seminary, Chicago, 1957).

Holocaust (*Shoah*): The term is used to describe the destruction of the Jews during World War II, 1939–1945. As a special designation, it encompasses the latter years of the broader term, the Nazi persecution of the Jews. See **The Nazi Persecution of the Jews: The Final Solution.**

"Jewish Question" ("Jewish problem"): In the context of the American Protestant press (1933–1945), the term reflects the discussion over the place of the Jews in a Western Christian nation, culture, or society. Related questions included anti-Semitism, assimilation, the Jews as a Chosen People of God, the Jew and biblical prophecy, the Jew and race, the question of an international Jewish conspiracy (alleged), the Jews in America, Judaism and Christianity, the Jews as "nation within a nation," the Jews as refugees, the religious beliefs and practices of Jews, and Zionism.

Kristallnacht: This term refers to the specific events of November 7–13, 1938, a time when a nationwide persecution and humiliation of Jews took place in Germany and Austria. Literally, the word means the Night of Broken Glass or the Night of Glass; this was taken from the smashing of the windows of Jewish homes, businesses, and synagogues that occurred during Kristallnacht.

Liberal: This term should be defined in relation to the period in which this study has been done; thus, it was the position held by theologians and churchmen that was open to the influences of Darwinism and of the German higher criticism and that brought into question the inerrancy of Scripture and the position espoused by conservative-evangelicals and fundamentalists. American Liberal theology formed the theological basis for modernism and for the opposition embodied in the fundamentalist-modernist controversy of 1910–1940. The philosophy embodied an optimistic view of human nature, and thereby it was a repudiation of the doctrines of original sin and human depravity. See **Fundamentalism; Modernism.**

Main-line Protestant: These were members of the Protestant denominations whose founding and growth formed the strength of Protestant denominationalism in the United States, for example, Presbyterians, Lutherans, Congregationalists, Methodists, and Episcopalians.

Millenial, Millenarian: (1) The term refers to the imminent Second Coming of Jesus Christ. (2) The term comes from *millennium* in a biblical context referring to the thousand-year reign of Jesus Christ to be inaugurated at the Second Coming. (3) Millenarianism was a distinct movement within British and American Protestantism, which began in the nineteenth century and continues to the present. Ernest Sandeen referred to this movement as "a church within a church" (Ernest R. Sandeen, *The Roots of Fundamentalism*. Chicago, The University of Chicago Press, 1970, chapter 15). See **Premillenial.**

Modernism: Again, this term should be defined in the context of the period in which this study was undertaken. Modernism was a term descriptive of those of liberal theological persuasion, those who practiced the Social Gospel commitment to humanitarian assistance and involvement in the political process, and those who were sympathetic to contemporary philosophy, science, and scholarship to the extent of modifying traditional conservative, evangelical views, or the fundamentals. *Modernist* and *Liberal* are both terms that are less relevant today than they were in the nineteenth and early twentieth centuries, and both may be best understood as the positions opposed by fundamentalists in the fundamentalist-modernist controversy, 1910–1940.

The Nazi persecution of the Jews: The term is used to describe the entire period of the Nazi political rule in Germany under Adolf Hitler, 1933–1945, during which Jews were systematically persecuted. This broader designation encompasses the Holocaust, 1939–1945.

Non-Aryan, non-Aryan Christian: These terms were commonly used in the American Protestant press during the Nazi era to refer to those persons excluded by the "Aryan paragraph" and the Nuremberg laws of 1935 as not being of "Aryan blood" or Germanic descent as defined by the laws. Specifically, *non-Aryan Christian* described baptized or converted Jews who were professing Christians but who were excluded by racial laws from the Church because of their being Jews.

Pre-Millenial: This was the view commonly held by millenarians that Jesus Christ will return to establish His thousand-year reign and thus the Second Coming of Christ.

Pre-Tribulation Rapture: There was a position held by some premillenialists stressing that a Secret Rapture, or meeting of the Bride of Christ, the true believers or true Church, would take place "in the air," inaugurating a seven-year period called the Tribulation, which would end with the Second Coming of Christ to establish His kingdom and inaugurate the thousand-year reign of Christ on the earth. Pre-Tribulation exponents were also premillenialists, and almost all were dispensationalists in interpretation of the Bible and aligned with the fundamentalist movement of the 1930s and 1940s. See **Secret Rapture.**

Scofield Reference Bible: C. I. Scofield added notes to the King James Version of the Bible, laying out a scheme of periodization or dispensations. The Scofield notes are in the form of an outline in both the Old and New Testaments setting forth the periods and also explanatory notes accompanying the outline setting forth the meaning of each dispensation, with cross references. The *Scofield Reference Bible* embodies the position of John Newton Darby (Darbyism) and is generally considered to be the single most influential publication in fundamentalism. It was first published in 1909 and is still being published.

Secret Rapture: In the American Protestant press, the fundamentalist periodicals often stressed dispensational teaching, premillenial interpretation of the Second Coming of Christ and the Secret Rapture, the latter view being that the Church was a spiritual entity not defined by churches or organizations but as believers. At the Second Coming, a first stage, or "Secret Rapture," would occur before the Second Coming of Christ as Messiah. Commonly, the Church as the Bride of Christ would be "caught up" secretly, at any moment, to "meet Christ in the air," thus, the "Secret Rapture." The role of the Jews in the fulfillment of prophecy was seen as important in gauging when the time for such an event might be "drawing nigh." See **Pre-Tribulation Rapture.**

Wannsee Conference: This conference was held on January 20, 1942, at Am Grossen Wannsee, the offices of the International Police Commission, was attended by fourteen persons representing various Nazi agencies and bureaus, and was conducted by Reinhard Heydrich. Adolf Eichmann served as secretary. Thirty copies of the minutes were made and distributed. Number 16 was used subsequently by the American prosecution in the Nuremberg trials. The plan embodied in the phrase, the Final

Solution, the planned extermination of the Jews, was presented and approved at this conference. The implementation of the program approved at the Wannsee Conference became one of the major tasks of the RSHA (Reich Security Main Office) and of Adolf Eichmann, coded IV-B-4 (Jews).

NOTES

Notes

Introduction

1. Lucy S. Dawidowicz, *The War against the Jews: 1933–1945*, New York, Holt, Rinehart and Winston, 1975, pp. 261–78.
2. Alan T. Davies, *Anti-Semitism and the Christian Mind*. New York, Herder and Herder, 1969, pp. 132–35.
3. "World Council Diary," *The Ecumenical Review* (April 1955), 284. (Quoted in Davies, p. 134.)
4. Davies, p. 136.
5. Roy and Alice L. Eckardt, "Again, Silence in the Churches," *The Christian Century* (July 26, August 2, 1967) 73–77, 78–82.
6. Ibid., p. 73.
7. Davies, p. 8.
8. Ibid.
9. Eckardt.
10. Franklin H. Littell, *Holocaust Studies Newsletter* (n.d.) 1:4.
11. Timothy L. Smith, *Revivalism and Social Reform*. New York, Abingdon Press, 1957, p. 9.

Chapter 1

1. William L. Shirer, *The Rise and Fall of the Third Reich*, 1st ed. New York, Simon and Shuster, 1959, p. 1133.
2. Ibid., pp. 1138–39.
3. Lucy S. Dawidowicz, *The War against the Jews: 1933–1945*. New York, Holt, Rinehart and Winston, 1975, pp. 261–78 and 357ff.
4. *The Evangelical Visitor, A Religious Journal* (February 13, 1933), 2. (Evangelical Visitor Publishing House [Brethren in Christ Publication Board], 301–305 North Elm Street, Nappanee, Indiana. Permanent Church Headquarters, Messiah Rescue and Benevolent Home, 1175 Bailey Street, Harrisburg, Pennsylvania.)
5. Ibid.
6. *The Christian Century: An Undenominational Journal of Religion* (February 8, 1933), 8. (Charles Clayton Morrison, editor, 407 South Dearborn Street, Chicago, Illinois.)
7. Shirer, pp. 191–95.
8. *The Sunday School Times* (March 11, 1933), 173. (Published weekly by the Sunday School Times Company, 323–327 North 13th Street, Philadelphia, Pennsylvania.)
9. Editorial, "The Third German Reich," *The Christian Century* (March 15, 1933), 352–53.
10. E. G. Homrighausen, "Hitler and German Religion," *The Christian Century* (March 29, 1933), 418–20.

11. The subject of the Church Struggle dominated in the American Protestant press throughout the Nazi era. The Church Struggle has also been the subject of innumerable books, articles, and doctoral theses, with substantial bibliographies and citations. For example: John S. Conway, *The Nazi Persecution of the Churches*, New York, Basic Books, 1968; Franklin H. Littell and Hubert G. Locke, editors, *The German Church Struggle and the Holocaust*, Detroit, Wayne State University Press, 1974; Guenter Lewy, *The Catholic Church and Nazi Germany*, New York, McGraw-Hill, 1964; Frederick K. Wentz, The Reaction of the Religious Press in America to the Emergence of Nazism (1933–1937), New Haven, Yale University, unpublished doctoral thesis, 1954.

12. Karl Stern, *The Pillar of Fire*. New York, Harcourt, Brace and Company, 1951, p. 132.

13. Dawidowicz, pp. 52–58.

14. Ibid., pp. 58–61.

15. "Germany as Seen by Newspaperman," *The Churchman* (October 15, 1933), 21; also an editorial on Mowrer, 7. (Mowrer spoke in New York City, sponsored by the National Conference of Christians and Jews, on October 3, 1933.)

16. "Germany Still Much Upset," *The Evangelical Visitor* (November 6, 1933), 354. (Official organ of the Brethren in Christ Church.)

17. "Hitler's Policy Rouses Protest: 'Cold Pogrom' against German Jews Threatens World with Return to Medievalism, Say Ministers," *The Christian Century* (May 24, 1933), 702. (The statement released by the National Conference of Jews and Christians was signed by "two dozen of the best known ministers in the United States.")

18. "Jews Protest Alleged Hitler Outrages," *The Christian Century* (April 5, 1933), 470 (report of protest in Chicago, March 23, 1933); "Protestants Attack Hitler's Antisemitism," *The Christian Century* (April 5, 1933), 474–75 (refers to Dr. Cadman and to the Federal Council of Churches; Dr. Cadman is S. Parkes Cadman); *The Christian Century* (April 12, 1933), 506, 510 (another report on a protest rally at Madison Square Garden and also a "huge mass meeting" held at Memphis, Tennessee, "to protest against the treatment of the Jews in Germany.")

19. "Dictators," *The Alliance Weekly* (May 6, 1933), 275; Alva J. McClain, "Hitler and God's Providence," *The Brethren Evangelist* (April 1, 1933), 2 (Suggests that Hitler is like the "'Assyrian' King of Isaiah's day," who was a "'rod' in the providential hand of God," carrying out the purpose of God.)

20. Frederick K. Wentz, in examining twenty-seven religious periodicals in America, 1933–1937, called such papers "right-wing, millenial Protestant journals, seeking signs of the times in contemporary events." An abstract of his thesis, The Reaction of the Religious Press in America to the Emergence of Nazism, is in *Dissertation Abstracts: Abstracts of Dissertations and Monographs in Microfilm*. Ann Arbor, Michigan, University Microfilm, volume XXV, number 6 (December 1964), p. 3723.

21. Editorial, "Christianity Being Denatured in Germany," *The Brethren Evangelist* (December 2, 1933), 3–4, 8. (An editorial article including paragraphs directly referring to Hitler's statements about Jews from *Mein Kampf*, then newly released in English translation by Houghton Mifflin. The editorial article quoted extensively a Dr. Frederick Lynch, who had reviewed the book [source of the review not identified]; the Lynch review was originally published in *The Reformed Church Messenger* [November 23, 1933], 2.)

22. R. C. Schiedt, "Germany and the Jewish Problem," *The Reformed Church Messenger* (May 4, 1933), 8. (Being of German extraction and having studied in Germany and receiving newspapers and personal letters from family and friends in Germany, Schiedt cited himself as an expert qualified to speak the truth about Germany.)

23. Ibid.

24. Editorial, "World Wrath at Hitler's Attack on German Jews," *The Christian Century* (April 5, 1933), 443.

25. Editorial, "Hitler Pursuing His Relentless Course," *The Presbyterian Banner* (July 13, 1933), 5.

26. Samuel McCrea Cavert, "Behind the Scenes in Germany," *The Lutheran Companion* (June 17, 1933), 750–51. (Also appeared in *The Reformed Church Messenger* [May 25, 1933], 9–10.)

27. Paul Hutchinson, "Germany Welcomes New Messiah," *The Christian Century* (August 16, 1933), 1031–33.

28. "Nazis and Jews," *The Christian Century* (November 15, 1933), 1448.

29. The concordat has been the subject of a number of monographs, including: Lewy; Conway; and Gordon L. Zahn, *German Catholics and Hitler's Wars*, New York, Sheed and Ward, 1962. Two very early studies were Paul F. Douglas, *God among the Germans*, Philadelphia, University of Philadelphia Press, 1935; and A. S. Duncan-Jones, *The Struggle for Religious Freedom in Germany*, London, Victor Gollancz, 1938 (reprinted by Greenwood Press Publishers, 1971).

30. Douglas, pp. 116–43.

31. The debate within and outside Germany was fierce and heated. Douglas described one such defense of the "Aryan clause" from "a verbatim paper . . . by a leading Berlin pastor" not otherwise identified. Ibid., pp. 131–37.

32. E. G. Homrighausen, "Hitler and the German Religion," *The Christian Century* (March 9, 1933), 418–20.

33. Reinhold Niebuhr, "Why German Socialism Crashed," *The Christian Century* (April 5, 1933), 451–53.

34. Editorial, "Jews and Jesus," *The Christian Century* (May 3, 1933), 582–84.

35. W. A. Visser't Hooft, "Christ or Caesar in Germany?" *The Christian Century* (May 3, 1933), 589–90.

36. Samuel McCrea Cavert, "Hitler and the German Churches," *The Christian Century* (May 24, 1933), 683–85. (Cavert did attempt to speak of what the churches had done on behalf of persecuted Jews but concluded that in the main they had been silent. See also an editorial, "Has Hitler Cowed the Churches?" *The Christian Century* [June 14, 1933], 775–77.)

37. The "German Christians" referred to by Niebuhr were members of those Protestant churches who aligned themselves with Hitler and who came to power in church elections in 1933. See Pfarrer Thom, "What Do 'German Christians' Want?" *The Presbyterian Banner* (August 3, 1933), 11–12. (The editors warned that this article, though released through the Evangelical Press Service at Berlin, "manifestly presents only one side of the subject." Thom was identified as being a member of an executive committee of the German Christian movement, "which works in apparent cooperation with the Hitler government." See also "The German Christians" and the editorial "The German Christians," *The Lutheran Companion* [June 17, 1933], 764–65, 771.)

38. Reinhold Niebuhr, "Religion and the New Germany," *The Christian Century* (June 28, 1933), 843–45.

39. "The National Evangelical Church of Germany," *The Lutheran Companion* (July 1, 1933), 828–29. (The entire section was signed with the initials I. O. N. and was evidently written by the compiler of news about Lutherans in other lands.)

40. "The Peril of the German Church," *Federal Council Bulletin* (October, 1933), 4–5.

41. Henry Smith Leiper, "The German Church Problem," *The Reformed Church Messenger* (November 16, 1933), 10. (See also the editorial "A Solemn Protest," *The Reformed Church Messenger* [October 19, 1933], 4.)

42. Editorial, "The Nazification of German Protestantism Continues," *The Christian Century* (September 16, 1933), 1164.

43. "Aryan Clause Brings Church Crisis," *The Christian Century* (October 11, 1933), 1279.

44. Editorial, *The Mennonite* (December 7, 1933), 1–2.

45. The status of the articles' writers should be noted. In the main, churchmen with impeccable international and national reputations were the authors of the more penetrating analyses of the emerging Church Struggle in Germany. Samuel McCrea Cavert was the general secretary of the Federal Council of Churches of Christ in America; W. A. Visser't Hooft was the secretary of the World Student Christian Federation and later became the general secretary of the World Council of Churches; Henry Smith Leiper was with the Federal Council of Churches and later with the World Council; Adolf Keller was the secretary of the Central Bureau for the Relief of the Evangelical Churches of Europe and later the associate general secretary of the Universal Christian Council for Life and Work of the World Council of Churches; Reinhold Niebuhr was a distinguished theologian from Union Theological Seminary in New York; and Dr. E. G. Homrighausen was identified in *The Reformed Church Messenger* of August 24, 1933, as "one of our most gifted young pastors."

46. The general tenor of the articles in the Lutheran press and in *The Reformed Church Messenger* tended to present analyses of events in the Protestant church in Germany that were between favorable and neutral since the Lutheran and Reformed churches in Germany were the largest Protestant groups by a wide margin. In 1933, with much of the Nazi-Hitler program for the churches just unfolding, such an attitude should not be surprising. Also, both groups in America tended to stress heavily that Hitler had saved Germany from Communism and the Bolshevist threat.

47. Frederick Lynch, "Hitler Tells His Own Story," *The Reformed Church Messenger* (November 23, 1933), 2. (As for *The Brown Book of the Hitler Terror*, it was something other than described by Lynch. Prepared by the World Committee for the Victims of German Fascism and first published in London by Victor Gollancz in September 1933, it was a documented record of events in Germany from the burning of the Reichstag to chapters entitled "Brutality and Torture," "The Persecution of the Jews," "The Concentration Camps," "Murder," "The German Workers Fight against Fascism," and an appendix, "List of Murders." Though Lynch dismissed it, with today's knowledge, it seems a credible statement of events in Germany.)

48. Editorial, "Christianity Being Denatured in Germany," *The Brethren Evangelist* (December 2, 1933), 3.

49. *The Christian Century* (July 12, 1933), 911.

50. Conrad Henry Moehlman's *The Christian Jewish Tragedy*, published in 1933, discussed at great length a revisionist view that Pilate and the Romans were really responsible for the death of Jesus, not the Jews. This whole refutation of the Jews as a "deicide people" was discussed in reviews in *The Christian Century* (September 6, 1933), 6; *Church Management* (November, 1933), 83; and *Federal Council Bulletin* (September, 1933), 13.

51. Editorials, "World Wrath at Hitler's Attack on Jews" and "A Need for Light, Not Heat," *The Christian Century* (April 5, 1933), 443.

52. Letter to the editor, "We Repeat: Light Not Heat," *The Christian Century* (April 26, 1933), 565.

53. Ibid.

54. Editorial, "Jews and Jesus," *The Christian Century* (May 3, 1933), 582–84.

55. Ibid.

56. Letter to the Editor, *The Christian Century* (May 17, 1933), 659–62.

57. Letter to the editor, "From Rabbi Isserman," *The Christian Century* (May 17, 1933), 659–60.

58. Letter to the editor, "From Rabbi Lyons," *The Christian Century* (May 17, 1933), 660–61.

59. Letter to the editor, "From Rabbi Fink," *The Christian Century* (May 17, 1933), 661–62.

60. Letter to the editor, "From a Christian Clergyman," *The Christian Century* (May 17, 1933), 662.

61. "Mass Meeting Protests Hitler's Anti-Jewish Program," *The Christian Century* (April 26, 1933), 574.

62. Letter to the editor, "Were German Jews Red?" *The Christian Century* (May 24, 1933), 694.

63. Robert E. Asher, "A Jew Protests against the Protestors," *The Christian Century* (April 12, 1933), 492–94.

64. Horst Von Maltitz, *The Evolution of Hitler's Germany: The Ideology, the Personality, the Moment.* New York, McGraw-Hill, 1973, pp. 132ff.

65. Letter to the editor, "Our 'Humanism' Runs Away!" *The Christian Century* (May 31, 1933), 727–28. (The editorial referred to in the letter was "Jews and Jesus," *The Christian Century* [May 3, 1933], 582–84.)

66. Letter to the editor, "Nothing Will Save Us But a Pogrom!" *The Christian Century* (June 28, 1933), 850.

67. Letter to the editor, "Adolph Hitler, Alias '666'," *The Christian Century* (June 7, 1933), 759.

68. "A New Antichrist," *Church Management* (August 1933), 566.

69. Letter to the editor, "Yes, Where Are You?" *The Christian Century* (June 21, 1933), 819.

70. Letter to the editor, "Refugees from Germany," *The Christian Century* (September 27, 1933), 1211.

71. Letter to the editor, "German Church Situation," *The Christian Century* (September 13, 1933), 1150.

72. "Letter to the editor, *The Reformed Church Messenger* (September 21, 1933), 13–14.

73. "A Protest by Chicago Church Federation," *The Hebrew Christian Alliance Quarterly* (June 1933), 40.

74. Editorial, "Jewish Persecutions," *The Lutheran* (April 6, 1933), 17.

75. Editorial, "Jews in Germany," *The Moody Bible Institute Monthly* (May 1933), 392.

76. Editorial, "The Jews in Germany," *The King's Business* (June 1933), 171.

77. *The Sunday School Times* (December 9, 1933), 778.

78. Editorial, "The State, the Church, the Synagogue," *The Lutheran* (June 8, 1933), 14–15.

79. Alf. Bergin, "Hitler and the Jews," *The Lutheran Companion* (September 2, 1933), 1105.

80. Editorial, *The Mennonite* (December 7, 1933), 1–2.

81. See note 46.

82. Adolph Keller, "Facts and Meaning of the German Revolution as Seen from a Neutral Point of View," *The Reformed Church Messenger* (April 27, 1933), 9–10.

83. R. C. Schiedt, "Germany and the Jewish Problem," *The Reformed Church Messenger* (May 4, 1933), 8.

84. *The Reformed Church Messenger* (April 6, 1933), 8.

85. E. G. Homrighausen, "Behind the German Jewish Problem, I, II," *The Reformed Church Messenger* (August 24, 1933), 9–11; (September 7, 1933), 8–9. (The two articles must be taken together, for the conclusions to both appear in the second article.)

86. Ibid., first article, 9.

87. Ibid., first article, 10.

88. *The Jews in Nazi Germany: The Factual Record of Their Persecution by the National Socialists,* the American Jewish Committee (171 Madison Avenue at 33rd Street, New York City) (June 9, 1933), 99; later in the fall, the American Jewish Committee also published *The Voice of Religion: The Views of Christian Religious Leaders on the Persecution of the Jews in Germany by the National Socialists.* (80,000 of the first title were printed; 10,000 of the second.)

89. Alva J. McClain, "Signs of the Times," *The Brethren Evangelist* (April 1, 1933), 2; Charles W. Mayes, "What of the Future," *The Brethren Evangelist* (July 22, 1933), 5–6.

90. Louis S. Bauman, "God and Gog, 1937(?)"; "Present Day Fulfillment of Proph-

ecy"; "Present Day Fulfillment of Prophecy" *The King's Business* (April–May 1933), 133–36; (June 1933), 180–82; (July 1933), 223–25.

91. Editorial, "Treatment of the Jews," *The Presbyterian* (April 27, 1933), 8; Editorial, "The Jew," *The Presbyterian* (November 9, 1933), 3–4.

92. Editorial, "Lo, the Poor Jew," *The Signs of the Times* (May 2, 1933), 16.

93. Editorial, "Dictators," *The Alliance Weekly* (May 6, 1933), 275.

94. Joseph R. Lewak, "The Sign of the Fig Tree," *The Alliance Weekly* (September 30, 1933), 613–14.

95. Editorial, "Millenialism Running Wild," *The Concordia Theological Monthly* (October 1933), 787–88.

96. Letter to the editor, "From Rabbi Fink," *The Christian Century* (May 17, 1933), 661–62.

97. "Israel and Her Messiah," *The Evangelical Visitor* (April 24, 1933), 131–32.

Chapter 2

1. Editorial, *The Arkansas Baptist* (March 22, 1934), 13.

2. *The Arkansas Baptist* (February 8, 1934), 6.

3. "A Challenge to Christendom," *Federal Council Bulletin* (February 1934), 5.

4. "Jewish Items," *The Alliance Weekly* (April 14, 1934), 236.

5. Editorial, "Paganism Increases," *The Alliance Weekly* (October 13, 1934), 651.

6. Louis S. Bauman, "The Great Dragon and the Woman Child—In 1934," *The King's Business* (March 1934), 94, 95.

7. Louis S. Bauman, "The Great Red Dragon and the Woman Child," *The King's Business* (May 1934), 179.

8. Franklin H. Littel, "The German Church Struggle and the Plight of the Jews," Philadelphia, Philadelphia Board of Education, 191.

9. J. H. Rushmore, "The World Congress in Berlin: Full Speed Ahead" and "Information for Attending the Baptist World Congress in Berlin," *The Baptist Herald* (January 15, 1934), 2.

10. Conrad Henry Moehlman, "The Baptists Are Going to Berlin," *The Christian Century* (February 7, 1934), 183–85.

11. G. B. Hopkins, "Baptists and Berlin," *The Watchman-Examiner* (March 1, 1934), 202.

12. "A Letter from Germany," *The Watchman-Examiner* (April 12, 1934), 395.

13. F. W. C. Meyer, "If the Baptists Meet in Berlin," letter to the editor, *The Christian Century* (February 21, 1934), 257.

14. Ibid.

15. Letter to the editor, "More Reasons Why the Baptists Are Going to Berlin," *The Christian Century* (May 9, 1934), 636. (The letter was signed by a committee of three, W. L. Spears, W. B. Hicks, and Thomas D. Denman.)

16. B. L. Bridges, "Baptists, Hitler and the Jews," *The Arkansas Baptist* (March 29, 1934), 16.

17. In the attribution of the *New York World*, no date or issue number was given. This strongly suggests that Bridges used this information without having seen the original in the *New York World* and that he was using some other unidentified source.

18. B. L. Bridges, "Baptists, Hitler and the Jews," *The Arkansas Baptist* (March 29, 1934), 16.

19. "Baptists and Berlin: A Statement on Behalf of the Baptist World Alliance," *The Baptist Herald* (April 15, 1934), 6.

20. *The Christian Century* (June 6, 1934), 779.

21. "The Baptist World Alliance," *The Alliance Weekly* (July 28, 1934), 466.

22. Editorial, "World Baptists Alliance Meets in Berlin," *The Christian Century* (Au-

gust 15, 1934), 1036–37. (A. W. Beaven was past-president of the Northern Baptist Convention and was elected a vice-president of the Baptist World Alliance in Berlin)

23. Editorial, "The Baptists in Berlin," *The Christian Century* (August 22, 1934), 1060.

24. On the page "Men and Things," the editors announced that Bradbury was to be their official reporter at the Berlin congress. *The Watchman-Examiner* (August 23, 1934), 914.

25. John W. Bradbury, "On to Berlin," *The Watchman-Examiner* (August 23, 1934), 923.

26. John W. Bradbury, "Report of the Baptist World Alliance: Berlin, Germany, August 4–10," *The Watchman-Examiner* (August 30, 1934), 947–51.

27. John W. Bradbury, "Berlin Congress Reflections and Experiences," *The Watchman-Examiner* (September 13, 1934), 996–97.

28. Herman von Berge, "What Think Ye of Germany," *The Baptist Herald* (November 15, 1934), 12–13.

29. Herman von Berge, "What Hitler Has Meant to Germany," *The Baptist Herald* (December 1, 1934), 3–4.

30. Ibid.

31. Herman von Berge, "The Price of Hitlerism," *The Baptist Herald* (December 12, 1934), 6–7.

32. Herman von Berge, "The Problem of the Jew in Germany," *The Baptist Herald* (January 1, 1935), 6–8.

33. Ibid., 7.

34. Ibid.

35. Ibid.

36. Ibid.

37. Ibid., 8.

38. Ibid.

39. Herman von Berge, "The Religious Situation in Germany," *The Baptist Herald* (January 15, 1935), 22–23.

40. Frank H. Woyke, "An Afternoon 'Unter den Linden'," *The Baptist Herald* (October 15, 1934), 7.

41. "The Call of the Berlin Congress: A Message from the Baptist World Alliance," *The Baptist Herald* (October 1, 1934), 9.

42. Earle Eubank, "The Baptists Went to Berlin," *The Christian Century* (September 19, 1934), 1170–72.

43. Ibid., 1172.

44. Ibid.

45. John D. Freeman, "Baptist World Alliance," *The Baptist and Reflector* (September 13, 1934), 1, 7.

46. Ibid.

47. John D. Freeman, "The Germany of Adolf Hitler," *The Baptist and Reflector* (September 20, 1934), 1, 6. (Reprinted in *The Arkansas Baptist* [November 15, 1934], 3–4.)

48. M. E. Dodd, "Impressions of the Baptist World Congress," *The Baptist and Reflector* (September 13, 1934), 5–6.

49. Ibid., 5.

50. Ibid., 6.

51. Letter to the editor, "Open Letter to Dr. Dodd, October 10, 1934," *The Baptist and Reflector* (November 8, 1934), 8. (Under the "Open Forum" head there appeared this disclaimer: "*The Baptist and Reflector* does not necessarily concur in all opinions expressed on this page.")

52. Ibid.

53. "Missions," *Christian Faith and Life* (October 1934), 258.

54. *The Hebrew Christian Alliance Quarterly* (January 1934), 39; *The Hebrew Lutheran* (April, October 1934) 2,2; *The Watchman-Examiner* (January 1, 1934), 4–5; *Federal Council Bulletin* (September 1934), 17.

55. *The Alliance Weekly* (April 29, 1934), 267; *The Presbyterian* (June 28, 1934), 14; *The Moody Bible Institute Monthly* (August 1934), 539.

56. Letter to the editor, *The Moody Bible Institute Monthly* (July 1934), 506.

57. John Haynes Holmes, "How Do I Know about Hitler?" *The Christian Century* (March 21, 1934), 391–92.

58. Ibid., 392.

59. Ibid.

60. Ibid.

61. Ibid.

62. Ewart Edmund Turner, "European War Not Inevitable: Berlin Correspondent Answering Questions Asked in America, Urges Taking Hitler's Peace Talk as Sincere," *The Christian Century* (March 21, 1934), 401–2.

63. Editorial, "The Jews in Germany," *The Moody Bible Institute Monthly* (December 1934), 151–52.

64. Solomon Birnbaum, "Conrad Hoffman's World Report on the Jews," *The Moody Bible Institute Monthly* (December 1934), 167.

65. *Federal Council Bulletin* (January 1934), 12, (February 1934), 13–14; *The Reformed Church Messenger* (January 25, 1934), 2. (Examples of reviews of the book by Charles S. Macfarland.)

66. Advertisement, *The Moody Bible Institute Monthly* (February 1934), inside back cover.

67. Will H. Houghton, "The Jew—His Present and Future"; "The Truth about Germany and the Jews"; "The Jewish Problem in Europe," *The Sunday School Times* (August 11, August 18, August 25, 1934), 511–12; 523, 527; 539–40.

68. Will H. Houghton, "The Truth about Germany and the Jews," *The Sunday School Times* (August 18, 1934), 523.

69. "Fearless Foe of Nazi Church Creed," *The Baptist Herald* (April 15, 1935), 121.

70. James M. Yard, "Underground Movement in Germany," letter to the editor, *The Christian Century* (January 2, 1935), 24.

71. Editorial, "Move the Olympics!" *The Christian Century* (August 7, 1935), 1007–8.

72. Letter to the editor, *The Christian Century* (August 21, 1935), 1064–65.

73. The editorials on the Olympic Games question were published in *The Christian Century* on August 7, 14, and 28; September 25; November 6 and 13; and December 4 and 11, all in 1935. The letters to the editor, on August 21, September 25, October 23, and December 18, 1935. The news items appeared on August 7 (1019), September 25 (1215), November 6 (1431), and December 4 (1566), 1935.

74. Russell J. Clinchy, "Leave the Olympics Alone," letter to the editor, *The Christian Century*, (October 23, 1935), 1350–51.

75. Editorial, "How Christians May Show Sympathy for Jews," *Federal Council Bulletin* (October 1935), 4–5.

76. Editorial, *The Friend* (August 15, 1935), 54; letter to the editor, "Olympic Games," *The Friend* (December 19, 1935), 215.

77. "The Truth about Conditions in Germany," *The Concordia Theological Monthly* (December 1935), 947–48.

78. "The End of National Socialism," *The Christian Century* (March 13, 1935), 326.

79. Editorial, "Naziism Reverts to Type in New Outbreak of Violence," *The Christian Century* (July 31, 1935), 980.

80. Editorial, "Nazi Intolerance Grows Clearer," *The Christian Century* (August 7, 1935), 1004.

81. H. R. Trauer, "Shows Plight of Germany's Jews: Streicher's Recent Charges Ludicrous—A Retired Professor Gives Testimony—Some 'Myths' Exploded," *The Christian Century* (September 11, 1935), 1150–51.

82. "Germany Nears Another Purge: Schact's Defiance of Jew-Baiters Evidence of Economic Stress—Prison Conference Packed by Nazis," *The Christian Century* (September 18, 1935), 1183–84.

83. "Nazi-Fury Breaks Out Again over German Jews," *The Friend of Zion* (September 1935), 48; "Germany," *The Friend of Zion* (December 1935), 71–72.

84. *The Reformed Church Messenger* (August 1; August 15, 1935), 19–21; Editorial, "Mind Your Own Business," *The Reformed Church Messenger* (August 22, 1935), 6; George W. Richards, "Leaves from a President's Diary," *The Reformed Church Messenger* (September 12, 1935), 7–8; Henry S. Leiper, "Church Leader Sees Reich Catholics Triumphing Over Nazis," *The Reformed Church Messenger* (September 12, 1935), 10–11; Samuel McCrea Cavert, "What the Tourist in Germany Does Not See," *The Reformed Church Messenger* (October 3, 1935), 7–8.

85. Samuel McCrea Cavert, "What the Tourist in Germany Does Not See," *The Reformed Church Messenger* (October 3, 1935), 7.

86. *The Sunday School Times* (January 5, 1935), 7.

87. J. Emlyn Williams, "Germany Spurns Foreign Opinion," *The Christian Century* (May 29, 1935), 738–39.

88. A. S. Eker, "Reich Continues Attack on Jews," *The Christian Century* (August 28, 1935), 1089–90.

89. Editorial, "Nazis Hold Party Congress," *The Christian Century* (September 25, 1935), 1196.

90. Ibid.

91. "Anti-Semitism—The Most Serious Obstacle to Jewish Evangelization: A Voice from Sweden," *The Friend of Zion* (September 1935), 44–46.

92. *The Watchman-Examiner* (September 26, 1935), 1068, and (October 3, 1935), 1092.

93. Julius S. Seebach, "In the World's Eye," *The Lutheran* (October 3, 1935), 10.

94. "New Anti-Jewish Decree" and "Who Are Jews?" *The Alliance Weekly* (December 14, 1935), 803.

95. A. S. Eker, "Nazis Woo and Warn Churches," *The Christian Century* (December 18, 1935), 1631–32.

96. Advertisement, *The Moody Bible Institute Monthly* (May 1935), 407. (Another paid advertisement appeared in the same periodical in the December 1935 issue, p. 163. Both advertisements were paid for by the American Board of Missions to the Jews, Brooklyn, New York, and were one-quarter-column ads.)

Chapter 3

1. "I Cannot Remain Silent: The High Commissioner Voices the Wrongs of German Jewry," *The Friend of Zion* (March 1936), 18–19.

2. The *Endlösung*, or Final Solution, as policy was adopted at the Wannsee Conference, January 20, 1942, but the plan in one form or another had been rumored since 1941. A detailed account of the Final Solution can be found in Lucy S. Dawidowicz, *The War against the Jews: 1933–1945*, part 1, "The Final Solution," New York, Holt, Rinehart and Winston, 1975, pp. 3–166, and in Raul Hilberg, *The Destruction of the European Jews*, Chicago, Quadrangle Books, 1961, pp. 257–66. Other descriptions are in Nora Levin, *The Holocaust: The Destruction of European Jewry, 1933–1945*, New York, Thomas Y. Crowell Company, 1968, *passim*; Arthur D. Morse, *While Six Million Died: A Chronicle of American Apathy* New York, Random House, 1968, pp. 289–310; and in the massive work by Gerald Reitlinger, *The Final Solution: An Attempt to Exterminate the Jews of Europe, 1939–1945*, 2nd rev. ed., New York, Thomas Yoseloff, 1968.

3. "Letter of Resignation of James G. McDonald, High Commissioner for Refugees (Jewish and Other) Coming from Germany: Addressed to the Secretary General of the League of Nations, with an Annex containing an analysis of the measures in Germany against 'non-Aryans,' and of their effects in creating refugees." *The Christian Century* (January 15, 1936) 99–127. (Annex published as part 2 of issue.)

4. Ibid., 103.

5. Ibid., 104.

6. Ibid., table of contents, 98.

7. Editorial, "Commissioner McDonald's Resignation," *The Christian Century* (January 15, 1936), 67.

8. *The Reformed Church Messenger* (January 9, 1936), 19.

9. Letter to the editor, "Could This Be Sarcasm?" *The Christian Century* (February 19, 1936), 300.

10. "I Cannot Remain Silent: The High Commissioner Voices the Wrongs of German Jewry," *The Friend of Zion* (March 1936), 18–19.

11. Ibid., 19.

12. Ibid.

13. Editorial, "The Jewish Problem," and Joseph Ernest McAfee, "An Open Letter to Rabbi Weisfeld," *The Christian Century* (April 29, 1936), 624–26, 632–33.

14. From its founding in 1928 until late 1938, the name National Conference of Jews and Christians was used. From 1939 to the present, the name National Conference of Christians and Jews, commonly called the NCCJ, has been used.

15. Joseph Ernest McAfee, "An Open Letter to Rabbi Weisfeld," *The Christian Century* (April 29, 1936), 633.

16. Ibid.

17. Ibid.

18. Editorial, "Jews, Christians and Democracy," *The Christian Century* (May 13, 1936), 698.

19. Louis L. Mann, "Jewish Integrity and Tolerance," *The Christian Century* (May 13, 1936), 703–5.

20. Abram Hirschberg (Temple Shalom, Chicago), "Identifying the Jew," letter to the editor, *The Christian Century* (May 6, 1936), 676; five letters to editor, (Wright, Zielonka, Niebuhr, Chase, Shulman), "The Jewish Problem," *The Christian Century* (May 27, 1936), 770–72.

21. Five letters to the editor, "The Jewish Problem," *The Christian Century* (June 10, 1936), 843–46.

22. Two letters to the editor, "The Jewish Problem," *The Christian Century* (June 10, 1936), 905.

23. Editorial, "Tolerance Is Not Enough," *The Christian Century* (July 1, 1936), 926–28.

24. J. E. McAfee, "No Tribal Diety," letter to the editor, *The Christian Century* (July 1, 1936), 943. (See also letters to the editor, *The Christian Century* [July 15, 1936], 991–92, and [July 29, 1936], 1040–41.)

25. Editorial, "Jewry and Democracy," *The Christian Century* (June 9, 1937), 734–36.

26. Ibid., 736.

27. Editorial, "Why Is Anti-Semitism?" and letter to the editor "From Rabbi Lazaron," *The Christian Century* (July 7, 1937), 862–64, 878–79.

28. This trip of the representatives of the three major faiths is described in the chapter, "An American Pilgrimage," in James E. Pitt, *Adventures in Brotherhood*, New York, Farrar, Straus and Company, 1955, 40–61.

29. Ibid.

30. Louis Minsky, "American Jews Take Stock," *The Christian Century* (May 26, 1937), 677–79.

31. Ibid.

32. See "News and the Churches," *Newsweek* (April 12, 1948), 76–77, for a brief history of the NCJC-RNS and of the role of Louis Minsky in its founding.

33. The newsletter of the National Conference of Jews and Christians (Winter 1938), p. 4, reported the change of name from the NCJC News Service to the Religious News Service (RNS).

34. *Advance* (September 1, 1936), 542; *Christendom* (Summer 1936), 727–30, a series of book reviews; *The Friend* (November 5, 1936), 162; *The Gospel Herald* (December 5, 1936), 27; *The Gospel Messenger* (April 11, 1936), 4; *The Lutheran* (March 26, July 11, 1936), 7, 7; *The Reformed Church Messenger* (July 16, October 1, 1936), 4, 3; *The Presbyterian* (May 7, 1936), 6; *The Watchman-Examiner* (October 29, 1936), 1196–97.

35. Editorial, "Fascism in America"; Guy Emery Shipler, Sr., "The Fascist Threat to America," *The Churchman* (February 1, 1937), 7, 14–16, (February 15, 1937), 9–11; (March 1, 1937), 14–16.

36. "Anti-Semitism," *The Churchman* (January 1, 1938), 20.

37. Editorial, "More from the Little Flower," *The Churchman* (September 15, 1938), 9.

38. Alfred Artyn Gross, "Manners and Morals of Anti-Semitism," *The Churchman* (November 15, 1938), 14–15.

39. "Lutheran Synods Score Anti-Semitism: Spokesman of Five Important Christian Groups Denounce Religious Intolerance," *The Hebrew Lutheran* (January 1937), 2.

40. See Donald P. Strong, *Organized Anti-Semitism in America: The Rise of Group Prejudice during the Decade 1930–40*, Washington, D.C., American Council on Public Affairs, 1941. (This book, and the series in *The Churchman*, reported extensively on Winrod.)

41. By the managing editor (Rev. A. J. Kligerman), "I Am Called Down by A Presbyterian Elder," *The Hebrew Christian Alliance Quarterly* (Winter 1937), 5–7.

42. Ibid., 6–7.

43. *Christendom* (Summer 1938), 477–79.

44. Orrie D. Yoder, "Three Big Questions for Jew Haters," *The Evangelical Visitor* (July 4, 1938), 15, 223.

45. Samuel McCrea Cavert, "The Church May Be Next: Anti-Semitism Leads to Anti-Christianity," *The Lutheran Companion* (October 20, 1938), 1323.

46. Al Segal, "How It Feels to Be a Jew," *The Mennonite* (August 16, 1938), 13–14.

47. "Jews in American Life," *Christendom* (Summer 1936), 727–30. (The four books reviewed were Baker, Hayes and Straus, *The American Way: A Study of Human Life*, Willet, Clark and Company; Everett R. Clinchy, *All in the Name of God*, John Day; Mordecai M. Kaplan, *Judaism as a Civilization: Toward a Reconstruction of American Jewish Life*, Macmillan Company, and *Judaism in Transition*, Covici, Friede. Baker [Newton D. Baker], Hayes [Carlton J. H. Hayes], and Straus [Robert W. Straus] were cochairmen of the National Conference of Jews and Christians [NCJC].)

48. Arno C. Gaebelein, "The Future Fulfillment of the Promises of Israel," parts 1 and 2; Albertus Pieters, "The Future of the Jews," *The Presbyterian* (May 7, May 14; June 11, 1936), 1, 11–12, 6–8; 1, 6–7.

49. See Samuel S. Cohen, "How Christian Missions Feels to a Jew," *The Christian Century*, (December 6, 1933), 1530–32. (This article briefly reviewed the origins of the movement begun at conferences in Budapest and Warsaw in 1927 and continued at a conference at Atlantic City, New Jersey, in 1931 and called the Christian Approach to the Jews. Cohen, in the article, spoke of "the Old Missions" and "the New Missions," describing the new approach but also, as a Jew, he was critical of both approaches.)

50. John Stuart Conning, "Why, They're Jews: The Challenge of American Jewry to the Church," *The Presbyterian* (October 22, 1936), 1–2.

51. Susie H. Keen, "Appreciation of the Jews," *The Gospel Herald* (December 5, 1936), 1719.

52. "Our Jewish Neighbors" and "Jewish Conference," *The Presbyterian* (September 23, September 30, 1937), 3, 22.

53. "Presbyterians and Jews Exchange Greetings," *The Watchman-Examiner* (July 1, 1937), 769.

54. B. A. M. Schapiro, "Is Usury of Jewish Origin?" *The Watchman-Examiner* (July 22, 1937), 843–44. (Schapiro was identified as a Christian Jew and a well-known writer of books and tracts for Jews.)

55. Louis S. Bauman, "Why I Believe the Second Coming of Christ Is Imminent," *The Brethren Evangelist* (April 25, 1936), 6–8, 12–13; "Today in the Light of Prophecy," *The Brethren Evangelist* (August 1, 1936), 8–11; "This Befogged and Befuddled World," *The King's Business* (June 1937), 209, 227–28; "The Old Serpent Crawls On," *The King's Business* (July 1937), 246–47. (In presenting his prophetic-millenial interpretation, Bauman continued to pay a great deal of attention to what was happening to Jews in Germany but always to make his central point—that persecution of the Jews, anti-

Semitic activity, and the return of the Jews to Palestine as refugees were "signs" of the end of the age, heralding the Second Coming of Christ. His position was consistently premillenial and dispensational, as also reflected in the Scofield Reference Bible.)

56. A. G. Fegert, "Zionism's Stupendous Failure to Acknowledge God" and "The Light of Prophecy at a Zionist Meeting," *The Sunday School Times* (October 30, November 6, 1937), 765–66; 783, 796–97.

57. George T. B. Davis, "The Glorious Future of the Jews," *The Sunday School Times* (December 18, 1937), 907–8. (The other articles were announced October 2 and 9, 1937, and begun on October 16, 1937. There were ten in all, running consecutively through December 18, 1937. They were all on Palestine and prophecy.)

58. Editorial, "Renewed Rioting in Palestine," *The Christian Century* (May 6, 1936), 651–52.

59. Editorial, "Renewed Rioting in Palestine," *The Lutheran Companion* (May 16, 1936), 610.

60. Khalil Totah, "Palestine Again," Wadi R. Tarazi, "Progress in Palestine"; Khalil Totah, "Peace or Truce in Palestine"; "A Quaker Mediator in Palestine," *The Friend* (August 13, November 19, December 3, 1936), 56–57; 180–81; 181–83; 196–97.

61. "Serious Disorders in Palestine," "Palestine Disorders," "Violence Continued Unabated," *The Friend of Zion* (June, September, November 1936), 47, 55, 72.

62. "Olympics, Propaganda and Fascism," *Advance* (January 1, 1936), 168; *The Friend of Zion* (May 1936), 40.

63. "Nazi Propaganda Rules Olympics," *The Christian Century* (March 11, 1936), 412.

64. "Germany Dons Olympic Dress," *The Christian Century* (August 5, 1936), 1065; Editorial, "Nordics and Negroes," *The Christian Century* (August 12, 1936), 1075.

65. Sherwood Eddy, "Germany in Olympic Dress," *The Christian Century* (September 2, 1936), 1154–55.

66. "Germany Pleased with Olympics," *The Christian Century* (September 9, 1936), 1204.

67. Editorial, *The Gospel Messenger* (August 29, 1936), 3.

68. Advertisements, *The King's Business* (May 1936), inside cover; *The Moody Bible Institute Monthly* (May, June 1936), 441, 489, inside back cover; *The Moody Bible Institute Monthly* (November 1937), 109; *The Sunday School Times* (November 20, 1937), 840.

69. "Germany Protests against Sympathy for Refugees," *The Christian Century* (April 29, 1937), 540–41; "Film on German Refugees," *Federal Council Bulletin* (May 1937), 12; "Germany Excited" and "Terrorism: Riverside Church Meeting Draws Attack by Nazis," *The Churchman* (May 1, 1937), 8–9, 18.

70. Announced in the *Federal Council Bulletin* (December 1937), 3–4, as "Churches Unite in Relief of War Sufferers."

71. "Exiles: A Christmas Appeal for Refugees from Germany," *The Churchman* (December 15, 1937), 20; "Christmas Appeals," *The Messenger* (formerly *The Reformed Church Messenger*) (December 16, 1937), 4.

72. "A Four-Power Pact in the Offing?" *The Presbyterian* (March 3, 1938), 5.

73. "Jews Must Quit," *The Presbyterian* (April 7, 1938), 6.

74. *The Presbyterian* (April 28, 1938), 2. (The figure given of 470,000 Jews receiving assistance is obviously a misprint. Probably the figure was 70,000 of the 176,000 Jews in Vienna who were being assisted by the Jewish Central Union.)

75. Dorothy Thompson, "We Know But One God," *The Christian Herald* (April 1938), 27; "Austria," *The Christian Herald* (May 1938), 9.

76. "Self-Destruction," *The Alliance Weekly* (May 14, 1938), 306.

77. Jacob Gertenhaus, "Israel Needs Prayers," *The Baptist and Reflector* (June 9, 1938), 1; *Hebrew Christian Alliance Quarterly* (Fall 1938), 14.

78. "Jewish Persecution Grows More Bitter," *The Christian Century* (February 23, 1938), 250.

79. Editorial, "First Rob the Jews and then Starve Them," *The Christian Century* (May 11, 1938), 581–82.

80. M. Zeidman, *The Jewish Peril,*" *The Hebrew Christian Alliance Quarterly* (Winter 1938), 23.

81. Louis S. Bauman, "The Time of Jacob's Trouble" (second in a series), *The Brethren Evangelist* (April 30, 1938), 10–11.

82. *The Friend* (August 11, 1938); *The Brethren Evangelist* (December 17, 1938), 2; "Italy Goes Race Pure and Anti-Semitic," *The Christian Century* (September 14, 1938), 1084; "Rome," *The Christian Herald* (September 1938), 9; "Racism—Issue in Fascist Italy," *Friend of Zion* (October 1938), 63; Louis A. Bauman, "The European Imbroglio," *The King's Business* (November 1938), 368–69, 398–99; "Anti-Semitism in Italy," *The Lutheran* (August 17, 1938), 12; "Racism Has Become an Issue in Fascist Italy," *The Lutheran Companion* August 11, 1938), 999; *The Messenger* (July 14, 1938), 21; "Jews in Italy" and "New Enemies for the Jews," *The Presbyterian* (August 18, September 15, 1938), 5, 5.

83. For a brief but accurate discussion of *Lebensraum*, see Dawidowicz, pp. 90–92.

84. William L. Shirer, *The Rise and Fall of the Third Reich*, 1st ed., New York, Simon and Schuster, 1959, pp. 357–427.

85. Sherwood Eddy, "The Critical Hour," *The Christian Century* (October 19, 1938), 1258–60.

86. The letters to the editor, all in *The Christian Century*, were published on the following dates: October 12, 1938, three letters, 1235–36; October 19, 1938, six letters, 1267–69; October 26, 1938, two letters, 1299, 1300; November 9, 1938, six letters, 1371–72; November 16, 1938, one letter, 1404; November 23, 1938, one letter, 1435–36; December 14, 1938, one letter, 1549–50; December 28, 1938, one letter, 1611.

87. Brackett Lewis, "What the Sudetans Want," *The Christian Century* (August 3, 1938), 938–39.

88. Editorial, "Tortured Minorities in Sudentanland," *The Christian Century* (November 2, 1938), 1315.

89. "A Day of Prayer for Victims of Racial and Religious Oppression," *Federal Council Bulletin* (November 1938), 9.

90. Letter to the editor, "A Voice from the Land of John Hus," *The Presbyterian* (September 22, 1938), 9–10. (Five members of the theology faculty at Prague signed the letter.)

91. "The Spiritual Front," *The Presbyterian* (October 20, 1938), 5.

92. Sherwood Eddy, "The Critical Hour," *The Christian Century* (October 19, 1938), 1258–60.

93. "Refugees: 400,000 Christians, 30,000 Jews Flee Sudentanland," *The Churchman* (November 15, 1938), 20–21.

94. "More Horror in Europe" and "The Voice of Protest," *Advance* (December 1, 1938), 540.

95. Editorial, "Germany Brutally Fulfills Prophecy," *The Sunday School Times* (November 26, 1938), 857–58.

96. Advertisement, *The Sunday School Times* (December 31, 1938), inside front cover, 956.

97. "It Is Hard to Believe" and "Roosevelt in Queer Diplomatic Moves," *The Lutheran Companion* (November 24, December 1, 1938), 1479, 1508.

98. Editorial, "Anxious Regrets," *The Lutheran* (November 23, 1938), 29.

99. Editorials, "Anti-Semitism," "Our Attitudes in the Present Crisis," "A Statement about Conditions in Germany," and "Persecution of Christians," *The Lutheran Herald* (November 29, 1938), 1199–1200.

100. Editorials, "Just Because They Are Jews," "Fear at the Shaking of a Leaf," "All Things Work Together for Good" and "How about the United States," *The Brethren Evangelist* (November 26, 1938), 3–4.

101. "Christians Unite in Sympathy for Jews," *Federal Council Bulletin* (December 1938), 9.

102. Editorial, "The Perennial Jewish Problem," *The Calvin Forum* (December 1938), 102.

103. "Persecution: McKee Gives Radio Talk on Plight of the Jews," "Emergency: Three Faiths Ask Funds to Aid Nazi Persecuted," "CLID: Statement Says Germany Should Pay Settlement Costs," and "Prayer: Bishop Mann Writes Prayer in Behalf of Persecuted Germans," *The Churchman* (December 1, 1938), 17–19.

104. "Pleas for the Persecuted: Well-known Bishops and Other Clergymen Comment on the Nazi Terror Perpetrated by the Fanatical Leaders of Germany," *The Churchman* (December 1, 1938), 10–11. (Ten Letters were published.)

105. "Disintegration: Bishops Hit Persecution and Fall of Diplomacy," *The Churchman* (December 1, 1938), 22–23.

106. Editorial, "The Necessity of Pessimism," *The Friend* (December 1, 1938), 182–83.

107. "The Refugees: A Word from the Service Committee," *The Friend* (December 1, 1938), 185.

108. "Anti-Semitic Rioting Flares in Germany," "Protest Wave Sweep in U.S.: Catholics and Protestants Ask Mercy for Jews—Trade Reprisals Urged" and "Jewish Situation in Brief," *The Friend of Zion* (December 1938), 77.

109. Editorial, "The German Pogrom," *The Messenger* (December 1, 1938), 4–5.

110. "The Unimaginative Nazis" and "Cities of Refuge"; "Third Reich Aroused" and "They Planned It That Way"; and "More Trouble for Jews," *The Presbyterian* (November 24, December 1, December 15, 1938), 5, 5, 5.

111. "Not All Germans . . . ," *The Presbyterian*, (December 29, 1938), 5.

112. Editorial, "Christian Sympathy for the Jews," *The Watchman-Examiner* (December 8, 1938), 1295.

113. *The Watchman-Examiner*, (December 1, December 8, 1938), 1265, 1287.

114. Letter to the editor, "Negroes Pray for Jews," *The Christian Century* (December 21, 1938), 1580.

115. "Hitler Demands Colonies or Else—," *The Christian Century* (November 23, 1938), 1419.

116. See Dawidowicz, pp. 100–101.

117. Editorial, "Terror in Germany," *The Christian Century* (November 23, 1938), 1422–23.

118. Ina Corinne Brown, "The Racial Branding Iron," *The Christian Century* (November 23, 1938), 1428–29.

119. "New York Aghast at New Pogroms: Protestants, Catholics and Jews Unite to Protest German Persecution—Urge U.S. to Act Officially," *The Christian Century*, (November 23, 1938), 1442–43.

120. "Rabbi Asks Mercy and Justice for Germany," *The Christian Century* (November 23, 1938), 1438.

121. Editorial, "Demonic Germany and the Predicament of Humanity," *The Christian Century* (November 30, 1938), 1456–58.

122. Editorial, "New Measures against the Jews," *The Christian Century* (December 7, 1938), 1485.

123. "Nazis Condemned by Carolinians," *The Christian Century* (December 7, 1938), 1521.

124. "And So Forth," *The Christian Century* (December 7, 1938), 1521.

125. "Leaders Urge Common Front," "Detroit Protests Nazi Pogroms," "New Trade Pact Stirs England," *The Christian Century* (December 7, 1938), 1513–14.

126. Editorial, "Pinpricks for German Jews," *The Christian Century* (December 14, 1938), 1535.

127. "Friends Reaffirm Stand on War," *The Christian Century* (December 14, 1938), 1551.

128. "English Protest Nazi Persecution," "Los Angeles Mass Meeting in Behalf of German Jews," *The Christian Century* (December 21, 1938), 1585, 1582.

129. "Relate Religion to World Plight," *The Christian Century* (December 21, 1938), 1583–84.

130. Letters to the editor, "Two Suggestions for Jewish Havens," "A Letter to the President," and "Not Pleased," *The Christian Century* (December 28, 1938), 1609–11.

131. James G. McDonald, *The Christian Century* (January 15, 1936), 102, 104.

132. Dawidowicz, pp. 99–100.

133. Quoted in Dawidowicz, p. 106.

134. Arthur Byrd McCormick, "Hitler's Speech," *The Presbyterian* (February 9, 1939), 5.

Chapter 4

1. This topic was discussed in Gerald Reitlinger, *The Final Solution: The Attempt to Exterminate the Jews of Europe, 1939–1945*, 2nd rev. ed., New York, Thomas Yoseloff, 1968, chapter 1, pp. 3–20, including a discussion of the "November Jews," the 9,815 Jews actually deported to Buchenwald, p. 16. For other figures on the number of deportations in 1938 and 1939, see *The Black Book: The Nazi Crime against the Jewish People*, New York, Duell, Sloan and Pearce, 1946, pp. 252–53.

2. The order was issued by Goering on July 31, 1941. See Raul Hilberg, *Documents of Destruction: Germany and Jewry, 1933–1945*, Chicago, Quadrangle Books, 1971, pp. 88–89.

3. The Wannsee Conference was described in detail in Hilberg, pp. 88–106, including the testimony of Adolph Eichmann at his trial from the transcript of June 26, 1961. (See also Raul Hilberg, *The Destruction of the European Jews*, Chicago, Quadrangle Books, 1961, pp. 264–65; Reitlinger, *passim*; and Lucy S. Dawidowicz, *The War against the Jews, 1933–1945*, New York, Holt, Rinehart, Winston, 1975, pp. 136–39, among others.) Thirty copies of the official minutes of the meeting were prepared and distributed, with copy number 16, coded as Nuremberg document NG-2586, eventually used in the Nuremberg trials.

4. Reitlinger, p. 2.

5. Editorial, "Refugee Plans Are Taking More Definite Form," *The Christian Century* (March 1, 1939), 268. (See also Dawidowicz, pp. 104–6, and Reitlinger, pp. 20–24).

6. Dawidowicz, p. 106.

7. "Concealed Threats behind Words," *The Christian Century* (January 11, 1939), 65.

8. "Rufus Jones Back from Germany: Reports Tentative Plans for Refugee Immigration," *The Christian Century* (January 18, 1939), 99.

9. Dawidowicz, pp. 99 and 104–5.

10. Hilberg, *Destruction of the European Jews*, pp. 262–63.

11. Editorial, *The Friend* (January 12, 1939), 246.

12. Rufus M. Jones, "The Visit to Germany," *The Friend* (January 12, 1939), 256.

13. Reitlinger, pp. 20–24.

14. Editorial, "The Beginning of the End?" *The Christian Herald* (January, 1939), 7.

15. Editorial, *The Evangelical Visitor* (February 13, 1939), 50.

16. "New Measures against the Jews," *The Friend of Zion* (January 1939), 7. (The item was reprinted from *The Christian Century*.)

17. "The Jews in Germany," *The Gospel Herald* (April 29, 1939), 578.

18. Advertisement, *The King's Business* (January 1938), 1.

19. Advertisement, *The Sunday School Times* (February 25, 1939), 137.

20. The two books were Leo Stein, *I Was In Hell with Niemoeller*, New York, Fleming H. Revell, 1942; and Martin Niemoeller, *God is My Fuehrer*, New York, Philosophical Library, 1942. There was some controversy over Stein's credentials, but the book was highly praised. See *Church Management* (May 1942), 35, and "I Was in Prison . . . ," *The Watchman-Examiner* (April 30, 1942), 418–19, for reviews of Stein's book and *The Concordia Theological Monthly* (April 1942), 317, for a review of Niemoeller's book. For information on the Church Struggle, Niemoeller, and the persecution of Roman Catholics,

see John S. Conway, *The Nazi Persecution of the Churches, 1933–1945*, New York, Basic Books, 1968, and Guenter Lewy, *The Catholic Church and Nazi Germany*, New York, McGraw-Hill, 1964.

21. See William Kinsey, "The Jews and the New Covenant," *The Gospel Messenger* (January 7, February 4, 1939), 10–11; 7–8. (There were four articles, but the first and fourth raised specific questions about the significance of the return of Jews to Palestine in relation to the teaching of prophecy and the fulfillment of a specific prophetic statement of the Bible, as interpreted by some.)

22. See editorials, *The Churchman* (January 1, February 1, February 15, March 1, March 15, June 1, August, September 1, October 1, 1939), 8, 9; 7, 9; 7, 7; 8, 9; 7, 9; 7; 7, 9; 7. Articles on fascism, Coughlin et al., *The Churchman* (January 15, February 1, March 15, May 1, June 1, June 15, September 1, 1939), 10–11; 10–12; 12–13; 13–14; 19–20; 10–11; 18–19 and 24–25. Five letters to the editor on fascism in America were published, *The Churchman* (January 1, January 15, February 1, July–August, 1939), 3–4; 3; 3, 4–5; 3. The cover photographs on two issues showed meetings of American Nazis, *The Churchman* (February 1, June 1, 1939).

23. Guy Emery Shipler, "Protestants and Anti-Semitism: What Christians Do to Spread and Combat Race Hatred," *The Churchman* (August 1940), 14–15; editorial, "What of Tomorrow," *The Churchman* (June 15, 1940), 7. (These are examples of the defense of clergymen who opposed anti-Semitism.)

24. Editorials, "Anti-Semitism Goes into High Gear" and "Dr. Ayer and Refugees," *The Churchman* (October 1, December 15, 1940), 7; 8. Articles on bigotry, Coughlin, and totalitarianism and a specific article on Nazis in America also appeared in *The Churchman* (January 1, February 1, September 15, October 1, October 15, 1940), *passim*.

25. William C. Kernan, "Catching Up with the Bund, Why Not Catch Up with Coughlin?" and Sigmund Livingston, "Anti-Semitism: A Mental Disorder, How It Can be Effectively Combated," *The Churchman* (September 1, October 15, 1943), 14–15; 12–13.

26. "Thirteenth Anniversary Marks Interest in Unity"; editorial, "The Christian Attitude toward Anti-Semitism"; "Repudiate Racialism in Church"; and "Combating Anti-Semitism," *Federal Council Bulletin* (January, February, June, September 1939), 7; 3; 9; 13.

27. "Condemnation of Anti-Semitism," *Federal Council Bulletin* (October 1941), 6.

28. Leo Polman, "To the Jew First"; editorial, "Wrong Idea about the Jews" and W. H. Schaffer, "Our Church and the Jews"; F. C. Imhof, "Conversion Miracles among Cleveland Jews"; editorials, "The Wandering Jew" and "God's Purpose"; Alfred Segal, "How It Feels to Be a Jew"; LeBaron W. Kinney, "Salvation Is of the Jew," *The Brethren Evangelist* (February 25, March 11, May 27, June 24, September 23, September 30, 1939), 7–8, 3–4, 10–12; 10–12; 3–4; 15–16; 2, 20.

29. Arthur Acy Rouner, "Jew and Christian Worshipping Together," *Advance* (April 1939), 181.

30. Pieter Smit, "The Remarkable Jew," Ina Corinne Brown, "Who Are the Jews," *The Baptist Herald* (October 15, 1939), 384–385, 389; 386 and 397; "The Thoughts of Justis Timberline: The Healing Jew," *The Christian Advocate* (March 9, 1939), 223; editorials, "Refugees: They are Not Taking Jobs from American Workers," "Christian Refugees: Their Future Is a Question Mark in Germany and Elsewhere," "Reich's Refugees: They Are Most Pitiful of War's Victims," "Local Churches and Refugees," *The Christian Advocate* (May 18, June 29, October 19, October 26, 1939), 477, 616, 1000, 1018.

31. Review of Jacques Maritain's *A Christian Looks at the Jewish Question*, *The Churchman* (September 15, 1939), 21. (The reviewer noted that Maritain represented an enlightened Roman Cahtolic viewpoint and that he also called for a reconciliation of Jews to Christianity, or Christian conversion, as a solution to the "Jewish question.")

32. Morris S. Lazaron, "Judaism a Universal Religion," *The Christian Century* (August 30, 1939), 1042–45. (Examples of editorials: "Rufus Jones Back from Germany" and "Quakers and Refugees," "Refugee Plans Are Taking a More Definite Shape," "Refugee

Children Await Action by Congress," "Help for the Helpless," *The Christian Century* [December 18, March 1, May 10, October 25, 1939], 80–81, 99, 268, 596, 1293–94. Examples of letters to the editor: "Poor Man's Sheep," "Unto the Least," "The Chosen People," *The Christian Century* [January 1, February 8, February 15, 1939], 125, 189, 219–20.)

33. George A. Sokolsky, "What Is a Jew?" *The Mennonite* (April 11, 1939), 4–6; "Evian Conference Committee to Aid Refugees by Raising Funds" and "The Thoughts of Justis Timberline: The Healing Jew," *The Messenger* (March 2; March 23, 1939), 24; 6. (For a full explanation of the international conference on the refugee crisis held in July 1938 at Evian-les-Bains, France, see Henry Feingold, *The Politics of Rescue*, New Brunswick, New Jersey, Rutgers University Press, 1970, pp. 20–24 and *passim*; Hans Habe, *The Mission*, New York, New American Library, 1967. Habe's book was a fictionalized account of a Jewish representation to the Evian Conference, a conference that proved to be largely ineffective in its attempts to solve the refugee crisis. For a note on Habe and *The Mission* see Dawidowicz, p. 190n.)

34. Jacob Pelz, "Jewish Situation and Christian Responsibility"; editorial, "Our Mission to Jews"; John Stuart Conning, "The Jew Today"; W. H. Jordan, "An Appeal to Jews"; Vartan Dikron Melconian, "A Summer Appeal to Jews in Philadelphia," *The Presbyterian* (April 6, May 4, June 8, July 6, August 24, 1939), 20–21; 4; 3; 23; 19.

35. For an account of the S.S. *St. Louis* and other ships carrying Jewish refugees, see Feingold, pp. 64–65.

36. Editorial, "A People without a Country," *The Lutheran Companion* (June 15, 1939), 740; letters to the editor, "Admit Jewish Refugees," *The Christian Advocate* (August 10, 1939), 769; editorial, "The Wandering Jew," *The Brethren Evangelist* (June 24, 1939), 3.

37. "Jews as God's Yardstick" and J. Wilbur Chapman, "The Jews," *The Gospel Herald* (August 22, September 5, 1942), 1185–86, 1256–58; A. J. Kligerman, "Israel's Position in Romans 11," *Moody Monthly* (September 1942), 16–17; Hyman Appelman, "Can Hitler Win the War?" *The Sunday School Times* (August 29, 1942), 679.

38. Roy L. Laurin, "How Much Prophecy," *The King's Business* (December 1939), 453.

39. Louis S. Bauman, "A Twenty-Seven-Centuries-Old Prophecy," "What Makes Folks Hate Us So?" and "The German-Russian Alliance," *The King's Business* (August, October, November 1939), 300–301, 325; 380, 402–3; 415, 444. (In *The Sunday School Times*, Bauman wrote six articles in 1940, all on prophetic themes, two in February, two in June, one in July, and one in August. The titles were new; the content was not. Bauman worked and reworked the same prophetic-dispensational-premillenial themes regardless of who published his articles.)

40. Dawidowicz, *passim*. (This was really the central thesis of her book, developed carefully and persuasively in the first major section, "The Final Solution," and in chapter 9 of the second major section, "Between Freedom and Ghetto, 1933–1938," pp. 169–96.)

41. Hilberg, *Destruction of the European Jews*, *passim*, and *Documents of Destruction*, *passim*.

42. "Adult Topic: Peter Preaches to Gentiles: Or a Faith That Breaks Down Racial Barriers," *Adult Class and Adult Leader* (March 1939), 49–53. (This publication was further identified as *A Journal of Christian Education and Church Work; with Study and Teaching Material for the Uniform [International] Lessons*, American Baptist Publications Society.)

43. For the numbers of Jews in Europe, east and west, see Dawidowicz, pp. 197–98, appendix A, "The Fate of the Jews in Hitler's Europe: By Country," pp. 357–401, and appendix B, "The Final Solution in Figures," pp. 402–3.

44. Henry Smith Leiper, "Don't Confuse Facts and Issues," *Advance* (April 1, 1939), 157. (See also *Advance* (January 1, February 1, 1938), 14; 62.)

45. Editorial, "Persecuted Israel," *The Alliance Weekly* (March 4, 1939), 131.

46. "Europe's Darkest Cloud," *The Alliance Weekly* (September 9, 1939), 571.

47. J. Hoffman Cohn, "The Jews in Europe," *The Brethren Evangelist* (March 25, 1939), 14–15. (Note the reference to the failure of the Evian Conference.)

48. "Germany," *The Brethren Evangelist* (April 1, 1939), 2.

49. *The Brethren Evangelist* (April 8, 1939), 2–3.

50. "Expectation of War, and Armageddon," "The Jew—An Internationalist," and "The Spirit of Antichrist Marches in Germany," *The Brethren Evangelist* (July 8, 1939), 5–7.

51. "Land Policy: Victims of New Plan Are Bohemia, Moravia, and Slovakia," *The Christian Advocate* (March 30, 1939), 301. (Earlier editorials mentioned Germany only; see "Pax Germanica: Hitler Proclaims It, to Consolidate His Gains," "Refugee Ransom: Nazi Leaders Would Use It to Stave Off Collapse"; W. Fay Butler, "One Blood"; Jacob Simpson Payton, "Washington Observations," *The Christian Advocate* (January 26, February 9, February 23, 1939), 85; 129; 173. George Mecklenburg described in detail the direct persecution of Jews in Austria based on his interviews with Jews while in Germany and Austria during the summer of 1938 in "Three Tragedies in Europe," *The Christian Adovcate* (March 30, 1939), 298.

52. "Globe-Scouring: Jews Are Doing It in Search of Settlement Territory," *The Christian Advocate* (July 13, 1939), 664.

53. "More Refugees: War Offers No Solutions to Tragic Problems," *The Christian Advocate* (November 2, 1939), 1052.

54. Editorial, "Ransoms Stimulate Kidnaping," *The Christian Century* (January 25, 1939), 109.

55. "Anti-Jewish Imredy Had a Jewish Ancestor," *The Christian Century* (March 1, 1939), 268–69.

56. "Jewish Refugees from Italy," *The Christian Century* (March 22, 1939), 371.

57. Albert Viton, "Memel: A Study in Nazi Terror," *The Christian Century* (April 5, 1939), 442–44.

58. "The Fate of Poland" and "Pious Propaganda Tried on American Ministers," *The Christian Century* (September 20, November 29, 1939), 1127, 1461.

59. "Pastor Debarred from the Reich," *The Christian Century* (September 20, 1939), 1149. (Mecklenberg had written articles, primarily for *The Christian Advocate*, telling of his clandestine interviews with Jews in Germany and Vienna.)

60. "Unpleasant Truths," *The Churchman* (October 1, 1939), 8.

61. R. M. Stephens, "Europe's Darkest Cloud," *The Hebrew Christian Alliance Quarterly* (Fall 1939), 26–27.

62. Editorial, "Suffering of the Jews," *The Watchman-Examiner* (December 28, 1939), 1392.

63. Dawidowicz, p. 202.

64. The details of the Evian Conference, the machinations and international politics and rivalries and the ultimate failure of the Intergovernmental Committee for Political Refugees (IGC) was described in Feingold, *passim*, and in Arthur D. Morse, *While Six Million Died: A Chronicle of American Apathy*, New York, Random House, 1968, pp. 199–220, 241–51.

65. Morse, pp. 250–51.

66. J. Hoffman Cohn, "The Jews in Europe," *The Brethren Evangelist* (March 25, 1939), 14–15.

67. Dawidowicz, pp. 160–62, described briefly this period of respite from persecution while the plans for Germany's future were being formulated.

68. For a description of the early deportation of Jews to Poland, see Reitlinger, "The First Deportations to Poland," pp. 42–53. (Reitlinger established the dates for these first deportations as being October 1939 to March 1940. He also confirmed that the "persistent rumors" of the editorial in *The Watchman-Examiner* for December 28, 1939, were based on fact; see p. 251.)

69. For a concise, accurate summation of the conquest of Poland, Denmark, Norway, and Western Europe, see Robert Payne, *The Life and Death of Adolf Hitler*, New York, Praeger Publishers, 1973. (Payne described these events in two chapters, "Blitzkrieg against Poland" and "Blitzkrieg against the West," pp. 357–85. Innumerable other ref-

erences could be cited, but Payne's account seems adequate for establishing the essential details of Hitler's conquest.)

70. Louis S. Bauman, "Israel's Day of Sorrow," editorial, *The Brethren Missionary Herald* (February 3, 1940), 3.

71. Editorial, "Hated of All Nations," *The Brethren Missionary Herald* (March 16, 1940), 3.

72. *The Brethren Missionary Herald* (April 20, 1940), 3.

73. Editorial, "Germans Bring 'Jim Crow' Cars to Warsaw," *The Christian Century* (January 31, 1940), 131.

74. Dr. Conrad J. Hoffman, Jr., was a recognized authority on world Jewry, serving the Board of Home Missions of the Presbyterian Church in the United States and the International Missionary Council on Jewish work. See "Consider Problem of Jewish Refugees," *The Christian Century* (February 21, 1940), 257.

75. Devere Allen, "Germans Reveal Peace Longing: Audience at Bach Mass Weeps at References to Good Will—Some Nazis Show Humane Spirit," *The Christian Century* (March 6, 1940), 328–29.

76. "Jewish Population in Reich Drastically Reduced," *The Christian Century* (April 17, 1940), 519.

77. "According to the 'White Book,'" *The Friend of Zion* (February 1940), 16.

78. Elias Newman, "A Piteous Cry for Help," *The Friend of Zion* (March 1940), 17–18.

79. *The Friend of Zion* (March 1940), 24.

80. "The Tragic Plight of the Jews in Central Europe," *The Friend of Zion* (April 1940), 28.

81. "The Bitterest Hour in Israel's History," *The Friend of Zion* (June 1940), 42–43.

82. "Walls," *The Lutheran Companion* (December 12, 1940), 1575.

83. Louis S. Bauman, "What? Then!" *The King's Business* (January 1940), 12, 36.

84. The supporting statement of the editor is bracketed in the article "Why the End of the Age Must Be Very Near," *The Sunday School Times* (February 3, 1940), 90. The more formal endorsement was entitled, "A Word by the Editor," *The Sunday School Times* (August 17, 1940), 647. (It should be noted that the figure "twenty-one articles" was a bit confusing in that the editor does not indicate where he began the count. There was some indication that articles from 1937 are included in this total, but it was not made clear.)

85. The articles by Louis S. Bauman were published under various titles in *The Sunday School Times* (February 3, February 10, June 15, June 29, July 20, and August 17, 1940). (Between February and June, Bauman was ill and so the series was delayed.)

86. Joseph Taylor Britan, "Continued Persecution of Jews in Europe," *The Sunday School Times* (March 16, 1940), 216–17; editorials, "Why the Jews Live" and "The Rescuing Jew," *The Sunday School Times* (August 17, December 28, 1940), 645, 1050.

87. Editorial, "The Unhappy Jew," *The Watchman-Examiner* (June 13, 1940), 665.

88. Geneva H. Kuhn, "Hear, O Israel!" *The Brethren Missionary Herald* (October 26, 1940), 11–12.

89. "Anguish: NNS Writer Reports the Known Facts of France," *The Churchman* (October 15, 1940), 26–27.

90. Douglas V. Steere, "In the Backwash of the War," *The Friend* (October 31, 1940), 151–54.

91. *The Friend* (November 28, 1940), 178.

92. "Jewish Tribulations," *The Alliance Weekly* (January 18, 1941), 34.

93. "The Jewish Dictation," *The Alliance Weekly* (May 10, 1941), 290–91.

94. For example, "Bergson's Last Testimony," *Advance* (February 1, 1941), 63. See also "Henri Bergson," *Current Religious Thought* (April 1941), I.

95. "The Lamps Are Going Out," *The Baptist and Reflector* (April 24, 1941), 7.

96. "Less German Persecution of Jews" contrasted with "Germany: NNS Informant Reveals Some Interesting Items," *The Churchman* (January 15, 1941), 7, 27.

97. "Horror: Protestant Pastor Works in Concentration Camps," *The Churchman* (March 15, 1941), 24–25.

98. "Jewish Annihilation," *The Friend of Zion* (April 1941), 31.

99. *The Friend of Zion* (June 1941), 47, *passim*.

100. Reported in Dawidowicz, p. 125. (Dawidowicz, Hilberg, and Reitlinger, among others, gave full descriptions of the *Einsatzgruppen*. The estimates are that 2 million Jews were exterminated by shootings and mass killings, including the use of gas vans, by these death squads.)

101. *The Friend of Zion* (December 1941), 86.

102. "A Yellow Badge as a 'Deterrent,'" *The Hebrew Christian Alliance Quarterly* (Fall 1941), 28–29.

103. Editorial, "Horror Stories from Poland," *The Christian Century* (December 9, 1942), 1518–19.

104. Editorial, "Polish Atrocities Are Entered in the Books," *The Christian Century* (December 30, 1942), 1611.

105. "Protest Swiss Anti-Semitism," *The Christian Century* (January 21, 1942), 92.

106. Editorial, "The Mind and Heartlessness of National Socialism," *The Christian Century* (May 20, 1942), 651.

107. Editorial, "Vichy's Persecution of Jews Brings Deserved Rebuke," *The Christian Century* (September 30, 1942), 1171.

108. Editorial, "All Dutch Christians Protest Jewish Exile," *The Christian Century* (October 7, 1942), 1203.

109. Editorial, "Laval—Anti-Humanitarian," *The Churchman* (October 1, 1942), 5.

110. William C. Kernan, "Beware of These Hitler Weapons: The Method Is First Hate then Murder," *The Churchman* (October 1, 1942), 7.

111. "Nazi Powers: Dr. Cavert Tells Story of Refugee Plight in Europe," *The Churchman* (December 15, 1942), 24. (See also "Dr. Cavert Reports on Refugees," *Federal Council Bulletin* [December 1942], 1–2; Samuel McCrea Cavert, "Christian Europe Today and Tomorrow," *The Messenger* [November 19, November 26, 1942], 7; 9–10; "Dr. Cavert Reports on Europe," *The Presbyterian* (December 10, 1942), 7.

112. *The Gospel Messenger* (September 12, 1942), 2.

113. William Bayles, "All Dominating Fear," *The Signs of the Times* (July 25, 1942), 3, 15.

114. Editorial, "Jews in Europe," *The Watchman-Examiner* (January 15, 1942), 56.

115. *The Watchman-Examiner* (October 1, 1942), 963.

116. Examples of paid advertisements published in *The King's Business* (May 1940), inside back cover; *The Watchman-Examiner* (May 23, 1940), 592; *Moody Monthly* (March 1940), 381; *The King's Business* (November 1940), 435; *The Sunday School Times* (September 14, 1940), 720; *The Presbyterian* (December 19, 1940), 23.

117. Advertisement, *Moody Monthly* (November 1941), 147.

118. Advertisement, *The Presbyterian* (December 11, 1941), 2.

119. "Horrors of Warsaw Ghetto Related by Woman Who Escaped to Palestine," *The Friend of Zion* (September 1942), 63. (See also the issues for January, March, April, May, July, September, and November 1942.)

120. "Persecution of the Jews: A Letter from the President of the Baptist World Alliance," *The Watchman-Examiner* (December 24, 1942), 1261.

Chapter 5

1. "Exiled German Lutheran Pastors Ask for Prayers for Suffering Jews," *Advance* (February 1, 1943), 63.

2. "Six Thousand Jews Executed Daily in Poland," *Advance* (April 1, 1943), 158.

3. "Modern Martyrdoms Multiply under Hitlerite Fury," "Quisling Plunders Missionary Treasury: Danish Bishop Writes Norwegian Churchmen," "Dutch Churchmen

Cheered by Release of Synodical Leaders," and "Extension of Quisling Pressure to Free Churches Feared," *Advance* (April 1, 1943), 158–59.

4. Ibid., 158.

5. "Echoes of Changes in Wholly Occupied France," *Advocate* (June 1, 1943), 256.

6. Letter to the editor, "From Rabbi Wise," *The Christian Century* (January 13, 1943), 53. (A discussion of the content of the editorial "Horror Stories from Poland" is in chapter 4; see also note 106 of chapter 4. See also Stephen S. Wise, *Challenging Years, The Autobiography of Stephen S. Wise*. New York, G. P. Putnam's Sons, 1949, pp. 274–79.)

7. "Rabbis Discuss Plan for Peace," *The Christian Century* (January 6, 1943), 26–28.

8. Editorial, "A Return to Barbarism in Eastern Europe," *The Christian Century* (February 3, 1943), 125.

9. Editorial, "The Chief Rabbi May Well Complain," *The Christian Century* (March 3, 1943), 253.

10. Editorial, "Britain to Transfer Jewish Children to Palestine," *The Christian Century* (March 10, 1943), 284.

11. R. Paul Miller, "I Sat Where They Sat," *The Brethren Missionary Herald* (January 16, 1943), 34.

12. Louis S. Bauman, "Still Blames Jews," editorial, *The Brethren Missionary Herald* (July 3, 1943), 403–4.

13. Editorial, "Israel's 'Day of Grief and Desperate Sorrow,'" *The Brethren Missionary Herald* (July 24, 1943), 451. (Reprinted in *The Gospel Herald* [January 8, 1944], 68–70, with the same title.)

14. Ibid.

15. Editorials, "The Agony and Suffering of Israel" and "Greatest Mass Murder in All History," *The Brethren Missionary Herald* (August 14, September 4, 1943), 501, 546.

16. "Liquidation of Warsaw Ghetto" and "Nazis Suffocate Jews in Groups of 500," *The Brethren Missionary Herald* (September 25, 1943), 605.

17. Editorial, "The Greatest War Casualties," *The Brethren Missionary Herald* (November 20, 1943), 712.

18. "Various Messages and Resolutions Adopted by the Council's Biennial Meeting," *Federal Council Bulletin* (January 1943), 12.

19. "Christian Concern for the Suffering Jews," *Federal Council Bulletin* (June 1943), 6.

20. "Observance of the Day of Compassion," *Federal Council Bulletin* (June 1943), 6.

21. Letter to the editor, "'Day of Compassion' Ignored," *The Christian Century* (June 2, 1943), 669. (The writer of the letter identified himself as Karl M. Chworowsky of the Flatbush Unitarian Church, Brooklyn, New York.)

22. "United States Will Aid Jews," *The Alliance Weekly* (September 1943), 746.

23. "What about Atrocities Now?" *The Baptist and Reflector* (June 10, 1943), 20.

24. Jacob T. Hoogstra, "The Jew—The Great 'Why' of History," *The Calvin Forum* (August-September 1943), 7–9.

25. William C. Kernan, "Lidice and the Jews: You, Christians, Also Are Responsible," *The Churchman* (January 1, 1943), 11.

26. Ibid., the last three paragraphs of the article.

27. "Declaration: Loyal German-Americans Appeal for Signatories," *The Churchman* (January 15, 1943), 17–18.

28. "Persecutions: Americans Must Demand Action in Behalf of Jews," *The Churchman* (March 15, 1943), 20.

29. Dorothy Moulton Mayer, "Blessed Are the Meek: Why Hitler Hates and Persecutes the Jews," *The Churchman* (April 1, 1943), 14–15.

30. "For Jews: Federal Council Seeks to Aid Those in Europe," *The Churchman* (April 1, 1943), 21–22.

31. Letter to the editor, "What about Christians?" *The Churchman* (May 1, 1943), 2.

32. "Persecution: Bishop Oldham Pleads for Jewish Sufferers," *The Churchman* (May 15, 1943), 21–22.

33. Editorial, "A Blot of Shame," *The Churchman* (December 15, 1943), 4–5.

34. "A Review of Religion, 1942–43," *Church Management* (July 1943), 10–11.

35. *The Concordia Theological Monthly* (July 1943), 519.

36. Abba Hillel Silver, "Plea for United Jewish Support of Palestine National Homeland," *Current Religious Thought* (December 1943), 5–9.

37. A. D. Cornett, "Is This War a Judgment of God?" *The Pulpit* (August 1943), 173–75.

38. "Nazis Continue Deportation of Thousands of Jews" and "Aliens Doomed," *The Friend of Zion* (January 1943), 7.

39. *The Friend of Zion* (February 1943), 15.

40. "Nazism, Anti-Christian as Well as Anti-Semitic" and "Extermination Job," *The Friend of Zion* (March 1943), 18–19. (First article reprinted from the *American Hebrew*, the second from a small monthly published in Los Angeles, *Prophecy Monthly*.)

41. *The Friend of Zion* (April 1943), 31.

42. *The Friend of Zion* (July 1943), 55.

43. "The American Jewish World" and "Jewish World News," *The Friend of Zion* (October and December 1943), 70–71, 95.

44. The editor, "Hitler Plans to Destroy European Jews," *The Hebrew Christian Alliance Quarterly* (Winter 1943), 25–26. (The editor of the winter 1943 issue probably was the Rev. David Bronstein; see *The Hebrew Christian Alliance Quarterly* [Summer 1943], 16.)

45. The general secretary, "The Jewish Tragedy," *The Hebrew Christian Alliance Quarterly* (Summer 1943), 17–18. (Morris Zeidman was the general secretary.)

46. Robert J. McConnell, "The Jew and Prophecy," *The Gospel Herald* (March 27, 1943), 464.

49. "Work and Workers: Israel's Only Hope," *The Gospel Herald* (August 28, 1943), 1218–20. (The article, really an editorial, was signed by Fred T. Mills, not otherwise identified.)

48. "Christians and Jews in Europe," *The Presbyterian* (January 14, 1943), 23.

49. "Against Nazi Jewish Oppression," *The Presbyterian* (April 8, 1943), 19.

50. Joseph Taylor Britan, "If by Any Means I Might Save Some," *The Presbyterian* (November 18, 1943), 6.

51. For example, *The Presbyterian* (May 27, 1943), 498, carried a small news item on Jews in Germany at the bottom of column two, stating that they were "doomed to death."

52. "Russia and Jews," *The Watchman-Examiner* (September 30, 1943), 1173.

53. "French Jews Suffering," *The Watchman-Examiner* (December 9, 1943), 1173.

54. Editorial, "Two Million Jews Have Been Liquidated," *The Christian Century* (May 5, 1943), 533.

55. Letter to the editor, "Either Zionism or Annihilation," *The Christian Century* (May 26, 1943), 639.

56. Editorial, "European Jews Are in a Desperate Plight," *The Christian Century* (September 8, 1943), 1004–5.

57. "Belgian Churches Continue Resistance to Nazi Anti-Semitism" and "Swedish Churches Show Increased Concern over Nazi Ideology," *Advance* (January 1, 1943), 14.

58. "More Churchmen Arrested," *Advance* (July 1943), 26.

59. "Dachau, Block 17," *The Friend* (February 4, 1943), 244–45.

60. "Protestant and Catholic Cooperation in the Occupied Countries," "Christian Ministry to Refugees in France," and "Church Opposition in Germany Becoming Increasingly Outspoken," *The Messenger* (January 12, 1943), 6–7.

61. *The Watchman-Examiner* (April 1, 1943), 294, third column, third full paragraph.

62. "Jewish Persecution," *The Churchman* (March 1, 1943), 27.

63. "Protest of Churches Is Not Underground" and "Add: Protest of Churches," *The Christian Century* (July 7, July 14, 1943), 789–90, 813.

64. "Intercede for Mercy for the People," *The Christian Century* (August 18, 1943), 949.

65. "Catholic Church Looks for Revival of Faith," *The Christian Century* (August 23, 1943), 975.

66. "Danes Aid Jews to Escape," *The Christian Century* (November 3, 1943), 1286–87.

67. Advertisement, *The King's Business* (September 1943), 355. (Other such advertisements can be found in the following Protestant periodicals for 1943. *The King's Business* [September, October, December 1943], 383, 384; 466; 472; *Moody Monthly* [July 1943], 639; *The Presbyterian* [November 18, December 16, 1943], 2; 2; *The Sunday School Times* [January 23, October 2, October 30, November 6, November 13, November 27, December 4, 1943], 76; 796; 883; 886, 900; 976; 978; 992; *The Watchman-Examiner* [January 14; December 16, 1934], 27, 29; 1194.)

68. Stephen E. Balogh, "Freedom to Worship God: Evangelical and Reformed Chaplain Arranges Jewish Holiday Worship Services on Soil of France," *The Messenger* (December 26, 1944), 20.

69. For example, "Kaj Munk: Anti-Nazi Danish Leader Found Murdered in Jutland," *The Churchman* (January 15, 1944), 21–22; and "Denmark: Kaj Munk, Anti-Nazi Clergyman Found Murdered," *The Living Church* (January 16, 1944), 8.

70. Editorial, "Vernichtungskommando," *The Brethren Missionary Herald* (March 4, 1944), 116–17.

71. "World Council Protests Persecution of Hungarian Jews," *The Messenger* (July 25, 1944), 27.

72. "Hungarian Americans Protest," *The Messenger* (August 22, 1944), 32. (The story of the Hungarian Jews is a special chapter in the history of the Holocaust; see André Biss, *A Million Jews to Save: Check to the Final Solution*, London, Hutchinson and Company, 1973.)

73. Editorial, "Biggest Atrocity Story Breaks in Poland," *The Christian Century* (September 13, 1944), 1045. (The reference at the end of the editorial was to the Polish uprising. See Michael Zylberberg, *A Warsaw Diary, 1939–1945*, London, Vallentine-Mitchell, 1969, pp. 153–81.)

74. "The Master Race," *The Churchman* (September 15, 1944), 6.

75. Editorial, "The Tragedy of Germany," *The Living Church* (September 17, 1944), 14–15.

76. "Germany: German People Guilty, Must Face Consequences," *The Living Church* (September 24, 1944), 8.

77. Editorial, "Murder, Inc.," *The Messenger* (October 3, 1944), 5–6.

78. "We Shall Not Stoop," *The Messenger* (October 3, 1944), 6.

79. *The Friend of Zion* (October 1944), 80.

80. Advertisements for 1944: *The King's Business* (January, April, October, December 1944), 37, 160, 341, 425; *Moody Monthly* (November 1944), 163; *The Presbyterian* (March 30, April 27, November 6, December 14, 1944), 19; 20; 2; 2; *The Sunday School Times* (January 1, January 15, January 22, February 19, March 25, April 15, June 10, June 17, July 15, September 23, October 21, November 4, November 11, December 2, December 9, December 16, 1944), 10; 44; 61; 130; 227; 281; 282; 431; 445; 511; 685; 765; 801; 810; 900; 902; 948; *The Watchman-Examiner* (February 10; April 13; May 11, 1944), 124; 340; 451.

81. "Suffering: Eye-Witness Story of Nazi Cruelty to Prisoners," *The Churchman* (February 1, 1944), 18–19.

Chapter 6

1. Henry Smith Leiper, "The World Council of Churches: What the Council Is Doing for Refugees," *The Churchman* (January 1, 1945), 11. (Published in *The Messenger* (January 23, 1945), 8–9, as "A World Council and a World of Refugees.")

2. Only a few examples can be cited. "Reconstruction: Aides Going to Europe," *Federal Council Bulletin* (May 1945), 9, a report of the sending of five young people to France to aid in reconstruction, rehabilitation, and refugee assistance work. "News of the World Council," *Federal Council Bulletin* (September 1945), 7–8, including details of a

centralized office and staff at the World Council headquarters in Geneva to coordinate all relief and reconstruction efforts in Europe. "Various Council Actions," *Federal Council Bulletin* (October 1945), 11, reporting on the executive committee's recommendation to send surplus food to Europe, support the UNRRA appeals for funds and all denominational efforts to raise funds for overseas relief aid, and offer the services of the council's Overseas Relief and Reconstruction Committee to those denominations having no such committee. Robert Root, "The Facts about Europe's Children," *Advance* (December 1945), 31–32, a detailed report, including naming Protestant, Catholic, and Jewish agencies and nonreligious groups who were cooperating in their aid to Europe's children. *The Christian Century, The Churchman, The Concordia Theological Monthly, The Evangelical Visitor, The Gospel Messenger, The Friend, The Living Church, The Lutheran Companion, The Lutheran Standard, The Messenger, The Presbyterian,* and *The Watchman-Examiner,* among others, published articles about aid to refugees in 1945.

3. Alice Shaffer, "These Are They Which Came Out of Great Tribulation," letter to the editor, *The Friend* (August 30, 1945), 71–73.

4. *The Evangelical Visitor* (April 9, 1945), 114–15.

5. *The Evangelical Visitor* (December 17 and December 31, 1945), 402, 409; 418. The later issue particularly reported on the immediate threat of mass starvation in Europe during the winter of 1945–1946.

6. M. Guy West, "With Malice toward None," *The Gospel Messenger* (September 8, 1945), 5–6.

7. The basic outline and purpose of the trip by the three Lutheran leaders was given in P. O. Bersell, "A Glimpse of War's Devastation. . . . We Saw Europe," *The Lutheran Companion* (May 9, 1945), 5–6. Later articles giving more detail were published in most of the Lutheran periodicals. Later in the year, reports of Lutheran work in Europe from S. M. C. Michelfelder, commissioner of the American Section of the Lutheran World Convention in Geneva, Switzerland, were published in Lutheran periodicals.

8. A. L. Warnshuis, "The Church Situation in Europe," *Lutheran Herald* (February 30, 1945), 154–56, 158; A. L. Warnshuis, "The New World of Tomorrow," *The Lutheran Standard* (March 17, 1945), 4–5; *The Lutheran Witness* (March 27, 1945), 103–4.

9. Lawrence Meyer, "Our Share in the Rebuilding of Europe," *The Lutheran Witness* (May 8, 1945), 151–52.

10. Samuel McCrea Cavert, "Hunger of Body and Soul: Christians of America Must Demonstrate Their Christianity in Healing Fellowship with Christians of Europe," *The Messenger* (March 6, 1945), 11–14.

11. P. O. Bersell, "What Shall We Do with Germany?" *The Lutheran Companion* (August 22, 1945), 6–7. (Reprinted from the *Lutheran Outlook* (June 1945), 176–77; also reprinted in *The Bond* (June 1945), 2, 5.)

12. Cecil Northcott, "The Treatment of Germany," *The Christian Century* (February 14, 1945), 204–5; Editorial, "Germany's Rehabilitation," *The Christian Century* (June 13, 1945), 702–3.

13. "Germany: Visiting Europeans See Problems Realistically," *The Churchman* (June 1, 1945), 21–22.

14. P. O. Bersell, "What Shall We Do with Germany?" *The Lutheran Companion* (August 22, 1945), 6–7.

15. Stewart W. Herman, *It's Your Souls We Want,* New York and London, Harper and Brothers, 1943.

16. Stewart W. Herman, *The Rebirth of the German Church,* New York and London, Harper and Brothers, 1946.

17. See "Background to a Journey," *The Lutheran Standard* (November 17, 1945), 13–14; and Paul C. Empie, "Background to a Journey, Part II," *The Lutheran Herald* (November 25, 1945), 941; and "Herman Takes Aid to Berlin Churches," *The Christian Century* (August 29, 1945), 988–89. Articles or notes by Herman were published as "Evangelical Church Seeks to Dispense with State Financial Aid," *The Living Church* (September 9, 1945), 7–8; "Clergyman Reports on Activity of German Churches," *The*

Messenger (October 16, 1945), 23; "Paris," *The Christian Century* (October 17, 1945), 1190–91, "News of the World Council," *Federal Council Bulletin,* (September, 1945), 7, which reports on Herman's appointment to the World Council's staff.

18. "Leaders on Important Mission Abroad," *Federal Council Bulletin* (May 1945), 7. (See also "Bishop Henry Knox Sherrill," *The Churchman* [June 15, 1945], 29–30; "Bishop Sherrill Gives Report on Observations of Visit," *The Living Church* [September 30, 1945], 3–5; "Statement of Delegates to Germany Representing the Federal Council of Churches: Issued on Their Return to America, December 10, 1945," *The Living Church* [December 30, 1945], 8; "American Churchmen Discuss Europe as They Saw It," *The Lutheran Standard* [December 29, 1945], 14.)

19. "Background to a Journey," *The Lutheran Standard* (November 17, 1945), 13–14; and Paul E. Empie, "Background to a Journey, Part II," *The Lutheran Herald* (November 25, 1945), 941. (See also Lawrence Meyer, "Our Share in Rebuilding Europe," *The Lutheran Witness* [May 8, 1945], 151–52; "From Our Representatives in Europe," *The Lutheran Witness* [November 6, 1945], 368–79; "With Drs. Behnken and Meyers in Europe," *The Lutheran Witness* [November 20, 1945], 383–84; "Berlin Letter," *The Lutheran Witness* [December 4, 1945], 401; and "Should Lutheranism in Germany Be Saved: Berlin in Retrospect," *The Lutheran Witness* [December 18, 1945], 415–16.)

20. "Dr. Cavert to Geneva," *The Presbyterian* (September 20, 1945), 23; "Dr. Cavert Reports on Europe's Needs," *Federal Council Bulletin* (December 1945), 6–7; Samuel McCrea Cavert, "The New Birth of the German Churches," *The Christian Century* (December 20, 1945), 1380–81. (See also "Background of a Journey," and Paul C. Empie, "Background of a Journey, Part II," *The Lutheran Standard* [November 17, 1945], 13–14; *The Lutheran Herald* [November 25, 1945], 941, and S. C. Michelfelder, "Church Leadership Reversed in Germany," *The Lutheran Companion* [September 26, 1945], 2; "Michelfelder Takes Part in Geneva Peace Service," *The Lutheran Standard* [October 13, 1945], 15; S. C. Michelfelder, "Steps in Rechristianization of Germany" *The Lutheran Standard* [September 1, September 8, September 15, 1945], 11, 13–14, 11–12.)

21. *The Watchman-Examiner* (November 1, 1945), 1050. (See also Ewart E. Turner, "Pastor Niemoeller Puts Blame on German People," *The Living Church* [October 28, 1945], 8–9.)

22. "Leaders on Important Mission Abroad," *Federal Council Bulletin* (May 1945), 7. (See also "From Our Chaplains," *The Alliance Weekly* [September 8, 1945], 283; George B. Wood, "An Evening with Bishop Dibelius," *The Living Church* [*October 14, 1945*], 10; Earl J. Stainbrook, "A Chaplain Views the Evangelical Church in Germany," *The Lutheran Standard* [August 11, 1945], 8–9; "Foreign War Emergency Relief" [the report by a chaplain of an offering made by his army unit for aid to German church rehabilitation], *The Presbyterian* [September 6, 1945], 11; "Chaplain's Report from Czechoslovakia," *The Watchman-Examiner* [July 19, 1945], 690.)

23. Elizabeth McCracken, "Visitors: World Council of Churches Deputation to New York City," *The Living Church* (May 27, 1945), 5–7; Henry Smith Leiper, "Visitors from Europe," *Advance* (July 1945), 9; "Visser't Hooft Tells Chicago of Europe's Churches," *The Christian Century* (June 20, 1945), 741; "Germany: Visiting European Churchmen See Problem Realistically," *The Churchman* (June 1, 1945), 21–22.

24. "Pastor Niemoeller Free," *The Lutheran Witness* (June 19, 1945), 200–201; "Pastor Niemoeller Free," *The Presbyterian* (May 17, 1945), 8; *The Watchman-Examiner* (July 12, 1945), 667.

25. Editorial, "Niemoeller Interviewed by Dorothy Thompson," *The Christian Century* (May 30, 1945), 645; F. B. Oxnam, "Niemoeller Today," *The Christian Century* (June 13, 1945), 705–6; Ben L. Rose, "As Niemoeller Sees Germany's Future," *The Christian Century* (October 10, 1945), 1155–56; Ewart E. Turner, "Pastor Niemoeller Puts Blame on German People," *The Christian Century* (October 28, 1945), 8–9; David L. Ostergren, "Germany's Hero, Pastor Martin Niemoeller," *The Lutheran Companion* (September 26, 1945), 7–8; David L. Ostergren, "An Intimate View of Martin Niemoeller," *The Lutheran Standard* (September 15, 1945), 7; "American Bishops Interview Niemoeller," *The Lu-*

theran Witness (June 19, 1945), 201; "For Christ and Humanity: Our Church in Service to a World Stricken by War: A Chaplain's Impressions of Our Program for German Rehabilitation" (includes an interview with Niemoeller), *The Lutheran Witness* (August 28, 1945), 280–81; Dorothy Thompson, "A Meeting with Niemoeller," *The Messenger* (June 26, 1945), 15–16; James L. Ewart, "Breakfast with Niemoeller," *The Presbyterian* (July 26, 1945), 8.

26. "Niemoeller," *The Christian Herald* (August 1945), 9; "Pastor Niemoeller and the Role of the Churches," *The Christian Century* (June 20, 1945), 724; Letter to the editor, "To Understand Niemoeller, Study Barth," *The Christian Century* (October 10, 1945), 1765–66; editorial, "Niemoeller Holds Church to Blame for War," *The Christian Century* (October 31, 1945), 1212; "Germany: Niemoeller and Others See Undemocratic Errors," *The Churchman* (October 1, 1945), 22; "Niemoeller: No German Has a Clear Conscience," *The Churchman* (November 1, 1945), 22; *The Gospel Messenger* (June 2, 1945), 2; "Niemoeller Preaches His First Sermon," *The Gospel Messenger* (December 8, 1945), 25; Martin Niemoeller, "The Spiritual Outlook in Germany," *The Living Church* (June 24, 1945), 9; "Pastor Niemoeller Gives News on Future of Church," *The Living Church* (September 23, 1945), 7; "Pastor Martin Niemoeller: Spiritual Outlook in Germany Not Hopeless," *The Lutheran Herald* (July 7, 1945), 4–5; "Niemoeller Returns to Berlin Parish," *The Lutheran Standard* (November 17, 1945), 14; "Martin Niemoeller: God Does Not Fail," *The Messenger* (July 24, 1945), 13; "Karl Barth Backs Niemoeller's Leadership," *The Messenger* (November 13, 1945), 27; "Niemoeller Preaches Sermon in Dahlem Church," *The Messenger* (November 13, 1945), 27; "Niemoeller Says He Sought to Overthrow Hitler" and "Niemoeller Gives Views on Future of German Church," *The Presbyterian* (September 27, 1945), 18; "Niemoeller's First Postwar Sermon," *The Sunday School Times* (June 30, 1945), 501; *The Watchman-Examiner* (July 12, 1945), 667, (September 20, 1945), 907; "Niemoeller Indicts Church," *The Watchman-Examiner* (November 8, 1945), 1079.

27. Letter to the editor, "Niemoeller for German President," *The Christian Century* (May 23, 1945), 631; letter to the editor, "Don't Bring Niemoeller Here," *The Christian Century* (June 27, 1945), 761; G. B. Oxnam, "The Attack on Niemoeller," *The Christian Century* (August 29, 1945), 977–78; editorial, "Why Attack Niemoeller?" *The Christian Century* (September 12, 1945), 1031–32; letter to the editor, "The Attack on Niemoeller" (the answer to the editorial in a letter from Rex Stout, chairman of the Writer's War Board, defending their attack on Niemoeller), *The Christian Century* (November 21, 1945), 1290–91; "Dr. Barth Backs Dr. Niemoeller's Church Leadership," *The Living Church* (October 28, 1945), 9; "The Campaign against Niemoeller," *The Lutheran Witness* (September 11, 1945), 297; "Observations" (on Niemoeller), *The Sabbath Recorder* (July 1945), 70–71.

28. "German Church Joins World Council," *The Christian Century* (December 5, 1945), 1356–57; Samuel McCrea Cavert, "The New Birth of the German Church," *The Christian Century* (December 12, 1945), 1380–81; Henry Smith Leiper, "The German Church Since V-E Day," *The Living Church* (November 11, 1945), 12.

29. "Prominent Pastor Executed by Nazis in April," *The Living Church* (June 17, 1945), 7; "Prominent German Pastor Was Executed by Nazis," *The Messenger* (June 26, 1945), 26; "Germany: World Council to Study Relationships with Germany," *The Living Church* (August 5, 1945), 7–8 (on Bonhoeffer and the World Council of Churches.)

30. Henry Smith Leiper, "News of the World Council," *Advance* (November 1945), 12–13; "Europe's Churches Called Stronger," *The Baptist and Reflector* (July 5, 1945), 7; "An Evangelical Voice out of Germany," "Peter's Observatory," and "Evangelical Church of Germany," *The Bond* (July, September, and December 1945), 2; 5; 6; "News of the World Council," "Various Council Actions," and "Repentence and Humiliation," *Federal Council Bulletin* (September, October, and December 1945), 7–8; 11; 4–5; Henry Smith Leiper, "The Restoration of Ecumenical Fellowship with German Churches" and "Church in Europe and Germany," *Christendom* (Autumn 1945), 494–502, 544–45; "Germany," *The Christian Herald* (November 1945), 10; editorial, "German's Regeneration"; "Oxnam Returns from Europe," editorial, "Penitence in German Churches"; "German

Protestants Reorganize"; "Geneva," "German Church Joins World Council"; Samuel McCrea Cavert, "The New Birth of the German Church"; Robert Root, "Barth Returns to Germany," *The Christian Century* (June 13, August 1, September 26, October 31, December 5, December 12, December 19, 1945), 702–3, 712; 877; 1084–85; 1224; 1357–58; 1380–81; 1411–13; "Madness: To Reeducate Germany from the Outside" and "Germany: Visiting Europeans See Problems Realistically"; "Bishop Wurm: German Protestants Seek Church State Separation"; "Germany: Youth Church Groups Are Reviving but on Probation"; "Guilty: A German Pastor Urges Repentence for Germans," *The Churchman* (June 1, June 15, July 1, August, 1945), 15, 21–22; 16; 24–25; 17; "Impressive Actions of German Church," *Church Management* (December 1945), 55; "The Christian Front in the Land of the Reformation," *The Concordia Theological Monthly* (June 1945), 419; "Youth Movement of Evangelicals in Germany," *The King's Business* (November 1945), 417. (Citations of a similar nature can be found in *The Living Church, The Lutheran Companion, The Lutheran Herald, The Lutheran Standard, The Lutheran Witness, The Messenger, The Presbyterian*, and *The Watchman-Examiner*. Citations are to the World Council of Churches, denominational leaders, chaplains, news correspondents (especially from the Religious News Service), Martin Niemoeller, Karl Barth, Henry Smith Leiper, A. L. Warnshuis, Samuel McCrea Cavert, Stewart W. Herman, and W. A. Visser't Hooft, as well as to leading German churchmen, such as Bishop Wurm, Bishop Dibelius, and Bishop Meiser.)

31. The actual figure is difficult to establish because some articles combine discussions of the reconstruction and rehabilitation of the German churches with information about relief aid and conditions in Europe. From the thirty-nine periodicals examined for 1945, a list by author, title, date, and page was made of those articles on the Church Struggle, primarily. Twenty-nine periodicals yielded 224 articles, including those on Niemoeller, or an average of 7.7 articles per periodical. Of the twenty-nine, *The Christian Century, The Churchman, The Living Church*, the Lutheran periodicals, *The Messenger, The Presbyterian*, and *The Watchman-Examiner* contained the greatest number. A total of 193 articles, or approximately 86 percent, of the articles were in six Lutheran periodicals and the six Protestant periodicals named above.

32. Hertzel Fishman, *American Protestantism and a Jewish State*, Detroit, Wayne State University Press, 1973.

33. Simon Wiesenthal, himself a survivor, was in and out of the displaced-person camps, some 200 of them in Germany and Austria, as he began his career as a "Nazi hunter." See Joseph Wechsberg, editor, *The Murderers among Us: The Simon Wiesenthal Memoirs*, New York, McGraw-Hill Book Company, 1967, 12. (See also the editorial, "Truman Orders Help for Displaced Persons," *The Christian Century* [October 10, 1945], 1148, in which the estimated number of displaced persons in the American zone are given—70,000 "unclassified" and 20,000 "stateless." Of the 90,000 included in the estimate, most were Jews. The editorial went on to quote Earl G. Harrison, President Truman's investigator, in his statement that it looked as though the Americans were treating the Jews as the Nazis had by keeping them in camps under guard, with the only difference being that they were no longer being exterminated, and in effect condoning the Nazi policies toward Jews.)

34. Henri Michel, *The Second World War* (American ed.), New York, Praeger Publishers, 1975, p. 558.

35. See Louis S. Snyder, *The War: A Concise History, 1939–1945*, New York, Simon and Schuster, 1960, pp. 419–20, and Michel, pp. 583–86, for concise descriptions of the Polish, or Warsaw, uprising. Michael Zylberberg, *A Warsaw Diary, 1939–1945*, London, Vallentine-Mitchell, 1969, pp. 153–92. told the story of the uprising as a participant and as a Jew who survived in and around Warsaw from 1939 to 1945.

36. Eugen Kogon, *The Theory and Practice of Hell: The German Concentration Camps and the System Behind Them*, New York, Berkley Medallion Books, 1958 (see particularly, "The End of the Camps," pp. 271–84); Martin Broszat, "The Concentration Camps, 1933–1945," in Helmut Krausnick, Hans Buchheim, Martin Broszat, and Hans-Adolf

Jacobsen, *Anatomy of the SS State*, New York, Walker and Company, 1965, pp. 397–504; and Wechsberg (see particularly, "A Profile of Simon Wiesenthal [Continued]" and "Simon Wiesenthal's Narrative," pp. 23–58.)
37. Kogon, pp. 273–74.
38. Broszat, p. 504.
39. Wechsberg, pp. 37–44.
40. "Dora Zaidenweber on How It Was," *Minneapolis Tribune, Picture Magazine* (Sunday, April 23, 1978), 10–28.
41. For general background on the progress of the war itself in late 1944 and in 1945, two primary sources were used, Snyder and Michel. (There are several other excellent histories of World War II, any one of which may be referred to.)
42. Editorial, "Have Jews a Citizenship?" *The Christian Century* (January 3, 1945), 4–5.
43. Cecil Northcott, "The Treatment of Germany," *The Christian Century* (February 14, 1945), 204–5.
44. "Jews Open Drive for Student Foundation," *The Christian Century* (February 21, 1945), 251.
45. "Aid Goes from Sweden to Interned Jews," *The Christian Century* (March 21, 1945), 377.
46. Editorial, "Warning from an Anti-Nazi," *The Christian Century* (April 18, 1945), 485.
47. "Catholic Clergy in Germany Are Persecuted," *The Christian Century* (April 18, 1945), 498.
48. Editorial, "Slamming the Door," *The Christian Century* (April 25, 1945), 513–15.
49. Ibid., 514.
50. "Regent," *The Christian Herald* (March 1945), 10. (A picture of Archbishop Damaskinos accompanied the article.)
51. George Kent, "Shepherds of the Underground," *The Christian Herald* (April 1945), 21–22, 65–66.
52. Stewart Herman, as told to Spencer Duryea, "Flaming Spirit," *The Christian Herald* (May 1945), 16–17, 66–67.
53. *The Churchman* (January 15, 1945), 29–30.
54. "Dangerous: French Clergyman Ran Refugee Organization," *The Churchman* (March 1, 1945), 22–23.
55. "Tribute: Dutch Are Praised for Opposing Anti-Semitism," *The Churchman* (April 15, 1945), 24.
56. *The Evangelical Visitor* (April 9, 1945), 114.
57. *The Gospel Messenger* (April 14, 1945), 2.
58. "Doors Closed," *The Friend of Zion* (February, 1945), 10, 15.
59. "Report and Greetings from the Rev. Jacob Bernheim," *The Hebrew Christian Alliance Quarterly* (Winter 1945), 18–19.
60. John Stuart Conning, "Israel! What of Tomorrow?" *The Hebrew Christian Alliance Quarterly* (Winter 1945), 28–30.
61. *The Hebrew Christian Alliance Quarterly* (Spring 1945), 24–26.
62. Ibid., 26.
63. "Report from Hungary," *The Presbyterian Register* (April 1945), 286.
64. Advertisement, *The King's Business* (February 1945), 41.
65. Advertisement, *The Sunday School Times* (January 20, 1945), 58.
66. Advertisement, *The Sunday School Times* (February 17, 1945), 124.
67. Advertisement, *The Sunday School Times* (March 17, 1945), 201.
68. Advertisement, *The Sunday School Times*, (March 31, 1945), 244.
69. Advertisement, *The Sunday School Times* (April 14, 1945), 284.
70. Advertisement, *The Sunday School Times* (September 1, 1945), 678.
71. Advertisement, *The Sunday School Times* (November 10, 1945), 897.
72. The eight periodicals containing items on the Nazi persecution of the Jews in

January through April of 1945 were *The Christian Century, The Christian Herald, The Churchman, The Evangelical Visitor, The Gospel Messenger, The Friend of Zion, The Hebrew Christian Alliance Quarterly,* and *The Presbyterian Register.* Two published paid advertisements, *The King's Business* and *The Sunday School Times.*

73. A reconstruction of the chronology of the evacuation and liberation of the forced labor camps, concentration camps, and death camps requires the use of several sources. No single such chronology seems to be available in standard histories of World War II or the standard works on the Nazi persecution of the Jews and on the Holocaust. Sources for chronology: Gerald Reitlinger, *The Final Solution: The Attempt to Exterminate the Jews of Europe, 1939–1945,* New York, Thomas Yoseloff, 1968, (2nd rev. ed.); Michel; Kogon; Helmut Krausnick, Hans Buchheim, Martin Groszat, and Hans-Adolf Jacobsen, *Anatomy of the SS State,* New York, Walker and Company, 1965; Raul Hilberg, *The Destruction of the European Jews,* Chicago, Quadrangle Books, 1961; Lucy S. Dawidowicz, *The War against the Jews, 1933–1945,* New York, Holt Rinehart and Winston, 1975; Nora Levin, *The Holocaust: The Destruction of European Jewry, 1933–1945,* New York, Thomas Y. Crowell Company, 1968.

74. Michel, map 13, p. 263.

75. Editorial, "Bringing Infamy Home to the Germans," *The Christian Century* (May 2, 1945), 541–42.

76. Editorial, "Gazing into the Pit," *The Christian Century* (May 9, 1945), 575–76.

77. Editorial, "Hell Hath Enlarged Herself," *The Churchman* (May 15, 1945), 4.

78. Editorial, "Think on This," *The Churchman* (May 15, 1945), 4.

79. Editorial, "The Shape of Buchenwald," *The Churchman* (May 15, 1945), 13.

80. Editorial, "England: Sees Lack of Moral Passion Helping Growth of Barbarism," *The Living Church* (May 20, 1945), 10.

81. Editorial, "Hope from Horror," *The Messenger* (May 15, 1945), 6–7.

82. The editor's remarks and "Gazing into the Pit," *The Messenger* (May 29, 1945), 4–5. ("Tottering on the Brink," *The Signs of the Times* [June 26, 1945], 2–3, was a virtual reprint of Morrison's editorial, with only a brief closing paragraph of agreement added.)

83. Editorial, "Judgment," *The Presbyterian Register* (August 1945), 312.

84. Editorial, "Let Us Maintain Our Honor," *The Sabbath Recorder* (May 7, 1945), 338.

85. Editorial, "So It Was True!" *The Signs of the Times* (May 22, 1945), 3.

86. Editorial, "Atrocities," *Advance* (March 1945), 2.

87. Editorial, "Atrocities That Weren't" *Advance* (October 1945), 23.

88. Gerhard E. Lenski, "A Word about Atrocities," *The Lutheran Standard* (June 2, 1945), 3.

89. Gerhard E. Lenski, "Atrocity Pictures," *The Lutheran Standard* (August 4, 1945), 3.

90. Editorial, "Theological Observer," *The Concordia Theological Monthly* (July 1945), 489–90.

91. Editorial, *The Mennonite* (June 3, 1945), 3.

92. James Morgan Read (Ph.D.) from *Who's Who in American College and University Administration,* New York, Crowell Collier Educational Corporation, 1970. (The last major position held by Read was that of president of Wilmington College, Wilmington, Delaware.)

93. James Morgan Read, *Atrocity Propaganda, 1914–1919,* New Haven, Yale University Press, 1941.

94. James Morgan Read, "Trials for War Criminals," *The Christian Century* (May 30, 1945), 651–53.

95. Editorial, "Reconciliation," *The Messenger* (June 26, 1945), 7.

96. "An Editor Speaks," *The Churchman* (August 1945), 5–6. (William C. Kernan, "No Moral Law: An Editor Warns America," *The Signs of the Times* [October 30, 1945], 3, was an only slightly revised republication of the editorial in *The Churchman.*)

97. Orlando J. Woodward, "From a Soldier in Europe on V-E Day," *The Gospel Messenger* (August 18, 1945), 11.

98. F. W. Van Houten, "Letter from Germany," *The Calvin Forum* (August-September 1945), 24–25.

99. Thomas P. Bailey, "Scenes Indescribable," *The Alliance Weekly* (June 16, 1945), 184.

100. George B. Wood, "German Concentration Camps," *The Living Church* (June 3, 1945), 3.

101. "Armed Forces: Chaplain Wood Officiates at Concentration Camp Burial," *The Living Church* (June 10, 1945), 9.

102. Donald G. Davis, "What I Saw at Buchenwald," *The Baptist Herald* (November 11, 1945), 6, 16.

103. See chapter 2. (The German Baptists took the name the North American Baptist Conference after World War II and moved their seminary from Rochester, New York, to Sioux Falls, South Dakota.)

104. Donald G. Davis, "What I Saw at Buchenwald," *The Baptist Herald* (November 11, 1945), 16.

105. Frank Woyke, "Helping Our Brethren in Need," *The Baptist Herald* (November 1, 1945), 4.

106. G. Bromley Oxnam, "Niemoeller Today," *The Christian Century* (June 13, 1945), 705–6.

107. Martin Niemoeller, "The Spiritual Outlook in Germany," *The Living Church* (June 24, 1945), 9. (Also published as Martin Niemoeller, "Spiritual Outlook in Germany Not Hopeless," *The Lutheran Standard* [July 7, 1945], 4–5, and Martin Niemoeller, "God Does Not Fail: Martin Niemoeller Sees the Foundations Gone but His Christian Faith Will Not Allow Him to Despair," *The Messenger* [July 24, 1945], 11–13. The Religious News Service had prepared the article for release.)

108. Editorial, "Murdering the Conscience," *The Lutheran Standard* (June 23, 1945). 9.

109. P. O. Bursell, "What Shall We Do with Germany," *The Lutheran Standard* (June 30, 1945), 4–5. (See also *The Bond* [June 1945], 2, 5.)

110. Martin Niemoeller, "The Spiritual Outlook in Germany," *The Living Church* (June 24, 1945), 9.

111. David L. Ostergren, "An Intimate View of Martin Niemoeller," *The Lutheran Standard* (September 15, 1945), 7.

112. David L. Ostergren, "Germany's Hero Pastor, Martin Niemoeller," *The Lutheran Companion* (September 26, 1945), 7–8.

113. Willis W. Willard, Jr., "Guilt for Atrocities," letter to the editor, *The Christian Century* (May 16, 1945), 606–7.

114. Woodrow W. Kern, "Saving Remnant," Letter to the editor, *The Christian Century* (May 16, 1945), 607.

115. Homer L. Rickel, "Missing the Main Point," letter to the editor, *The Christian Century* (May 16, 1945), 607.

116. Millard J. Gordanier, "Expanding the Lesson" and Eloise Hollett Davison, "Do We Fear to Speak?" letters to the editor, *The Christian Century* (May 30, 1945), 655.

117. William W. Fowler, "Two Answers," Letter to the editor, *The Churchman* (June 1, 1945), 2.

118. Joseph A. Leighton, "Hitler and the Germans," letter to the editor, *The Churchman* (June 1, 1945), 3.

119. David D. and Helen E. Baker, "The Unfinished Experiment in Freedom," *The Messenger* (September 4, 1945), 16–20.

120. Fredi Baum, "I Didn't Want to Believe It," *The Messenger* (October 2, 1945), 11–13.

121. Edward L. R. Elson, "The Clerical Colony at Dachau," *The Christian Century* (August 22, 1945), 956–58.

122. Published by the Jewish Black Book Committee as *The Black Book: The Nazi Crime against the Jewish People*, New York, Duell, Sloan and Pearce, 1946.

123. Vassilli Grossman, "Report from Treblinka," *The Churchman* (October 1, 1945), 10–11.

124. Editorial, "Atrocities," *Advance* (March 1945), 2.

125. Editorial, "Buchenwald," *The Presbyterian* (April 26, 1945), 4.

126. Editorial, "Disregard for Human Life," *The Watchman-Examiner* (November 8, 1945), 1080.

127. *The King's Business* (July 1945), 254.

128. "The Jewish Problem," *The Watchman-Examiner* (October 25, 1945), 1032–33.

129. Advertisement, *Moody Monthly* (June 1945), 602.

130. Advertisement, *The King's Business* (February 1945), 41.

131. Advertisement, *The King's Business* (October 1945), 393.

132. Advertisement, *The King's Business* (December 1945), 484.

133. Advertisements in *The Sunday School Times* (January 20, February 17, March 17, March 31, April 14, September 1, October 6, November 10, November 17, December 8, December 29, 1945), 58, 124, 201, 244, 678, 783, 887, 897, 920, 997, 1069. (The sponsoring agencies were the International Hebrew Christian Alliance, the Friends of Israel Missionary and Relief Society, and the Bethel Mission of Eastern Europe.)

134. Editorial, "Gazing into The Pit," *The Christian Century* (May 9, 1945), 575–76.

135. Editorial, "So It Was True!" *The Signs of the Times* (May 22, 1945), 3–4.

Chapter 7

1. See John Toland, *Adolf Hitler*, New York, Ballantine Books, 1976, pp. 289 and 300, for the dates and the circumstances of the first German publication of *Main Kampf*.

2. For examples of journals with regularly published sections of letters to the editor, see *The Christian Century* ("Correspondence"), *The Churchman* ("The Open Forum"), *The Friend* ("Correspondence").

3. "Notes from Our Chaplains" in *The Alliance Weekly* was an example of a special section set up for the publication of news from military personnel (in this instance, chaplains).

4. See "News of the Christian World," *The Christian Century*; "The World Church," *Advance*; "This Week's Comments," *The Alliance Weekly*; "News Digest of the Month," *The Christian Herald*; "People, Opinion, Events," *The Churchman*; "The Bible in the News," *The King's Business*; "Here and There on the Christian Front," *The Lutheran Herald*; "News of the Religious World," *The Messenger*, "Editorial Notes," *Moody Monthly*; "As I See It," *The Presbyterian Banner*; "The Commentator," *The Presbyterian*; "The Flight of Time: A Survey of World Events," *The Signs of the Times*; "A Survey of Religious Life and Thought," *The Sunday School Times*; and "Men and Things," *The Watchman-Examiner*. As the Religious News Service began to supply more and more information to the religious press, occasionally attribution would be included on these pages to the RNS.

5. The role of the SS police as special police units responsible only to Hitler and Himmler by secret order (August 17, 1938) was discussed in a summary in Hans Dietrich Bracher, *The German Dictatorship*, New York, Praeger Publishers, 1970, pp. 409–31, and more fully in Hans Buchheim, "The SS—Instrument of Domination," In Helmut Krausnick, Hans Buchheim, Martin Broszat, and Hans-Adolf Jacobsen, *Anatomy of the SS State*, New York, Walker and Company, 1965, pp. 127–371, and Gerald Reitlinger, *The SS: Alibi of a Nation, 1922–1945*, London, William Heinemann, 1956.

6. The role of secrecy in the Nazi policy of extermination of all groups, including Jews, was discussed fully in Bracher, pp. 420–31.

7. Raul Hilberg, *The Destruction of the European Jews*, Chicago, Quadrangle Books, 1961, pp. 32, 134–37.

8. Ibid., p. 266.

9. Quoted in Helmut Krausnick, "The Persecution of the Jews" and in Hans Buchheim, "Command and Compliance," in Krausnick, et al., pp. 123 and 359.

10. Buchheim, "Command and Compliance," p. 359.

11. Bracher, pp. 420–21.

12. Editorial, "How Hell was Enlarged," *The Churchman* (May 15, 1945), 4.

13. Bruno Bettelheim and Morris Janowitz, *Social Change and Prejudice, Including the Dynamics of Prejudice*, Glencoe, Illinois, the Free Press of Glencoe, 1964; pp. 130–35 and *passim*.

14. For example, "A Protest by Chicago Church Federation," *The Hebrew Christian Alliance Quarterly* (June 1933), 40.

15. See Henry Feingold, *The Politics of Rescue*, New Brunswick, New Jersey, Rutgers University Press, 1973, *passim*.

16. See chapter 1, pp. 9-14.

17. See chapter 3, pp. 84-89.

18. The career of James G. McDonald in relation to his efforts to aid refugees from Germany and from the Nazi persecution was told briefly in Arthur D. Morse, *While Six Million Died: A Chronicle of American Apathy*, New York, Random House, 1968, *passim*; specific reference to the letter of resignation and its reception and to the subsequent actions of the League of Nations can be found in Morse, pp. 187–98.

19. See chapter 2, pp. 65-67.

20. See chapter 3, pp. 102-3.

21. See chapter 2, pp. 69-70, and *The Moody Bible Institute Monthly* (February 1934).

22. Editorial, "Suffering of the Jews," *The Watchman-Examiner* (December 28, 1939), 1392.

23. Elias Newman, "A Piteous Cry for Help," *The Friend of Zion* (March 1940), 17–18.

24. Yevgeny Yevtushenko, "Babi Yar," quoted in Nora Levin, *The Holocaust: The Destruction of European Jewry, 1933–1945*, New York, Thomas Y. Crowell Company, 1968, pp. 255–56. The poem was quoted in the context of a discussion of Babi Yar as an example of the killing operation carried out by Einsatzgruppen C and D in the Soviet Ukraine and in eastern Galicia.)

25. Editorial, "Horror Stories from Poland," *The Christian Century* (December 9, 1942), 1518–19.

26. William C. Kernan, "Beware of These Hitler Weapons: The Method Is First Hate Then Murder," *The Churchman* (October 1, 1942), 7.

27. Editorial, "Polish Atrocities Are Entered in the Books," *The Christian Century* (December 30, 1942), 1611.

28. "Persecution of the Jews: A Letter from the President of the Baptist World Alliance," *The Watchman-Examiner* (December 24, 1942), 1261.

29. Lucy S. Dawidowicz, *The Jewish Presence*, New York, Holt, Rinehart and Winston, 1977, p. 291.

30. "Six Thousand Jews Executed Daily in Poland," *Advance* (April 1, 1943), 158.

31. For a discussion of the debate over the use of Zyklon B and carbon monoxide in the gas chambers, see Gerald Reitlinger, *The Final Solution: The Attempt to Exterminate the Jews of Europe, 1939–1945*, 2nd rev. ed., New York, Thomas Yoseloff, 1968, pp. 154–64.

32. Editorial, "Israel's 'Day of Grief and Desperate Sorrow,'" *The Brethren Missionary Herald* (July 24, 1943), 451.

33. "Nazis Suffocate Jews in Groups of 500," *The Brethren Missionary Herald* (September 25, 1943), 605.

34. Ernest R. Sandeen called the Scofield Reference Bible "the most influential single publication in millenarian and Fundamentalist historiography"; see Ernest R. Sandeen, *The Roots of Fundamentalism: British and American Millenarianism, 1800–1930*, Chicago, the University of Chicago Press, 1970. See also Clarence Bass, *Backgrounds of Dispensationalism*, Grand Rapids, Michigan, William B. Eerdmans Company, 1960; C. Norman Draus, *Dispensationalism in America: Its Rise and Development*, Richmond, Virginia, John Knox Press, 1958; William C. McLoughlin, *Modern Revivalism: Charles Grandison Finney to Billy Graham*, New York, Ronald Press, 1958.

35. See chapter 4 notes 73–80 for references to the editorials and articles on Majdanek.

36. Editorial, "Gazing into the Pit," *The Christian Century* (May 9, 1945), 575–76.

37. Editorial, "So It Was True!" *The Signs of the Times* (May 22, 1945), 3.

38. F. W. Van Houten, "Letter from Germany," *The Calvin Forum* (August–September 1945), 24–25.

39. Donald G. Davis, "What I Saw at Buchenwald," *The Baptist Herald* (November 11, 1945), 6, 16.

40. Placed by the American Board of Missions to the Jews, the advertisement appeared on the inside back cover page of *The Moody Bible Institute Monthly* (February 1934).

41. A total of seventy-seven paid advertisements were noted in the text and cited in the notes, with the publication, date, and page. There were more paid advertisements in the American Protestant religious periodicals examined from 1934 through 1945, but often they were the same advertisement published in more than one periodical, so only a primary reference was made to these. For 1943, 1944, and 1945, all paid advertisements were cited.

42. "A Challenge to Christendom," *Federal Council Bulletin* (February 1934), 5.

Chapter 8

1. The editor, "Hitler Plans to Destroy European Jews," *The Hebrew Christian Alliance Quarterly* (Winter 1943), 25–26. A delegation of Jewish leaders visited President Roosevelt on December 8, 1942. The statement left with President Roosevelt was later published by the American Jewish Committee as *Hitler's Black Record: The Documented Story of Nazi Atrocities against the Jews*, New York, American Jewish Committee, 1943.

2. The editor, "Hitler Plans to Destroy European Jewry," *The Hebrew Christian Alliance Quarterly* (Winter 1943), 26.

3. R. Paul Miller, ed., "The Greatest War Casualties," *The Brethren Missionary Herald* (November 20, 1943), 712.

4. 16 million divided by 6 million equals 26.666 percent.

5. *The Churchman* (August 1945), 56.

6. Elie Wiesel, "Solitude and Madness," an address given at the Annual Bernhard E. Olson Scholars' Conference on the Church Struggle and the Holocaust, March 5, 1975, New York City.

7. Rufus M. Jones, "The Visit to Germany," *The Friend* (January 12, 1939), 256; "Rufus Jones Back from Germany: Reports Tentative Plans for Refugee," *The Christian Century* (January 18, 1939), 99.

8. J. Hoffman Cohn, "The Jews of Europe," *The Brethren Evangelist* (March 25, 1939), 14–15. (The conference was held July 6–15, 1938, at the Hotel Royal, Evian-les-Bains, France.)

9. George M. Kren and Leon Rappaport, "Victims: The Fallacy of Innocence," *Societas* (Spring 1974), 111–29.

10. "England: Sees Lack of Moral Passion Helping Growth of Barbarism," *The Living Church* (May 20, 1945), 10.

11. The "Jewish sufferings of the past few years" of prophetic interpretation of the death camps and their meaning were from "The Jewish Problem," *The Watchman-Examiner* (October 25, 1945), 1032–33.

12. Luke 10:29–37, for the parable of the Good Samaritan.

13. Editorial, "So It Was True!" *The Signs of the Times* (May 22, 1945), 3; editorial, "Gazing into the Pit," *The Christian Century* (May 9, 1945), 575–76.

14. "Think on This," *The Churchman* (May 15, 1945), 4.

15. Victor Buksbazen, "Happenings in Israel," *The Hebrew Christian Alliance Quarterly* (Spring 1945), 24–26.

16. Horace J. Fuller, "The Atomic Bomb and the Church," *Advance* (October 1945), 29–30.

17. Editorial, "Atomic Bomb Shocks World," *The Brethren Missionary Herald* (September 29, 1945), 606.

18. Editorial, "Atomic Bomb Loosed against Japan," *The Christian Century* (August 15, 1945), 923.

19. Editorials, "On the Brink of Peace," "The World Left by the War," "Man and the Atom," and "The Church's Responsibility," *The Christian Century* (August 22, 1945), 947–53.

20. Editorial, "America's Atomic Atrocity," *The Christian Century* (August 29, 1945), 974–76.

21. Letters to the editor, "On the Atomic Bomb," *The Christian Century* (August 29, 1945), 982–84.

22. Letter to the editor by Fred Eastman, *The Christian Century* (August 29, 1945), 983.

23. "Leaders Protest Atomic Bombs," *The Christian Century* (August 29, 1945), 985.

24. *The Christian Century* (August 29, 1945), 985.

25. Editorials, "New Wine for New Bottles" and "Atom Bomb: Reflections of Religious Leaders Here and Abroad"; "Security: Human Brotherhood Must Control the Atomic Bomb"; Joseph A. Leighton, "Doom or Dawn: The World's Obsolete Nationalism," *The Churchman* (September 1, September 15, October 15, 1945), 4–5; 16–17; 18–19; 9.

26. "The Atomic Bomb and the Cessation of Hostilities," *The Concordia Theological Monthly* (October 1945), 703.

27. George W. Phillips, "At the Portals of Tomorrow," *Current Religious Thought* (December 1945), 1–6.

28. Editorial; Richard M. Fagley, "The Atomic Bomb and the Crisis of Man"; and letters to the editor, *The Friend* (September 13, 1945), 82; 90–92; 108–9.

29. Editorial, "Our Tragic Victory," *The Lutheran Companion* (September 26, 1945), 8.

30. Richard M. Fagley, "The Atomic Bomb and the Crisis of Man," *The Lutheran Standard* (September 29, 1945), 4–5.

31. Editorial, "Remorse in Victory," *The Messenger* (September 18, 1945), 4.

32. Editorials, *Moody Monthly* (October 1945), 57.

33. Marshall Wingfield, "The Atomic Bomb and Its Implications," *The Pulpit* (October 1945), 227–29.

34. William B. Ziff, "Palestine in the Present Crisis," *The Voice of Christian America: Proceedings of the National Conference on Palestine*, Washington, D.C., March 9, 1944, 13–14.

35. Alfred Kazin, "In Every Voice, In Every Ban," *New Republic* (January 10, 1944), 44–46.

36. Robert A. Ashworth, letter to the editor, *The Reformed Church Messenger* (September 21, 1933), 13–14. (The Belloc article quoted by Ashworth was published in part in *The Voice of Religion: The Views of Christian Religious Leaders on the Persecution of the Jews in Germany by the National Socialists*. New York, the American Jewish Committee, 1933, p. 7, and was taken from Hilaire Belloc, "The Persecution of the Jews," *America* [July 22, 1933], 367–69.)

BIBLIOGRAPHY

Bibliography

ARTICLES

Alexander, Edward, "Imagining the Holocaust: Mr. Sammler's Planet, and Others," *Judaism* (Summer 1973), 288–300.

Braatz, Werner E., "The *Völkish* Ideology and Anti-Semitism in Germany," *YIVO Annual of Jewish Social Science*, volume XV, pp. 166–87. New York, YIVO Institute for Jewish Research, 1974.

Braham, Randolph L., "The Holocaust in Hungary: An Historical Interpretation of the Role of the Hungarian Radical Right," *Societas* (Summer 1972), 195–220.

Cain, Seymour, "The Question and the Answer after Auschwitz," *Judaism* (Summer 1971), 263–78.

Clifford, Clark M., "Recognizing Israel: The Behind-the-Scenes Struggle in 1948 between the President and State Department," *American Heritage* (April 1977), 4–11.

Cohen, Israel, "The Doom of European Jewry," *The Contemporary Review* (February 1943), 5.

Eckardt, A. Roy, "The Question Still Remains" (book review essay on Carlo Falconi's *The Silence of Pius XII*), *Judaism* (Winter 1971), 502–5.

Eckardt, Roy and Alice L., "Again, Silence in Churches," *The Christian Century* (July 26, August 2, 1967), 73–77, 78–82.

Eckardt, Alice and Roy, "How German Thinkers View the Holocaust," *Christian Century* (March 17, 1976), 249–52.

Edelsheim-Muehsam, Margaret, "Reactions of the Jewish Press to the Nazi Challenge," *Year Book V*, 1960, pp. 308–29. Leo Baeck Institute Year Book, New York, East and West Library, 1960.

Elias, Joseph, "Dealing with 'Churban Europa,'" *The Jewish Observer* (October 1977), 10–18.

Fackenheim, Emil L., Richard H. Poplin, George Steiner, and Elie Wiesel, "Jewish Values in the Post-Holocaust Future," *Judaism* (Summer 1967), 266–99.

Fackenheim, Emil, "On the Self-exposure of Faith to the Modern Secular World: Philosophical Reflections in the Light of Jewish Experience," *Daedulus* (Winter 1967), 216n.

Fackenheim, Emil L., "The People Israel Lives," in Frank Ephraim Talmage, editor, *Disputation and Dialogue: Readings in Jewish-Christian Encounter*, pp. 296–308. New York. KTAV Publishing House, Anti-Defamation League of B'nai B'rith, 1975.

Bibliographical note: References to the items used from American Protestant periodicals appear only in the notes.

Fleishner, Eva, "The Crucifixion of the Jews" (book review essay on Franklin H. Littell's *The Crucifixion of the Jews*), *Cross Currents* (Spring 1975), 101–3; also in *CCI Notebook* (March 1976), 5–6.

Garber, Frederick, "The Art of Elie Wiesel," *Judaism* (Summer 1973), 301–8.

Garvie, A. E., "The Jewish Problem," in *The International Review of Missions* (April 1941), 216–24.

Gordis, Robert, "A Cruel God or None—Is There No Other Choice?" *Judaism* (Fall 1972), 277–84.

Gottlieb, Moshe, "Boycott, Rescue and Ransom: The Threefold Dilemma of American Jewry in 1938–1939," *YIVO Annual of Jewish Social Science*, volume XV, pp. 235–79. New York, YIVO Institute for Jewish Research, 1974.

Greenberg, Irving, "Judaism and Christianity after the Holocaust," *Journal of Ecumenical Studies* (Fall 1975), 521–51.

Halperin, Irving, "On Stepping into the 'Fiery Gates,'" *Judaism* (Fall 1972), 405–8.

"The Holocaust: Auschwitz . . . Buchenwald . . . Dachau, Why It Happened—What It Means Today," *DISCOVER: The Sunday Bulletin* (July 17, 1977), 6–17.

"The Holocaust" in Leo W. Schwarz, editor, *The Jewish Caravan: Great Stories of Twenty-five Centuries*, pp. 689–733. New York, Holt, Rinehart and Winston, 1963.

"The Holocaust through Christian Eyes," *Judaism* (Spring 1976), 131.

Hutner, Yitzchok, "Holocaust," *The Jewish Observer* (October 1977), 3–9. (Prepared in English translation by Rabbis Chaim Feurman and Yaakov Feitman.)

Kaleska, Nina, "Nobody Who Wasn't There Can Ever Understand," *Friday Forum, A Supplement to the Jewish Exponent* (October 26, 1973), 1–4.

Kazin, Alfred, "In Every Voice, In Every Ban," *New Republic* (January 10, 1944), 44–46.

Kirman, Joseph M., "A Note on Friedrich Paulsen," in *YIVO Annual of Jewish Social Science*, volume XV, pp. 367–72. New York: YIVO Institute for Jewish Research, 1974.

Korman, Gerd, "The Holocaust in American Historical Writing," *Societas* (Summer 1974), 251–70.

Korman, Gerd, "Warsaw Plus Thirty: Some Perceptions in the Sources and Written History of the Ghetto Uprising," in *YIVO Annual of Jewish Social Science*, volume XV, pp. 280–96. New York, YIVO Institute for Jewish Research, 1974.

Kren, George M., and Leon Rappaport, "Victims: The Fallacy of Innocence," *Societas* (Spring 1974), 111–29.

Lapide, Pinchas, "Christians and Jews—A New Protestant Beginning," *Journal of Ecumenical Studies* (Fall 1975), 485–92.

Lazin, Frederick A., "Put Not Your Faith in Princes," (book review essay of Henry Feingold's *The Politics of Rescue*), *Judaism* (Winter 1977), 505–7.

Levine, Herbert S., "Comments," *Societas* (Summer 1974), 271–77.

Lewy, Guenther, and John M. Snoek, "The Holocaust and the Christians Churches: Roman Catholics, Protestant, Eastern Orthodox," *Encyclopedia Judaica*, volume 8, pp. 910–16. New York, Macmillan Company, 1971.

Lincoln, Timothy Dwight, "Two Philosophies of Jewish History after the Holocaust," *Judaism* (Spring 1976), 150–57.

Littell, Franklin H., "Christians and Jews in the Historical Process," *Judaism* (Summer 1973), 263–77.

Littell, Franklin H., "Ethics after Auschwitz," *Worldview* (September 1975), 22–26.

Littell, Franklin H., "The German Church Struggle and the Plight of the Jews," a paper prepared for the World Congress of Jewish Studies, Jerusalem, August 8–12, 1977. Philadelphia, Department of Instructional Materials, Philadelphia Board of Education, 1977.

Littell, Franklin H., *Holocaust Studies Newsletter* (n.d.), 1:4.

Littell, Franklin H., "Uprooting Antisemitism: A Call to Christians," *Journal of Church and State* (Winter 1975), 15–24.

Litvak, Joseph, "Holocaust, Rescue From," *Encyclopedia Judaica*, volume 8, pp. 905–10. New York, Macmillan Company, 1971.

Luckens, Michael J., "Reaction to a Meeting with Elie Wiesel, *Judaism* (Summer 1971), 365–68.

Luther, Martin, "On the Jews and Their Lies," *Luther's Works*, volume 47, pp. 121–306. American Edition/The Christian and Society.

Mager, John G., "Nazis, Jews, and the War: What the Lutheran Witness Said, 1934–1935," *American Lutheran* (November 1964), 10–12.

Mashberg, Michael, "American Diplomacy and the Jewish Refugee, 1938–1939," in *YIVO Annual of Jewish Social Science*, volume XV, pp. 339–65. New York, YIVO Institute for Jewish Research, 1974.

Meier, Peg, "30 Years Later, Memories of War Remain," *Minneapolis Tribune* (August 31, 1975), 1E, 4E.

Morgenthau, Henry, Jr., "The Morgenthau Diaries: The Refugee Run-Around," *Collier's* (November 1, 1947), 22–23, 62, 65.

Parker, Frank S., "A Visit to Majdanek," *Judaism* (Spring 1976), 158–66.

Robinson, Jacob, "Holocaust," *Encyclopedia Judaica*, volume 8, pp. 828–905. New York, Macmillan Company, 1971.

Rosenbloom, Noah H., "The Threnodist of the Holocaust," *Judaism*, (Spring 1977), 232–47.

Rosenfeld, Alvin H., "On Holocaust and History," *SHOAH: A Review of Holocaust Studies and Commemorations* (Summer 1978), 19.

Sandmel, Samuel, "A Passionate Statement" (book review essay of Franklin H. Littell's *The Crucifixion of the Jews*), *Judaism* (Spring 1976), 123–25.

Steckel, Charles W., "God and the Holocaust," *Judaism* (Summer 1971), 279–85.

Steiner, George, "Jewish Values in the Post-Holocaust Future," *Judaism* (Summer 1967), 266–99.

Tiefel, Hans O., "Holocaust Interpretations and Religious Assumptions," *Judaism* (Spring 1976), 135–49.

Trunk, Isaiah, "The Jewish Councils in Eastern Europe under Nazi Rule (An Attempt at a Synthesis)," *Societas* (Summer 1972), 221–39.

Unsdorfer, Simcha Bunem, "Thumb Prints," *The Jewish Observer* (October 1977), 19–20.

Voss, Carl Herman, "Holocaust Conference in Hamburg," *Journal of Ecumenical Studies* (Fall 1975), 634–38.

Warnshuis, A. Livingston, "The Voice of the Martyrs," *Collier's* (April 7, 1945), 16, 65.

Willis, Robert E., "Auschwitz and the Nurturing of Conscience," *Religion and Life* (Winter 1975), 432–47.

Willis, Robert E., "Christian Theology after Auschwitz," *Journal of Ecumenical Studies* (Fall 1975), 493–519.

Wolf, Arnold Jacob, "Jewish Theology after the Death Camps," (a book review essay of Richard L. Rubenstein's *After Auschwitz*), *Judaism* (Spring 1967), 233–36.

Wyschogrod, Michael, "Faith and the Holocaust," *Judaism* (Summer 1977), 286–94.

Zaidenweber, Dora, "How It Was," *Minneapolis Tribune, Picture Magazine* (Sunday, April 23, 1975), 10–28.

BOOKS

Abel, Ernest L., *The Roots of Anti-Semitism*. London, Associated University Presses, 1975.

The American Jewish Year Book, 5704, volume 45, Harry Schneiderman, editor, for the American Jewish Committee. New York, the Jewish Publication Society, 1944.

Annual Reports of the Federal Council of Churches of Christ in America. New York, Federal Council of Churches of Christ in America, 1933 through 1946.

Asch, Sholem, *One Destiny: An Epistle to the Christians*. New York, G. P. Putnam's Sons, 1945.

Barth, Karl, *Trouble and Promise in the Struggle of the German Church*. Oxford University Press, American Section of the Universal Christian Council.

Bass, Clarence, *Backgrounds of Dispensationalism*. Grand Rapids, Michigan, William B. Eerdmans Company, 1960.

Berdyaev, Nicolas, *Christianity and Anti-Semitism*. Aldington, Kent, The Hand and Flower Press, 1952.

Berkovits, Eliezer, *Faith after the Holocaust*. New York, KTAV Publishing House, 1973.

Berkovits, Eliezer, *God, Man and History: A Jewish Interpretation*. New York, Jonathan David Publishers, 1959.

Bettelheim, Bruno, and Morris Janowitz, *Social Change and Prejudice, Including the Dynamics of Prejudice*. Glencoe, Illinois, Free Press of Glencoe, 1964.

Biss, André, *A Million Jews to Save: Check to the Final Solution*. London, Hutchinson and Company, 1973.

The Black Book: The Nazi Crime against the Jewish People. New York, Duell, Sloan and Pearce, 1946.

The Black Book of Poland. New York, the Polish Information Center, 1942.

Boorstin, Daniel J., George Mayberry, and John Rackliffe, *Anti-Semitism: A Threat to Democracy*. Wakefield, Massachusetts, 1939.

Bracher, Hans Dietrich, *The German Dictatorship*. New York, Praeger Publishers, 1970.

The Brown Book of the Hitler Terror. London, Victor Gollancz, 1933.

Browne, Benjamin P., *Christian Journalism for Today*. Philadelphia, Judson Press, 1952.

Cantrill, Hadley, editor, *Public Opinion, 1935–1946*. Princeton, New Jersey, Princeton University Press, 1951.

The Case of Civilization against Hitlerism, New York, Robert O. Ballou, 1934. (Statement of the American Jewish Congress rally held at Madison Square Garden, March 7, 1934.)

Cavert, Samuel McCrea, *Church Cooperation and Unity in America: A Historical Review, 1900–1970*. New York, Association Press, 1970.

Clinchy, Everett R., *All in the Name of God*. New York, John Day, 1934.

Cohen, Naomi W., *Not Free to Desist the American Jewish Committee, 1906–1966*. Philadelphia, the Jewish Publication Society of America, 1972.

Conway, John S., *The Nazi Persecution of the Churches, 1933–1945*. New York, Basic Books, 1968. (Also published in London, Weidenfeld and Nicolson, 1968.)

Davies, Alan T., *Anti-Semitism and the Christian Mind*. New York, Herder and Herder, 1969.

Dawidowicz, Lucy S., *The Jewish Presence*. New York, Holt, Rinehart and Winston, 1977.

Dawidowicz, Lucy S., *The War against the Jews: 1933–1945*. Holt, Rinehart and Winston, 1975.

Des Pres, Terence, *The Survivor: An Anatomy of the Death Camps*. New York, Oxford University Press, 1976.

Dissertation Abstracts: Abstracts of Dissertations and Monographs in Microfilm. Ann Arbor, Michigan, University Microfilm, volume XXV, number 6 (December 1964).

Donat, Alexander, *The Holocaust Kingdom*. New York, Holt, Rinehart and Winston, 1963.

Douglas, Paul F., *God among the Germans*. Philadelphia, University of Philadelphia Press, 1935.

Duncan-Jones, A. S. *The Struggle for Religious Freedom in Germany*. London, Victor Gollancz 1938. (Reprinted by Greenwood Press Publishers, 1971.)

Dushaw, Amos I., *Anti-Semitism—The Voice of Folly and Fanaticism*. Tolerance Press, 1943.

Eckardt, A. Roy, *Christianity and the Children of Israel*. London, King's Crown Press, 1948.

Faulhaber, Cardinal Michael von, *Judaism, Christianity, and Germany: Advent Sermons Preached in St. Michael's, Munich*, George D. Smith, translator. New York, Macmillan, 1934.

Feingold, Henry, *The Politics of Rescue*. New Brunswick, New Jersey, Rutgers University Press, 1970.

Fishman. Hertzel, *American Protestantism and a Jewish State*. Detroit, Wayne State University Press, 1973.

Fleischner, Eva, editor, *Auschwitz: Beginning of a New Era, Reflections on the Holocaust*. New York, KTAV Publishing House, 1977.

Fleischner, Eva, *Judaism in German Christian Theology since 1945: Christianity and Israel Considered in Terms of Mission*. Metuchen, New Jersey, The American Theological Library Association, 1975.

Flora, Bruce H., *The Rise and Development of Anti-Semitism*. Chicago, unpublished B.D. thesis, Bethany Biblical Seminary, 1942.

Friedlander, Albert H., *Out of the Whirlwind, A Reader of Holocaust Literature*. New York: Doubleday and Company, 1968.

Friedlander, Henry, *On the Holocaust: A Critique of the Treatment of the Holocaust in History Textbooks Accompanied by an Annotated Bibliography*. New York, Anti-Defamation League of B'nai B'rith, 1972.

Friedman, Saul S., *No Haven for the Oppressed: United States Policy toward Jewish Refugees, 1933–1945*. Detroit, Wayne State University Press, 1973.

Glattstein, Jacob, Israel Knox, and Samuel Margoshes, editors, *Anthology of Holocaust Literature*. Philadelphia, the Jewish Publication Society of America, 1968.

Gordis, Robert, and Ruth B. Waxman, editors, *Faith and Reason, Essays in Judaism*. New York, KTAV Publishing House, 1973.

Habe, Hans, *The Mission*. New York, New American Library, 1967.

Herman, S. N., *Reaction of Jews to Anti-Semitism*. Johannesburg, South Africa, Witwatersrand University Press, 1945.

Herman, Stewart W., *It's Your Souls We Want*. New York and London, Harper and Brothers, 1943.

Herman, Stewart W., *The Rebirth of the German Church*. New York and London, Harper and Brothers, 1946.

Hero, Alfred O., Jr., *American Religious Groups View Foreign Policy: Trends in Rank-and-File Opinion, 1937–1969*. Durham, North Carolina, Duke University Press, 1973.

Hilberg, Raul, *The Destruction of the European Jews*. Chicago, Quadrangle Books, 1961.

Hilberg, Raul, *Documents of Destruction: Germany and Jewry, 1933–1945*. Chicago, Quadrangle Books, 1971.

Himmelfarb, Milton, *The Jews of Modernity*. New York, Basic Books, 1973.

Hitler's Black Record: The Documented Story of Nazi Atrocities against the Jews. New York, the American Jewish Congress, 1943.

Hoffman, Conrad, Jr., *The Jews Today: A Call to Christian Action*. New York, Friendship Press, 1941.

Holborn, Louise W., *The International Refugee Organization: A Specialized Agency of the United Nations, Its History and Its Work, 1946–1952*. London, Oxford University Press, 1956.

The Holocaust. Jerusalem, Yad Vashem, 1975

358   BIBLIOGRAPHY

Isaac, Jules, *Jesus and Israel*. New York, Holt, Rinehart and Winston, 1959.
Isaac, Jules, *The Teaching of Contempt: The Christian Roots of Anti-Semitism*. New York, Holt, Rinehart and Winston, 1964.
The Jewish Situation in Germany. New York, the American Jewish Committee, 1934.
The Jews in Nazi Germany: The Factual Record of Their Persecution by the National Socialists. New York, the American Jewish Committee, 1933.
The Jews in Nazi Germany: A Handbook of Facts Concerning Their Present Condition. New York, the American Jewish Committee, 1935.
Joffroy, Pierre, *A Spy for God: The Ordeal of Kurt Gerstein*. Translated by Norman Denny. New York; Harcourt, Brace, Jovanovich, 1970.
Kaplan, Chaim A., *Scroll of Agony: The Warsaw Diary of Chaim A. Kaplan*. New York, Macmillan Company, 1965.
Kaul, Leo, *Why Is the Jew Persecuted Today?* Published by the author, Chicago, 1939.
Keller, Adolph, *Christian Europe Today*. New York, Harper and Brothers, 1942.
Keller, Adolph, *Religion and Revolution: Problems of Contemporary Christianity and the European Scene*. New York, Fleming H. Revell, 1934.
Kogon, Eugen, *The Theory and Practice of Hell: The German Concentration Camps and the System behind Them*. New York, Berkley Medallion Books, 1958.
Krausnick, Helmut, Hans Buchheim, Martin Broszat, and Hans-Adolf Jacobsen, *Anatomy of the SS State*. New York, Walker and Company, 1965.
Kraus, C. Norman, *Dispensationalism in America: Its Rise and Development*. Richmond, Virginia, John Knox Press, 1958.
Lazaron, Morris S., *Common Ground: A Plea for Intelligent Americanism*. Liveright, 1938.
Leboucher, Fernande, *Incredible Mission*. Garden City, New York: Doubleday and Company, 1969.
Leiper, Henry, *Churchmen Who Defy Hitler*. New York, National Conference of Christians and Jews, 1941 or 1942.
Levi, Primo, *The Truce: A Survivor's Journey Home from Auschwitz*. London, the Bodley Head, 1963.
Levin, Nora, *The Holocaust: The Destruction of European Jewry, 1933–1945*. New York, Thomas Y. Crowell Company, 1968.
Lewy, Guenter, *The Catholic Church and Nazi Germany*. New York, McGraw-Hill, 1964.
Liptzin, Solomon, *Germany's Stepchildren*. New York: the Jewish Publication Society of America, 1945.
Littell, Franklin H., and Hubert G. Locke, editors, *The German Church Struggle and the Holocaust*. Detroit, Wayne State University Press, 1974.
McClaskey, Beryl, *The History of U.S. Policy and Program in the Field of Religious Affairs under the Office of the U.S. High Commissioner of Germany*. Office of the High Commissioner for Germany, 1951.
Macfarland, Charles S. *New Church and New Germany: A Study of Church and State*. Toronto, Macmillan, 1934.
McLoughlin, William C., *Modern Revivalism: Charles Grandison Finney to Billy Graham*. New York, Ronald Press, 1958.
McPherson, Charles S., *I Was in Prison*. New York: Fleming H. Revell, 1939 or 1940.
Maltitz, Horst Von, *The Evolution of Hitler's Germany: The Ideology, the Personality, the Moment*. New York: McGraw-Hill Book Company, 1973.
Maritain, Jacques, *A Christian Looks at the Jewish Question*. New York, Longmans, Green and Company, 1939.
Marty, Martin E., John G. Deedy, Jr., David Wolf Silverman, and Robert Lekachman, *The Religious Press in America*. New York, Holt, Rinehart and Winston, 1963.
Mathews, Basil, *The Jews and the World Ferment*, New York Friendship Press, 1934 or 1935.
Michel, Henri, *The Second World War* (American edition). New York, Praeger Publishers, 1975.

Moehlman, Conrad Henry, *The Christian Jewish Tragedy: A Study in Religious Prejudice.* New York, Printing House of Leo Hart, 1933.

Morais, Vamberto, *A Short History of Anti-Semitism.* New York, W. W. Norton and Company, 1976.

Morse, Arthur D., *While Six Million Died: A Chronicle of American Apathy.* New York, Random House, 1968.

Nazi Massacre of the Jews and Others: Some Practical Proposals for Immediate Rescue Made by the Archbishop of Canterbury and Lord Rochester in Speeches on March 23rd 1943 in the House of Lords. London, Victor Gollancz, 1943.

Neusner, Jacob, editor, *Understanding Jewish Theology: Classical Issues and Modern Perspectives.* New York, KTAV Publishing House and Anti-Defamation League of B'nai B'rith, 1973.

Niebuhr, Reinhold, *Christianity and Power Politics* New York, Charles Scribner's Sons, 1940.

Niemoeller, Martin, *God Is My Fuehrer,* New York, Philosophical Library, 1942.

Noakes, Jeremy, and Geoffrey Pridham, *Documents on Nazism, 1919–1945.* New York, Viking Press, 1975.

Oldham, J. H. *The Oxford Conference* (official report). New York, Willit, Clark and Company, 1937.

Olson, Bernhard E., *Faith and Prejudice: Intergroup Problems in Protestant Curricula.* New Haven and London, Yale University Press, 1963.

Orphaned Missions: The War in Europe Challenges Maintenance of the Christian World Community. New York, International Missionary Council, n.d. (probably 1941).

Payne, Robert, *The Life and Death of Adolf Hitler.* New York, Praeger Publishers, 1973.

Philipson, David, *The Jew in America* (Popular Studies in Judaism). Cincinnati, Ohio, Union of American Hebrew Congregations, n.d., (probably 1939 or 1940).

Pitt, James E., *Adventures in Brotherhood.* New York, Farrar, Straus, and Company, 1955.

Pulzer, P. G. J., *The Rise of Political Anti-Semitism in Germany and Austria.* New York, John Wiley & Sons, 1964.

Questions and Answers Concerning the Jew. Chicago, Anti-Defamation League of B'nai B'rith, 1944.

Rabinowitz, Dorothy, *New Lives: Survivors of the Holocaust Living in America.* New York, Alfred A. Knopf, 1976.

Read, James Morgan, *Atrocity Propaganda, 1914–1919.* New Haven, Connecticut, Yale University Press, 1941.

Reitlinger, Gerald, *The Final Solution: The Attempt to Exterminate the Jews of Europe, 1939–1945,* 2nd rev. ed. New York, Thomas Yoseloff, 1968.

Reitlinger, Gerald, *The SS: Alibi of a Nation, 1922–1945.* London, William Heinemann, 1956.

Ribalow, Harold U., editor, *Mid-Century: An Anthology of Jewish Life and Culture in Our Times.* New York, Beechhurst Press, 1955.

Roy, Ralph Lord, *Apostles of Discord: A Study of Organized Bigotry and Disruption on the Fringes of Protestantism.* Boston, Beacon Press, 1953.

Ruether, Rosemary Radford, *Faith and Fratricide: The Theological Roots of Anti-Semitism.* New York, Seabury Press, 1974.

Rubenstein, Richard L., *After Auschwitz: Radical Theology and Contemporary Judaism.* New York: Bobbs-Merrill, 1966.

Rubenstein, Richard L., *The Cunning of History: The Holocaust and the American Future.* New York, Harper and Row, 1975.

Sandeen, Ernest R., *The Roots of Fundamentalism: British and American Millenarianism, 1800–1930.* Chicago, University of Chicago Press, 1970.

Schwartz, Leo W., editor, *The Jewish Caravan: Great Stories of Twenty-five Centuries.* New York, Holt, Rinehart and Winston, 1963.

Schwartz, Leo W., *The Root and the Bough: The Epic of an Enduring People.* New York, Rinehart and Company, 1949.

360   BIBLIOGRAPHY

Shirer, William L., *Berlin Diary; The Journal of a Foreign Correspondent, 1934–1940.* New York, Alfred A. Knopf, 1941.

Shirer, William L., *The Rise and Fall of the Third Reich,* 1st ed. New York, Simon and Schuster, 1959.

Smith, Timothy L., *Revivalism and Social Reform.* New York, Abingdon Press, 1957.

Snoek, Johan M., *The Grey Book.* Assen, The Netherlands, Royal Van Gorcum, 1968.

Snyder, Louis S., *The War: A Concise History, 1939–1945.* New York, Simon and Schuster, 1960.

Spotts, Frederic, *The Churches and Politics in Germany.* Middletown, Connecticut, Wesleyan University Press, 1973.

Steckel, Charles W., *Destruction and Survival.* Los Angeles, Delmar Publishing Company, 1973.

Stein, Leo, *I Was in Hell with Niemoeller.* New York, Fleming H. Revell, 1942.

Steinberg, Lucien, *Not as a Lamb: The Jews against Hitler.* London, D. C. Heath, 1970.

Steiner, Jean-Francois, *Treblinka.* New York, Simon and Schuster, 1967.

Stember, Charles Herbert, and Others, *Jews in the Mind of America.* New York, Basic Books, 1966.

Stern, Karl, *The Pillar of Fire.* New York, Harcourt, Brace and Company, 1951.

The Story of Christian Science Wartime Activities, 1939–1946. Boston, the Christian Science Publishing Society, 1947. (There is no mention of the Jews, assistance to Jews, Jews as refugees, or of contact with or concern for the plight of Jews. There is one reference to atrocities committed in prison camps in Germany as a matter of "photographic record" [p. 330] but no direct description or comment on the camps.)

Strober, Gerald R., *Portrait of the Elder Brother: Jews and Judaism in Protestant Teaching Materials.* New York: the American Jewish Committee and the National Conference of Christians and Jews, 1972.

Strong, Donald P. *Organized Anti-Semitism in America: The Rise of Group Prejudice during the Decade 1930–1940.* Washington, D.C., American Council on Public Affairs, 1941.

Suhl, Yuri, *They Fought Back: The Story of the Jewish Resistance in Nazi Europe.* New York: Crown Publishers, 1965.

Survey Data for Trend Analysis: An Index of Repeated Questions in U.S. National Surveys Held by the Roper Public Opinion Research Center. SSRC and the Roper Public Opinion Research Center, 1974.

Svensbye, Lloyd, The History of Developing Social Responsibility among Lutherans in America from 1930 to 1960, with Reference to the American Lutheran Church, the Augustana Lutheran Church, the Evangelical Lutheran Church, and the United Lutheran Church in America. Unpublished Ph.D. thesis, New York, Union Theological Seminary, 1966.

Talmadge, Frank Ephraim, editor, *Disputation and Dialogue: Readings in Jewish-Christian Encounter.* New York, KTAV Publishing House, Anti-Defamation League of B'nai B'rith, 1975.

Toland, John, *Adolf Hitler.* New York, Ballantine Books, 1976.

Tuman, Melvin M., *An Inventory and Appraisal of Research on American Anti-Semitism.* New York, Freedom Books, 1961.

Van Passen, Pierre, and James Waterman Wise, editors, *Nazism: An Assault on Civilization.* New York, Harrison Smith and Robert Haas, 1934.

Vogt, Hannah, *The Burden of Guilt: A Short History of Germany, 1914–1945.* New York, Oxford University Press, 1964.

The Voice of Christian America: Proceedings of the National Conference on Palestine, Washington, D.C., March 9, 1974.

The Voice of Religion: The Views of Christian Religious Leaders on the Persecution of the Jews in Germany by the National Socialists. New York, the American Jewish Committee, 1933.

Wells, Leon, *The Janowska Road*. New York, Leon Wells, 1963.

Wentz, Frederick K., The Reaction of the Religious Press in America to the Emergence of Nazism (1933–1937). New Haven, Yale University, unpublished Ph.D. thesis, 1954.

Wechsberg, Joseph, editor, *The Murderers among Us: The Simon Wiesenthal Memoirs*. New York, McGraw-Hill Book Company, 1967.

Who's Who in American College and University Administration. New York, Crowell Collier Educational Corporation, 1970.

Wilson, Dwight, *Armageddon Now! The Premillenarian Response to Russia and Israel Since 1917*. Grand Rapids, Michigan, Baker Book House, 1977.

Wise, Stephen S., *Challenging Years: The Autobiography of Stephen S. Wise*. New York, G. P. Putnam's Sons, 1949.

YIVO Annual of Jewish Social Science, volume XV. New York, YIVO Institute for Jewish Research, 1974.

Zahn, Gordon L., *German Catholics and Hitler's Wars*. New York, Sheed and Ward, 1962.

Zimmels, J. H., *The Echo of the Nazi Holocaust in Rabbinic Literature*. New York, KTAV Publishing House, 1975.

Zylberberg, Michael, *A Warsaw Diary, 1939–1945*. London, Vallentine-Mitchell, 1969.

INDEX

Index

Aasgard, J. A., 210
Africa, as a refugee site for Jews, 104, 118, 131
Aftonbladt (Stockholm, Sweden), 192
Alaska, as refugee site for Jews, 131
Albany Jewish Congress, 186
All in the Name of God (Clinchy), 69
Allgemeine Evangelisch-Luth. Kirchenzeitung, 16
Allen, Devere, 147
Am Grossen Wannsee, 124, 180. *See also* Final Solution
American Baptist Foreign Mission Society, 53
American Board of Missions to the Jews, 70, 103, 111, 129, 162, 195
American Christian Committee for German Refugees, 104
American Church in Berlin, 210
American Committee for Christian Refugees, 161, 204
American Committee on Religious Rights and Minorities, 11
American Friends' Service Committee, 113, 125, 126, 167, 193
American Institute on Judaism and a Just and Enduring Peace, 176
American Jewish Committee, 36, 51, 271
American Jewish Conference (New York City), 187
American Jewish Congress, 10, 186, 192, 271
American Lutheran Church, 96
American Olympic Committee, 102
American Palestine Committee, 298
American Protestantism and the American State (Fishman), 213
Anatomy of the SS State (Krausnick, et al.), 215

Anti-Defamation League of B'nai B'rith, 133
Anti-Semitism, 10–11, 26–27, 40, 44, 45, 46, 47–48, 53, 58, 59, 64, 89, 93, 96, 99–100, 158, 184, 186, 230, 253, 269–70, 272, 274; in America, 26–27, 35–36, 37, 38, 47, 69, 93–94, 94–98, 111, 117, 118, 132, 133–34, 181, 186; in Germany, 6, 7–8, 15, 34, 58, 59, 60, 62, 64, 75, 89, 100, 230, 264; in Europe, 6, 70, 103, 109, 161
Antonescu, Ion, 155
Appelman, Hyman, 137
Arab-Jewish conflict (*1936–1938*), 101, 134
Arab nationalism, 101–2
Arkansas Baptist Convention, 51
Army Prayer Book, 198
"Aryan clause" ("Aryan paragraph"), 3, 13, 14, 15, 16, 17, 18, 37, 42, 43, 86, 258, 265, 267, 268, 271, 283
Asch, Sholom, 222
Asher, Robert, 25
Ashton, Frederick Alfred, 24
Ashworth, Robert A., 3, 29–30, 65–67, 273, 300
Asmussen, Herman, 211
Associated Press, 68, 114
Atom bomb, 295–98
Atrocity stories, 9, 11, 12–13, 21, 30, 35, 37, 56, 59, 68, 157, 171, 172, 185, 189–90, 199–200, 202, 208, 212, 229, 231, 233, 234, 235, 236, 238, 239, 243, 247, 274, 278, 282, 289
Augustana Swedish Synod, 96, 97, 111, 206
Auschwitz, 199, 202, 215, 222, 224, 226, 252, 281, 289, 295
Australia, as a refugee site for Jews, 104, 131

365